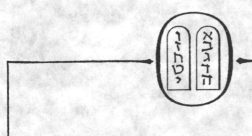

PRESENTED TO

_____

BY

_____

_____

DATE

THE WRITINGS

כתובים

KETHUBIM

THE WRITINGS

כתובים

KETHUBIM

A new translation of
THE HOLY SCRIPTURES
according to the Masoretic text

THIRD SECTION

THE JEWISH PUBLICATION SOCIETY OF AMERICA

PHILADELPHIA

ISBN 0–8276–0202–2 (cloth-bound)
ISBN 0–8276–0203–0 (leather-bound)
Library of Congress Catalog Card No. 81–85106
Manufactured in the United States of America

PREFACE

The committee of translators for *The Writings–Kethubim*—the third part of the Hebrew Bible—was set up in 1966 by The Jewish Publication Society of America. It comprised professors Moshe Greenberg (now of the Hebrew University), Jonas C. Greenfield (now of the Hebrew University), and Nahum M. Sarna (of Brandeis University). Associated with them were rabbis Saul Leeman, Martin Rozenberg, and David Shapiro, representing the three sections of organized Jewish life in America. Chaim Potok served as secretary of the committee.

The Five Megilloth, which form a part of *The Writings*, have been translated by an earlier committee and were published separately, together with the Book of Jonah, in 1969. This translation was done by the following committee: H. L. Ginsberg as editor-in-chief, Harry M. Orlinsky as fellow editor, and associated with them, Max Arzt, Bernard J. Bamberger, Harry Freedman, and Solomon Grayzel.

The present English rendering of *The Writings* is a new version, not a revision of an earlier translation. It is based on the traditional Masoretic Hebrew text—its consonants, vowels, and syntactical divisions—although on occasion the traditional accentuation has been disregarded for an alternative construction of a verse that appeared to yield a better sense. Such departures from the traditional accentuation often were made by many earlier Jewish commentators and translators.

The entire gamut of biblical interpretation, ancient and modern, Jewish and non-Jewish, has been consulted, and whenever possible, the results of modern study of the languages and cultures of the ancient Near East have been brought to bear on the biblical word. In choosing between alternatives, however, just as antiquity was not in itself a disqualification, so modernity was not in itself a recommendation. When the present translation diverges from recent renderings (as it frequently does), this is due as much to our judgment that certain innovations, though interesting, are too speculative for adoption in the present state of knowledge as it is due to our commitment to the received Hebrew text, a commitment not made by most recent translations.

For many passages, our as yet imperfect understanding of the language of the Bible or what appears to be some disorder in the Hebrew text makes sure translation impossible. Our uncertainty is indicated in a note, where the Hebrew text permits, and alternative renderings sometimes have been offered. Emendations of the text are not proposed, however, and notes are kept to a minimum.

The style of the translation is modern literary English. An effort has been made to retain the imagery of the Hebrew rather than to render it by English equivalents and approximations alien to the biblical world. Consistency in rendering Hebrew terms was an aim but not a rule. Where its employment would have resulted in encumbered or awkward language, it was abandoned. Several passages in *The Writings* are very similar to passages in *The Torah* and *The Prophets.* The rendering of these passages in *The Writings* generally follows the wording in the earlier books. On occasion, owing to various considerations, divergences in style and translation will be found. For example, in the presentation of the poetry of the Psalms, it was deemed fitting, because of their liturgical use, to depart from the practice followed elsewhere in this work, and to indicate the thought units through appropriate indentation.

The interpretation of the text and meaning of *The Writings* presented us with extraordinary, and at times insuperable, difficulties. We know, too, that we have not conveyed the fullness of the Hebrew, with its ambiguities, its overtones, and the richness that it carries from centuries of use. Still, we hope to have transmitted something of the directness, the simplicity, and the uniquely Israelite expression of piety that are so essential to the sublimity of the Hebrew Bible.

We give thanks to God, who has enabled us to complete this sacred task.

מנחם אב תשל״ט
August 1979

CONTENTS

THE WRITINGS – KETHUBIM

תהילים	PSALMS	1–196
משלי	PROVERBS	197–257
איוב	JOB	259–331
שיר השירים	THE SONG OF SONGS	333–349
רות	RUTH	351–359
איכה	LAMENTATIONS	361–379
קהלת	ECCLESIASTES	381–401
אסתר	ESTHER	403–419
דניאל	DANIEL	421–451
עזרא	EZRA	453–473
נחמיה	NEHEMIAH	475–503
דברי הימים א	I CHRONICLES	505–557
דברי הימים ב	II CHRONICLES	559–624

תהילים

PSALMS

תהילים

PSALMS

BOOK ONE

1 Happy is the man who has not followed the counsel of the
wicked,
or taken the path of sinners,
or joined the company of the insolent;
2 rather, the teaching of the LORD is his delight,
and he studies[a] that teaching day and night.
3 He is like a tree planted beside streams of water,
that yields its fruit in season,
whose foliage never fades,
and whatever [b-]it produces thrives.[-b]

4 Not so the wicked;
rather, they are like chaff that wind blows away.
5 Therefore the wicked will not survive judgment,
nor will sinners, in the assembly of the righteous.
6 For the LORD cherishes the way of the righteous,
but the way of the wicked is doomed.

2 Why do nations assemble,
and peoples plot[a] vain things;
2 kings of the earth take their stand,
and regents intrigue together
against the LORD and against His anointed?
3 "Let us break the cords of their yoke,
shake off their ropes from us!"

---

[a] *Or "recites"; lit. "utters."*
[b-b] *Or "he does prospers."*

[a] *Lit. "utter."*

⁴ He who is enthroned in heaven laughs;
  the Lord mocks at them.
⁵ Then He speaks to them in anger,
  terrifying them in His rage,
⁶ "But I have installed My king
  on Zion, My holy mountain!"
⁷ Let me tell of the decree:
  the LORD said to me,
  b-"You are My son,
  I have fathered you this day.*-b*
⁸ Ask it of Me,
  and I will make the nations your domain;
  your estate, the limits of the earth.
⁹ You can smash them with an iron mace,
  shatter them like potter's ware."

¹⁰ So now, O kings, be prudent;
  accept discipline, you rulers of the earth!
¹¹ Serve the LORD in awe;
  c-tremble with fright,*-c*
¹² *d*-pay homage in good faith,*-d*
  lest He be angered, and your way be doomed
  in the mere flash of His anger.
  Happy are all who take refuge in Him.

3 A psalm of David when he fled from his son Absalom.

² O LORD, my foes are so many!
  Many are those who attack me;
³ many say of me,
  "There is no deliverance for him through
  God."   *Selah.ᵃ*

---

b-b Compare II Sam. 7.14, and Ps. 89.27ff.
c-c Meaning of Heb. uncertain; others "rejoice with trembling."
d-d Meaning of Heb. uncertain.

ᵃ A liturgical direction of uncertain meaning.

4

⁴ But You, O Lᴏʀᴅ, are a shield about me,
    my glory, He who holds my head high.
⁵ I cry aloud to the Lᴏʀᴅ,
    and He answers me from His holy mountain.   *Selah.*
⁶ I lie down and sleep and wake again,
    for the Lᴏʀᴅ sustains me.
⁷ I have no fear of the myriad forces
    arrayed against me on every side.

⁸ Rise, O Lᴏʀᴅ!
  Deliver me, O my God!
  For You slap all my enemies in the face;[b]
  You break the teeth of the wicked.
⁹ Deliverance is the Lᴏʀᴅ's;
    Your blessing be upon Your people!   *Selah.*

4 *a-*For the leader; with instrumental music.*-a* A psalm of David.

² Answer me when I call,
    O God, my vindicator!
  You freed me from distress;
    have mercy on me and hear my prayer.
³ You men, how long will my glory be mocked,
    will you love illusions,
    have recourse to frauds?   *Selah.*
⁴ Know that the Lᴏʀᴅ singles out the faithful for Himself;
    the Lᴏʀᴅ hears when I call to Him.
⁵ So tremble, and sin no more;
    ponder it on your bed, and sigh.[b]
⁶ Offer sacrifices in righteousness
    and trust in the Lᴏʀᴅ.

⁷ Many say, "O for good days!"
  *c-*Bestow Your favor on us,*-c* O Lᴏʀᴅ.

[b] *Lit. "cheek."*

ᵃ⁻ᵃ *Meaning of Heb. uncertain.*
[b] *Others "be still."*
ᶜ⁻ᶜ *Lit. "Lift up the light of Your countenance upon us"; cf. Num. 6.25f.*

⁸ You put joy into my heart
   when their grain and wine show increase.
⁹ Safe and sound, I lie down and sleep,
   d-for You alone, O LORD, keep me secure.⁻*d*

5 *a*-For the leader; on *nehiloth.*⁻*a* A psalm of David.

² Give ear to my speech, O LORD;
   consider my utterance.
³ Heed the sound of my cry,
   my king and God,
   for I pray to You.
⁴ Hear my voice, O LORD, at daybreak;
   at daybreak I plead before You, and wait.

⁵ For You are not a God who desires wickedness;
   evil cannot abide with You;
⁶   wanton men cannot endure in Your sight.
   You detest all evildoers;
⁷   You doom those who speak lies;
   murderous, deceitful men the LORD abhors.

⁸ But I, through Your abundant love, enter Your house;
   I bow down in awe at Your holy temple.
⁹ O LORD, *b*-lead me along Your righteous [path]⁻*b*
   because of my watchful foes;
   make Your way straight before me.
¹⁰ For there is no sincerity on their lips;*c*
   their heart is [filled with] malice;
   their throat is an open grave;
   their tongue slippery.
¹¹ Condemn them, O God;
   let them fall by their own devices;
   cast them out for their many crimes,

d-d *Or "for You, O LORD, keep me alone and secure."*

a-a *Meaning of Heb. uncertain.*
b-b *Or "as You are righteous, lead me."*
c *Lit. "mouth."*

6

for they defy You.
12 But let all who take refuge in You rejoice,
   ever jubilant as You shelter them;
   and let those who love Your name exult in You.
13 For You surely bless the righteous man, O LORD,
   encompassing him with favor like a shield.

6 *a*-For the leader; with instrumental music on the *sheminith.*-*a*
A psalm of David.

2 O LORD, do not punish me in anger,
   do not chastise me in fury.
3 Have mercy on me, O LORD, for I languish;
   heal me, O LORD, for my bones shake with terror.
4 My whole being is stricken with terror,
   while You, LORD—O, how long!
5 O LORD, turn! Rescue me!
   Deliver me as befits Your faithfulness.
6 For there is no praise of You among the dead;
   in Sheol, who can acclaim You?

7 I am weary with groaning;
   every night I drench my bed,
   I melt my couch in tears.
8 My eyes are wasted by vexation,
   worn out because of all my foes.
9 Away from me, all you evildoers,
   for the LORD heeds the sound of my weeping.
10 The LORD heeds my plea,
   the LORD accepts my prayer.
11 All my enemies will be frustrated and stricken with terror;
   they will turn back in an instant, frustrated.

a-a Meaning of Heb. uncertain.

7

7 *a-Shiggaion* of David,*-a* which he sang to the LORD, concerning Cush, a Benjaminite.

> 2 O LORD, my God, in You I seek refuge;
>   deliver me from all my pursuers and save me,
> 3 lest, like a lion, they tear me apart,
>   rending in pieces, and no one save me.
> 4 O LORD, my God, if I have done such things,
>   if my hands bear the guilt of wrongdoing,
> 5 if I have dealt evil to my ally,
>   —*b-*I who rescued my foe without reward*-b*—
> 6 then let the enemy pursue and overtake me;
>   let him trample my life to the ground,
>   and lay my body in the dust.   *Selah.*

> 7 Rise, O LORD, in Your anger;
>   assert Yourself *c-*against the fury of my foes;*-c*
>   bestir Yourself on my behalf;
>   You have ordained judgment.
> 8 *a-*Let the assembly of peoples gather about You,
>   with You enthroned above, on high.*-a*
> 9 The LORD judges the peoples;
>   vindicate me, O LORD,
>   for the righteousness and blamelessness that are mine.
> 10 Let the evil of the wicked come to an end,
>   but establish the righteous;
>   he who probes the mind and conscience*d* is God the
>   righteous.
> 11 *e-*I look to God to shield me;*-e*

---

a-a *Meaning of Heb. uncertain.*
b-b *Meaning of Heb. uncertain; others "or stripped my foe clean."*
c-c *Or "in Your fury against my foes."*
d *Lit. "kidneys."*
e-e *Cf. Ibn Ezra and Kimhi; lit. "My shield is upon God."*

the deliverer of the upright.
12 God vindicates the righteous;
God *f*-pronounces doom*-f* each day.
13 *g*-If one does not turn back, but whets his sword,
bends his bow and aims it,
14 then against himself he readies deadly weapons,
and makes his arrows sharp.*-g*
15 See, he hatches evil, conceives mischief,
and gives birth to fraud.
16 He has dug a pit and deepened it,
and will fall into the trap he made.
17 His mischief will recoil upon his own head;
his lawlessness will come down upon his skull.
18 I will praise the LORD for His righteousness,
and sing a hymn to the name of the LORD Most High.

8 *a*-For the leader; on the *gittith.*-*a* A psalm of David.

2 O LORD, our Lord,
How majestic is Your name throughout the earth,
b-You who have covered the heavens with Your
splendor!*-b*
3 *a*-From the mouths of infants and sucklings
You have founded strength on account of Your foes,
to put an end to enemy and avenger.*-a*
4 When I behold Your heavens, the work of Your fingers,
the moon and stars that You set in place,
5 what is man that You have been mindful of him,
mortal man that You have taken note of him,
6 that You have made him little less than divine,*c*

---

f-f Others "has indignation."
g-g Meaning of vv. *13–14* uncertain; an alternate rendering, with God as the main subject,
is:*13* If one does not turn back, He whets His sword, /bends His bow and aims it; /*14* deadly
weapons He prepares for him, /and makes His arrows sharp.

a-a Meaning of Heb. uncertain.
b-b Meaning of Heb. uncertain; or "You whose splendor is celebrated all over the heavens!"
c Or "the angels."

and adorned him with glory and majesty;
7 You have made him master over Your handiwork,
laying the world at his feet,
8 sheep and oxen, all of them,
and wild beasts, too;
9 the birds of the heavens, the fish of the sea,
whatever travels the paths of the seas.
10 O LORD, our Lord, how majestic is Your name
throughout the earth!

9 *a-*For the leader; *'almuth labben.-a* A psalm of David.

2 I will praise You, LORD, with all my heart;
I will tell all Your wonders.
3 I will rejoice and exult in You,
singing a hymn to Your name, O Most High.

4 When my enemies retreat,
they stumble to their doom at Your presence.
5 For You uphold my right and claim,
enthroned as righteous judge.
6 You blast the nations;
You destroy the wicked;
You blot out their name forever.
7 *b-*The enemy is no more—
ruins everlasting;
You have torn down their cities;
their very names are lost.*-b*
8 But the LORD abides forever;
He has set up His throne for judgment;
9 it is He who judges the world with righteousness,
rules the peoples with equity.
10 The LORD is a haven for the oppressed,
a haven in times of trouble.
11 Those who know Your name trust You,

a-a *Meaning of Heb. uncertain; some mss. and ancient versions,* 'al muth labben, *as though "over the death of the son."*
b-b *Meaning of Heb. uncertain.*

for You do not abandon those who turn to You, O LORD.

12 Sing a hymn to the LORD, ^cwho reigns in Zion;^{-c}
  declare His deeds among the peoples.

13 ^{d-}For He does not ignore the cry of the afflicted;
  He who requites bloodshed is mindful of them.^{-d}

14 Have mercy on me, O LORD;
  see my affliction at the hands of my foes,
  You who lift me from the gates of death,

15 so that in the gates of ^{e-}Fair Zion^{-e}
  I might tell all Your praise,
  I might exult in Your deliverance.

16 The nations sink in the pit they have made;
  their own foot is caught in the net they have hidden.

17 The LORD has made Himself known:
  He works judgment;
  the wicked man is snared by his own
  devices.   *Higgaion.^b Selah.*

18 Let the wicked be ^f in Sheol,
  all the nations who ignore God!

19 Not always shall the needy be ignored,
  nor the hope of the afflicted forever lost.

20 Rise, O LORD!
  Let not men have power;
  let the nations be judged in Your presence.

21 ^{b-}Strike fear into them,^{-b} O LORD;
  let the nations know they are only men.   *Selah.*

10 Why, O LORD, do You stand aloof,
  heedless in times of trouble?

2 The wicked in his arrogance hounds the lowly—
  ^{a-}may they be caught in the schemes they devise!^{-a}

^{c-c} *Or "O you who dwell in Zion."*
^{d-d} *Order of Hebrew clauses inverted for clarity.*
^{e-e} *Lit. "the Daughter of Zion."*
^f *Others "return to."*

^{a-a} *Or "they (i.e. the lowly) are caught by the schemes they devised."*

3 *b-*The wicked crows about his unbridled lusts;
   the grasping man reviles and scorns the LORD.
4 The wicked, arrogant as he is,
   in all his scheming [thinks],*-b*
   "He does not call to account;
   *c-*God does not care."*-c*
5 His ways prosper at all times;
   Your judgments are far beyond him;
   he snorts at all his foes.
6 He thinks, "I shall not be shaken,
   through all time never be in trouble."
7 His mouth is full of oaths, deceit, and fraud;
   mischief and evil are under his tongue.
8 He lurks in outlying places;
   from a covert he slays the innocent;
   his eyes spy out the hapless.
9 He waits in a covert like a lion in his lair;
   waits to seize the lowly;
   he seizes the lowly as he pulls his net shut;
10   he stoops, he crouches,
   *b-*and the hapless fall prey to his might.*-b*
11 He thinks, "God is not mindful,
   He hides His face, He never looks."
12 Rise, O LORD!
   *d-*Strike at him,*-d* O God!
   Do not forget the lowly.
13 Why should the wicked man scorn God,
   thinking You do not call to account?
14 You do look!
   You take note of mischief and vexation!
   *b-*To requite is in Your power.*-b*
   To You the hapless can entrust himself;
   You have ever been the orphan's help.
15 O break the power of the wicked and evil man,

b-b Meaning of Heb. uncertain.
c-c Lit. "There is no God."
d-d Lit. "Lift Your hand."

so that when You *e*-look for-*e* his wickedness
You will find it no more.

16 The LORD is king for ever and ever;
the nations will perish from His land.
17 You will listen to the entreaty of the lowly, O LORD,
You will make their hearts firm;
You will incline Your ear
18 to champion the orphan and the downtrodden,
b-that men who are of the earth tyrannize no more.-*b*

11 For the leader. Of David.

In the LORD I take refuge;
how can you say to me,
"Take to *a*-the hills like a bird!-*a*
2 For see, the wicked bend the bow,
they set their arrow on the string
to shoot from the shadows at the upright.
3 *b*-When the foundations are destroyed,
what can the righteous man do?"-*b*

4 The LORD is in His holy palace;
the LORD—His throne is in heaven;
His eyes behold, His gaze searches mankind.
5 The LORD seeks out the righteous man,
but loathes the wicked one who loves injustice.
6 He will rain down upon the wicked blazing coals and
sulfur;
a scorching wind shall be *c*-their lot.-*c*
7 For the LORD is righteous;
He loves righteous deeds;
the upright shall behold His face.

e-e A play on **darash**, *which in vv. 4, 13 means "to call to account."*

a-a *Meaning of Heb. uncertain; lit. "your hill, bird!"*
b-b *Or "For the foundations are destroyed; what has the Righteous One done?" Or "If the foundations are destroyed, what has the righteous man accomplished?"*
c-c *Lit. "the portion of their cup."*

12 For the leader; on the *sheminith*. A psalm of David.

² Help, O LORD!
For the faithful are no more;
the loyal have vanished from among men.
³ Men speak lies to one another;
their speech is smooth;
they talk with duplicity.
⁴ May the LORD cut off all flattering lips,
every tongue that speaks arrogance.
⁵ They say, "By our tongues we shall prevail;
with lips such as ours, who can be our master?"

⁶ "Because of the groans of the plundered poor and needy,
I will now act," says the LORD.
a-"I will give help," He affirms to him.*-a*
⁷ The words of the LORD are pure words,
silver purged in an earthen crucible,
refined sevenfold.
⁸ You, O LORD, will keep them,
guarding each *a-*from this age*-a* evermore.
⁹ On every side the wicked roam
*a-*when baseness is exalted among men.*-a*

13 For the leader. A psalm of David.

² How long, O LORD; will You ignore me forever?
How long will You hide Your face from me?
³ How long will I have cares on my mind,
grief in my heart all day?
How long will my enemy have the upper hand?
⁴ Look at me, answer me, O LORD, my God!

___

a-a Meaning of Heb. uncertain.

Restore the luster to my eyes,
    lest I sleep the sleep of death;
5   lest my enemy say, "I have overcome him,"
    my foes exult when I totter.
6 But I trust in Your faithfulness,
    my heart will exult in Your deliverance.
I will sing to the LORD,
    for He has been good to me.

14 *a*For the leader. Of David.

The benighted man thinks,
    b-"God does not care."-*b*
Man's deeds are corrupt and loathsome;
    no one does good.
2 The LORD looks down from heaven on mankind
    to find a man of understanding,
    a man mindful of God.
3 All have turned bad,
    altogether foul;
    there is none who does good,
    not even one.
4 Are they so witless, all those evildoers,
    who devour my people as they devour food,
    and do not invoke the LORD?
5 There they will be seized with fright,
    for God is present in the circle of the righteous.
6 You may set at naught the counsel of the lowly,
    but the LORD is his refuge.

7 O that the deliverance of Israel might come from Zion!
When the LORD restores the fortunes of His people,
    Jacob will exult, Israel will rejoice.

---

a *Cf. Ps. 53.*
b-b *Lit. "There is no God"; cf. Ps. 10.4.*

15 A psalm of David.

LORD, who may sojourn in Your tent,
who may dwell on Your holy mountain?
2 He who lives without blame,
who does what is right,
and in his heart acknowledges the truth;
3 *a*-whose tongue is not given to evil;-*a*
who has never done harm to his fellow,
or borne reproach for [his acts toward] his neighbor;
4 for whom a contemptible man is abhorrent,
but who honors those who fear the LORD;
who stands by his oath even to his hurt;
5 who has never lent money at interest,
or accepted a bribe against the innocent.
The man who acts thus shall never be shaken.

16 A *michtam*ᵃ of David.

Protect me, O God, for I seek refuge in You.
2 I say to the LORD,
"You are my Lord, *b*-my benefactor;
there is none above You."-*b*
3 *c*-As to the holy and mighty ones that are in the land,
my whole desire concerning them is that
4 those who espouse another [god]
may have many sorrows!-*c*
I will have no part of their bloody libations;
their names will not pass my lips.

___

ᵃ⁻ᵃ *Meaning of Heb. uncertain; or "who has no slander upon his tongue."*

ᵃ *Meaning of Heb. uncertain.*
ᵇ⁻ᵇ *Others "I have no good but in You."*
ᶜ⁻ᶜ *Meaning of Heb. uncertain; "holy and mighty ones" taken as epithets for divine beings;
cf. qedoshim in Ps. 89.6, 8, and 'addirim in I Sam. 4.8.*

5 The LORD is my allotted share and portion;^d
  You control my fate.
6 Delightful country has fallen to my lot;
  lovely indeed is my estate.
7 I bless the LORD who has guided me;
  my conscience^e admonishes me at night.
8 I am ever mindful of the LORD's presence;
  He is at my right hand; I shall never be shaken.
9 So my heart rejoices,
  my whole being exults,
  and my body rests secure.
10 For You will not abandon me to Sheol,
  or let Your faithful one see the Pit.
11 You will teach me the path of life.
  In Your presence is perfect joy;
  delights are ever in Your right hand.

17 A prayer of David.

  Hear, O LORD, what is just;
  heed my cry, give ear to my prayer,
  uttered without guile.
2 My vindication will come from You;
  Your eyes will behold what is right.
3 You have visited me at night, probed my mind,
  You have tested me and found nothing amiss;
  ^a-I determined that my mouth should not transgress.
4 As for man's dealings,
  in accord with the command of Your lips,^{-a}
  I have kept in view the fate^b of the lawless.
5 My feet have held to Your paths;
  my legs have not given way.

6 I call on You;
  You will answer me, God;

^d *Lit. "cup."*
^e *Lit. "kidneys."*

^{a-a} *Meaning of Heb. uncertain.*
^b *Cf. Prov. 1.19; lit. "paths."*

turn Your ear to me,
hear what I say.
7 Display Your faithfulness in wondrous deeds,
You who deliver with Your right hand
those who seek refuge from assailants.
8 Guard me like the apple of Your eye;
hide me in the shadow of Your wings
9 from the wicked who despoil me,
c-my mortal enemies who-*c* encircle me.
10 *a*-Their hearts are closed to pity;-*a*
they mouth arrogance;
11 now they hem in our feet on every side;
they set their eyes roaming over the land.
12 He is like a lion eager for prey,
a king of beasts lying in wait.

13 Rise, O LORD! Go forth to meet him.
Bring him down;
rescue me from the wicked with Your sword,
14 *a*-from men, O LORD, with Your hand,
from men whose share in life is fleeting.
But as to Your treasured ones,
fill their bellies.-*a*
Their sons too shall be satisfied,
and have something to leave over for their young.
15 Then I, justified, will behold Your face;
awake, I am filled with the vision of You.

18 *a*For the leader. Of David, the servant of the LORD, who addressed the words of this song to the LORD after the LORD had saved him from the hands of all his enemies and from the clutches of Saul.
2 He said:
b-I adore you, O LORD, my strength,-*b*

c-c *Or "from my enemies who avidly."*

a *This poem occurs again at II Sam. 22, with a number of variations, some of which are cited in the following notes.*
b-b *Not in II Sam. 22.2.*

3 O LORD, my crag, my fortress, my rescuer,
  my God, my rock in whom I seek refuge,
  my shield, my ^{c-}mighty champion,^{-c} my haven.
4 ^{d-}All praise! I called on the LORD^{-d}
  and was delivered from my enemies.
5 Ropes^e of Death encompassed me;
  torrents of Belial^f terrified me;
6   ropes of Sheol encircled me;
  snares of Death confronted me.
7 In my distress I called on the LORD,
  cried out to my God;
  in His temple He heard my voice;
  my cry to Him reached His ears.
8 Then the earth rocked and quaked;
  the foundations of the mountains shook,
  rocked by His indignation;
9   smoke went up from His nostrils,
  from His mouth came devouring fire;
  live coals blazed forth from Him.
10 He bent the sky and came down,
  thick cloud beneath His feet.
11 He mounted a cherub and flew,
  gliding on the wings of the wind.
12 He made darkness His screen;
  dark thunderheads, dense clouds of the sky
  were His pavilion round about Him.
13 Out of the brilliance before Him,
  hail and fiery coals ^{g-}pierced His clouds.^{-g}
14 Then the LORD thundered from heaven,
  the Most High gave forth His voice—
  ^{h-}hail and fiery coals.^{-h}

^{c-c} *Lit. "horn of rescue."*
^{d-d} *Construction of Heb. uncertain.*
^e *II Sam. 22.5, "breakers."*
^f *I.e., the netherworld, like "Death" and "Sheol."*
^{g-g} *II Sam. 22.13, "blazed."*
^{h-h} *Not in II Sam. 22.14.*

¹⁵ He let fly His shafts and scattered them;
He discharged lightning and routed them.
¹⁶ The ocean bed was exposed;
the foundations of the world were laid bare
by Your mighty roaring, O LORD,
at the blast of the breath of Your nostrils.
¹⁷ He reached down from on high, He took me;
He drew me out of the mighty waters;
¹⁸ He saved me from my fierce enemy,
from foes too strong for me.
¹⁹ They confronted me on the day of my calamity,
but the LORD was my support.
²⁰ He brought me out to freedom;
He rescued me because He was pleased with me.

²¹ The LORD rewarded me according to my merit;
He requited the cleanness of my hands;
²² for I have kept to the ways of the LORD,
and have not been guilty before my God;
²³ for I am mindful of all His rules;
I have not disregarded His laws.
²⁴ I have been blameless toward Him,
and have guarded myself against sinning;
²⁵ and the LORD has requited me according to my merit,
the cleanness of my hands in His sight.

²⁶ With the loyal, You deal loyally;
with the blameless man, blamelessly.
²⁷ With the pure, You act purely,
and with the perverse, You are wily.
²⁸ It is You who deliver lowly folk,
but haughty eyes You humble.
²⁹ It is You who light my lamp;
the LORD, my God, lights up my darkness.
³⁰ With You, I can rush a barrier;[i]

ⁱ *Cf. note to II Sam. 22.30; or "troop."*

with my God I can scale a wall;

31 the way of God is perfect;
the word of the LORD is pure;
He is a shield to all who seek refuge in Him.

32 Truly, who is a god except the LORD,
who is a rock but our God?—

33 the God who girded me with might,
who made my way perfect;

34 who made my legs like a deer's,
and let me stand firm on the *j* heights;

35 who trained my hands for battle;
my arms can bend a bow of bronze.

36 You have given me the shield of Your protection;
Your right hand has sustained me,
Your care*k* has made me great.

37 You have let me stride on freely;
my feet have not slipped.

38 I pursued my enemies and overtook them;
I did not turn back till I destroyed them.

39 I struck them down,
and they could rise no more;
they lay fallen at my feet.

40 You have girded me with strength for battle,
brought my adversaries low before me,

41 made my enemies turn tail before me;
I wiped out my foes.

42 They cried out, but there was none to deliver;
[cried] to the LORD, but He did not answer them.

43 I ground them fine as windswept dust;
I trod them flat as dirt of the streets.

44 You have rescued me from the strife of people;
You have set me at the head of nations;
peoples I knew not must serve me.

45 At the mere report of me they are submissive;
foreign peoples cower before me;

j *Taking* bamothai *as a poetic form of* bamoth; *cf. Hab. 3.19; others "my."*
k *Meaning of Heb. uncertain; others "condescension."*

46   foreign peoples lose courage,
       l-and come trembling out of their strongholds.*-l*

47 The LORD lives! Blessed is my rock!
   Exalted be God, my deliverer,
48   the God who has vindicated me
       and made peoples subject to me,
49   who rescued me from my enemies,
       who raised me clear of my adversaries,
       saved me from lawless men.
50 For this I sing Your praise among the nations, LORD,
   and hymn Your name:
51   *m*-He accords great victories-*m* to His king,
       keeps faith with His anointed,
       with David and his offspring forever.

19 For the leader. A psalm of David.

2 The heavens declare the glory of God,
  the sky proclaims His handiwork.
3 Day to day makes utterance,
  night to night speaks out.
4 There is no utterance,
  there are no words,
  a-whose sound goes unheard.-*a*
5 Their voice*b* carries throughout the earth,
  their words to the end of the world.
  He placed in them*c* a tent for the sun,
6   who is like a groom coming forth from the chamber,
      like a hero, eager to run his course.
7 His rising-place is at one end of heaven,
  and his circuit reaches the other;
  nothing escapes his heat.

---

l-l *Meaning of Heb. uncertain.*
m-m *II Sam. 22.51, "Tower of victory."*

a-a *With Septuagint, Symmachus, and Vulgate; or "their sound is not heard."*
b *Cf. Septuagint, Symmachus, and Vulgate; Arabic* qawwah, *"to shout."*
c *Viz. the heavens.*

8 The teaching of the LORD is perfect,
    renewing life;
    the decrees of the LORD are enduring,
    making the simple wise;
9 The precepts of the LORD are just,
    rejoicing the heart;
    the instruction of the LORD is lucid,
    making the eyes light up.
10 The fear of the LORD is pure,
    abiding forever;
    the judgments of the LORD are true,
    righteous altogether,
11   more desirable than gold,
    than much fine gold;
    sweeter than honey,
    than drippings of the comb.
12 Your servant pays them heed;
    in obeying them there is much reward.
13 Who can be aware of errors?
    Clear me of unperceived guilt,
14   and from d-willful sins-d keep Your servant;
    let them not dominate me;
    then shall I be blameless
    and clear of grave offense.
15 May the words of my mouth
    and the prayer of my heart e
    be acceptable to You,
    O LORD, my rock and my redeemer.

20 For the leader. A psalm of David.

2 May the LORD answer you in time of trouble,
    the name of Jacob's God keep you safe.
3 May He send you help from the sanctuary,

d-d Or "arrogant men"; cf. Ps. 119.51.
e For leb as a source of speech, see note to Eccl. 5.1.

and sustain you from Zion.
4 May He receive the tokens*a* of all your meal offerings,
and approve*b* your burnt offerings.   *Selah.*
5 May He grant you your desire,
and fulfill your every plan.
6 May we shout for joy in your victory,
arrayed by standards in the name of our God.
May the LORD fulfill your every wish.

7 Now I know that the LORD will give victory to His
anointed,
will answer him from His heavenly sanctuary
with the mighty victories of His right arm.
8 They [call] on chariots, they [call] on horses,
but we call on the name of the LORD our God.
9 They collapse and lie fallen,
but we rally and gather strength.
10 *c-*O LORD, grant victory!
May the King answer us when we call.*-c*

21 For the leader. A psalm of David.

2 O LORD, the king rejoices in Your strength;
how greatly he exults in Your victory!
3 You have granted him the desire of his heart,
have not denied the request of his lips.   *Selah.*
4 You have proffered him blessings of good things,
have set upon his head a crown of fine gold.
5 He asked You for life; You granted it;
a long life, everlasting.
6 Great is his glory through Your victory;
You have endowed him with splendor and majesty.
7 You have made him blessed forever,

---

a *Reference to* azkara, *"token portion" of meal offering; Lev. 2.2, 9, 16, etc.*
b *Meaning of Heb. uncertain.*
c-c *Or, in the light of v. 7, "O LORD, grant victory to the king; may He answer us when we call."*

gladdened him with the joy of Your presence.
8 For the king trusts in the LORD;
Through the faithfulness of the Most High
he will not be shaken.
9 Your hand is equal to all Your enemies;
Your right hand overpowers Your foes.
10 You set them ablaze like a furnace
a-when You show Your presence.-*a*
The LORD in anger destroys them;
fire consumes them.
11 You wipe their offspring from the earth,
their issue from among men.
12 For they schemed against You;
they laid plans,
but could not succeed.
13 *b*-For You make them turn back-*b*
by Your bows aimed at their face.
14 Be exalted, O LORD, through Your strength;
we will sing and chant the praises of Your mighty deeds.

22 For the leader; on *a*-ayyeleth ha-shahar.-*a* A psalm of David.

2 My God, my God,
why have You abandoned me;
why so far from delivering me
and from my anguished roaring?
3 My God,
I cry by day—You answer not;
by night, and have no respite.

4 *b*-But You are the Holy One,
enthroned,
the Praise of Israel.-*b*
5 In You our fathers trusted;

---

a-a *Or, "at the time of Your anger."*
b-b *Meaning of Heb. uncertain.*

a-a *Meaning of Heb. uncertain.*
b-b *Or "But You are holy, enthroned upon the praises of Israel."*

they trusted, and You rescued them.
6 To You they cried out
and they escaped;
in You they trusted
and were not disappointed.

7 But I am a worm, less than human;
scorned by men, despised by people.
8 All who see me mock me;
c-they curl their lips,-*c*
they shake their heads.
9 "Let him commit himself to the LORD;
let Him rescue him,
let Him save him,
for He is pleased with him."
10 You *a*-drew me-*a* from the womb,
made me secure at my mother's breast.
11 I became Your charge at birth;
from my mother's womb You have been my God.
12 Do not be far from me,
for trouble is near,
and there is none to help.
13 Many bulls surround me,
mighty ones of Bashan encircle me.
14 They open their mouths at me
like tearing, roaring lions.
15 *d*-My life ebbs away:-*d*
all my bones are disjointed;
my heart is like wax,
melting within me;
16 my vigor dries up like a shard;
my tongue cleaves to my palate;
You commit me to the dust of death.
17 Dogs surround me;
a pack of evil ones closes in on me,

c-c *Lit. "they open wide with a lip."*
d-d *Lit. "I am poured out like water."*

e-like lions [they maul] my hands and feet.*-e*

18 I take the count of all my bones
  while they look on and gloat.
19 They divide my clothes among themselves,
  casting lots for my garments.

20 But You, O LORD, be not far off;
  my strength, hasten to my aid.
21 Save my life from the sword,
  my precious life *f* from the clutches of a dog.
22 Deliver me from a lion's mouth;
  from the horns of wild oxen rescue*g* me.
23 Then will I proclaim Your fame to my brethren,
  praise You in the congregation.

24 You who fear the LORD, praise Him!
  All you offspring of Jacob, honor Him!
  Be in dread of Him, all you offspring of Israel!
25 For He did not scorn, He did not spurn
  the plea*h* of the lowly;
  He did not hide His face from him;
  when he cried out to Him, He listened.
26 *i*-Because of You I offer praise-*i* in the great congregation;
  I pay my vows in the presence of His worshipers.
27 Let the lowly eat and be satisfied;
  let all who seek the LORD praise Him.
  Always be of good cheer!
28 Let all the ends of the earth pay heed and turn to the LORD,
  and the peoples of all nations prostrate themselves be-
    fore You;
29   for kingship is the LORD'S

---

e-e With Rashi; cf. Isa. 38.13.
f Lit. "only one."
g Lit. "answer."
h Or "plight."
i-i Lit. "From You is my praise."

and He rules the nations.
³⁰ *j*-All those in full vigor shall eat and prostrate themselves;
all those at death's door, whose spirits flag,
shall bend the knee before Him.*j*
³¹ Offspring shall serve Him;
the LORD's fame shall be proclaimed to the generation
³² to come;
they shall tell of His beneficence
to people yet to be born,
for He has acted.

23 A psalm of David.

The LORD is my shepherd;
I lack nothing.
² He makes me lie down in green pastures;
He leads me to *a*-water in places of repose;-*a*
³ He renews my life;
He guides me in right paths
as befits His name.
⁴ Though I walk through *b*-a valley of deepest darkness,-*b*
I fear no harm, for You are with me;
Your rod and Your staff—they comfort me.

⁵ You spread a table for me in full view of my enemies;
You anoint my head with oil;
my drink is abundant.
⁶ Only goodness and steadfast love shall pursue me
all the days of my life,
and I shall dwell in the house of the LORD
for many long years.

---

^{j-j} *Meaning of Heb. uncertain; others "All the fat ones of the earth shall eat and worship;/All they that go down to the dust shall kneel before Him,/Even he that cannot keep his soul alive."*

^{a-a} *Others "still waters."*
^{b-b} *Others "the valley of the shadow of death."*

24 Of David. A psalm.

The earth is the LORD's and all that it holds,
　the world and its inhabitants.
2 For He founded it upon the ocean,
　set it on the nether-streams.

3 Who may ascend the mountain of the LORD?
　Who may stand in His holy place?—
4 He who has clean hands and a pure heart,
　who has not taken a false oath by My[a] life
　or sworn deceitfully.
5 He shall carry away a blessing from the LORD,
　a just reward from God, his deliverer.
6 Such is the circle[b] of those who turn to Him,
　Jacob, who seek Your presence.　　　　　　*Selah.*

7 O gates, lift up your heads!
　Up high, you everlasting doors,
　　so the King of glory may come in!
8 Who is the King of glory?—
　the LORD, mighty and valiant,
　the LORD, valiant in battle.
9 O gates, lift up your heads!
　Lift them up, you everlasting doors,
　　so the King of glory may come in!
10 Who is the King of glory?—
　the LORD of hosts,
　He is the King of glory!　　　　　　*Selah.*

___

[a] *Ancient versions and some mss. read "His."*
[b] *Lit. "generation."*

25 Of David.

א   O Lord, I set my hope on You;
ב 2 my God, in You I trust;
      may I not be disappointed,
      may my enemies not exult over me.
ג 3 O let none who look to You be disappointed;
      let the faithless be disappointed, empty-handed.
ד 4 Let me know Your paths, O Lord;
      teach me Your ways;
הו 5 guide me in Your true way and teach me,
      for You are God, my deliverer;
      it is You I look to at all times.
ז 6 O Lord, be mindful of Your compassion
      and Your faithfulness;
      they are old as time.
ח 7 Be not mindful of my youthful sins and transgressions;
      in keeping with Your faithfulness consider what is in my
        favor,
      as befits Your goodness, O Lord.
ט 8 Good and upright is the Lord;
      therefore He shows sinners the way.
י 9 He guides the lowly in the right path,
      and teaches the lowly His way.
כ 10 All the Lord's paths are steadfast love
      for those who keep the decrees of His covenant.
ל 11 As befits Your name, O Lord,
      pardon my iniquity though it be great.
מ 12 Whoever fears the Lord,
      he shall be shown what path to choose.
נ 13 He shall live a happy life,
      and his children shall inherit the land.
ס 14 The counsel[a] of the Lord is for those who fear Him;

---

[a] Or "secret."

to them He makes known His covenant.
ע 15 My eyes are ever toward the LORD,
    for He will loose my feet from the net.
פ 16 Turn to me, have mercy on me,
    for I am alone and afflicted.
צ 17 *b*-My deep distress-*b* increases;
    deliver me from my straits.
ר 18 Look at my affliction and suffering,
    and forgive all my sins.
  19 See how numerous my enemies are,
    and how unjustly they hate me!
ש 20 Protect me and save me;
    let me not be disappointed,
    for I have sought refuge in You.
ת 21 May integrity and uprightness watch over me,
    for I look to You.
  22 O God, redeem Israel
    from all its distress.

26 Of David.

Vindicate me, O LORD,
    for I have walked without blame;
    I have trusted in the LORD;
    I have not faltered.
2 Probe me, O LORD, and try me,
    test my *a*-heart and mind;-*a*
3   *b*-for my eyes are on Your steadfast love;
    I have set my course by it.-*b*
4 I do not consort with scoundrels,
    or mix with hypocrites;
5   I detest the company of evil men,
    and do not consort with the wicked;
6   I wash my hands in innocence,

b-b *Lit. "The distress of my heart."*

a-a *Lit. "kidneys and heart."*
b-b *Or "I am aware of Your faithfulness, and always walk in Your true [path]."*

and walk around Your altar,
7   raising my voice in thanksgiving,
    and telling all Your wonders.
8 O LORD, I love Your temple abode,
    the dwelling-place of Your glory.
9 Do not sweep me away with sinners,
        or [snuff out] my life with murderers,
10   who have schemes at their fingertips,
    and hands full of bribes.
11 But I walk without blame;
    redeem me, have mercy on me!
12 My feet are on level ground.
    In assemblies I will bless the LORD.

27   Of David.

The LORD is my light and my help;
    whom should I fear?
The LORD is the stronghold of my life,
    whom should I dread?
2 When evil men assail me
    a-to devour my flesh-*a*—
    it is they, my foes and my enemies,
    who stumble and fall.
3 Should an army besiege me,
    my heart would have no fear;
    should war beset me,
    still would I be confident.

4 One thing I ask of the LORD,
    only that do I seek:
    to live in the house of the LORD
    all the days of my life,
    to gaze upon the beauty of the LORD,

---

a-a *Or "to slander me"; cf. Dan. 3.8; 6.25.*

b-to frequent-*b* His temple.
5 He will shelter me in His pavilion
on an evil day,
grant me the protection of His tent,
raise me high upon a rock.
6 Now is my head high
over my enemies roundabout;
I sacrifice in His tent with shouts of joy,
singing and chanting a hymn to the LORD.

7 Hear, O LORD, when I cry aloud;
have mercy on me, answer me.
8 *b*-In Your behalf-*b* my heart says:
"Seek My face!"
O LORD, I seek Your face.
9 Do not hide Your face from me;
do not thrust aside Your servant in anger;
You have ever been my help.
Do not forsake me, do not abandon me,
O God, my deliverer.
10 Though my father and mother abandon me,
the LORD will take me in.
11 Show me Your way, O LORD,
and lead me on a level path
because of my watchful foes.
12 Do not subject me to the will of my foes,
for false witnesses and unjust accusers
have appeared against me.
13 Had I not the assurance
that I would enjoy the goodness of the LORD
in the land of the living . . .

14 Look to the LORD;
be strong and of good courage!
O look to the LORD!

b-b *Meaning of Heb. uncertain.*

28 Of David.

O Lord, I call to You;
   my rock, do not disregard me,
   for if You hold aloof from me,
   I shall be like those gone down into the Pit.
2 Listen to my plea for mercy
   when I cry out to You,
   when I lift my hands
   toward Your inner sanctuary.
3 Do not *a-count me-a* with the wicked and evildoers
   who profess goodwill toward their fellows
   while malice is in their heart.
4 Pay them according to their deeds,
   their malicious acts;
   according to their handiwork pay them,
   give them their deserts.
5 For they do not consider the Lord's deeds,
   the work of His hands.
May He tear them down,
   never to rebuild them!
6 Blessed is the Lord,
   for He listens to my plea for mercy.
7 The Lord is my strength and my shield;
   my heart trusts in Him.
I was helped,*b* and my heart exulted,
   so I will glorify Him with my song.
8 The Lord is *c-their strength;-c*
   He is a stronghold for the deliverance of His anointed.
9 Deliver and bless Your very own people;
   tend them and sustain them forever.

---

a-a *Or "drag me off"; meaning of Heb. uncertain.*
b *Or "strengthened."*
c-c *Septuagint, Saadia, and others render, and some mss. read,* 'oz le'ammo, *"the strength of His people."*

29 A psalm of David.

Ascribe to the LORD, O divine beings,
    ascribe to the LORD glory and strength.
2 Ascribe to the LORD the glory of His name;
    bow down to the LORD, majestic in holiness.
3 The voice of the LORD is over the waters;
    the God of glory thunders,
    the LORD, over the mighty waters.
4 The voice of the LORD is power;
    the voice of the LORD is majesty;
5   the voice of the LORD breaks cedars;
    the LORD shatters the cedars of Lebanon.
6 *a*-He makes Lebanon skip like a calf,-*a*
    Sirion, like a young wild ox.
7 The voice of the LORD kindles flames of fire;
8   the voice of the LORD convulses the wilderness;
    the LORD convulses the wilderness of Kadesh;
9   the voice of the LORD causes hinds to calve,
    b-and strips forests bare;-*b*
    while in His temple all say "Glory!"
10 The LORD sat enthroned at the Flood;
    the LORD sits enthroned, king forever.

11 May the LORD grant strength to His people;
    may the LORD bestow on His people well-being.

30 A psalm of David. A song for the dedication of the House.*a*

2 I extol You, O LORD,
    for You have lifted me up,
    and not let my enemies rejoice over me.

a-a *Lit. "He makes them skip like a calf, Lebanon and Sirion, etc."*
b-b *Or "brings ewes to early birth."*

a *I.e. the Temple.*

³ O Lord, my God,
    I cried out to You,
    and You healed me.
⁴ O Lord, You brought me up from Sheol,
    preserved me from going down into the Pit.

⁵ O you faithful of the Lord, sing to Him,
    and praise His holy name.
⁶ For He is angry but a moment,
    and when He is pleased there is life.
    ᵇOne may lie down weeping at nightfall;⁻ᵇ
    but at dawn there are shouts of joy.

⁷ When I was untroubled,
    I thought, "I shall never be shaken,"
⁸   for You, O Lord, when You were pleased,
    made [me]ᶜ firm as a mighty mountain.
    When You hid Your face,
    I was terrified.
⁹ I called to You, O Lord;
    to my Lord I made appeal,
¹⁰   "What is to be gained from my death,ᵈ
    from my descent into the Pit?
    Can dust praise You?
    Can it declare Your faithfulness?
¹¹ Hear, O Lord, and have mercy on me;
    O Lord, be my help!"

¹² You turned my lament into dancing,
    you undid my sackcloth and girded me with joy,
¹³   that [my] whole being might sing hymns to You
        endlessly;
    O Lord my God, I will praise You forever.

ᵇ⁻ᵇ *Or "Weeping may linger for the night."*
ᶜ *Following Saadia, R. Isaiah of Trani; cf. Ibn Ezra.*
ᵈ *Lit. "blood."*

31 For the leader. A psalm of David.

2 I seek refuge in You, O Lord;
    may I never be disappointed;
    as You are righteous, rescue me.
3 Incline Your ear to me;
    be quick to save me;
    be a rock, a stronghold for me,
    a citadel, for my deliverance.
4 For You are my rock and my fortress;
    You lead me and guide me as befits Your name.
5 You free me from the net laid for me,
    for You are my stronghold.
6 Into Your hand I entrust my spirit;
    You redeem me, O Lord, faithful God.
7 I detest those who rely on empty folly,
    but I trust in the Lord.
8 Let me exult and rejoice in Your faithfulness
    when You notice my affliction,
    are mindful of my deep distress,
9   and do not hand me over to my enemy,
    but *-grant me relief.-*

10 Have mercy on me, O Lord,
    for I am in distress;
    my eyes are wasted by vexation,
    -my substance and body too.-
11 My life is spent in sorrow,
    my years in groaning;
    my strength fails because of my iniquity,
    my limbs waste away.
12 Because of all my foes
    I am the particular butt of my neighbors,

a-a Lit. *"make my feet stand in a broad place."*
b-b *Meaning of Heb. uncertain.*

a horror to my friends;
those who see me on the street avoid me.
¹³ I am put out of mind like the dead;
I am like an object given up for lost.
¹⁴ I hear the whisperings of many,
intrigue ᶜ on every side,
as they scheme together against me,
plotting to take my life.

¹⁵ But I trust in You, O LORD;
I say, "You are my God!"
¹⁶ My fate is in Your hand;
save me from the hand of my enemies and pursuers.
¹⁷ Show favor to Your servant;
as You are faithful, deliver me.
¹⁸ O LORD, let me not be disappointed when I call You;
let the wicked be disappointed;
let them be silenced in Sheol;
¹⁹ let lying lips be stilled
that speak haughtily against the righteous
with arrogance and contempt.
²⁰ How abundant is the good
that You have in store for those who fear You,
that You do in the full view of men
for those who take refuge in You.
²¹ You grant them the protection of Your presence
ᵇ⁻against scheming men;⁻ᵇ
You shelter them in Your pavilion
from contentious tongues.
²² Blessed is the LORD,
for He has been wondrously faithful to me,
a veritable bastion.
²³ Alarmed, I had thought,
"I am thrust out of Your sight";
yet You listened to my plea for mercy
when I cried out to You.

ᶜ Others "terror."

²⁴ So love the LORD, all you faithful;
   the LORD guards the loyal,
   and more than requites
   him who acts arrogantly.
²⁵ Be strong and of good courage,
   all you who wait for the LORD.

32 Of David. ᵃ⁻A *maskil.*⁻ᵃ

Happy is he whose transgression is forgiven,
   whose sin is covered over.
² Happy the man whom the LORD does not hold guilty,
   and in whose spirit there is no deceit.

³ As long as I said nothing,
   my limbs wasted away
   from my anguished roaring all day long.
⁴ For night and day
   Your hand lay heavy on me;
   my vigor waned
   as in the summer drought.   *Selah.*
⁵ Then I acknowledged my sin to You;
   I did not cover up my guilt;
   I resolved, "I will confess my transgressions to the
      LORD,"
   and You forgave the guilt of my sin.   *Selah.*
⁶ Therefore let every faithful man pray to You
   ᵇ⁻upon discovering [his sin],⁻ᵇ
   that the rushing mighty waters
   not overtake him.
⁷ You are my shelter;
   You preserve me from distress;
   You surround me with the joyous shouts of
      deliverance.   *Selah.*

ᵃ⁻ᵃ *Meaning of Heb. uncertain.*
ᵇ⁻ᵇ *Meaning of Heb. uncertain; others "in a time when You may be found."*

8 Let me enlighten you
   and show you which way to go;
   let me offer counsel; my eye is on you.
9 Be not like a senseless horse or mule
   a-whose movement must be curbed by bit and bridle;-*a*
   c-far be it from you!-*c*
10 Many are the torments of the wicked,
   but he who trusts in the LORD
   shall be surrounded with favor.
11 Rejoice in the LORD and exult, O you righteous;
   shout for joy, all upright men!

33   Sing forth, O you righteous, to the LORD;
     it is fit that the upright acclaim Him.
2 Praise the LORD with the lyre;
   with the ten-stringed harp sing to Him;
3   sing Him a new song;
     play sweetly with shouts of joy.
4 For the word of the LORD is right;
   His every deed is faithful.
5 He loves what is right and just;
   the earth is full of the LORD's faithful care.
6 By the word of the LORD the heavens were made,
   by the breath of His mouth, all their host.
7 He heaps up the ocean waters like a mound,
   stores the deep in vaults.

8 Let all the earth fear the LORD;
   let all the inhabitants of the world dread Him.
9 For He spoke, and it was;
   He commanded, and it endured.
10 The LORD frustrates the plans of nations,
   brings to naught the designs of peoples.
11 What the LORD plans endures forever,
   what He designs, for ages on end.

c-c Meaning of Heb. uncertain; for this rendering cf. Ibn Ezra.

12 Happy the nation whose God is the Lord,
the people He has chosen to be His own.
13 The Lord looks down from heaven;
He sees all mankind.
14 From His dwelling-place He gazes
on all the inhabitants of the earth—
15 He who fashions the hearts of them all,
who discerns all their doings.

16 Kings are not delivered by a large force;
warriors are not saved by great strength;
17 horses are a false hope for deliverance;
for all their great power they provide no escape.
18 Truly the eye of the Lord is on those who fear Him,
who wait for His faithful care
19 to save them from death,
to sustain them in famine.
20 We set our hope on the Lord,
He is our help and shield;
21 in Him our hearts rejoice,
for in His holy name we trust.
22 May we enjoy, O Lord, Your faithful care,
as we have put our hope in You.

34 Of David, *a*-when he feigned madness in the presence of
Abimelech, who turned him out, and he left.*-a*

א   2 I bless the Lord at all times;
praise of Him is ever in my mouth.
ב   3 I glory in the Lord;
let the lowly hear it and rejoice.
ג   4 Exalt the Lord with me;
let us extol His name together.
ד   5 I turned to the Lord, and He answered me;
He saved me from all my terrors.

a-a *Cf. I Sam. 21.14ff.*

ה   ⁶ Men look to Him and are radiant;
ו   let their faces not be downcast.
ז   ⁷ Here was a lowly man who called,
      and the LORD listened,
      and delivered him from all his troubles.
ח   ⁸ The angel of the LORD camps around those who fear Him
      and rescues them.
ט   ⁹ Taste and see how good the LORD is;
      happy the man who takes refuge in Him!
י   ¹⁰ Fear the LORD, you His consecrated ones,
      for those who fear Him lack nothing.
כ   ¹¹ Lions have been reduced to starvation,
      but those who turn to the LORD shall not lack any good.
ל   ¹² Come, my sons, listen to me;
      I will teach you what it is to fear the LORD.
מ   ¹³ Who is the man who is eager for life,
      who desires years of good fortune?
נ   ¹⁴ Guard your tongue from evil,
      your lips from deceitful speech.
ס   ¹⁵ Shun evil and do good,
      seek amity*b* and pursue it.
ע   ¹⁶ The eyes of the LORD are on the righteous,
      His ears attentive to their cry.
פ   ¹⁷ The face of the LORD is set against evildoers,
      to erase their names from the earth.
צ   ¹⁸ They*c* cry out, and the LORD hears,
      and saves them from all their troubles.
ק   ¹⁹ The LORD is close to the brokenhearted;
      those crushed in spirit He delivers.
ר   ²⁰ Though the misfortunes of the righteous be many,
      the LORD will save him from them all,
ש   ²¹   keeping all his bones intact,
      not one of them being broken.
ת   ²² One misfortune is the deathblow of the wicked;
      the foes of the righteous shall be ruined.

b *Or "integrity."*
c *Viz. the righteous of v. 16.*

23 The LORD redeems the life of His servants;
all who take refuge in Him shall not be ruined.

35 Of David.

O LORD, strive with my adversaries,
give battle to my foes,
2 take up shield and buckler,
and come to my defense;
3 ready the spear and javelin
against my pursuers;
tell me, "I am your deliverance."
4 Let those who seek my life
be frustrated and put to shame;
let those who plan to harm me
fall back in disgrace.
5 Let them be as chaff in the wind,
the LORD's angel driving them on.
6 Let their path be dark and slippery,
with the LORD's angel in pursuit.
7 For without cause they hid a net to trap me;
without cause they dug a pit*a* for me.
8 Let disaster overtake them unawares;
let the net they hid catch them;
let them fall into it when disaster [strikes].
9 Then shall I exult in the LORD,
rejoice in His deliverance.
10 All my bones shall say,
"LORD, who is like You?
You save the poor from one stronger than he,
the poor and needy from his despoiler."

11 Malicious witnesses appear
who question me about things I do not know.
12 They repay me evil for good,

a Transferred from first clause for clarity.

43

[seeking] my bereavement.
13 Yet, when they were ill,
my dress was sackcloth,
I kept a fast—
b-may what I prayed for happen to me!-*b*
14 I walked about as though it were my friend or my brother;
I was bowed with gloom, like one mourning for his
mother.
15 But when I stumble, they gleefully gather;
wretches gather against me,
I know not why;
c-they tear at me without end.
16 With impious, mocking grimace-*c*
they gnash their teeth at me.

17 O Lord, how long will You look on?
Rescue me *c*-from their attacks,-*c*
my precious life, from the lions,
18 that I may praise You in a great congregation,
acclaim You in a mighty throng.
19 Let not my treacherous enemies rejoice over me,
or those who hate me without reason wink their eyes.
20 For they do not offer amity,
but devise fraudulent schemes against harmless folk.
21 They open wide their mouths at me,
saying, "Aha, aha, we have seen it!"

22 You have seen it, O LORD;
do not hold aloof!
O Lord, be not far from me!
23 Wake, rouse Yourself for my cause,
for my claim, O my God and my Lord!
24 Take up my cause, O LORD my God, as You are
beneficent,
and let them not rejoice over me.

b-b *Meaning of Heb. uncertain; lit. "my prayer returns upon my bosom."*
c-c *Meaning of Heb. uncertain.*

²⁵ Let them not think,
"Aha, just what we wished!"
Let them not say,
"We have destroyed him!"
²⁶ May those who rejoice at my misfortune
be frustrated and utterly disgraced;
may those who vaunt themselves over me
be clad in frustration and shame.
²⁷ May those who desire my vindication
sing forth joyously;
may they always say,
"Extolled be the LORD
who desires the well-being of His servant,"
²⁸   while my tongue shall recite Your beneficent acts,
Your praises all day long.

36   For the leader. Of the servant of the LORD, of David.

² ᵃ-I know-ᵃ what Transgression says to the wicked;
he has no sense of the dread of God,
³   ᵇ-because its speech is seductive to him
till his iniquity be found out and he be hated.-ᵇ
⁴ His words are evil and deceitful;
he will not consider doing good.
⁵ In bed he plots mischief;
he is set on a path of no good,
he does not reject evil.

⁶ O LORD, Your faithfulness reaches to heaven;
Your steadfastness to the sky;
⁷   Your beneficence is like the high mountains;
Your justice like the great deep;
man and beast You deliver, O LORD.
⁸ How precious is Your faithful care, O God!

ᵃ-ᵃ *Lit. "In my heart is."*
ᵇ-ᵇ *Meaning of Heb. uncertain.*

45

Mankind shelters in the shadow of Your wings.
⁹ They feast on the rich fare of Your house;
    You let them drink at Your refreshing stream.
¹⁰ With You is the fountain of life;
    by Your light do we see light.
¹¹ Bestow Your faithful care on those devoted to You,
    and Your beneficence on upright men.
¹² Let not the foot of the arrogant tread on me,
    or the hand of the wicked drive me away.
¹³ There lie the evildoers, fallen,
    thrust down, unable to rise.

37   Of David.

א   Do not be vexed by evil men;
    do not be incensed by wrongdoers;
  ² for they soon wither like grass,
    like verdure fade away.
ב ³ Trust in the LORD and do good,
    abide in the land and remain loyal.
  ⁴ Seek the favor of the LORD,
    and He will grant you the desires of your heart.
ג ⁵ Leave all*ᵃ* to the LORD;
    trust in Him; He will do it.
  ⁶ He will cause your vindication to shine forth like the light,
    the justice of your case, like the noonday sun.
ד ⁷ Be patient and wait for the LORD,
    do not be vexed by the prospering man
    who carries out his schemes.

ה ⁸ Give up anger, abandon fury,
    do not be vexed;
    it can only do harm.
  ⁹ For evil men will be cut off,

ᵃ *Lit. "your way."*

but those who look to the LORD—
they shall inherit the land.

ו ¹⁰ A little longer and there will be no wicked man;
you will look at where he was—
he will be gone.

¹¹ But the lowly shall inherit the land,
and delight in abundant well-being.

ז ¹² The wicked man schemes against the righteous,
and gnashes his teeth at him.

¹³ The Lord laughs at him,
for He knows that his day will come.

ח ¹⁴ The wicked draw their swords, bend their bows,
to bring down the lowly and needy,
to slaughter *ᵇ*upright men.*ᵇ*

¹⁵ Their swords shall pierce their own hearts,
and their bows shall be broken.

ט ¹⁶ Better the little that the righteous man has
than the great abundance of the wicked.

¹⁷ For the arms of the wicked shall be broken,
but the LORD is the support of the righteous.

י ¹⁸ The LORD is concerned for the needs*ᶜ* of the blameless;
their portion lasts forever;

¹⁹   they shall not come to grief in bad times;
in famine, they shall eat their fill.

כ ²⁰ But the wicked shall perish,
and the enemies of the LORD shall be consumed,
like meadow grass*ᵈ* consumed in smoke.

ל ²¹ The wicked man borrows and does not repay;
the righteous is generous and keeps giving.

²² Those blessed by Him shall inherit the land,
but those cursed by Him shall be cut off.

מ ²³ The steps of a man are made firm by the LORD,
when He delights in his way.

²⁴ Though he stumbles, he does not fall down,
for the LORD gives him support.

ᵇ⁻ᵇ *Lit. "those whose way is upright."*
ᶜ *Lit. "days."*
ᵈ *Meaning of Heb. uncertain.*

נ ²⁵ I have been young and am now old,
but I have never seen a righteous man abandoned,
or his children seeking bread.
²⁶ He is always generous, and lends,
and his children are held blessed.

ס ²⁷ Shun evil and do good,
and you shall abide forever.
²⁸ For the LORD loves what is right,
He does not abandon His faithful ones.
They are preserved forever,
while the children of the wicked will be cut off.
²⁹ The righteous shall inherit the land,
and abide forever in it.

פ ³⁰ The mouth of the righteous utters wisdom,
and his tongue speaks what is right.
³¹ The teaching of his God is in his heart;
his feet do not slip.

צ ³² The wicked watches for the righteous,
seeking to put him to death;
³³ the LORD will not abandon him to his power;
He will not let him be condemned in judgment.

ק ³⁴ Look to the LORD and keep to His way,
and He will raise you high that you may inherit the land;
when the wicked are cut off, you shall see it.

ר ³⁵ I saw a wicked man, powerful,
well-rooted like a robust native tree.
³⁶ Suddenly he vanished and was gone;
I sought him, but he was not to be found.

ש ³⁷ Mark the blameless, note the upright,
for there is a future for the man of integrity.
³⁸ But transgressors shall be utterly destroyed,
the future of the wicked shall be cut off.

ת ³⁹ The deliverance of the righteous comes from the LORD,
their stronghold in time of trouble.
⁴⁰ The LORD helps them and rescues them,

rescues them from the wicked and delivers them,
for they seek refuge in Him.

38 A psalm of David. *Lehazkir.*[a]

² O LORD, do not punish me in wrath;
do not chastise me in fury.
³ For Your arrows have struck me;
Your blows have fallen upon me.
⁴ There is no soundness in my flesh because of Your rage,
no wholeness in my bones because of my sin.
⁵ For my iniquities have [b]overwhelmed me;[b]
they are like a heavy burden, more than I can bear.
⁶ My wounds stink and fester
because of my folly.
⁷ I am all bent and bowed;
I walk about in gloom all day long.
⁸ For my sinews are full of fever;
there is no soundness in my flesh.
⁹ I am all benumbed and crushed;
I roar because of the turmoil in my mind.

¹⁰ O Lord, You are aware of all my entreaties;
my groaning is not hidden from You.
¹¹ My mind reels;
my strength fails me;
my eyes too have lost their luster.
¹² My friends and companions stand back from my
affliction;
my kinsmen stand far off.
¹³ Those who seek my life lay traps;
those who wish me harm speak malice;
they utter deceit all the time.
¹⁴ But I am like a deaf man, unhearing,

[a] *Meaning of Heb. uncertain.*
[b-b] *Lit. "passed over my head."*

like a dumb man who cannot speak up;
15 I am like one who does not hear,
who has no retort on his lips.
16 But I wait for You, O LORD;
You will answer, O Lord, my God.
17 For I fear they will rejoice over me;
when my foot gives way they will vaunt themselves
against me.
18 For I am on the verge of collapse;
my pain is always with me.
19 I acknowledge my iniquity;
I am fearful over my sin;
20 for my mortal enemies are numerous;
my treacherous foes are many.
21 Those who repay evil for good
harass me for pursuing good.

22 Do not abandon me, O LORD;
my God, be not far from me;
23 hasten to my aid,
O Lord, my deliverance.

39 For the leader; for *Jeduthun.* A psalm of David.

2 I resolved I would watch my step
lest I offend by my speech;
I would keep my mouth muzzled
while the wicked man was in my presence.
3 I was dumb, silent;
I was very*a* still
while my pain was intense.
4 My mind was in a rage,
my thoughts were all aflame;
I spoke out:

---

a *Cf. use of* ṭwb *in Hos. 10.1; Jonah 4.4.*

5   Tell me, O LORD, what my term is,
    what is the measure of my days;
    I would know how fleeting my life is.
6 You have made my life just handbreadths long;
    its span is as nothing in Your sight;
    b-no man endures any longer than a breath.-*b*   *Selah.*
7 Man walks about as a mere shadow;
    mere futility is his hustle and bustle,
    amassing and not knowing who will gather in.
8 What, then, can I count on, O Lord?
    In You my hope lies.
9 Deliver me from all my transgressions;
    make me not the butt of the benighted.
10 I am dumb, I do not speak up,
    for it is Your doing.
11 Take away Your plague from me;
    I perish from Your blows.
12 You chastise a man in punishment for his sin,
    consuming like a moth what he treasures.
    No man is more than a breath.   *Selah.*

13 Hear my prayer, O LORD;
    give ear to my cry;
    do not disregard my tears;
    for like all my forebears
    I am an alien, resident with You.
14 Look away from me, *b*-that I may recover,-*b*
    before I pass away and am gone.

40 For the leader. A psalm of David.

2 I put my hope in the LORD;
    He inclined toward me,
    and heeded my cry.

b-b *Meaning of Heb. uncertain.*

³ He lifted me out of the miry pit,
   the slimy clay,
   and set my feet on a rock,
   steadied my legs.
⁴ He put a new song into my mouth,
   a hymn to our God.
   May many see it and stand in awe,
   and trust in the LORD.
⁵ Happy is the man who makes the LORD his trust,
   who turns not to the arrogant or to followers of falsehood.
⁶ ᵃ-You, O LORD my God, have done many things;
   the wonders You have devised for us
   cannot be set out before You;⁻ᵃ
   I would rehearse the tale of them,
   but they are more than can be told.
⁷ ᵇ-You gave me to understand that⁻ᵇ
   You do not desire sacrifice and meal offering;
   You do not ask for burnt offering and sin offering.
⁸ Then I said,
   ᵇ-"See, I will bring a scroll recounting what befell
   me."⁻ᵇ
⁹ To do what pleases You, my God, is my desire;
   Your teaching is in my inmost parts.
¹⁰ I proclaimed [Your] righteousness in a great
    congregation;
    see, I did not withhold my words;
    O LORD, You must know it.
¹¹ I did not keep Your beneficence to myself;
    I declared Your faithful deliverance;
    I did not fail to speak of Your steadfast love in a great
    congregation.
¹² O LORD, You will not withhold from me Your
    compassion;
    Your steadfast love will protect me always.

ᵃ⁻ᵃ Or "You, O LORD my God, have done many things—the wonders You have devised for
us; none can equal You."
ᵇ⁻ᵇ Meaning of Heb. uncertain.

¹³ For misfortunes without number envelop me;
   my iniquities have caught up with me;
   I cannot see;
   they are more than the hairs of my head;
   c-I am at my wits' end.-*c*
¹⁴ *d*O favor me, LORD, and save me;   .
   O LORD, hasten to my aid.
¹⁵ Let those who seek to destroy my life
   be frustrated and disgraced;
   let those who wish me harm
   fall back in shame.
¹⁶ Let those who say "Aha! Aha!" over me
   be desolate because of their frustration.
¹⁷ But let all who seek You be glad and rejoice in You;
   let those who are eager for Your deliverance always say,
   "Extolled be the LORD!"
¹⁸ But I am poor and needy;
   may the Lord devise [deliverance] for me.
   You are my help and my rescuer;
   my God, do not delay.

41   For the leader. A psalm of David.

² Happy is he who is thoughtful of the wretched;
   in bad times may the LORD keep him from harm.
³ May the LORD guard him and preserve him;
   and may he be thought happy in the land.
   Do not subject him to the will of his enemies.
⁴ The LORD will sustain him on his sickbed;
   a-You shall wholly transform his bed of suffering.-*a*
⁵ I said, "O LORD, have mercy on me,
   heal me, for I have sinned against You."
⁶ My enemies speak evilly of me,
   "When will he die and his name perish?"

---

c-c Or "my courage fails me."
d With vv. 14–18, cf. Ps. 70.

a-a Meaning of Heb. uncertain.

7 If one comes to visit, he speaks falsely;
   his mind stores up evil thoughts;
   once outside, he speaks them.
8 All my enemies whisper together against me,
   imagining the worst for me.
9 "Something baneful has settled in him;
   he'll not rise from his bed again."
10 My ally in whom I trusted,
   even he who shares my bread,
   a-has been utterly false to me.*-a*
11 But You, O LORD, have mercy on me;
   let me rise again and repay them.
12 Then shall I know that You are pleased with me:
   when my enemy cannot shout in triumph over me.
13 You will support me because of my integrity,
   and let me abide in Your presence forever.

14 Blessed is the LORD, God of Israel,
   from eternity to eternity.
   Amen and Amen.

BOOK TWO

42 For the leader. A *maskil* of the Korahites.

2 Like a hind crying for water,*a*
   my soul cries for You, O God;
3   my soul thirsts for God, the living God;
   O when will I come to appear before God!
4 My tears have been my food day and night;
   I am ever taunted with, "Where is your God?"
5 When I think of this, I pour out my soul:
   how I *b*-walked with the crowd, moved with them,*-b*
   the festive throng, to the House of God

a Lit. "watercourses."
b-b Meaning of Heb. uncertain.

54

with joyous shouts of praise.
6 Why so downcast, my soul,
   why disquieted within me?
  Have hope in God;
    I will yet praise Him
    c-for His saving presence.-*c*

7 O my God, my soul is downcast;
   therefore I think of You
   in this land of Jordan and Hermon,
   in Mount Mizar,
8   where deep calls to deep
    in the roar of *b*-Your cataracts;-*b*
    all Your breakers and billows have swept over me.
9 By day may the LORD vouchsafe His faithful care,
    so that at night a song to Him may be with me,
    a prayer to the God of my life.
10 I say to God, my rock,
    "Why have You forgotten me,
    why must I walk in gloom,
    oppressed by my enemy?"
11 *b*-Crushing my bones,-*b*
    my foes revile me,
    taunting me always with, "Where is your God?"
12 Why so downcast, my soul,
    why disquieted within me?
  Have hope in God;
    I will yet praise Him,
    my ever-present help, my God.

43 *a*Vindicate me, O God,
     champion my cause
     against faithless people;
     rescue me from the treacherous, dishonest man.

c-c *Several ancient versions and Heb. mss. connect the first word in v. 7 with the end of 6,*
reading yeshu'ot panai we'Elohai, *"my ever-present help, my God," as in vv. 12 and*
Ps. 43.5.

a *A continuation of Ps. 42.*

55

2 For You are my God, my stronghold;
  why have You rejected me?
Why must I walk in gloom,
  oppressed by the enemy?
3 Send forth Your light and Your truth;
  they will lead me;
  they will bring me to Your holy mountain,
  to Your dwelling-place,
4   that I may come to the altar of God,
  God, my delight, my joy;
  that I may praise You with the lyre,
  O God, my God.
5 Why so downcast, my soul,
  why disquieted within me?
Have hope in God;
  I will yet praise Him,
  my ever-present help, my God.

44 For the leader. Of the Korahites. A *maskil.*

2 We have heard, O God,
  our fathers have told us
  the deeds You performed in their time,
  in days of old.
3 With Your hand You planted them,
  displacing nations;
  You brought misfortune on peoples,
  and drove them out.
4 It was not by their sword that they took the land,
  their arm did not give them victory,
  but Your right hand, Your arm, and Your goodwill,
  for You favored them.
5 You are my king, O God;
  decree victories for Jacob!

6 Through You we gore our foes;
   by Your name we trample our adversaries;
7   I do not trust in my bow;
   it is not my sword that gives me victory;-
8   You give us victory over our foes;
   You thwart those who hate us.
9 In God we glory at all times,
   and praise Your name unceasingly.   *Selah.*

10 Yet You have rejected and disgraced us;
   You do not go with our armies.
11 You make us retreat before our foe;
   our enemies plunder us at will.
12 You let them devour us like sheep;
   You disperse us among the nations.
13 You sell Your people for no fortune,
   You set no high price on them.
14 You make us the butt of our neighbors,
   the scorn and derision of those around us.
15 You make us a byword among the nations,
   a laughingstock*a* among the peoples.
16 I am always aware of my disgrace;
   I am wholly covered with shame
17   at the sound of taunting revilers,
   in the presence of the vengeful foe.

18 All this has come upon us,
   yet we have not forgotten You,
   or been false to Your covenant.
19 Our hearts have not gone astray,
   nor have our feet swerved from Your path,
20   though You cast us, crushed, to where the *b*-sea
   monster*-b* is,
   and covered us over with deepest darkness.
21 If we forgot the name of our God

---

a *Lit. "a wagging of the head."*
b-b *Heb.* tannim=tannin, *as in Ezek. 29.3 and 32.2.*

and spread forth our hands to a foreign god,
22 God would surely search it out,
for He knows the secrets of the heart.
23 It is for Your sake that we are slain all day long,
that we are regarded as sheep to be slaughtered.

24 Rouse Yourself; why do You sleep, O Lord?
Awaken, do not reject us forever!
25 Why do You hide Your face,
ignoring our affliction and distress?
26 We lie prostrate in the dust;
our body clings to the ground.
27 Arise and help us,
redeem us, as befits Your faithfulness.

45
For the leader; *a*-on *shoshannim.*-*a* Of the Korahites. A *maskil.*
A love song.

2 My heart is astir with gracious words;
I speak my poem to a king;
my tongue is the pen of an expert scribe.

3 You are fairer than all men;
your speech is endowed with grace;
rightly has God given you an eternal blessing.
4 Gird your sword upon your thigh, O hero,
in your splendor and glory;
5 *a*-in your glory, win success;
ride on in the cause of truth and meekness and right;
and let your right hand lead you to awesome deeds.-*a*
6 Your arrows, sharpened,
b-[pierce] the breast of the king's enemies;
peoples fall at your feet.-*b*
7 Your *c*-divine throne-*c* is everlasting;

a-a *Meaning of Heb. uncertain.*
b-b *Order of Heb. clauses inverted for clarity.*
c-c *Cf. I Chron. 29.23.*

your royal scepter is a scepter of equity.
8 You love righteousness and hate wickedness;
rightly has God, your God, chosen to anoint you
with oil of gladness over all your peers.
9 All your robes [are fragrant] with
myrrh and aloes and cassia;
from ivoried palaces
lutes entertain you.
10 Royal princesses are your favorites;
the consort stands at your right hand,
decked in gold of Ophir.

11 Take heed, lass, and note,
incline your ear:
forget your people and your father's house,
12 and let the king be aroused by your beauty;
since he is your lord, bow to him.
13 O Tyrian lass,
the wealthiest people will court your favor with gifts,
14 a-goods of all sorts.

The royal princess,
her dress embroidered with golden mountings,
15 is led inside to the king;-a
maidens in her train, her companions,
are presented to you.
16 They are led in with joy and gladness;
they enter the palace of the king.
17 Your sons will succeed your ancestors;
you will appoint them princes throughout the land.

18 I commemorate your fame for all generations,
so peoples will praise you forever and ever.

46 For the leader. Of the Korahites; ᵃ⁻on *alamoth.*⁻ᵃ A song.

2 God is our refuge and stronghold,
   a help in trouble, very near.
3 Therefore we are not afraid
   though the earth reels,
   though mountains topple into the sea—
4   its waters rage and foam;
   in its swell mountains quake.   *Selah.*

5 There is a river whose streams gladden God's city,
   the holy dwelling-place of the Most High.
6 God is in its midst, it will not be toppled;
   by daybreak God will come to its aid.
7 Nations rage, kingdoms topple;
   at the sound of His thunder the earth dissolves.
8 The LORD of hosts is with us;
   the God of Jacob is our haven.   *Selah.*

9 Come and see what the LORD has done,
   how He has wrought desolation on the earth.
10 He puts a stop to wars throughout the earth,
   breaking the bow, snapping the spear,
   consigning wagons to the flames.
11 "Desist! Realize that I am God!
   I dominate the nations;
   I dominate the earth."
12 The LORD of hosts is with us;
   the God of Jacob is our haven.   *Selah.*

ᵃ⁻ᵃ *Meaning of Heb. uncertain.*

47   For the leader. Of the Korahites. A psalm.

2 All you peoples, clap your hands,
    raise a joyous shout for God.
3 For the LORD Most High is awesome,
    great king over all the earth;
4   He subjects peoples to us,
    sets nations at our feet.
5 He chose our heritage for us,
    the pride of Jacob whom He loved.   *Selah.*

6 God ascends midst acclamation;
    the LORD, to the blasts of the horn.
7 Sing, O sing to God;
    sing, O sing to our king;
8   for God is king over all the earth;
    sing a hymn.[a]
9 God reigns over the nations;
    God is seated on His holy throne.
10 The great of the peoples are gathered together,
    the retinue of Abraham's God;
    for the guardians of the earth belong to God;
    He is greatly exalted.

48   A song. A psalm of the Korahites.

2 The LORD is great and much acclaimed
    in the city of our God,
    His holy mountain—
3   fair-crested, joy of all the earth,
    Mount Zion, summit of Zaphon,[a]
    city of the great king.

---

[a] *Heb.* maskil, *a musical term of uncertain meaning.*
[a] *A term for the divine abode.*

4 Through its citadels, God has made Himself known
as a haven.
5 See, the kings joined forces;
they advanced together.
6 At the mere sight of it they were stunned,
they were terrified, they panicked;
7 they were seized there with a trembling,
like a woman in the throes of labor,
8 as the Tarshish fleet was wrecked
in an easterly gale.*b*
9 The likes of what we heard we have now witnessed
in the city of the LORD of hosts,
in the city of our God—
may God preserve it forever! *Selah.*

10 In Your temple, God,
we meditate upon Your faithful care.
11 The praise of You, God, like Your name,
reaches to the ends of the earth;
Your right hand is filled with beneficence.
12 Let Mount Zion rejoice!
Let the towns*c* of Judah exult,
because of Your judgments.

13 Walk around Zion,
circle it;
count its towers,
14 take note of its ramparts;
d-go through-*d* its citadels,
that you may recount it to a future age.
15 For God—He is our God forever;
He will lead us *d*-evermore.-*d*

b *See I Kings 22.49.*
c *Or "women."*
d-d *Meaning of Heb. uncertain.*

49 For the leader. Of the Korahites. A psalm.

2 Hear this, all you peoples;
    give ear, all inhabitants of the world,
3   men of all estates,
    rich and poor alike.
4 My mouth utters wisdom,
    my speech[a] is full of insight.
5 I will turn my attention to a theme,
    set forth my lesson to the music of a lyre.

6 In time of trouble, why should I fear
    the encompassing evil of those who would
       supplant me—
7   men who trust in their riches,
    who glory in their great wealth?
8 [b-]Ah, it[-b] cannot redeem a man,
    or pay his ransom to God;
9   the price of life is too high;
    and so one ceases to be, forever.
10 Shall he live eternally,
    and never see the grave?
11 For one sees that the wise die,
    that the foolish and ignorant both perish,
    leaving their wealth to others.
12 Their grave[c] is their eternal home,
    the dwelling-place for all generations
    of those once famous on earth.
13 Man does not abide in honor;
    he is like the beasts that perish.

14 Such is the fate of those who are self-confident,
    [d-]the end of those pleased with their own talk.[-d] Selah.

---

[a] Lit. "utterance of my heart"; on leb, cf. Ps. 19.15.
[b-b] Or "A brother."
[c] Taken with ancient versions and medieval commentators as the equivalent of qibram.
[d-d] Meaning of Heb. uncertain.

¹⁵ Sheeplike they head for Sheol,
with Death as their shepherd.
The upright shall rule over them at daybreak,
*d-*and their form shall waste away in Sheol
till its nobility be gone.*-d*
¹⁶ But God will redeem my life from the clutches of Sheol,
for He will take me.   *Selah.*

¹⁷ Do not be afraid when a man becomes rich,
when his household goods increase;
¹⁸   for when he dies he can take none of it along;
his goods cannot follow him down.
¹⁹ Though he congratulates himself in his lifetime
—*d-*"They must admit that you did well by yourself"*-d*—
²⁰   yet he must join the company of his ancestors,
who will never see daylight again.
²¹ Man does not understand honor;
he is like the beasts that perish.

50 A psalm of Asaph.

*a-*God, the LORD God*-a* spoke
and summoned the world from east to west.
² From Zion, perfect in beauty,
God appeared
³   —let our God come and not fail to act!
Devouring fire preceded Him;
it stormed around Him fiercely.
⁴ He summoned the heavens above,
and the earth, for the trial of His people.
⁵ "Bring in My devotees,
who made a covenant with Me over sacrifice!"

a-a Heb. 'El 'Elohim YHWH.

64

⁶ Then the heavens proclaimed His righteousness,
    for He is a God who judges.   *Selah.*

⁷ "Pay heed, My people, and I will speak,
    O Israel, and I will arraign you.
    I am God, your God.
⁸ I censure you not for your sacrifices,
    and your burnt offerings, made to Me daily;
⁹   I claim no bull from your estate,
    no he-goats from your pens.
¹⁰ For Mine is every animal of the forest,
    the beasts on ᵇ⁻a thousand mountains.⁻ᵇ
¹¹ I know every bird of the mountains,
    the creatures of the field are subject to Me.
¹² Were I hungry, I would not tell you,
    for Mine is the world and all it holds.
¹³ Do I eat the flesh of bulls,
    or drink the blood of he-goats?
¹⁴ Sacrifice a thank offering to God,
    and pay your vows to the Most High.
¹⁵ Call upon Me in time of trouble;
    I will rescue you, and you shall honor Me."

¹⁶ And to the wicked, God said:
    "Who are you to recite My laws,
    and mouth the terms of My covenant,
¹⁷   seeing that you spurn My discipline,
    and brush My words aside?
¹⁸ When you see a thief, you fall in with him,
    and throw in your lot with adulterers;
¹⁹   you devote your mouth to evil,
    and yoke your tongue to deceit;
²⁰   you are busy maligning your brother,
    defaming the son of your mother.

ᵇ⁻ᵇ *Meaning of Heb. uncertain.*

²¹ If I failed to act when you did these things,
you would fancy that I was like you;
so I censure you and confront you with charges.
²² Mark this, you who are unmindful of God,
lest I tear you apart and no one save you.

²³ He who sacrifices a thank offering honors Me,
*ᵇ*and to him who improves his way*⁻ᵇ*
I will show the salvation of God."

51 For the leader. A psalm of David, ² when Nathan the
prophet came to him after he had come to Bathsheba.*ᵃ*

³ Have mercy upon me, O God,
as befits Your faithfulness;
in keeping with Your abundant compassion,
blot out my transgressions.
⁴ Wash me thoroughly of my iniquity,
and purify me of my sin;
⁵ for I recognize my transgressions,
and am ever conscious of my sin.
⁶ Against You alone have I sinned,
and done what is evil in Your sight;
so You are just in Your sentence,
and right in Your judgment.
⁷ Indeed I was born with iniquity;
with sin my mother conceived me.
⁸ *ᵇ*Indeed You desire truth about that which is hidden;
teach me wisdom about secret things.*⁻ᵇ*

⁹ Purge me with hyssop till I am pure;
wash me till I am whiter than snow.
¹⁰ Let me hear tidings of joy and gladness;
let the bones You have crushed exult.

ᵃ *Cf. II Sam. 12.*
ᵇ⁻ᵇ *Meaning of Heb. uncertain.*

11 Hide Your face from my sins;
   blot out all my iniquities.
12 Fashion a pure heart for me, O God;
   create in me a steadfast spirit.
13 Do not cast me out of Your presence,
   or take Your holy spirit away from me.
14 Let me again rejoice in Your help;
   let a vigorous spirit sustain me.
15 I will teach transgressors Your ways,
   that sinners may return to You.

16 Save me from bloodguilt,
   O God, God, my deliverer,
   that I may sing forth Your beneficence.
17 O LORD, open my lips,
   and let my mouth declare Your praise.
18 You do not want me to bring sacrifices;
   You do not desire burnt offerings;
19 True sacrifice to God is a contrite spirit;
   God, You will not despise
   a contrite and crushed heart.

20 May it please You to make Zion prosper;
   rebuild the walls of Jerusalem.
21 Then You will want sacrifices offered in righteousness,
   burnt and whole offerings;
   then bulls will be offered on Your altar.

52 For the leader. A *maskil* of David, 2 when Doeg the Edomite came and informed Saul, telling him, "David came to Ahimelech's house."*a*

3 Why do you boast of your evil, brave fellow?
   God's faithfulness *b*-never ceases.*-b*

---

a *Cf. I Sam. 22.9 ff.*
b-b *Lit. "is all the day."*

⁴ Your tongue devises mischief,
 like a sharpened razor that works treacherously.
⁵ You prefer evil to good,
 the lie, to speaking truthfully.   *Selah.*
⁶ You love all pernicious words,
 treacherous speech.
⁷ So God will tear you down for good,
 will break you and pluck you from your tent,
 and root you out of the land of the living. *Selah.*
⁸ The righteous, seeing it, will be awestruck;
 they will jibe at him, saying,
⁹ "Here was a fellow who did not make God his refuge,
 but trusted in his great wealth,
 relied upon his mischief."

¹⁰ But I am like a thriving olive tree in God's house;
 I trust in the faithfulness of God forever and ever.
¹¹ I praise You forever, for You have acted;
 ᶜ-I declare that Your name is good-ᶜ
 in the presence of Your faithful ones.

53 ᵃFor the leader; on *mahalath.*ᵇ A *maskil* of David.

² The benighted man thinks,
 ᶜ-"God does not care."-ᶜ
Man's wrongdoing is corrupt and loathsome;
 no one does good.
³ The Lᴏʀᴅ looks down from heaven on mankind
 to find a man of understanding,
 a man mindful of God.
⁴ Everyone is dross,
 altogether foul;
 there is none who does good,
 not even one.

ᶜ-ᶜ *Meaning of Heb. uncertain; others "I will wait for Your name for it is good."*
ᵃ *Cf. Ps. 14.*
ᵇ *Meaning of Heb. unknown.*
ᶜ-ᶜ *Lit. "There is no God"; cf. Ps. 10.4.*

5 Are they so witless, those evildoers,
   who devour my people as they devour food,
   and do not invoke God?
6 There they will be seized with fright
   —*d*-never was there such a fright—
   for God has scattered the bones of your besiegers;
   you have put them to shame,-*d*
   for God has rejected them.

7 O that the deliverance of Israel might come from Zion!
   When God restores the fortunes of His people,
   Jacob will exult, Israel will rejoice.

54   For the leader; with instrumental music. A *maskil* of David, 2 when the Ziphites came and told Saul, "Know, David is in hiding among us."*a*

3 O God, deliver me by Your name;
   by Your power vindicate me.
4 O God, hear my prayer;
   give ear to the words of my mouth.
5 For strangers have risen against me,
   and ruthless men seek my life;
   they are unmindful of God.   *Selah.*

6 See, God is my helper;
   the LORD is my support.
7 He will repay the evil of my watchful foes;
   by Your faithfulness, destroy them!
8 Then I will offer You a free-will sacrifice;
   I will praise Your name, LORD, for it is good,
9   for it has saved me from my foes,
   and let me gaze triumphant upon my enemies.

d-d *Meaning of Heb. uncertain.*
a *Cf. I Sam. 23.19.*

55 For the leader; with instrumental music. A *maskil* of David.

² Give ear, O God, to my prayer;
do not ignore my plea;
³ pay heed to me and answer me.
I am tossed about, complaining and moaning
⁴ at the clamor of the enemy,
because of the oppression of the wicked;
for they bring evil upon me
and furiously harass me.
⁵ My heart is convulsed within me;
terrors of death assail me.
⁶ Fear and trembling invade me;
I am clothed with horror.
⁷ I said,
"O that I had the wings of a dove!
I would fly away and find rest;
⁸ surely, I would flee far off;
I would lodge in the wilderness;   *Selah.*
⁹ I would soon find me a refuge
from the sweeping wind,
from the tempest."

¹⁰ O LORD, confound their speech, confuse it!
For I see lawlessness and strife in the city;
¹¹ day and night they make their rounds on its walls;
evil and mischief are inside it.
¹² Malice is within it;
fraud and deceit never leave its square.

¹³ It is not an enemy who reviles me
—I could bear that;
it is not my foe who vaunts himself against me

—I could hide from him;
14 but it is you, my equal,
   my companion, my friend;
15 sweet was our fellowship;
   we walked together in God's house.
16 Let Him incite death against them;
   may they go down alive into Sheol!
   For where they dwell,
   there evil is.

17 As for me, I call to God;
   the LORD will deliver me.
18 Evening, morning, and noon,
   I complain and moan,
   and He hears my voice.
19 He redeems me unharmed
   from the battle against me;
   *ait is as though many are on my side.*ᵃ
20 God who has reigned from the first,
   who will have no successor,
   hears and humbles those who have no fear of
   God.   *Selah.*

21 Heᵇ harmed his ally,
   he broke his pact;
22 his talk was smoother than butter,
   yet his mind was on war;
   his words were more soothing than oil,
   yet they were drawn swords.

23 Cast your burden on the LORD and He will sustain you;
   He will never let the righteous man collapse.
24 For You, O God, will bring them down to the nethermost
      Pit—
   those murderous, treacherous men;

ᵃ⁻ᵃ *Meaning of Heb. uncertain.*
ᵇ *I.e. the friend of v. 14.*

they shall not live out half their days;
but I trust in You.

56 For the leader; *a*-on *jonath elem rehokim.*-*a* Of David. A *michtam;* when the Philistines seized him in Gath.

² Have mercy on me, O God,
    for men persecute me;
    all day long my adversary oppresses me.
³ My watchful foes persecute me all day long;
    many are my adversaries, O Exalted One.
⁴ When I am afraid, I trust in You,
⁵   in God, whose word I praise,
    in God I trust;
    I am not afraid;
    what can mortals*b* do to me?
⁶ All day long *a*-they cause me grief in my affairs,-*a*
    they plan only evil against me.
⁷ They plot, they lie in ambush;
    they watch my every move, hoping for my death.
⁸ Cast them out for their evil;
    subdue peoples in Your anger, O God.

⁹ *a*-You keep count of my wanderings;
    put my tears into Your flask,
    into Your record.-*a*
¹⁰ Then my enemies will retreat when I call on You;
    this I know, that God is for me.
¹¹ In God, whose word I praise,
    in the LORD, whose word I praise,
¹²   in God I trust;
    I am not afraid;
    what can man do to me?
¹³ I must pay my vows to You, O God;

a-a *Meaning of Heb. uncertain.*
b *Lit. "flesh."*

I will render thank offerings to You.
14 For You have saved me from death,
my foot from stumbling,
that I may walk before God in the light of life.

57 For the leader; *a-al tashheth.-a* Of David. A *michtam;* when he
fled from Saul into a cave.

2 Have mercy on me, O God, have mercy on me,
for I seek refuge in You,
I seek refuge in the shadow of Your wings,
until danger passes.
3 I call to God Most High,
to God who is good to me.
4 He will reach down from heaven and deliver me:
God will send down His steadfast love;
my persecutor reviles.   *Selah.*

5 As for me, I lie down among man-eating lions
whose teeth are spears and arrows,
whose tongue is a sharp sword.
6 Exalt Yourself over the heavens, O God,
let Your glory be over all the earth!
7 They prepared a net for my feet *b-to ensnare me;-b*
they dug a pit for me,
but they fell into it.   *Selah.*

8 *c*My heart is firm, O God;
my heart is firm;
I will sing, I will chant a hymn.
9 Awake, O my soul!
Awake, O harp and lyre!
I will wake the dawn.
10 I will praise You among the peoples, O LORD;

a-a *Meaning of Heb. uncertain.*
b-b *Cf. Mishnaic Heb.* kefifah, *a wicker basket used in fishing.*
c *With vv. 8–12, cf. Ps. 108.2–6.*

I will sing a hymn to You among the nations;
11 for Your faithfulness is as high as heaven;
Your steadfastness reaches to the sky.
12 Exalt Yourself over the heavens, O God,
let Your glory be over all the earth!

58 For the leader; *al tashheth*. Of David. A *michtam*.

2 *ᵃ*-O mighty ones,-*ᵃ* do you really decree what is just?
Do you judge mankind with equity?
3 In your minds you devise wrongdoing in the land;
ᵃ-with your hands you deal out lawlessness.-*ᵃ*
4 The wicked are defiant from birth;
the liars go astray from the womb.
5 Their venom is like that of a snake,
a deaf viper that stops its ears
6 so as not to hear the voice of charmers
or the expert mutterer of spells.

7 O God, smash their teeth in their mouth;
shatter the fangs of lions, O LORD;
8 let them melt, let them vanish like water;
let Him aim His arrows that they be cut down;
9 *ᵃ*-like a snail that melts away as it moves;-*ᵃ*
like a woman's stillbirth, may they never see the sun!
10 Before *ᵃ*-the thorns grow into a bramble,
may He whirl them away alive in fury.-*ᵃ*

11 The righteous man will rejoice when he sees revenge;
he will bathe his feet in the blood of the wicked.
12 Men will say,
"There is, then, a reward for the righteous;
there is, indeed, divine justice on earth."

ᵃ-ᵃ *Meaning of Heb. uncertain.*

59 For the leader; *al tashheth.* Of David. A *michtam;* when Saul sent men to watch his house in order to put him to death.[a]

2 Save me from my enemies, O my God;
   secure me against my assailants.
3 Save me from evildoers;
   deliver me from murderers.
4 For see, they lie in wait for me;
   fierce men plot against me
   for no offense of mine,
   for no transgression, O LORD;
5   for no guilt of mine
   do they rush to array themselves against me.
   Look, rouse Yourself on my behalf!
6 You, O LORD God of hosts,
   God of Israel,
   bestir Yourself to bring all nations to account;
   have no mercy on any treacherous villain.   *Selah.*

7 They come each evening growling like dogs,
   roaming the city.
8 They rave with their mouths,
   [b]sharp words[b] are on their lips;
   [they think,] "Who hears?"
9 But You, O LORD, laugh at them;
   You mock all the nations.

10 O my[c] strength, I wait for You;
   for God is my haven.
11 My faithful God will come to aid me;
   God will let me gloat over my watchful foes.
12 Do not kill them lest my people be unmindful;
   with Your power make wanderers of them;

[a] *Cf. I Sam. 19.11.*
[b-b] *Lit. "swords."*
[c] *With several mss.; cf. v. 18; lit. "His."*

75

bring them low, O our shield, the Lord,
13   because of their sinful mouths,
the words on their lips.
Let them be trapped by their pride,
and by the imprecations and lies they utter.
14 In Your fury put an end to them;
put an end to them that they be no more;
that it may be known to the ends of the earth
that God does rule over Jacob.   *Selah.*

15 They come each evening growling like dogs,
roaming the city.
16 They wander in search of food;
and whine if they are not satisfied.
17 But I will sing of Your strength,
extol each morning Your faithfulness;
for You have been my haven,
a refuge in time of trouble.

18 O my strength, to You I sing hymns;
for God is my haven, my faithful God.

60   For the leader; on *a-shushan eduth.-a* A *michtam* of David (to be taught), 2 when he fought with Aram-Naharaim and Aram-Zobah, and Joab returned and defeated Edom—[an army] of twelve thousand men—in the Valley of Salt.*b*

3 O God, You have rejected us,
You have made a breach in us;
You have been angry;
restore us!
4 You have made the land quake;
You have torn it open.
Mend its fissures,

a-a *Meaning of Heb. uncertain.*
b *Cf. II Sam. 8; I Chron. 18.*

for it is collapsing.
5 You have made Your people suffer hardship;
c-You have given us wine that makes us reel.-c
6 a-Give those who fear You because of Your truth
a banner for rallying.-a   Selah.
7 d That those whom You love might be rescued,
deliver with Your right hand and answer me.

8 God promised e-in His sanctuary-e
that I would exultingly divide up Shechem,
and measure the Valley of Sukkoth;
9   Gilead and Manasseh would be mine,
Ephraim my chief stronghold,
Judah my scepter;
10   Moab would be my washbasin;
on Edom I would cast my shoe;
acclaim me, O Philistia!

11 Would that I were brought to the bastion!
Would that I were led to Edom!

12 But You have rejected us, O God;
God, You do not march with our armies.
13 Grant us Your aid against the foe,
for the help of man is worthless.
14 With God we shall triumph;
He will trample our foes.

61   For the leader; with instrumental music. Of David.

2 Hear my cry, O God,
heed my prayer.
3 From the end of the earth I call to You;
when my heart is faint,

c-c Or "You have sated Your people with a bitter draft."
d Cf. Ps. 108.7–14.
e-e Or "by His holiness."

You lead me to a rock that is high above me.
4 For You have been my refuge,
    a tower of strength against the enemy.
5 O that I might dwell in Your tent forever,
    take refuge under Your protecting wings.   *Selah.*

6 O God, You have heard my vows;
    grant the request*a* of those who fear Your name.
7 Add days to the days of the king;
    may his years extend through generations;
8   may he dwell in God's presence forever;
    appoint*b* steadfast love to guard him.
9 So I will sing hymns to Your name forever,
    as I fulfill my vows day after day.

62   For the leader; on *Jeduthun.* A psalm of David.

2 Truly my soul waits quietly for God;
    my deliverance comes from Him.
3 Truly He is my rock and deliverance,
    my haven; I shall never be shaken.
4 How long will all of you attack*a* a man,
    to crush*a* him, as though he were
    a leaning wall, a tottering fence?
5 They lay plans to topple him from his rank;
    they delight in falsehood;
    they bless with their mouths,
    while inwardly they curse.   *Selah.*

6 Truly, wait quietly for God, O my soul,
    for my hope comes from Him.
7 He is my rock and deliverance,
    my haven; I shall not be shaken.
8 I rely on God, my deliverance and glory,

ᵃ *Taking the noun* yršt *as an alternate form of* 'ršt; *cf. Ps. 21.3.*
ᵇ *Meaning of Heb. uncertain.*

ᵃ *Meaning of Heb. uncertain.*

    my rock of strength;
    in God is my refuge.
9 Trust in Him at all times, O people;
    pour out your hearts before Him;
    God is our refuge.   *Selah.*

10 Men are mere breath;
    mortals, illusion;
    placed on a scale all together,
    they weigh even less than a breath.
11 Do not trust in violence,
    or put false hopes in robbery;
    if force bears fruit pay it no mind.
12 One thing God has spoken;
    two things have I heard:
    that might belongs to God,
13   and faithfulness is Yours, O Lord,
    to reward each man according to his deeds.

63   A psalm of David, when he was in the Wilderness of Judah.

2 God, You are my God;
    I search for You,
    my soul thirsts for You,
    my body yearns for You,
    as a parched and thirsty land that has no water.
3 I shall behold You in the sanctuary,
    and see Your might and glory,
4 Truly Your faithfulness is better than life;
    my lips declare Your praise.
·5 I bless You all my life;
    I lift up my hands, invoking Your name.
6 I am sated as with a *ª-rich feast,-ª*
    I sing praises with joyful lips

ª-ª *Lit. "suet and fat."*

7 when I call You to mind upon my bed,
when I think of You in the watches of the night;
8 for You are my help,
and in the shadow of Your wings
I shout for joy.
9 My soul is attached to You;
Your right hand supports me.

10 May those who seek to destroy my life
enter the depths of the earth.
11 May they be gutted by the sword;
may they be prey to jackals.
12 But the king shall rejoice in God;
all who swear by Him shall exult,
when the mouth of liars is stopped.

64 For the leader. A psalm of David.

2 Hear my voice, O God, when I plead;
guard my life from the enemy's terror.
3 Hide me from a band of evil men,
from a crowd of evildoers,
4 who whet their tongues like swords;
they aim their arrows—cruel words—
5 to shoot from hiding at the blameless man;
they shoot him suddenly and without fear.
6 *a*-They arm themselves with an evil word;
when they speak, it is to conceal traps;-*a*
they think, "Who will see them?"
7 *b*Let the wrongdoings they have concealed,*c*
each one inside him, his secret thoughts,
be wholly exposed.
8 God shall shoot them with arrows;
they shall be struck down suddenly.

a-a *Meaning of Heb. uncertain.*
b *Meaning of verse uncertain.*
c *Reading* ṭamnu *with some mss. (cf. Minhat Shai) and Rashi; most printed editions,* tamnu,
traditionally rendered "they have accomplished."

9 Their tongue shall be their downfall;
    all who see them shall recoil in horror;
10   all men shall stand in awe;
    they shall proclaim the work of God
    and His deed which they perceived.
11 The righteous shall rejoice in the LORD,
    and take refuge in Him;
    all the upright shall exult.

65 For the leader. A psalm of David. A song.

2 Praise befits You in Zion, O God;
    vows are paid to You;
3   all mankind[a] comes to You,
    You who hear prayer.
4 When all manner of sins overwhelm me,
    it is You who forgive our iniquities.
5 Happy is the man You choose and bring near
    to dwell in Your courts;
    may we be sated with the blessings of Your house,
    Your holy temple.

6 Answer us with victory through awesome deeds,
    O God, our deliverer,
    in whom all the ends of the earth
    and the distant seas
    put their trust;
7   who by His power fixed the mountains firmly,
    who is girded with might,
8   who stills the raging seas,
    the raging waves,
    and tumultuous peoples.
9 Those who live at the ends of the earth are awed by Your
    signs;

a *Lit. "flesh."*

You make the lands of sunrise and sunset shout for joy.
10 You take care of the earth and irrigate it;
 You enrich it greatly,
 with the channel of God full of water;
 You provide grain for men;
 for so do You prepare it.
11 Saturating its furrows,
 leveling its ridges,
 You soften it with showers,
 You bless its growth.
12 You crown the year with Your bounty;
 fatness is distilled in Your paths;
13 the pasturelands distill it;
 the hills are girded with joy.
14 The meadows are clothed with flocks,
 the valleys mantled with grain;
 they raise a shout, they break into song.

66 For the leader. A song. A psalm.

2 Raise a shout for God, all the earth;
 sing the glory of His name,
 make glorious His praise.
3 Say to God,
 "How awesome are Your deeds,
 Your enemies cower before Your great strength;
4 all the earth bows to You,
 and sings hymns to You;
 all sing hymns to Your name."   *Selah.*

5 Come and see the works of God,
 who is held in awe by men for His acts.
6 He turned the sea into dry land;

they crossed the river on foot;
we therefore rejoice in Him.
7 He rules forever in His might;
His eyes scan the nations;
let the rebellious not assert themselves.   *Selah.*

8 O peoples, bless our God,
celebrate His praises,
9 who has granted us life,
and has not let our feet slip.

10 You have tried us, O God,
refining us, as one refines silver.
11 You have caught us in a net,
a-caught us in trammels.-*a*
12 You have let men ride over us;
we have endured fire and water,
and You have brought us through to prosperity.

13 I enter Your house with burnt offerings,
I pay my vows to You,
14 [vows] that my lips pronounced,
that my mouth uttered in my distress.
15 I offer up fatlings to You,
with the odor of burning rams;
I sacrifice bulls and he-goats.   *Selah.*

16 Come and hear, all God-fearing men,
as I tell what He did for me.
17 I called aloud to Him,
glorification on my tongue.
18 Had I an evil thought in my mind,
the LORD would not have listened.
19 But God did listen;
He paid heed to my prayer.

a-a *Lit. "put a trammel on our loins."*

20 Blessed is God who has not turned away my prayer,
or His faithful care from me.

67 For the leader; with instrumental music. A psalm. A song.

2 May God be gracious to us and bless us;
may He show us favor, *Selah.*
3 that Your way be known on earth,
Your deliverance among all nations.

4 Peoples will praise You, O God;
all peoples will praise You.
5 Nations will exult and shout for joy,
for You rule the peoples with equity,
You guide the nations of the earth. *Selah.*
6 The peoples will praise You, O God;
all peoples will praise You.

7 May the earth yield its produce;
may God, our God, bless us.
8 May God bless us,
and be revered to the ends of the earth.

68 *a*For the leader. Of David. A psalm. A song.

2 God will arise,
His enemies shall be scattered,
His foes shall flee before Him.
3 Disperse them as smoke is dispersed;
as wax melts at fire,
so the wicked shall perish before God.
4 But the righteous shall rejoice;

a *The coherence of this psalm and the meaning of many of its passages are uncertain.*

they shall exult in the presence of God;
they shall be exceedingly joyful.

5 Sing to God, chant hymns to His name;
extol Him who rides the clouds;
the LORD is His name.
Exult in His presence—
6 the father of orphans, the champion of widows,
God, in His holy habitation.
7 God restores the lonely to their homes,
sets free the imprisoned, safe and sound,
while the rebellious must live in a parched land.

8 O God, when You went at the head of Your army,
when You marched through the desert, *Selah.*
9 the earth trembled, the sky rained because of God,
yon Sinai, because of God, the God of Israel.
10 You released a bountiful rain, O God;
when Your own land languished, You sustained it.
11 Your tribe dwells there;
O God, in Your goodness You provide for the needy.

12 The LORD gives a command;
the women who bring the news are a great host:
13 "The kings and their armies are in headlong flight;
housewives are sharing in the spoils;
14 even for those of you who lie among the sheepfolds
there are wings of a dove sheathed in silver,
its pinions in fine gold."
15 When Shaddai scattered the kings,
it seemed like a snowstorm in Zalmon.

16 O majestic mountain, Mount Bashan;
O jagged mountain, Mount Bashan;
17 why so hostile, O jagged mountains,

85

toward the mountain God desired as His dwelling?
The LORD shall abide there forever.

¹⁸ God's chariots are myriads upon myriads,
thousands upon thousands;
the Lord is among them as in Sinai in holiness.

¹⁹ You went up to the heights, having taken captives,
having received tribute of men,
even of those who rebel
against the LORD God's abiding there.

²⁰ Blessed is the LORD.
Day by day He supports us,
God, our deliverance.   *Selah.*

²¹ God is for us a God of deliverance;
GOD the Lord provides an escape from death.

²² God will smash the heads of His enemies,
the hairy crown of him who walks about in his guilt.

²³ The LORD said, "I will retrieve from Bashan,
I will retrieve from the depths of the sea;

²⁴ that your feet may wade through blood;
that the tongue of your dogs may have its portion of
your enemies."

²⁵ Men see Your processions, O God,
the processions of my God, my king,
into the sanctuary.

²⁶ First come singers, then musicians,
amidst maidens playing timbrels.

²⁷ In assemblies bless God,
the LORD, O you who are from the fountain of Israel.

²⁸ There is little Benjamin who rules them,
the princes of Judah who command them,
the princes of Zebulon and Naphtali.

²⁹ Your God has ordained strength for you,
    the strength, O God,
    which You displayed for us
³⁰   from Your temple above Jerusalem.
    The kings bring You tribute.
³¹ Blast the beast of the marsh,
    the herd of bulls among the peoples, the calves,
    till they come cringing with pieces of silver.
    Scatter the peoples who delight in wars!
³² Tribute-bearers shall come from Egypt;
    Cush shall hasten its gifts to God.

³³ O kingdoms of the earth,
    sing to God;
    chant hymns to the Lord,   *Selah.*
³⁴   to Him who rides the ancient highest heavens,
    who thunders forth with His mighty voice.
³⁵ Ascribe might to God,
    whose majesty is over Israel,
    whose might is in the skies.
³⁶ You are awesome, O God, in Your holy places;
    it is the God of Israel who gives might and power to the
      people.
    Blessed is God.

69   For the leader. On *shoshannim.*[a] Of David.

² Deliver me, O God,
    for the waters have reached my neck;
³   I am sinking into the slimy deep
    and find no foothold;
    I have come into the watery depths;
    the flood sweeps me away.
⁴ I am weary with calling;

[a] *Meaning of Heb. uncertain.*

my throat is dry;
my eyes fail
while I wait for God.
5 More numerous than the hairs of my head
are those who hate me without reason;
many are those who would destroy me,
my treacherous enemies.
Must I restore what I have not stolen?

6 God, You know my folly;
my guilty deeds are not hidden from You.
7 Let those who look to You,
O LORD, God of hosts,
not be disappointed on my account;
let those who seek You,
O God of Israel,
not be shamed because of me.
8 It is for Your sake that I have been reviled,
that shame covers my face;
9 I am a stranger to my brothers,
an alien to my kin.
10 My zeal for Your house has been my undoing;
the reproaches of those who revile You have fallen upon
me.
11 When I wept and fasted,
I was reviled for it.
12 I made sackcloth my garment;
I became a byword among them.
13 Those who sit in the gate talk about me;
I am the taunt of drunkards.

14 As for me, may my prayer come to You, O LORD,
at a favorable moment;
O God, in Your abundant faithfulness,
answer me with Your sure deliverance.

¹⁵ Rescue me from the mire;
   let me not sink;
   let me be rescued from my enemies,
   and from the watery depths.
¹⁶ Let the floodwaters not sweep me away;
   let the deep not swallow me;
   let the mouth of the Pit not close over me.
¹⁷ Answer me, O LORD,
   according to Your great steadfastness;
   in accordance with Your abundant mercy
   turn to me;
¹⁸   do not hide Your face from Your servant,
   for I am in distress;
   answer me quickly.
¹⁹ Come near to me and redeem me;
   free me from my enemies.

²⁰ You know my reproach,
   my shame, my disgrace;
   You are aware of all my foes.
²¹ Reproach breaks my heart,
   I am in despair;^a
   I hope for consolation, but there is none,
   for comforters, but find none.
²² They give me gall for food,
   vinegar to quench my thirst.
²³ May their table be a trap for them,
   a snare for their allies.
²⁴ May their eyes grow dim so that they cannot see;
   may their loins collapse continually.
²⁵ Pour out Your wrath on them;
   may Your blazing anger overtake them;
²⁶   may their encampments be desolate;
   may their tents stand empty.
²⁷ For they persecute those You have struck;

they talk about the pain of those You have felled.
²⁸ Add that to their guilt;
   let them have no share of Your beneficence;
²⁹   may they be erased from the book of life,
   and not be inscribed with the righteous.

³⁰ But I am lowly and in pain;
   Your help, O God, keeps me safe.
³¹ I will extol God's name with song,
   and exalt Him with praise.
³² That will please the LORD more than oxen,
   than bulls with horns and hooves.
³³ The lowly will see and rejoice;
   you who are mindful of God, take heart!
³⁴ For the LORD listens to the needy,
   and does not spurn His captives.

³⁵ Heaven and earth shall extol Him,
   the seas, and all that moves in them.
³⁶ For God will deliver Zion
   and rebuild the cities of Judah;
   they shall live there and inherit it;
³⁷   the offspring of His servants shall possess it;
   those who cherish His name shall dwell there.

70 For the leader. Of David. *Lehazkir.*ᵃ

² ᵇHasten, O God, to save me;
   O LORD, to aid me!
³ Let those who seek my life
   be frustrated and disgraced;
   let those who wish me harm,
   fall back in shame.

ᵃ *Meaning of Heb. uncertain.*
ᵇ *Cf. Ps. 40. 14–18.*

90

⁴ Let those who say, "Aha! Aha!"
    turn back because of their frustration.

⁵ But let all who seek You be glad and rejoice in You;
    let those who are eager for Your deliverance always say,
    "Extolled be God!"
⁶ But I am poor and needy;
    O God, hasten to me!
You are my help and my rescuer;
    O LORD, do not delay.

71   I seek refuge in You, O LORD;
    may I never be disappointed.
² As You are beneficent, save me and rescue me;
    incline Your ear to me and deliver me.
³ Be a sheltering rock for me to which I may always repair;
    decree my deliverance,
    for You are my rock and my fortress.
⁴ My God, rescue me from the hand of the wicked,
    from the grasp of the unjust and the lawless.

⁵ For You are my hope,
    O Lord GOD,
    my trust from my youth.
⁶ While yet unborn, I depended on You;
    in the womb of my mother, You were my support;[a]
    I sing Your praises always.
⁷ I have become an example for many,
    since You are my mighty refuge.
⁸ My mouth is full of praise to You,
    glorifying You all day long.
⁹ Do not cast me off in old age;
    when my strength fails, do not forsake me!

---

[a] *Meaning of Heb. uncertain.*

¹⁰ For my enemies talk against me;
 those who wait for me are of one mind,
¹¹   saying, "God has forsaken him;
 chase him and catch him,
 for no one will save him!"
¹² O God, be not far from me;
 my God, hasten to my aid!
¹³ Let my accusers perish in frustration;
 let those who seek my ruin be clothed in reproach and
 disgrace!

¹⁴ As for me, I will hope always,
 and add to the many praises of You.
¹⁵ My mouth tells of Your beneficence,
 of Your deliverance all day long,
 though I know not how to tell it.
¹⁶ I come with praise of Your mighty acts, O Lord GOD;
 I celebrate Your beneficence, Yours alone.
¹⁷ You have let me experience it, God, from my youth;
 until now I have proclaimed Your wondrous deeds,
¹⁸   and even in hoary old age do not forsake me, God,
 until I proclaim Your strength to the next generation,
¹⁹   Your mighty acts, to all who are to come,
 Your beneficence, high as the heavens, O God,
 You who have done great things;
 O God, who is Your peer!
²⁰ You who have made me undergo many troubles and mis-
 fortunes
 will revive me again,
 and raise me up from the depths of the earth.
²¹ You will grant me much greatness,
 You will turn and comfort me.
²² Then I will acclaim You to the music of the lyre
 for Your faithfulness, O my God;
 I will sing a hymn to You with a harp,

O Holy One of Israel.
²³ My lips shall be jubilant, as I sing a hymn to You,
my whole being, which You have redeemed.
²⁴ All day long my tongue shall recite Your beneficent acts,
how those who sought my ruin were frustrated and disgraced.

72 Of Solomon.

O God, endow the king with Your judgments,
the king's son with Your righteousness;
² that he may judge Your people rightly,
Your lowly ones, justly.
³ Let the mountains produce well-being for the people,
the hills, the reward of justice.
⁴ Let him champion the lowly among the people,
deliver the needy folk,
and crush those who wrong them.
⁵ Let them fear You as long as the sun shines,
while the moon lasts, generations on end.
⁶ Let him be like rain that falls on a mown field,
like a downpour of rain on the ground,
⁷ that the righteous may flourish in his time,
and well-being abound, till the moon is no more.
⁸ Let him rule from sea to sea,
from the river to the ends of the earth.
⁹ Let desert-dwellers kneel before him,
and his enemies lick the dust.
¹⁰ Let kings of Tarshish and the islands pay tribute,
kings of Sheba and Seba offer gifts.
¹¹ Let all kings bow to him,
and all nations serve him.

¹² For he saves the needy who cry out,
the lowly who have no helper.

¹³ He cares about the poor and the needy;
He brings the needy deliverance.
¹⁴ He redeems them from fraud and lawlessness;
ᵃ‑the shedding of their blood weighs heavily
upon him.‑ᵃ

¹⁵ So let him live, and receive gold of Sheba;
let prayers for him be said always,
blessings on him invoked at all times.
¹⁶ ᵇ‑Let abundant grain be in the land, to the tops of the
mountains;
let his crops thrive like the forest of Lebanon;
and let men sprout up in towns like country grass.
¹⁷ May his name be eternal;
while the sun lasts, may his name endure;‑ᵇ
let men invoke his blessedness upon themselves;
let all nations count him happy.

¹⁸ Blessed is the Lord God, God of Israel,
who alone does wondrous things;
¹⁹ Blessed is His glorious name forever;
His glory fills the whole world.
Amen and Amen.

²⁰ End of the prayers of David son of Jesse.

BOOK THREE

73 A psalm of Asaph.

God is truly good to Israel,
to those whose heart is pure.
² As for me, my feet had almost strayed,
my steps were nearly led off course,

ᵃ‑ᵃ *Or "their life is precious in his sight."*
ᵇ‑ᵇ *Meaning of some Heb. phrases in these verses uncertain.*

3 for I envied the wanton;
   I saw the wicked at ease.
4 Death has no pangs for them;
   their body is healthy.
5 They have no part in the travail of men;
   they are not afflicted like the rest of mankind.
6 So pride adorns their necks,
   lawlessness enwraps them as a mantle.
7 *a*-Fat shuts out their eyes;
   their fancies are extravagant.-*a*
8 They scoff and plan evil;
   from their eminence they plan wrongdoing.
9 They set their mouths against heaven,
   and their tongues range over the earth.
10 *a*-So they pound His people again and again,
   until they are drained of their very last tear.-*a*
11 Then they say, "How could God know?
   Is there knowledge with the Most High?"
12 Such are the wicked;
   ever tranquil, they amass wealth.

13 It was for nothing that I kept my heart pure
   and washed my hands in innocence,
14   seeing that I have been constantly afflicted,
      that each morning brings new punishments.
15 Had I decided to say these things,
   I should have been false to the circle of Your disciples.
16 So I applied myself to understand this,
   but it seemed a hopeless task
17   till I entered God's Sanctuary
      and reflected on their fate.

18 You surround them with flattery;
   You make them fall through blandishments.
19 How suddenly are they ruined,

a-a *Meaning of Heb. uncertain.*

95

wholly swept away by terrors.

20 *a*-When You are aroused You despise their image,
as one does a dream after waking, O LORD.*-a*

21 My mind was stripped of its reason,
b-my feelings were numbed.*-b*
22 I was a dolt, without knowledge;
I was brutish toward You.

23 Yet I was always with You,
You held my right hand;
24 You guided me by Your counsel
c-and led me toward honor.*-c*
25 Whom else have I in heaven?
And having You, I want no one on earth.
26 My body and mind fail;
but God is the stay*d* of my mind, my portion forever.
27 Those who keep far from You perish;
You annihilate all who are untrue to You.
28 As for me, nearness to God is good;
I have made the Lord GOD my refuge,
that I may recount all Your works.

74 A *maskil* of Asaph.

Why, O God, do You forever reject us,
do You fume in anger at the flock that You tend?
2 Remember the community You made Yours long ago,
Your very own tribe that You redeemed,
Mount Zion, where You dwell.
3 *a*-Bestir Yourself*-a* because of the *b*-perpetual tumult,*-b*
all the outrages of the enemy in the sanctuary.
4 Your foes roar inside Your meeting-place;
they take their signs for true signs.

b-b Lit. "I was pierced through in my kidneys."
c-c Meaning of Heb. uncertain; others "And afterward receive me with glory."
d Lit. "rock."

a-a Lit. "Lift up Your feet."
b-b Meaning of Heb. uncertain.

5 *b-*It is like men wielding axes
against a gnarled tree;
6   with hatchet and pike
they hacked away at its carved work.*-b*
7 They made Your sanctuary go up in flames;
they brought low in dishonor the dwelling-place of
Your presence.
8 They resolved, "Let us destroy them altogether!"
They burned all God's tabernacles in the land.
9 No signs appear for us;
there is no longer any prophet;
no one among us knows for how long.

10 Till when, O God, will the foe blaspheme,
will the enemy forever revile Your name?
11 Why do You hold back Your hand, Your right hand?
*b-*Draw it out of Your bosom!*-b*

12 O God, my king from of old,
who brings deliverance throughout the land;
13   it was You who drove back the sea with Your might,
who smashed the heads of the monsters in the waters;
14   it was You who crushed the heads of Leviathan,
who left him as food for *c-*the denizens of the desert;*-c*
15   it was You who released springs and torrents,
who made mighty rivers run dry;
16   the day is Yours, the night also;
it was You who set in place the orb of the sun;
17   You fixed all the boundaries of the earth;
summer and winter—You made them.

18 Be mindful of how the enemy blasphemes the LORD,
how base people revile Your name.
19 Do not deliver Your dove to the wild beast;
do not ignore forever the band of Your lowly ones.
20 Look to the covenant!

c-c Or "seafaring men"; meaning of Heb. uncertain.

For the dark places of the land are full of the haunts of
lawlessness.
21 Let not the downtrodden turn away disappointed;
let the poor and needy praise Your name.
22 Rise, O God, champion Your cause;
be mindful that You are blasphemed by base men all day
long.
23 Do not ignore the shouts of Your foes,
the din of Your adversaries that ascends all the time.

75

For the leader; *al tashheth.*
A psalm of Asaph, a song.

2 We praise You, O God;
we praise You;
Your presence is near;
men tell of Your wondrous deeds.

3 "At the time I choose,
I will give judgment equitably.
4 Earth and all its inhabitants dissolve;
it is I who keep its pillars firm.   Selah.
5 To wanton men I say, 'Do not be wanton!'
to the wicked, 'Do not lift up your horns!' "

6 Do not lift your horns up high
a-in vainglorious bluster.*-a*
7 For what lifts a man comes not from the east
or the west or the wilderness;*b*
8 for God it is who gives judgment;
He brings down one man, He lifts up another.
9 There is a cup in the LORD's hand
with foaming wine fully mixed;
from this He pours;
all the wicked of the earth drink,

a-a *Lit. "with arrogant neck you speak."*
b *Reading* midbār *with many mss.*

draining it to the very dregs.
¹⁰ As for me, I will declare forever,
  I will sing a hymn to the God of Jacob.

¹¹ "All the horns of the wicked I will cut;
  but the horns of the righteous shall be lifted up."

76 For the leader; with instrumental music.
  A psalm of Asaph, a song.

² God has made Himself known in Judah,
  His name is great in Israel;
³   Salem became His abode;
  Zion, His den.
⁴ There He broke the fiery arrows of the bow,
  the shield and the sword of war.   *Selah.*

⁵ You were resplendent,
  glorious, on the mountains of prey.
⁶ The stout-hearted were despoiled;
  they were in a stupor;
  the bravest of men could not lift a hand.
⁷ At Your blast, O God of Jacob,
  horse and chariot lay stunned.
⁸ O You! You are awesome!
  Who can withstand You
  when You are enraged?
⁹ In heaven You pronounced sentence;
  the earth was numbed with fright
¹⁰   as God rose to execute judgment,
  to deliver all the lowly of the earth.   *Selah.*

¹¹ ᵃ⁻The fiercest of men shall acknowledge You,
  when You gird on the last bit of fury.⁻ᵃ

ᵃ⁻ᵃ *Meaning of Heb. uncertain.*

¹² Make vows and pay them to the LORD your God;
a-all who are around Him shall bring tribute to
the Awesome One.-*a*
¹³ He curbs the spirit of princes,
inspires awe in the kings of the earth.

77 For the leader; on *Jeduthun.* Of Asaph. A psalm.

² I cry aloud to God;
I cry to God that He may give ear to me.
³ In my time of distress I turn to the Lord,
a-with my hand [uplifted];
[my eyes] flow all night without respite;-*a*
I will not be comforted.
⁴ I call God to mind, I moan,
I complain, my spirit fails.   *Selah.*

⁵ You have held my eyelids open;
I am overwrought, I cannot speak.
⁶ My thoughts turn to days of old,
to years long past.
⁷ I recall at night their gibes at me;
I commune with myself;
my spirit inquires,
⁸   "Will the Lord reject forever
and never again show favor?
⁹ Has His faithfulness disappeared forever?
Will His promise be unfulfilled for all time?
¹⁰ Has God forgotten how to pity?
Has He in anger stifled His compassion?"   *Selah.*
¹¹ And I said, *a*-"It is my fault
that the right hand of the Most High has changed."-*a*

ᵃ⁻ᵃ *Meaning of Heb. uncertain.*
ᵃ⁻ᵃ *Meaning of Heb. uncertain.*

¹² I recall the deeds of the LORD;
yes, I recall Your wonders of old;
¹³ I recount all Your works;
I speak of Your acts.
¹⁴ O God, Your ways are holiness;
what god is as great as God?
¹⁵ You are the God who works wonders;
You have manifested Your strength among the peoples.
¹⁶ By Your arm You redeemed Your people,
the children of Jacob and Joseph.   *Selah.*
¹⁷ The waters saw You, O God,
the waters saw You and were convulsed;
the very deep quaked as well.
¹⁸ Clouds streamed water;
the heavens rumbled;
Your arrows flew about;
¹⁹ Your thunder rumbled like wheels;
lightning lit up the world;
the earth quaked and trembled.
²⁰ Your way was through the sea,
Your path, through the mighty waters;
Your tracks could not be seen.
²¹ You led Your people like a flock
in the care of Moses and Aaron.

78 A *maskil* of Asaph.

Give ear, my people, to my teaching,
turn your ear to what I say.
² I will expound a theme,
hold forth on the lessons of the past,
³ things we have heard and known,
that our fathers have told us.

⁴ We will not withhold them from their children,
  telling the coming generation
  the praises of the Lord and His might,
  and the wonders He performed.
⁵ He established a decree in Jacob,
  ordained a Teaching in Israel,
  charging our fathers
  to make them known to their children,
⁶   that a future generation might know
  —children yet to be born—
  and in turn tell their children
⁷   that they might put their confidence in God,
  and not forget God's great deeds,
  but observe His commandments,
⁸   and not be like their fathers,
  a wayward and defiant generation,
  a generation whose heart was inconstant,
  whose spirit was not true to God.

⁹ Like the Ephraimite bowmen
  who played false in the day of battle,
¹⁰   they did not keep God's covenant,
  they refused to follow His instruction;
¹¹   they forgot His deeds
  and the wonders that He showed them.
¹² He performed marvels in the sight of their fathers,
  in the land of Egypt, the plain of Zoan.
¹³ He split the sea and took them through it;
  He made the waters stand like a wall.
¹⁴ He led them with a cloud by day,
  and throughout the night by the light of fire.
¹⁵ He split rocks in the wilderness
  and gave them drink as if from the great deep.
¹⁶ He brought forth streams from a rock
  and made them flow down like a river.

17 But they went on sinning against Him,
   defying the Most High in the parched land.
18 To test God was in their mind
   when they demanded food for themselves.
19 They spoke against God, saying,
   "Can God spread a feast in the wilderness?
20 True, He struck the rock and waters flowed,
   streams gushed forth;
   but can He provide bread?
   Can He supply His people with meat?"
21 The LORD heard and He raged;
   fire broke out against Jacob,
   anger flared up at Israel,
22   because they did not put their trust in God,
   did not rely on His deliverance.
23 So He commanded the skies above,
   He opened the doors of heaven
24   and rained manna upon them for food,
   giving them heavenly grain.
25 Each man ate a hero's meal;
   He sent them provision in plenty.
26 He set the east wind moving in heaven,
   and drove the south wind by His might.
27 He rained meat on them like dust,
   winged birds like the sands of the sea,
28   making them come down inside His camp,
   around His dwelling-place.
29 They ate till they were sated;
   He gave them what they craved.
30 They had not yet wearied of what they craved,
   the food was still in their mouths
31   when God's anger flared up at them.
   He slew their sturdiest,
   struck down the youth of Israel.

³² Nonetheless, they went on sinning
and had no faith in His wonders.
³³ He made their days end in futility,
their years in sudden death.
³⁴ When He struck*a* them, they turned to Him
and sought God once again.
³⁵ They remembered that God was their rock,
God Most High, their Redeemer.
³⁶ Yet they deceived Him with their speech,
lied to Him with their words;
³⁷ their hearts were inconstant toward Him;
they were untrue to His covenant.
³⁸ But He, being merciful, forgave iniquity
and would not destroy;
He restrained His wrath time and again
and did not give full vent to His fury;
³⁹ for He remembered that they were but flesh,
a passing breath that does not return.

⁴⁰ How often did they defy Him in the wilderness,
did they grieve Him in the wasteland!
⁴¹ Again and again they tested God,
vexed*b* the Holy One of Israel.
⁴² They did not remember His strength,
or the day He redeemed them from the foe;
⁴³ how He displayed His signs in Egypt,
His wonders in the plain of Zoan.
⁴⁴ He turned their rivers into blood;
He made their waters undrinkable.
⁴⁵ He inflicted upon them swarms of insects to devour them,
frogs to destroy them.
⁴⁶ He gave their crops over to grubs,
their produce to locusts.
⁴⁷ He killed their vines with hail,
their sycamores *c*-with frost.-*c*

---

a Lit. "killed."
b Or "set a limit to."
c-c Meaning of Heb. uncertain.

⁴⁸ He gave their beasts over to hail,
their cattle to lightning bolts.
⁴⁹ He inflicted His burning anger upon them,
wrath, indignation, trouble,
a band of deadly messengers.
⁵⁰ He cleared a path for His anger;
He did not stop short of slaying them,
but gave them over to pestilence.
⁵¹ He struck every firstborn in Egypt,
the first fruits of their vigor in the tents of Ham.
⁵² He set His people moving like sheep,
drove them like a flock in the wilderness.
⁵³ He led them in safety; they were unafraid;
as for their enemies, the sea covered them.
⁵⁴ He brought them to His holy realm,ᵈ
the mountain His right hand had acquired.
⁵⁵ He expelled nations before them,
ᵉ⁻settled the tribes of Israel in their tents,
allotting them their portion by the line.⁻ᵉ

⁵⁶ Yet they defiantly tested God Most High,
and did not observe His decrees.
⁵⁷ They fell away, disloyal like their fathers;
they played false like a treacherous bow.
⁵⁸ They vexed Him with their high places;
they incensed Him with their idols.
⁵⁹ God heard it and was enraged;
He utterly rejected Israel.
⁶⁰ He forsook the tabernacle of Shiloh,
the tent He had set among men.
⁶¹ He let His mightⁱ go into captivity,
His glory into the hands of the foe.
⁶² He gave His people over to the sword;
He was enraged at His very own.
⁶³ Fire consumed their young men,

ᵈ Or "hill" with Septuagint and Saadia.
ᵉ⁻ᵉ Inverted for clarity.
ⁱ I.e. the Ark; cf. Ps. 132.8.

and their maidens *g*-remained unwed.-*g*
64 Their priests fell by the sword,
and their widows could not weep.

65 The Lord awoke as from sleep,
like a warrior *c*-shaking off-*c* wine.
66 He beat back His foes,
dealing them lasting disgrace.
67 He rejected the clan of Joseph;
He did not choose the tribe of Ephraim.
68 He did choose the tribe of Judah,
Mount Zion, which He loved.
69 He built His sanctuary like the heavens,
like the earth that He established forever.
70 He chose David, His servant,
and took him from the sheepfolds.
71 He brought him from minding the nursing ewes
to tend His people Jacob, Israel, His very own.
72 He tended them with blameless heart;
with skillful hands he led them.

79 A psalm of Asaph.

O God, heathens have entered Your domain,
defiled Your holy temple,
and turned Jerusalem into ruins.
2 They have left Your servants' corpses
as food for the fowl of heaven,
and the flesh of Your faithful for the wild beasts.
3 Their blood was shed like water around Jerusalem,
with none to bury them.
4 We have become the butt of our neighbors,
the scorn and derision of those around us.

g-g Lit. "had no nuptial song."

⁵ How long, O LORD, will You be angry forever,
 will Your indignation blaze like fire?
⁶ Pour out Your fury on the nations that do not know You,
 upon the kingdoms that do not invoke Your name,
⁷ for they have devoured Jacob
 and desolated his home.
⁸ Do not hold our former iniquities against us;
 let Your compassion come swiftly toward us,
 for we have sunk very low.
⁹ Help us, O God, our deliverer,
 for the sake of the glory of Your name.
 Save us and forgive our sin,
 for the sake of Your name.
¹⁰ Let the nations not say, "Where is their God?"
 Before our eyes let it be known among the nations
 that You avenge the spilled blood of Your servants.
¹¹ Let the groans of the prisoners reach You;
 reprieve those condemned to death,
 as befits Your great strength.
¹² Pay back our neighbors sevenfold
 for the abuse they have flung at You, O LORD.
¹³ Then we, Your people,
 the flock You shepherd,
 shall glorify You forever;
 for all time we shall tell Your praises.

80 For the leader; on *shoshannim, eduth.* Of Asaph. A psalm.

² Give ear, O shepherd of Israel
 who leads Joseph like a flock!
 Appear, You who are enthroned on the cherubim,
³ at the head of Ephraim, Benjamin, and Manasseh!
 Rouse Your might and come to our help!

4 Restore us, O God;
show Your favor that we may be delivered.

5 O Lord, God of hosts,
how long will You be wrathful
toward the prayers of Your people?
6 You have fed them tears as their daily bread,
made them drink great measures of tears.
7 You set us at strife with our neighbors;
our enemies mock us at will.
8 O God of hosts, restore us;
show Your favor that we may be delivered.

9 You plucked up a vine from Egypt;
You expelled nations and planted it.
10 You cleared a place for it;
it took deep root and filled the land.
11 The mountains were covered by its shade,
mighty cedars by its boughs.
12 Its branches reached the sea,
its shoots, the river.
13 Why did You breach its wall
so that every passerby plucks its fruit,
14 wild boars gnaw at it,
and creatures of the field feed on it?

15 O God of hosts, turn again,
look down from heaven and see;
take note of that vine,
16 the stock planted by Your right hand,
the stem[a] you have taken as Your own.
17 For it is burned by fire and cut down,
perishing before Your angry blast.
18 Grant Your help[b] to the man at Your right hand,
the one You have taken as Your own.

a *Lit. "son."*
b *Lit. "hand."*

¹⁹ We will not turn away from You;
   preserve our life that we may invoke Your name.
²⁰ O Lᴏʀᴅ, God of hosts, restore us;
   show Your favor that we may be delivered.

81

For the leader; on the *gittith*. Of Asaph.

² Sing joyously to God, our strength;
   raise a shout for the God of Jacob.
³ Take up the song,
   sound the timbrel,
   the melodious lyre and harp.
⁴ Blow the horn on the new moon,
   on the full moon for our feast day.
⁵ For it is a law for Israel,
   a ruling of the God of Jacob;
⁶   He imposed it as a decree upon Joseph
   when *ᵃ⁻he went forth from⁻ᵃ* the land of Egypt;
   I heard a language that I knew not.

⁷ I relieved his shoulder of the burden,
   his hands were freed from the basket.
⁸ In distress you called and I rescued you;
   I answered you from the *ᵇ⁻secret place of thunder⁻ᵇ*
   I tested you at the waters of Meribah.   *Selah.*

⁹ Hear, My people, and I will admonish you;
   Israel, if you would but listen to Me!
¹⁰ You shall have no foreign god,
   you shall not bow to an alien god.
¹¹ I the Lᴏʀᴅ am your God
   who brought you out of the land of Egypt;
   open your mouth wide and I will fill it.

ᵃ⁻ᵃ *Or "He went forth against."*
ᵇ⁻ᵇ *Meaning of Heb. uncertain.*

¹² But My people would not listen to Me,
Israel would not obey Me.
¹³ So I let them go after their willful heart
that they might follow their own devices.
¹⁴ If only My people would listen to Me,
if Israel would follow My paths,
¹⁵   then would I subdue their enemies at once,
strike their foes again and again.
¹⁶ Those who hate the LORD shall cower before Him;
their doom shall be eternal.
¹⁷ He fed them*ᶜ* the finest wheat;
I sated you with honey from the rock.

82   A psalm of Asaph.

God stands in the divine assembly;
among the divine beings He pronounces judgment.
² How long will you judge perversely,
showing favor to the wicked?   *Selah.*
³ Judge the wretched and the orphan,
vindicate the lowly and the poor,
⁴   rescue the wretched and the needy;
save them from the hand of the wicked.

⁵ They neither know nor understand,
they go about in darkness;
all the foundations of the earth totter.
⁶ I had taken you for divine beings,
sons of the Most High, all of you;
⁷   but you shall die as men do,
fall like any prince.

⁸ Arise, O God, judge the earth,
for all the nations are Your possession.

ᶜ *Lit. "him," i.e. Israel.*

83 A song, a psalm of Asaph.

2 O God, do not be silent;
do not hold aloof;
do not be quiet, O God!
3 For Your enemies rage,
Your foes *a*-assert themselves.*-a*
4 They plot craftily against Your people,
take counsel against Your treasured ones.
5 They say, "Let us wipe them out as a nation;
Israel's name will be mentioned no more."
6 Unanimous in their counsel
they have made an alliance against You—
7 the clans of Edom and the Ishmaelites,
Moab and the Hagrites,
8 Gebal, Ammon, and Amalek,
Philistia with the inhabitants of Tyre;
9 Assyria too joins forces with them;
they give support to the sons of Lot.   *Selah.*

10 Deal with them as You did with Midian,
with Sisera, with Jabin,
at the brook Kishon—
11 who were destroyed at En-dor,
who became dung for the field.
12 Treat their great men like Oreb and Zeeb,
all their princes like Zebah and Zalmunna,
13 who said, "Let us take the meadows of God
as our possession."
14 O my God, make them like thistledown,
like stubble driven by the wind.
15 As a fire burns a forest,
as flames scorch the hills,
16 pursue them with Your tempest,

---

a-a Lit. "lift up the head."

terrify them with Your storm.
17 Cover[b] their faces with shame
so that they seek Your name, O LORD.
18 May they be frustrated and terrified,
disgraced and doomed forever.
19 May they know
that Your name, Yours alone, is the LORD,
supreme over all the earth.

84 For the leader; on the *gittith*. Of the Korahites. A psalm.

2 How lovely is Your dwelling-place,
O LORD of hosts.
3 I long, I yearn for the courts of the LORD;
my body and soul shout for joy to the living God.
4 Even the sparrow has found a home,
and the swallow a nest for herself
in which to set her young,
near Your altar, O LORD of hosts,
my king and my God.
5 Happy are those who dwell in Your house;
they forever praise You.   *Selah.*

6 Happy is the man who finds refuge in You,
whose mind is on the [pilgrim] highways.
7 They pass through the Valley of Baca,
a-regarding it as a place of springs,
as if the early rain had covered it with blessing.-*a*
8 They go from *b*-rampart to rampart,-*b*
appearing before God in Zion.
9 O LORD, God of hosts,
hear my prayer;
give ear, O God of Jacob.   *Selah.*

b *Lit. "Fill."*

a-a *Meaning of Heb. uncertain.*
b-b *Others "strength to strength."*

¹⁰ O God, behold our shield,
 look upon the face of Your anointed.

¹¹ Better one day in Your courts than a thousand [anywhere
  else];
 I would rather stand at the threshold of God's house
  than dwell in the tents of the wicked.
¹² For the L ORD God is sun*ᶜ* and shield;
 the L ORD bestows grace and glory;
 He does not withhold His bounty from those who live
  without blame.

¹³ O L ORD of hosts,
 happy is the man who trusts in You.

85 For the leader. Of the Korahites. A psalm.

² O L ORD, You *ᵃ-will favor-ᵃ* Your land,
 restore*ᵇ* Jacob's fortune;
³ You *ᶜ-will forgive-ᶜ* Your people's iniquity,
 pardon*ᵈ* all their sins;   *Selah.*
⁴ You *ᵉ-will withdraw-ᵉ* all Your anger,
 turn*ᶠ* away from Your rage.
⁵ Turn again, O God, our helper,
 revoke Your displeasure with us.
⁶ Will You be angry with us forever,
 prolong Your wrath for all generations?
⁷ Surely You will revive us again,

ᶜ Or "bulwark," with Targum; cf. Isa. 54.12.

ᵃ⁻ᵃ Or "have favored."
ᵇ Or "have restored."
ᶜ⁻ᶜ Or "have forgiven."
ᵈ Or "have pardoned."
ᵉ⁻ᵉ Or "have withdrawn."
ᶠ Or "have turned."

so that Your people may rejoice in You.
8 Show us, O Lord, Your faithfulness;
    grant us Your deliverance.

9 Let me hear what God, the Lord, will speak;
    He will promise well-being to His people, His faithful
    ones;
    may they not turn to folly.
10 His help is very near those who fear Him,
    to make His glory dwell in our land.
11 Faithfulness and truth meet;
    justice and well-being kiss.
12 Truth springs up from the earth;
    justice looks down from heaven.
13 The Lord also bestows His bounty;
    our land yields its produce.
14 Justice goes before Him
    as He sets out on His way.

86   A prayer of David.

Incline Your ear, O Lord,
    answer me,
    for I am poor and needy.
2 Preserve my life, for I am steadfast;
    O You, my God,
    deliver Your servant who trusts in You.
3 Have mercy on me, O Lord,
    for I call to You all day long;
4   bring joy to Your servant's life,
    for on You, Lord, I set my hope.
5 For You, Lord, are good and forgiving,
    abounding in steadfast love to all who call on You.
6 Give ear, O Lord, to my prayer;

heed my plea for mercy.
7 In my time of trouble I call You,
  for You will answer me.

8 There is none like You among the gods, O LORD,
  and there are no deeds like Yours.
9 All the nations You have made
  will come to bow down before You, O LORD,
  and they will pay honor to Your name.
10 For You are great and perform wonders;
  You alone are God.

11 Teach me Your way, O LORD;
  I will walk in Your truth;
  let my heart be undivided in reverence for Your name.
12 I will praise You, O LORD, my God, with all my heart
  and pay honor to Your name forever.
13 For Your steadfast love toward me is great;
  You have saved me from the depths of Sheol.

14 O God, arrogant men have risen against me;
  a band of ruthless men seek my life;
  they are not mindful of You.
15 But You, O LORD, are a God
  compassionate and merciful,
  slow to anger, abounding in steadfast love and faithful-
    ness.
16 Turn to me and have mercy on me;
  grant Your strength to Your servant
  and deliver the son of Your maidservant.
17 Show me a sign of Your favor,
  that my enemies may see and be frustrated
  because You, O LORD, have given me aid and comfort.

87 *a*1-2   Of the Korahites. A psalm. A song.

b-The LORD loves the gates of Zion,
His foundation on the holy mountains,-*b*
more than all the dwellings of Jacob.
3 Glorious things are spoken of you,
O city of God.   *Selah.*
4 I mention Rahab*c* and Babylon among those who acknowledge Me;
Philistia, and Tyre, and Cush—each was born there.
5 Indeed, it shall be said of Zion,
"Every man was born there."
d-He, the Most High, will preserve it.-*d*
6 The LORD will inscribe in the register of peoples
that each was born there.   *Selah.*
7 Singers and dancers alike [will say]:
"All my roots*e* are in You."

88   A song. A psalm of the Korahites. For the leader; *a*-on
mahalath leannoth.-*a* A *maskil* of Heman the Ezrahite.

2 O LORD, God of my deliverance,
b-when I cry out in the night-*b* before You,
3   let my prayer reach You;
incline Your ear to my cry.

---

a The meaning of many passages in this psalm is uncertain.
b-b Order of lines inverted for clarity.
c A primeval monster; here, a poetic term for Egypt; cf. Isa. 30.7.
d-d Or "He will preserve it supreme."
e Lit. "sources."

a-a Meaning of Heb. uncertain.
b-b Or "by day I cry out [and] by night."

⁴ For I am sated with misfortune;
   I am at the brink of Sheol.
⁵ I am numbered with those who go down to the Pit;
   I am a helpless man
⁶   abandoned*c* among the dead,
   like bodies lying in the grave
   of whom You are mindful no more,
   and who are cut off from Your care.
⁷ You have put me at the bottom of the Pit,
   in the darkest places, in the depths.
⁸ Your fury lies heavy upon me;
   You afflict me with all Your breakers.   *Selah.*
⁹ You make my companions shun me;
   You make me abhorrent to them;
   I am shut in and do not go out.
¹⁰ My eyes pine away from affliction;
   I call to You, O LORD, each day;
   I stretch out my hands to You.

¹¹ Do You work wonders for the dead?
   Do the shades rise to praise You?   *Selah.*
¹² Is Your faithful care recounted in the grave,
   Your constancy in the place of perdition?
¹³ Are Your wonders made known in the netherworld,*d*
   Your beneficent deeds in the land of oblivion?

¹⁴ As for me, I cry out to You, O LORD;
   each morning my prayer greets You.
¹⁵ Why, O LORD, do You reject me,
   do You hide Your face from me?
¹⁶ From my youth I have been afflicted
   and near death;
   I suffer Your terrors *ᵉ*wherever I turn.*ᵉ*
¹⁷ Your fury overwhelms me;
   Your terrors destroy me.

c Lit. "released."
d Lit. "darkness."
e-e Following Saadia; meaning of Heb. uncertain.

¹⁸ They swirl about me like water all day long;
   they encircle me on every side.
¹⁹ You have put friend and neighbor far from me
   and my companions out of my sight./

89 A *maskil* of Ethan the Ezrahite.

² I will sing of the LORD's steadfast love forever;
   to all generations I will proclaim Your faithfulness with
      my mouth.
³ I declare, "Your steadfast love is confirmed forever;
   there in the heavens You establish Your faithfulness."

⁴ "I have made a covenant with My chosen one;
   I have sworn to My servant David:
⁵   I will establish your offspring forever,
   I will confirm your throne for all generations." *Selah.*

⁶ Your wonders, O LORD, are praised by the heavens,
   Your faithfulness, too, in the assembly of holy beings.
⁷ For who in the skies can equal the LORD,
   can compare with the LORD among the divine beings,
⁸   a God greatly dreaded in the council of holy beings,
   held in awe by all around Him?
⁹ O LORD, God of hosts,
   who is mighty like You, O LORD?
   Your faithfulness surrounds You;
¹⁰   You rule the swelling of the sea;
   when its waves surge, You still them.
¹¹ You crushed Rahab; he was like a corpse;
   with Your powerful arm You scattered Your enemies.
¹² The heaven is Yours,
   the earth too;
   the world and all it holds—
   You established them.

ᶠ *Lit. "into darkness."*

¹³ North and south—
    You created them;
    Tabor and Hermon sing forth Your name.
¹⁴ Yours is an arm endowed with might;
    Your hand is strong;
    Your right hand, exalted.
¹⁵ Righteousness and justice are the base of Your throne;
    steadfast love and faithfulness stand before You.

¹⁶ Happy is the people who know the joyful shout;
    O LORD, they walk in the light of Your presence.
¹⁷ They rejoice in Your name all day long;
    they are exalted through Your righteousness.
¹⁸ For You are their strength in which they glory;
    our horn is exalted through Your favor.
¹⁹ Truly our shield is of the LORD,
    our king, of the Holy One of Israel.

²⁰ Thenᵃ You spoke to Your faithful ones in a vision
    and said, "I have conferred power upon a warrior;
    I have exalted one chosen out of the people.
²¹ I have found David, My servant;
    anointed him with My sacred oil.
²² My hand shall be constantly with him,
    and My arm shall strengthen him.
²³ No enemy shall ᵇ⁻oppress him,⁻ᵇ
    no vile man afflict him.
²⁴ I will crush his adversaries before him;
    I will strike down those who hate him.
²⁵ My faithfulness and steadfast love shall be with him;
    his horn shall be exalted through My name.
²⁶ I will set his hand upon the sea,
    his right hand upon the rivers.
²⁷ He shall say to Me,
    'You are my father, my God, the rock of my deliverance.'
²⁸ I will appoint him firstborn,

ᵃ *Referring to vv. 4–5; cf. II Sam. 7.1–17.*
ᵇ⁻ᵇ *Meaning of Heb. uncertain.*

highest of the kings of the earth.
29 I will maintain My steadfast love for him always;
     My covenant with him shall endure.
30 I will establish his line forever,
     his throne, as long as the heavens last.
31 If his sons forsake My teaching
     and do not live by My rules;
32   if they violate My laws,
     and do not observe My commands,
33   I will punish their transgression with the rod,
     their iniquity with plagues.
34 But I will not take away My steadfast love from him;
     I will not betray My faithfulness.
35 I will not violate My covenant,
     or change what I have uttered.
36 I have sworn by My holiness, once and for all;
     I will not be false to David.
37 His line shall continue forever,
     his throne, as the sun before Me,
38   as the moon, established forever,
     an enduring witness in the sky."   *Selah.*

39 Yet You have rejected, spurned,
     and become enraged at Your anointed.
40 You have repudiated the covenant with Your servant;
     You have dragged his dignity in the dust.
41 You have breached all his defenses,
     shattered his strongholds.
42 All who pass by plunder him;
     he has become the butt of his neighbors.
43 You have exalted the right hand of his adversaries,
     and made all his enemies rejoice.
44 You have turned back the blade of his sword,
     and have not sustained him in battle.
45 You have brought *b*-his splendor-*b* to an end
     and have hurled his throne to the ground.

⁴⁶ You have cut short the days of his youth;
  You have covered him with shame.   *Selah.*
⁴⁷ How long, O LORD; will You forever hide Your face,
  will Your fury blaze like fire?
⁴⁸ O remember *ᵇ*how short my life is;*⁻ᵇ*
  why should You have created every man in vain?
⁴⁹ What man can live and not see death,
  can save himself from the clutches of Sheol?   *Selah.*
⁵⁰ O LORD, where is Your steadfast love of old
  which You swore to David in Your faithfulness?
⁵¹ Remember, O LORD, the abuse flung at Your servants
  *ᵇ*that I have borne in my bosom [from]
    many peoples,*⁻ᵇ*
⁵² how Your enemies, O LORD, have flung abuse,
  abuse at Your anointed at every step.

⁵³ Blessed is the LORD forever.
  Amen and Amen.

BOOK FOUR

90 A prayer of Moses, the man of God.

  O Lord, You have been our refuge in every generation.
² Before the mountains came into being,
  before You brought forth the earth and the world,
  from eternity to eternity You are God.

³ You return man to dust;*ᵃ*
  You decreed, "Return you mortals!"
⁴ *ᵇ*For in Your sight a thousand years
  are like yesterday that has past,
  like a watch of the night.
⁵ You engulf men in sleep;*⁻ᵇ*
  at daybreak they are like grass that renews itself;

ᵃ Or "contrition."
ᵇ⁻ᵇ Meaning of Heb. uncertain.

6 at daybreak it flourishes anew;
  by dusk it withers and dries up.
7 So we are consumed by Your anger,
  terror-struck by Your fury.
8 You have set our iniquities before You,
  our hidden sins in the light of Your face.
9 All our days pass away in Your wrath;
  we spend our years like a sigh.
10 The span of our life is seventy years,
  or, given the strength, eighty years;
  but the *b*-best of them-*b* are trouble and sorrow.
  They pass by speedily, and we *c*-are in darkness.-*c*
11 Who can know Your furious anger?
  Your wrath matches the fear of You.
12 Teach us to count our days rightly,
  that we may obtain a wise heart.

13 Turn, O LORD!
  How long?
  Show mercy to Your servants.
14 Satisfy us at daybreak with Your steadfast love
  that we may sing for joy all our days.
15 Give us joy for as long as You have afflicted us,
  for the years we have suffered misfortune.
16 Let Your deeds be seen by Your servants,
  Your glory by their children.
17 May the favor of the LORD, our God, be upon us;
  let the work of our hands prosper,
  O prosper the work of our hands!

91 O you who dwell in the shelter of the Most High
  and abide in the protection of Shaddai—
2   I say of the LORD, my refuge and stronghold,

c-c Or "fly away."

my God in whom I trust,
3 that He will save you from the fowler's trap,
from the destructive plague.
4 He will cover you with His pinions;
you will find refuge under His wings;
His fidelity is an encircling shield.
5 You need not fear the terror by night,
or the arrow that flies by day,
6 the plague that stalks in the darkness,
or the scourge that ravages at noon.
7 A thousand may fall at your left side,
ten thousand at your right,
but it shall not reach you.
8 You will see it with your eyes,
you will witness the punishment of the wicked.
9 Because you took the LORD—my refuge,
the Most High—as your haven,
10 no harm will befall you,
no disease touch your tent.
11 For He will order His angels
to guard you wherever you go.
12 They will carry you in their hands
lest you hurt your foot on a stone.
13 You will tread on cubs and vipers;
you will trample lions and asps.

14 "Because he is devoted to Me I will deliver him;
I will keep him safe, for he knows My name.
15 When he calls on Me, I will answer him;
I will be with him in distress;
I will rescue him and make him honored;
16 I will let him live to a ripe old age,
and show him My salvation."

92 A psalm. A song; for the sabbath day.

² It is good to praise the LORD,
    to sing hymns to Your name, O Most High,
³   to proclaim Your steadfast love at daybreak,
    Your faithfulness each night
⁴   with a ten-stringed harp,
    with voice and lyre together.

⁵ You have gladdened me by Your deeds, O LORD;
    I shout for joy at Your handiwork.
⁶ How great are Your works, O LORD,
    how very subtle ^a Your designs!
⁷ A brutish man cannot know,
    a fool cannot understand this:
⁸   though the wicked sprout like grass,
    though all evildoers blossom,
    it is only that they may be destroyed forever.

⁹ But You are exalted, O LORD, for all time.

¹⁰ Surely, Your enemies, O LORD,
    surely, Your enemies perish;
    all evildoers are scattered.
¹¹ You raise my horn high like that of a wild ox;
    I am soaked in freshening oil.
¹² I shall see the defeat of my watchful foes,
    hear of the downfall of the wicked who beset me.
¹³ The righteous bloom like a date-palm;
    they thrive like a cedar in Lebanon;
¹⁴   planted in the house of the LORD,
    they flourish in the courts of our God.
¹⁵ In old age they still produce fruit;

^a *Or "profound."*

they are full of sap and freshness,
16 attesting that the LORD is upright,
my rock, in whom there is no wrong.

93

The LORD is king,
He is robed in grandeur;
the LORD is robed,
He is girded with strength.
The world stands firm;
it cannot be shaken.
2 Your throne stands firm from of old;
from eternity You have existed.
3 The ocean sounds, O LORD,
the ocean sounds its thunder,
the ocean sounds its pounding.
4 Above the thunder of the mighty waters,
more majestic than the breakers of the sea
is the LORD, majestic on high.
5 Your decrees are indeed enduring;
holiness befits Your house,
O LORD, for all times.

94

God of retribution, LORD,
God of retribution, appear!
2 Rise up, judge of the earth,
give the arrogant their deserts!
3 How long shall the wicked, O LORD,
how long shall the wicked exult,
4 shall they utter insolent speech,
shall all evildoers vaunt themselves?
5 They crush Your people, O LORD,
they afflict Your very own;
6 they kill the widow and the stranger;

they murder the fatherless,
7 thinking, "The LORD does not see it,
the God of Jacob does not pay heed."

8 Take heed, you most brutish people;
fools, when will you get wisdom?
9 Shall He who implants the ear not hear,
He who forms the eye not see?
10 Shall He who disciplines nations not punish,
He who instructs men in knowledge?
11 The LORD knows the designs of men to be futile.

12 Happy is the man whom You discipline, O LORD,
the man You instruct in Your teaching,
13 to give him tranquillity in times of misfortune,
until a pit be dug for the wicked.
14 For the LORD will not forsake His people;
He will not abandon His very own.
15 Judgment shall again accord with justice
and all the upright shall rally to it.

16 Who will take my part against evil men?
Who will stand up for me against wrongdoers?
17 Were not the LORD my help,
I should soon dwell in silence.
18 When I think my foot has given way,
Your faithfulness, O LORD, supports me.
19 When I am filled with cares,
Your assurance soothes my soul.

20 Shall the seat of injustice be Your partner,
that frames mischief by statute?
21 They band together to do away with the righteous;
they condemn the innocent to death.
22 But the LORD is my haven;
my God is my sheltering rock.

23 He will make their evil recoil upon them,
   annihilate them through their own wickedness;
   the LORD our God will annihilate them.

95 Come, let us sing joyously to the LORD,
   raise a shout for our rock and deliverer;
2   let us come into His presence with praise;
   let us raise a shout for Him in song!
3 For the LORD is a great God,
   the great king of all divine beings.
4 In His hand are the depths of the earth;
   the peaks of the mountains are His.
5 His is the sea, He made it;
   and the land, which His hands fashioned.

6 Come, let us bow down and kneel,
   bend the knee before the LORD our maker,
7   for He is our God,
   and we are the people He tends, the flock in His care.
   O, if you would but heed His charge this day:
8   Do not be stubborn as at Meribah,
   as on the day of Massah, in the wilderness,
9   when your fathers put Me to the test,
   tried Me, though they had seen My deeds.
10 Forty years I was provoked by that generation.
   I thought, "They are a senseless people;
   they would not know My ways."
11 Concerning them I swore in anger,
   "They shall never come to My resting-place!"

96 *a*Sing to the LORD a new song,
   sing to the LORD, all the earth.
2 Sing to the LORD, bless His name,
   proclaim His victory day after day.

a *Cf. I Chron. 16.23–33.*

3 Tell of His glory among the nations,
His wondrous deeds, among all peoples.
4 For the LORD is great and much acclaimed,
He is held in awe by all divine beings.
5 All the gods of the peoples are mere idols,
but the LORD made the heavens.
6 Glory and majesty are before Him;
strength and splendor are in His temple.

7 Ascribe to the LORD, O families of the peoples,
ascribe to the LORD glory and strength.
8 Ascribe to the LORD the glory of His name,
bring tribute and enter His courts.
9 Bow down to the LORD majestic in holiness;
tremble in His presence, all the earth!
10 Declare among the nations, "The LORD is king!"
the world stands firm; it cannot be shaken;
He judges the peoples with equity.
11 Let the heavens rejoice and the earth exult;
let the sea and all within it thunder,
12 the fields and everything in them exult;
then shall all the trees of the forest shout for joy
13 at the presence of the LORD, for He is coming,
for He is coming to rule the earth;
He will rule the world justly
and its peoples in faithfulness.

97 The LORD is king!
Let the earth exult,
the many islands rejoice!
2 Dense clouds are around Him,
righteousness and justice are the base of His throne.
3 Fire is His vanguard,
burning His foes on every side.

⁴ His lightnings light up the world;
the earth is convulsed at the sight;
⁵ mountains melt like wax at the LORD's presence,
at the presence of the Lord of all the earth.
⁶ The heavens proclaim His righteousness
and all peoples see His glory.
⁷ All who worship images,
who vaunt their idols,
are dismayed;
all divine beings bow down to Him.
⁸ Zion, hearing it, rejoices,
the towns*a* of Judah exult,
because of Your judgments, O LORD.
⁹ For You, LORD, are supreme over all the earth;
You are exalted high above all divine beings.

¹⁰ O you who love the LORD, hate evil!
He guards the lives of His loyal ones,
saving them from the hand of the wicked.
¹¹ Light is sown for the righteous,
radiance*b* for the upright.
¹² O you righteous, rejoice in the LORD
and acclaim His holy name!

98 A psalm.

Sing to the LORD a new song,
for He has worked wonders;
His right hand, His holy arm,
has won Him victory.
² The LORD has manifested His victory,
has displayed His triumph in the sight of the nations.
³ He was mindful of His steadfast love and faithfulness
toward the house of Israel;

a Or "women."
b Others "joy."

all the ends of the earth beheld the victory of our God.
4 Raise a shout to the LORD, all the earth,
   break into joyous songs of praise!
5 Sing praise to the LORD with the lyre,
   with the lyre and melodious song.
6 With trumpets and the blast of the horn
   raise a shout before the LORD, the king.
7 Let the sea and all within it thunder,
   the world and its inhabitants;
8   let the rivers clap their hands,
   the mountains sing joyously together
9   at the presence of the LORD,
   for He is coming to rule the earth;
   He will rule the world justly,
   and its peoples with equity.

99   ^{a-}The LORD, enthroned on cherubim, is king,
   peoples tremble, the earth quakes.^{-a}
2 The LORD is great in Zion,
   and exalted above all peoples.
3 They praise Your name as great and awesome;
   He is holy!

4 ^{b-}Mighty king^{-b} who loves justice,
   it was You who established equity,
   You who worked righteous judgment in Jacob.
5 Exalt the LORD our God
   and bow down to His footstool;
   He is holy!

6 Moses and Aaron among His priests,
   Samuel, among those who call on His name—
   when they called to the LORD,
   He answered them.

^{a-a} *Clauses transposed for clarity.*
^{b-b} *Meaning of Heb. uncertain.*

⁷ He spoke to them in a pillar of cloud;
   they obeyed His decrees,
   the law He gave them.
⁸ O Lord our God, You answered them;
   You were a forgiving God for them,
   but You exacted retribution for their misdeeds.

⁹ Exalt the Lord our God,
   and bow toward His holy hill,
   for the Lord our God is holy.

100   A psalm ᵃ⁻for praise.⁻ᵃ

Raise a shout for the Lord, all the earth;
²   worship the Lord in gladness;
   come into His presence with shouts of joy.
³ Acknowledge that the Lord is God;
   He made us and ᵇ⁻we are His,⁻ᵇ
   His people, the flock He tends.
⁴ Enter His gates with praise,
   His courts with acclamation.
Praise Him!
Bless His name!
⁵ For the Lord is good;
   His steadfast love is eternal;
   His faithfulness is for all generations.

101   Of David. A psalm.

I will sing of faithfulness and justice;
   I will chant a hymn to You, O Lord.
² I will study the way of the blameless;
   when shall I attain it?

ᵃ⁻ᵃ *Traditionally, "for the thanksgiving offering."*
ᵇ⁻ᵇ *So qere; kethib and some ancient versions "not we ourselves."*

I will live without blame within my house.
3 I will not set before my eyes anything base;
I hate crooked dealing;
I will have none of it.
4 Perverse thoughts will be far from me;
I will know nothing of evil.
5 He who slanders his friend in secret I will destroy;
I cannot endure the haughty and proud man.
6 My eyes are on the trusty men of the land,
to have them at my side.
He who follows the way of the blameless
shall be in my service.
7 He who deals deceitfully
shall not live in my house;
he who speaks untruth
shall not stand before my eyes.
8 Each morning I will destroy
all the wicked of the land,
to rid the city of the LORD
of all evildoers.

102 A prayer of the lowly man when he is faint and pours forth his plea before the LORD.

2 O LORD, hear my prayer;
let my cry come before You.
3 Do not hide Your face from me
in my time of trouble;
turn Your ear to me;
when I cry, answer me speedily.
4 For my days have vanished like smoke
and my bones are charred like a hearth.
5 My body is stricken and withered like grass;
a-too wasted-*a* to eat my food;

---

a-a *Others "I forget."*

6   on account of my vehement groaning
    my bones *b*-show through my skin.*-b*
7 I am like a great owl in the wilderness,
    an owl among the ruins.
8 I lie awake; I am like
    a lone bird upon a roof.
9 All day long my enemies revile me;
    my deriders use my name to curse.
10 For I have eaten ashes like bread
    and mixed my drink with tears,
11   because of Your wrath and Your fury;
    for You have cast me far away.
12 My days are like a lengthening shadow;
    I wither like grass.

13 But You, O LORD, are enthroned forever;
    Your fame endures throughout the ages.
14 You will surely arise and take pity on Zion,
    for it is time to be gracious to her;
    the appointed time has come.
15 Your servants take delight in its stones,
    and cherish its dust.
16 The nations will fear the name of the LORD,
    all the kings of the earth, Your glory.
17 For the LORD has built Zion;
    He has appeared in all His glory.
18 He has turned to the prayer *c*-of the destitute*-c*
    and has not spurned their prayer.
19 May this be written down for a coming generation,
    that people yet to be created may praise the LORD.
20 For He looks down from His holy height;
    the LORD beholds the earth from heaven
21   to hear the groans of the prisoner,
    to release those condemned to death;
22   that the fame of the LORD may be recounted in Zion,

---

b-b Lit. "*cling to my flesh.*"
c-c Meaning of Heb. uncertain.

His praises in Jerusalem,
23 when the nations gather together,
the kingdoms, to serve the LORD.

24 He drained my strength in mid-course,
He shortened my days.
25 I say, "O my God, do not take me away
in the midst of my days,
You whose years go on for generations on end.
26 Of old You established the earth;
the heavens are the work of Your hands.
27 They shall perish, but You shall endure;
they shall all wear out like a garment;
You change them like clothing and they pass away.
28 But You are the same, and Your years never end.
29 May the children of Your servants dwell securely
and their offspring endure in Your presence."

103 Of David.

Bless the LORD, O my soul,
all my being, His holy name.
2 Bless the LORD, O my soul
and do not forget all His bounties.
3 He forgives all your sins,
heals all your diseases.
4 He redeems your life from the Pit,
surrounds you with steadfast love and mercy.
5 He satisfies you with good things in *a*-the prime of life,-*a*
so that your youth is renewed like the eagle's.

6 The LORD executes righteous acts
and judgments for all who are wronged.
7 He made known His ways to Moses,

a-a *Meaning of Heb. uncertain.*

His deeds to the children of Israel.
8 The LORD is compassionate and gracious,
slow to anger, abounding in steadfast love.
9 He will not contend forever,
or nurse His anger for all time.
10 He has not dealt with us according to our sins,
nor has He requited us according to our iniquities.
11 For as the heavens are high above the earth,
so great is His steadfast love toward those who fear Him.
12 As east is far from west,
so far has He removed our sins from us.
13 As a father has compassion for his children,
so the LORD has compassion for those who fear Him.
14 For He knows how we are formed;
He is mindful that we are dust.

15 Man, his days are like those of grass;
he blooms like a flower of the field;
16 a wind passes by and it is no more,
its own place no longer knows it.
17 But the LORD's steadfast love is for all eternity
toward those who fear Him,
and His beneficence is for the children's children
18 of those who keep His covenant
and remember to observe His precepts.
19 The LORD has established His throne in heaven,
and His sovereign rule is over all.

20 Bless the LORD, O His angels,
mighty creatures who do His bidding,
ever obedient to His bidding;
21 bless the LORD, all His hosts,
His servants who do His will;
22 bless the LORD, all His works,

through the length and breadth of His realm;
bless the LORD, O my soul.

104 Bless the LORD, O my soul;
O LORD, my God, You are very great;
You are clothed in glory and majesty,
2 wrapped in a robe of light;
You spread the heavens like a tent cloth.
3 He sets the rafters of His lofts in the waters,
makes the clouds His chariot,
moves on the wings of the wind.
4 He makes the winds His messengers,
fiery flames His servants.
5 He established the earth on its foundations,
so that it shall never totter.
6 You made the deep cover it as a garment;
the waters stood above the mountains.
7 They fled at Your blast,
rushed away at the sound of Your thunder,
8 —mountains rising, valleys sinking—
to the place You established for them.
9 You set bounds they must not pass
so that they never again cover the earth.

10 You make springs gush forth in torrents;
they make their way between the hills,
11 giving drink to all the wild beasts;
the wild asses slake their thirst.
12 The birds of the sky dwell beside them
and sing among the foliage.
13 You water the mountains from Your*a* lofts;
the earth is sated from the fruit of Your work.
14 You make the grass grow for the cattle,
and herbage for man's labor

a Lit. "His."

that he may get food out of the earth—
15 wine that cheers the hearts of men
    b-oil that makes the face shine,-*b*
    and bread that sustains man's life.
16 The trees of the LORD drink their fill,
    the cedars of Lebanon, His own planting,
17   where birds make their nests;
    the stork has her home in the junipers.
18 The high mountains are for wild goats;
    the crags are a refuge for rock-badgers.

19 He made the moon to mark the seasons;
    the sun knows when to set.
20 You bring on darkness and it is night,
    when all the beasts of the forests stir.
21 The lions roar for prey,
    seeking their food from God.
22 When the sun rises, they come home
    and couch in their dens.
23 Man then goes out to his work,
    to his labor until the evening.

24 How many are the things You have made, O LORD;
    You have made them all with wisdom;
    the earth is full of Your creations.
25 There is the sea, vast and wide,
    with its creatures beyond number,
    living things, small and great.
26 There go the ships,
    and Leviathan that You formed to sport with.
27 All of them look to You
    to give them their food when it is due.
28 Give it to them, they gather it up;
    open Your hand, they are well satisfied;
29   hide Your face, they are terrified;

b-b *Lit. "to make the face shine from oil."*

take away their breath, they perish
and turn again into dust;
30 send back Your breath, they are created,
and You renew the face of the earth.

31 May the glory of the LORD endure forever;
may the LORD rejoice in His works!
32 He looks at the earth and it trembles;
He touches the mountains and they smoke.

33 I will sing to the LORD as long as I live;
all my life I will chant hymns to my God.
34 May my prayer be pleasing to Him;
I will rejoice in the LORD.
35 May sinners disappear from the earth,
and the wicked be no more.
Bless the LORD, O my soul.
Hallelujah.

105 Praise the LORD;
call on His name;
proclaim His deeds among the peoples.
2 Sing praises to Him;
speak of all His wondrous acts.
3 Exult in His holy name;
let all who seek the LORD rejoice.
4 Turn to the LORD, to His might;[a]
seek His presence constantly.
5 Remember the wonders He has done,
His portents and the judgments He has pronounced,
6 O offspring of Abraham, His servant,
O descendants of Jacob, His chosen ones.

7 He is the LORD our God;
His judgments are throughout the earth.

_____
a *I.e. the Ark; cf. Ps. 78. 61; Ps. 132. 8.*

8 He is ever mindful of His covenant,
the promise He gave for a thousand generations,
9 that He made with Abraham,
swore to Isaac,
10 and confirmed in a decree for Jacob,
for Israel, as an eternal covenant,
11 saying, "To you I will give the land of Canaan
as your allotted heritage."

12 They were then few in number,
a mere handful, sojourning there,
13 wandering from nation to nation,
from one kingdom to another.
14 He allowed no one to oppress them;
He reproved kings on their account,
15 "Do not touch My anointed ones;
do not harm My prophets."

16 He called down a famine on the land,
destroyed every staff of bread.
17 He sent ahead of them a man,
Joseph, sold into slavery.
18 His feet were subjected to fetters;
an iron collar was put on his neck.
19 Until his prediction came true
the decree of the LORD purged him.
20 The king sent to have him freed;
the ruler of nations released him.
21 He made him the lord of his household,
empowered him over all his possessions,
22 to discipline his princes at will,
to teach his elders wisdom.
23 Then Israel came to Egypt;
Jacob sojourned in the land of Ham.

²⁴ He made His people very fruitful,
more numerous than their foes.
²⁵ ᵇ-He changed their heart-ᵇ to hate His people,
to plot against His servants.
²⁶ He sent His servant Moses,
and Aaron, whom He had chosen.
²⁷ They performed His signs among them,
His wonders, against the land of Ham.
²⁸ He sent darkness; it was very dark;
ᶜ-did they not defy His word?-ᶜ
²⁹ He turned their waters into blood
and killed their fish.
³⁰ Their land teemed with frogs,
even the rooms of their king.
³¹ Swarms of insects came at His command,
lice, throughout their country.
³² He gave them hail for rain,
and flaming fire in their land.
³³ He struck their vines and fig trees,
broke down the trees of their country.
³⁴ Locusts came at His command,
grasshoppers without number.
³⁵ They devoured every green thing in the land;
they consumed the produce of the soil.
³⁶ He struck down every firstborn in the land,
the first fruit of their vigor.
³⁷ He led Israelᵈ out with silver and gold;
none among their tribes faltered.
³⁸ Egypt rejoiced when they left,
for dread of Israelᵈ had fallen upon them.

³⁹ He spread a cloud for a cover,
and fire to light up the night.
⁴⁰ They asked and He brought them quail,
and satisfied them with food from heaven.

ᵇ⁻ᵇ Or "Their heart changed."
ᶜ⁻ᶜ Meaning of Heb. uncertain.
ᵈ Lit. "them."

⁴¹ He opened a rock so that water gushed forth;
   it flowed as a stream in the parched land.
⁴² Mindful of His sacred promise
   to His servant Abraham,
⁴³   He led His people out in gladness,
   His chosen ones with joyous song.
⁴⁴ He gave them the lands of nations;
   they inherited the wealth of peoples,
⁴⁵   that they might keep His laws
   and observe His teachings.
   Hallelujah.

106 Hallelujah.

Praise the LORD for He is good;
His steadfast love is eternal.
² Who can tell the mighty acts of the LORD,
   proclaim all His praises?

³ Happy are those who act justly,
   who do right at all times.
⁴ Be mindful of me, O LORD, when You favor Your people;
   take note of me when You deliver them,
⁵   that I may enjoy the prosperity of Your chosen ones,
   share the joy of Your nation,
   glory in Your very own people.

⁶ We have sinned like our forefathers;
   we have gone astray, done evil.
⁷ Our forefathers in Egypt did not perceive Your wonders;
   they did not remember Your abundant love,
   but rebelled at the sea, at the Sea of Reeds.
⁸ Yet He saved them, as befits His name,
   to make known His might.
⁹ He sent His blast against the Sea of Reeds;

it became dry;
He led them through the deep as through a wilderness.
10 He delivered them from the foe,
redeemed them from the enemy.
11 Water covered their adversaries;
not one of them was left.
12 Then they believed His promise,
and sang His praises.
13 But they soon forgot His deeds;
they would not wait to learn His plan.
14 They were seized with craving in the wilderness,
and put God to the test in the wasteland.
15 He gave them what they asked for,
then made them waste away.
16 There was envy of Moses in the camp,
and of Aaron, the holy one of the LORD.
17 The earth opened up and swallowed Dathan,
closed over the party of Abiram.
18 A fire blazed among their party,
a flame that consumed the wicked.
19 They made a calf at Horeb
and bowed down to a molten image.
20 They exchanged their glory
for the image of a bull that feeds on grass.
21 They forgot God who saved them,
who performed great deeds in Egypt,
22 wondrous deeds in the land of Ham,
awesome deeds at the Sea of Reeds.
23 He would have destroyed them
had not Moses His chosen one
confronted Him in the breach
to avert His destructive wrath.
24 They rejected the desirable land,
and put no faith in His promise.
25 They grumbled in their tents

and disobeyed the LORD.
26 So He raised His hand in oath
to make them fall in the wilderness,
27 to disperse^a their offspring among the nations
and scatter them through the lands.
28 They attached themselves to Baal Peor,
ate sacrifices offered to the dead.
29 They provoked anger by their deeds,
and a plague broke out among them.
30 Phinehas stepped forth and intervened,
and the plague ceased.
31 It was reckoned to his merit
for all generations, to eternity.
32 They provoked wrath at the waters of Meribah
and Moses suffered on their account,
33 because they rebelled against Him
and he spoke rashly.

34 They did not destroy the nations
as the LORD had commanded them,
35 but mingled with the nations
and learned their ways.
36 They worshiped their idols,
which became a snare for them.
37 Their own sons and daughters
they sacrificed to demons.
38 They shed innocent blood,
the blood of their sons and daughters,
whom they sacrificed to the idols of Canaan;
so the land was polluted with bloodguilt.
39 Thus they became defiled by their acts,
debauched through their deeds.
40 The LORD was angry with His people
and He abhorred His inheritance.
41 He handed them over to the nations;

a *Cf. Targum, Kimhi.*

their foes ruled them.
42 Their enemies oppressed them
    and they were subject to their power.
43 He saved them time and again,
    but they were deliberately rebellious,
    and so they were brought low by their iniquity.
44 When He saw that they were in distress,
    when He heard their cry,
45   He was mindful of His covenant
    and in His great faithfulness relented.
46 He made all their captors kindly disposed toward them.

47 Deliver us, O Lord our God,
    and gather us from among the nations,
    to acclaim Your holy name,
    to glory in Your praise.

48 Blessed is the Lord, God of Israel,
    From eternity to eternity.
    Let all the people say, "Amen."
    Hallelujah.

BOOK FIVE

107 "Praise the Lord, for He is good;
    His steadfast love is eternal!"
2 Thus let the redeemed of the Lord say,
    those He redeemed from adversity,
3   whom He gathered in from the lands,
    from east and west,
    from the north and from the sea.

4 Some lost their way in the wilderness,
    in the wasteland;

they found no settled place.
5 Hungry and thirsty,
   their spirit failed.
6 In their adversity they cried to the LORD,
   and He rescued them from their troubles.
7 He showed them a direct way
   to reach a settled place.
8 Let them praise the LORD for His steadfast love,
   His wondrous deeds for mankind;
9   for He has satisfied the thirsty,
   filled the hungry with all good things.

10 Some lived in deepest darkness,
   bound in cruel irons,
11   because they defied the word of God,
   spurned the counsel of the Most High.
12 He humbled their hearts through suffering;
   they stumbled with no one to help.
13 In their adversity they cried to the LORD,
   and He rescued them from their troubles.
14 He brought them out of deepest darkness,
   broke their bonds asunder.
15 Let them praise the LORD for His steadfast love,
   His wondrous deeds for mankind,
16   For He shattered gates of bronze,
   He broke their iron bars.

17 There were fools who suffered for their sinful way,
   and for their iniquities.
18 All food was loathsome to them;
   they reached the gates of death.
19 In their adversity they cried to the LORD
   and He saved them from their troubles.
20 He gave an order and healed them;
   He delivered them from the pits.[a]

a *Viz. of death.*

²¹ Let them praise the LORD for His steadfast love,
His wondrous deeds for mankind.
²² Let them offer thanksgiving sacrifices,
and tell His deeds in joyful song.

²³ Others go down to the sea in ships,
ply their trade in the mighty waters;
²⁴   they have seen the works of the LORD
and His wonders in the deep.
²⁵ By His word He raised a storm wind
that made the waves surge.
²⁶ Mounting up to the heaven,
plunging down to the depths,
disgorging in their misery,
²⁷   they reeled and staggered like a drunken man,
all their skill to no avail.
²⁸ In their adversity they cried to the LORD,
and He saved them from their troubles.
²⁹ He reduced the storm to a whisper;
the waves were stilled.
³⁰ They rejoiced when all was quiet,
and He brought them to the port they desired.
³¹ Let them praise the LORD for His steadfast love,
His wondrous deeds for mankind.
³² Let them exalt Him in the congregation of the people,
acclaim Him in the assembly of the elders.

³³ He turns the rivers into a wilderness,
springs of water into thirsty land,
³⁴   fruitful land into a salt marsh,
because of the wickedness of its inhabitants.
³⁵ He turns the wilderness into pools,
parched land into springs of water.
³⁶ There He settles the hungry;
they build a place to settle in.

37 They sow fields and plant vineyards
    that yield a fruitful harvest.
38 He blesses them and they increase greatly;
    and He does not let their cattle decrease,
39   after they had been few and crushed
    by oppression, misery, and sorrow.
40 He pours contempt on great men
    and makes them lose their way in trackless deserts;
41   but the needy He secures from suffering,
    and increases their families like flocks.

42 The upright see it and rejoice;
    the mouth of all wrongdoers is stopped.
43 The wise man will take note of these things;
    he will consider the steadfast love of the LORD.

108   A song. A psalm of David.

2 *a*My heart is firm, O God;
    I will sing and chant a hymn with all my soul.
3 Awake, O harp and lyre!
    I will wake the dawn.
4 I will praise You among the peoples, O LORD,
    sing a hymn to You among the nations;
5   for Your faithfulness is higher than the heavens;
    Your steadfastness reaches to the sky.
6 Exalt Yourself over the heavens, O God;
    let Your glory be over all the earth!
7 *b*That those whom You love may be rescued,
    deliver with Your right hand and answer me.

8 God promised *c*in His sanctuary*c*
    that I would exultingly divide up Shechem,
    and measure the Valley of Sukkoth;

a *With vv. 2–6, cf. Ps. 57.8–12.*
b *With vv. 7–14, cf. Ps. 60.7–14.*
c-c *Or "by His holiness."*

9   Gilead and Manasseh would be mine,
     Ephraim my chief stronghold,
     Judah my scepter;
10   Moab would be my washbasin;
     on Edom I would cast my shoe;
     I would raise a shout over Philistia.
11 Would that I were brought to the bastion!
     Would that I were led to Edom!

12 But You have rejected us, O God;
     God, You do not march with our armies.
13 Grant us Your aid against the foe,
     for the help of man is worthless.
14 With God we shall triumph;
     He will trample our foes.

109   For the leader. Of David. A psalm.

O God of my praise,
     do not keep aloof,
2   for the wicked and the deceitful
     open their mouth against me;
     they speak to me with lying tongue.
3 They encircle me with words of hate;
     they attack me without cause.
4 They answer my love with accusation
     *a-*and I must stand judgment.*-a*
5 They repay me with evil for good,
     with hatred for my love.

6 Appoint a wicked man over him;
     may an accuser stand at his right side;
7   may he be tried and convicted;
     may he be judged and found guilty.

a-a *Or "but I am all prayer"; meaning of Heb. uncertain, but see v. 7.*

8 May his days be few;
    may another take over *b*-his position.-*b*
9 May his children be orphans,
    his wife a widow.
10 May his children wander from their hovels,
    begging in search of [bread].
11 May his creditor seize all his possessions;
    may strangers plunder his wealth.
12 May no one show him mercy;
    may none pity his orphans;
13   may his posterity be cut off;
    may their names be blotted out in the next generation.
14 May God be ever mindful of his father's iniquity,
    and may the sin of his mother not be blotted out.
15 May the LORD be aware of them always
    and cause their names to be cut off from the earth,
16   because he was not minded to act kindly,
    and hounded to death the poor and needy man,
    one crushed in spirit.
17 He loved to curse—may a curse come upon him!
He would not bless—may blessing be far from him!
18 May he be clothed in a curse like a garment,
    may it enter his body like water,
    his bones like oil.
19 Let it be like the cloak he wraps around him,
    like the belt he always wears.
20 May the LORD thus repay my accusers,
    all those who speak evil against me.

21 Now You, O God, my Lord,
    act on my behalf as befits Your name.
Good and faithful as You are, save me.
22 For I am poor and needy,
    and my heart is pierced within me.
23 I fade away like a lengthening shadow;

b-b Meaning of Heb. uncertain.

149

I am shaken off like locusts.
²⁴ My knees give way from fasting;
my flesh is lean, has lost its fat.
²⁵ I am the object of their scorn;
when they see me, they shake their head.
²⁶ Help me, O LORD, my God;
save me in accord with Your faithfulness,
²⁷ that men may know that it is Your hand,
that You, O LORD, have done it.
²⁸ Let them curse, but You bless;
let them rise up, but come to grief,
while Your servant rejoices.
²⁹ My accusers shall be clothed in shame,
wrapped in their disgrace as in a robe.

³⁰ My mouth shall sing much praise to the LORD;
I will acclaim Him in the midst of a throng,
³¹ because He stands at the right hand of the needy,
to save him from those who would condemn him.

110 Of David. A psalm.

The LORD said to my lord,
"Sit at My right hand
while I make your enemies your footstool."

² The LORD will stretch forth from Zion your mighty
scepter;
hold sway over your enemies!
³ ᵃ⁻Your people come forward willingly on your day of battle.
In majestic holiness, from the womb,
from the dawn, yours was the dew of youth.⁻ᵃ

ᵃ⁻ᵃ *Meaning of Heb. uncertain.*

⁴ The LORD has sworn and will not relent,
"You are a priest forever, *-a rightful king by My
decree."*-ᵇ

⁵ The Lord is at your right hand.
He crushes kings in the day of His anger.

⁶ He works judgment upon the nations,
heaping up bodies,
crushing heads far and wide.

⁷ He drinks from the stream on his way;
therefore he holds his head high.

111

Hallelujah.

א I praise the LORD with all my heart

ב   in the assembled congregation of the upright.

ג ² The works of the LORD are great,

ד   *-within reach of all who desire them.*-ᵃ

ה ³ His deeds are splendid and glorious;

ו   His beneficence is everlasting;

ז ⁴ He has won renown for His wonders.

ח   The LORD is gracious and compassionate;

ט ⁵ He gives food to those who fear Him;

י   He is ever mindful of His covenant.

כ ⁶ He revealed to His people His powerful works,

ל   in giving them the heritage of nations.

מ ⁷ His handiwork is truth and justice;

נ   all His precepts are enduring,

ס ⁸ well-founded for all eternity,

ע   wrought of truth and equity.

פ ⁹ He sent redemption to His people;

צ   He ordained His covenant for all time;

ק   His name is holy and awesome.

ר ¹⁰ The beginningᵇ of wisdom is the fear of the LORD;

ש   all who practice it gain sound understanding.

ת   Praise of Him is everlasting.

ᵇ⁻ᵇ *Or "after the manner of Melchizedek."*

ᵃ⁻ᵃ *Meaning of Heb. uncertain.*
ᵇ *Or "chief part."*

112 Hallelujah.

א Happy is the man who fears the LORD,
ב   who is ardently devoted to His commandments.
ג 2 His descendants will be mighty in the land,
ד   a blessed generation of upright men.
ה 3 Wealth and riches are in his house,
ו   and his beneficence lasts forever.
ז 4 a-A light shines-a for the upright in the darkness;
ח   he is gracious, compassionate, and beneficent.
ט 5 All goes well with the man who lends generously,
י   who conducts his affairs with equity.
כ 6 He shall never be shaken;
ל   the beneficent man will be remembered forever.
מ 7 He is not afraid of evil tidings;
נ   his heart is firm, he trusts in the LORD.
ס 8 His heart is resolute, he is unafraid;
ע   in the end he will see the fall of his foes.
פ 9 He gives freely to the poor;
צ   his beneficence lasts forever;
ק   his horn is exalted in honor.
ר 10 The wicked man shall see it and be vexed;
ש   he shall gnash his teeth; his courage shall fail.
ת   The desire of the wicked shall come to nothing.

113 Hallelujah.

O servants of the LORD, give praise;
praise the name of the LORD.
2 Let the name of the LORD be blessed
now and forever.
3 From east to west
the name of the LORD is praised.

a-a Or "He shines as a light."

⁴ The Lᴏʀᴅ is exalted above all nations;
  His glory is above the heavens.
⁵ Who is like the Lᴏʀᴅ our God,
  who, enthroned on high,
⁶   sees what is below,
  in heaven and on earth?
⁷ He raises the poor from the dust,
  lifts up the needy from the refuse heap
⁸   to set them with the great,
  with the great men of His people.
⁹ He sets the childless woman among her household
  as a happy mother of children.
  Hallelujah.

114

When Israel went forth from Egypt,
  the house of Jacob from a people of strange speech,
²   Judah became His ᵃ-holy one,-ᵃ
  Israel, His dominion.
³ The sea saw them and fled,
  Jordan ran backward,
⁴   mountains skipped like rams,
  hills like sheep.
⁵ What alarmed you, O sea, that you fled,
  Jordan, that you ran backward,
⁶   mountains, that you skipped like rams,
  hills, like sheep?
⁷ Tremble, O earth, at the presence of the Lᴏʀᴅ,
  at the presence of the God of Jacob,
⁸   who turned the rock into a pool of water,
  the flinty rock into a fountain.

ᵃ⁻ᵃ *Or "sanctuary."*

115 Not to us, O LORD, not to us
but to Your name bring glory
for the sake of Your love and Your faithfulness.
2 Let the nations not say,
"Where now is their God?"
3 when our God is in heaven
and all that He wills He accomplishes.
4 *a*Their idols are silver and gold,
the work of men's hands.
5 They have mouths, but cannot speak,
eyes, but cannot see;
6 they have ears, but cannot hear,
noses, but cannot smell;
7 they have hands, but cannot touch,
feet, but cannot walk;
they can make no sound in their throats.
8 Those who fashion them,
all who trust in them,
shall become like them.
9 O Israel, trust in the LORD!
He is their help and shield.
10 O house of Aaron, trust in the LORD!
He is their help and shield.
11 O you who fear the LORD, trust in the LORD!
He is their help and shield.

12 The LORD is mindful of us.
He will bless us;
He will bless the house of Israel;
He will bless the house of Aaron;
13 He will bless those who fear the LORD,
small and great alike.

a With vv. 4–11, cf. Ps. 135.15–20.

14 May the LORD increase your numbers,
   yours and your children's also.
15 May you be blessed by the LORD,
   Maker of heaven and earth.
16 The heavens belong to the LORD,
   but the earth He gave over to man.
17 The dead cannot praise the LORD,
   nor any who go down into silence.
18 But we will bless the LORD
   now and forever.
   Hallelujah.

116 *a*-I love the LORD
      for He hears-*a* my voice, my pleas;
  2   for He turns His ear to me
      whenever I call.
  3 The bonds of death encompassed me;
      the torments of Sheol overtook me.
      I came upon trouble and sorrow
  4   and I invoked the name of the LORD,
      "O LORD, save my life!"

  5 The LORD is gracious and beneficent;
      our God is compassionate.
  6 The LORD protects the simple;
      I was brought low and He saved me.
  7 Be at rest, once again, O my soul,
      for the LORD has been good to you.
  8 You*b* have delivered me from death,
      my eyes from tears,
      my feet from stumbling.
  9 I shall walk before the LORD
      in the lands of the living.
  10 *c*-I trust [in the LORD];

a-a *Heb. transposed for clarity. Others "I would love that the* LORD *hear," etc.*
b *I.e. God.*
c-c *Meaning of Heb. uncertain.*

out of great suffering I spoke^{-c}
11 and said rashly,
"All men are false."

12 How can I repay the LORD
for all His bounties to me?
13 I raise the cup of deliverance
and invoke the name of the LORD.
14 I will pay my vows to the LORD
in the presence of all His people.
15 The death of His faithful ones
is grievous in the LORD's sight.

16 O LORD,
I am Your servant,
Your servant, the son of Your maidservant;
You have undone the cords that bound me.
17 I will sacrifice a thank offering to You
and invoke the name of the LORD.
18 I will pay my vows to the LORD
in the presence of all His people,
19 in the courts of the house of the LORD,
in the midst of^d Jerusalem.
Hallelujah.

117 Praise the LORD, all you nations;
extol Him, all you peoples,
2 for great is His steadfast love toward us;
the faithfulness of the LORD endures forever.
Hallelujah.

^d Others "of you."

118 Praise the LORD, for He is good,
His steadfast love is eternal.
2 Let Israel declare,
"His steadfast love is eternal."
3 Let the house of Aaron declare,
"His steadfast love is eternal."
4 Let those who fear the LORD declare,
"His steadfast love is eternal."

5 In distress I called on the LORD;
the Lord answered me and brought me relief.
6 The LORD is on my side,
I have no fear;
what can man do to me?
7 With the LORD on my side as my helper,
I will see the downfall of my foes.

8 It is better to take refuge in the LORD
than to trust in mortals;
9 it is better to take refuge in the LORD
than to trust in the great.

10 All nations have beset me;
by the name of the LORD I will surely *a-*cut them
down.*-a*
11 They beset me, they surround me;
by the name of the LORD I will surely cut them down.
12 They have beset me like bees;
they shall be extinguished like burning thorns;
by the name of the LORD I will surely cut them down.

13 You*b* pressed me hard,
I nearly fell;

---

a-a *Meaning of* 'amilam *in this and the following two verses uncertain.*
b *I.e. the enemy.*

but the Lord helped me.
14 The Lord is my strength and might;*c*
He has become my deliverance.

15 The tents of the victorious*d* resound with joyous shouts of
deliverance,
"The right hand of the Lord is triumphant!
16 The right hand of the Lord is exalted!
The right hand of the Lord is triumphant!"

17 I shall not die but live
and proclaim the works of the Lord.
18 The Lord punished me severely,
but did not hand me over to death.

19 Open the gates of victory*e* for me
that I may enter them and praise the Lord.
20 This is the gateway to the Lord—
the victorious*d* shall enter through it.

21 I praise You, for You have answered me,
and have become my deliverance.
22 The stone which the builders rejected
has become the chief cornerstone.
23 This is the Lord's doing;
it is marvelous in our sight.
24 This is the day that the Lord has made—
let us exult and rejoice on it.

25 O Lord, deliver us!
O Lord, let us prosper!

26 May he who enters be blessed in the name of the Lord;
we bless you from the House of the Lord.
27 The Lord is God;

c Others "song."
d Or "righteous."
e Or "righteousness."

He has given us light;
ᶠbind the festal offering to the horns of the altar with
   cords.ᶠ
28 You are my God and I will praise You;
   You are my God and I will extol You.
29 Praise the LORD for He is good,
   His steadfast love is eternal.

119 א Happy are those whose way is blameless,
   who follow the teaching of the LORD.
 2 Happy are those who observe His decrees,
   who turn to Him wholeheartedly.
 3 They have done no wrong,
   but have followed His ways.
 4 You have commanded that Your precepts
   be kept diligently.
 5 Would that my ways were firm
   in keeping Your laws;
 6 then I would not be ashamed
   when I regard all Your commandments.
 7 I will praise You with a sincere heart
   as I learn Your just rules.
 8 I will keep Your laws;
   do not utterly forsake me.

 ב 9 How can a young man keep his way pure?—
   by holding to Your word.
10 I have turned to You with all my heart;
   do not let me stray from Your commandments.
11 In my heart I treasure Your promise;
   therefore I do not sin against You.
12 Blessed are You, O LORD;
   train me in Your laws.
13 With my lips I rehearse

ᶠ⁻ᶠ *Meaning of Heb. uncertain.*

all the rules You proclaimed.
14 I rejoice over the way of Your decrees
as over all riches.
15 I study Your precepts;
I regard Your ways;
16 I take delight in Your laws;
I will not neglect Your word.

ג 17 Deal kindly with Your servant,
that I may live to keep Your word.
18 Open my eyes, that I may perceive
the wonders of Your teaching.
19 I am only a sojourner in the land;
do not hide Your commandments from me.
20 My soul is consumed with longing
for Your rules at all times.
21 You blast the accursed insolent ones
who stray from Your commandments.
22 Take away from me taunt and abuse,
because I observe Your decrees.
23 Though princes meet and speak against me,
Your servant studies Your laws.
24 For Your decrees are my delight,
my intimate companions.

ד 25 My soul clings to the dust;
revive me in accordance with Your word.
26 I have declared my way, and You have answered me;
train me in Your laws.
27 Make me understand the way of Your precepts,
that I may study Your wondrous acts.
28 I am racked with grief;
sustain me in accordance with Your word.
29 Remove all false ways from me;
favor me with Your teaching.

³⁰ I have chosen the way of faithfulness;
I have set Your rules before me.
³¹ I cling to Your decrees;
O LORD, do not put me to shame.
³² I eagerly pursue Your commandments,
for You broaden my understanding.

ה ³³ Teach me, O LORD, the way of Your laws;
I will observe them ᵃ⁻to the utmost.⁻ᵃ
³⁴ Give me understanding, that I may observe Your
teaching
and keep it wholeheartedly.
³⁵ Lead me in the path of Your commandments,
for that is my concern.
³⁶ Turn my heart to Your decrees
and not to love of gain.
³⁷ Avert my eyes from seeing falsehood;
by Your ways preserve me.
³⁸ Fulfill Your promise to Your servant,
which is for those who worship You.
³⁹ Remove the taunt that I dread,
for Your rules are good.
⁴⁰ See, I have longed for Your precepts;
by Your righteousness preserve me.

ו ⁴¹ May Your steadfast love reach me, O LORD,
Your deliverance, as You have promised.
⁴² I shall have an answer for those who taunt me,
for I have put my trust in Your word.
⁴³ Do not utterly take the truth away from my mouth,
for I have put my hope in Your rules.
⁴⁴ I will always obey Your teaching,
forever and ever.
⁴⁵ I will walk about at ease,
for I have turned to Your precepts.

ᵃ⁻ᵃ *Meaning of Heb. uncertain.*

46 I will speak of Your decrees,
and not be ashamed in the presence of kings.
47 I will delight in Your commandments,
which I love.
48 I reach out for Your commandments, which I love;
I study Your laws.

ז 49 Remember Your word to Your servant
through which You have given me hope.
50 This is my comfort in my affliction,
that Your promise has preserved me.
51 Though the arrogant have cruelly mocked me,
I have not swerved from Your teaching.
52 I remember Your rules of old, O LORD,
and find comfort in them.
53 I am seized with rage
because of the wicked who forsake Your teaching.
54 Your laws are *b*-a source of strength to me-*b*
wherever I may dwell.
55 I remember Your name at night, O LORD,
and obey Your teaching.
56 This has been my lot,
for I have observed Your precepts.

ח 57 The LORD is my portion;
I have resolved to keep Your words.
58 I have implored You with all my heart;
have mercy on me, in accordance with Your promise.
59 I have considered my ways,
and have turned back to Your decrees.
60 I have hurried and not delayed
to keep Your commandments.
61 Though the bonds of the wicked are coiled round me,
I have not neglected Your teaching.
62 I arise at midnight to praise You
for Your just rules.

b-b *Or "songs for me."*

162

⁶³ I am a companion to all who fear You,
    to those who keep Your precepts.
⁶⁴ Your steadfast love, O LORD, fills the earth;
    teach me Your laws.

ט ⁶⁵ You have treated Your servant well,
    according to Your word, O LORD.
⁶⁶ Teach me good sense and knowledge,
    for I have put my trust in Your commandments.
⁶⁷ Before I was humbled I went astray,
    but now I keep Your word.
⁶⁸ You are good and beneficent;
    teach me Your laws.
⁶⁹ Though the arrogant have accused me falsely,
    I observe Your precepts wholeheartedly.
⁷⁰ Their minds are thick like fat;
    as for me, Your teaching is my delight.
⁷¹ It was good for me that I was humbled,
    so that I might learn Your laws.
⁷² I prefer the teaching You proclaimed
    to thousands of gold and silver pieces.

י ⁷³ Your hands made me and fashioned me;
    give me understanding that I may learn Your command-
      ments.
⁷⁴ Those who fear You will see me and rejoice,
    for I have put my hope in Your word.
⁷⁵ I know, O LORD, that Your rulings are just;
    rightly have You humbled me.
⁷⁶ May Your steadfast love comfort me
    in accordance with Your promise to Your servant.
⁷⁷ May Your mercy reach me, that I might live,
    for Your teaching is my delight.
⁷⁸ Let the insolent be dismayed, for they have
    wronged me without cause;
    I will study Your precepts.

79 May those who fear You,
   those who know Your decrees,
   turn again to me.
80 May I wholeheartedly follow Your laws
   so that I do not come to grief.

 כ 81 I long for Your deliverance;
   I hope for Your word.
82 My eyes pine away for Your promise;
   I say, "When will You comfort me?"
83 Though I have become like a water-skin dried in smoke,
   I have not neglected Your laws.
84 How long has Your servant to live?
   when will You bring my persecutors to judgment?
85 The insolent have dug pits for me,
   flouting Your teaching.
86 All Your commandments are enduring;
   I am persecuted without cause; help me!
87 Though they almost wiped me off the earth,
   I did not abandon Your precepts.
88 As befits Your steadfast love, preserve me,
   so that I may keep the decree You proclaimed.

ל 89 The LORD exists forever;
   Your word stands firm in heaven.
90 Your faithfulness is for all generations;
   You have established the earth, and it stands.
91 They stand this day to [carry out] Your rulings,
   for all are Your servants.
92 Were not Your teaching my delight
   I would have perished in my affliction.
93 I will never neglect Your precepts,
   for You have preserved my life through them.
94 I am Yours; save me!
   For I have turned to Your precepts.

95 The wicked hope to destroy me,
    but I ponder Your decrees.
96 I have seen that all things have their limit,
    but Your commandment is broad beyond measure.

מ 97 O how I love Your teaching!
    It is my study all day long.
98 Your commandments make me wiser than my enemies;
    they always stand by me.
99 I have gained more insight than all my teachers,
    for Your decrees are my study.
100 I have gained more understanding than my elders,
    for I observe Your precepts.
101 I have avoided every evil way
    so that I may keep Your word.
102 I have not departed from Your rules,
    for You have instructed me.
103 How pleasing is Your word to my palate,
    sweeter than honey.
104 I ponder Your precepts;
    therefore I hate every false way.

נ 105 Your word is a lamp to my feet,
    a light for my path.
106 I have firmly sworn
    to keep Your just rules.
107 I am very much afflicted;
    O Lord, preserve me in accordance with Your word.
108 Accept, O Lord, my free-will offerings;
    teach me Your rules.
109 Though my life is always in danger,
    I do not neglect Your teaching.
110 Though the wicked have set a trap for me,
    I have not strayed from Your precepts.
111 Your decrees are my eternal heritage;

they are my heart's delight.
¹¹² I am resolved to follow Your laws
-to the utmost- forever.

ע ¹¹³ I hate men of divided heart,
but I love Your teaching.
¹¹⁴ You are my protection and my shield;
I hope for Your word.
¹¹⁵ Keep away from me, you evildoers,
that I may observe the commandments of my God.
¹¹⁶ Support me as You promised, so that I may live;
do not thwart my expectation.
¹¹⁷ Sustain me that I may be saved,
and I will always muse upon Your laws.
¹¹⁸ You reject all who stray from Your laws,
for they are false and deceitful.
¹¹⁹ You do away with the wicked as if they were dross;
rightly do I love Your decrees.
¹²⁰ My flesh creeps from fear of You;
I am in awe of Your rulings.

ע ¹²¹ I have done what is just and right;
do not abandon me to those who would wrong me.
¹²² Guarantee Your servant's well-being;
do not let the arrogant wrong me.
¹²³ My eyes pine away for Your deliverance,
for Your promise of victory.
¹²⁴ Deal with Your servant as befits Your steadfast love;
teach me Your laws.
¹²⁵ I am Your servant;
give me understanding,
that I might know Your decrees.
¹²⁶ It is a time to act for the LORD,
for they have violated Your teaching.
¹²⁷ Rightly do I love Your commandments

more than gold, even fine gold.
¹²⁸ Truly ^{c-}by all [Your] precepts I walk straight;^{-c}
I hate every false way.

 פ ¹²⁹ Your decrees are wondrous;
rightly do I observe them.
¹³⁰ ^{d-}The words You inscribed give^{-d} light,
and grant understanding to the simple.
¹³¹ I open my mouth wide, I pant,
longing for Your commandments.
¹³² Turn to me and be gracious to me,
as is Your rule with those who love Your name.
¹³³ Make my feet firm through Your promise;
do not let iniquity dominate me.
¹³⁴ Redeem me from being wronged by man,
that I may keep Your precepts.
¹³⁵ Show favor to Your servant,
and teach me Your laws.
¹³⁶ My eyes shed streams of water
because men do not obey Your teaching.

צ ¹³⁷ You are righteous, O LORD;
Your rulings are just.
¹³⁸ You have ordained righteous decrees;
they are firmly enduring.
¹³⁹ I am consumed with rage
over my foes' neglect of Your words.
¹⁴⁰ Your word is exceedingly pure,
and Your servant loves it.
¹⁴¹ Though I am belittled and despised,
I have not neglected Your precepts.
¹⁴² Your righteousness is eternal;
Your teaching is true.
¹⁴³ Though anguish and distress come upon me,
Your commandments are my delight.

^{c-c} Or "I declare all [Your] precepts to be just."
^{d-d} With Targum; or "The exposition of Your words gives"; meaning of Heb. uncertain.

¹⁴⁴ Your righteous decrees are eternal;
　　give me understanding, that I might live.

ק ¹⁴⁵ I call with all my heart;
　　answer me, O LORD,
　　that I may observe Your laws.
¹⁴⁶ I call upon You; save me,
　　that I may keep Your decrees.
¹⁴⁷ I rise before dawn and cry for help;
　　I hope for Your word.
¹⁴⁸ My eyes greet each watch of the night,
　　as I meditate on Your promise.
¹⁴⁹ Hear my voice as befits Your steadfast love;
　　O LORD, preserve me, as is Your rule.
¹⁵⁰ Those who pursue intrigue draw near;
　　they are far from Your teaching.
¹⁵¹ You, O LORD, are near,
　　and all Your commandments are true.
¹⁵² I know from Your decrees of old
　　that You have established them forever.

ר ¹⁵³ See my affliction and rescue me,
　　for I have not neglected Your teaching.
¹⁵⁴ Champion my cause and redeem me;
　　preserve me according to Your promise.
¹⁵⁵ Deliverance is far from the wicked,
　　for they have not turned to Your laws.
¹⁵⁶ Your mercies are great, O LORD;
　　as is Your rule, preserve me.
¹⁵⁷ Many are my persecutors and foes;
　　I have not swerved from Your decrees.
¹⁵⁸ I have seen traitors and loathedᵉ them,
　　because they did not keep Your word in mind.
¹⁵⁹ See that I have loved Your precepts;
　　O LORD, preserve me, as befits Your steadfast love.

ᵉ Or "have contended with."

168

¹⁶⁰ Truth is the essence of Your word;
Your just rules are eternal.

ע ¹⁶¹ Princes have persecuted me without reason;
my heart thrills at Your word.
¹⁶² I rejoice over Your promise
as one who obtains great spoil.
¹⁶³ I hate and abhor falsehood;
I love Your teaching.
¹⁶⁴ I praise You seven times each day
for Your just rules.
¹⁶⁵ Those who love Your teaching enjoy well-being;
they encounter no adversity.
¹⁶⁶ I hope for Your deliverance, O LORD;
I observe Your commandments.
¹⁶⁷ I obey Your decrees
and love them greatly.
¹⁶⁸ I obey Your precepts and decrees;
all my ways are before You.

ת ¹⁶⁹ May my plea reach You, O LORD;
grant me understanding according to Your word.
¹⁷⁰ May my petition come before You;
save me in accordance with Your promise.
¹⁷¹ My lips shall pour forth praise,
for You teach me Your laws.
¹⁷² My tongue shall declare Your promise,
for all Your commandments are just.
¹⁷³ Lend Your hand to help me,
for I have chosen Your precepts.
¹⁷⁴ I have longed for Your deliverance, O LORD;
Your teaching is my delight.
¹⁷⁵ Let me live, that I may praise You;
may Your rules be my help;
¹⁷⁶ I have strayed like a lost sheep;

search for Your servant,
for I have not neglected Your commandments.

120 A song of ascents.[a]

In my distress I called to the LORD
and He answered me.
2 O LORD, save me from treacherous lips,
from a deceitful tongue!
3 What can you profit,
what can you gain,
O deceitful tongue?
4 A warrior's sharp arrows,
with hot coals of broom-wood.

5 Woe is me, that I live with Meshech,
that I dwell among the clans of Kedar.
6 Too long have I dwelt with those who hate peace.
7 I am all peace;
but when I speak,
they are for war.

121 A song for ascents.

I turn my eyes to the mountains;
from where will my help come?
2 My help comes from the LORD,
maker of heaven and earth.
3 He will not let your foot give way;
your guardian will not slumber.
4 See, the guardian of Israel
neither slumbers nor sleeps!
5 The LORD is your guardian,
the LORD is your protection

---

[a] *A term of uncertain meaning.*

at your right hand.
6 By day the sun will not strike you,
nor the moon by night.
7 The LORD will guard you from all harm;
He will guard your life.
8 The LORD will guard your going and coming
now and forever.

122 A song of ascents. Of David.

1 rejoiced when they said to me,
"We are going to the house of the LORD."
2 Our feet stood inside your gates, O Jerusalem,
3 Jerusalem built up, a city knit together,
4 to which tribes would make pilgrimage,
the tribes of the LORD,
—as was enjoined upon Israel—
to praise the name of the LORD.
5 There the thrones of judgment stood,
thrones of the house of David.
6 Pray for the well-being of Jerusalem:
"May those who love you be at peace.
7 May there be well-being within your ramparts,
peace in your citadels."
8 For the sake of my kin and friends,
I pray for your well-being;
9 for the sake of the house of the LORD our God,
I seek your good.

123 A song of ascents.

To You, enthroned in heaven,
I turn my eyes.
2 As the eyes of slaves follow their master's hand,

as the eyes of a slave-girl follow the hand of her mistress,
so our eyes are toward the Lord our God,
awaiting His favor.
³ Show us favor, O Lord,
show us favor!
We have had more than enough of contempt.
⁴ Long enough have we endured
the scorn of the complacent,
the contempt of the haughty.

124 A song of ascents. Of David.

Were it not for the Lord, who was on our side,
let Israel now declare,
² were it not for the Lord, who was on our side
when men assailed us,
³ they would have swallowed us alive
in their burning rage against us;
⁴ the waters would have carried us off,
the torrent would have swept over us;
⁵ over us would have swept
the seething waters.
⁶ Blessed is the Lord, who did not let us
be ripped apart by their teeth.
⁷ We are like a bird escaped from the fowler's trap;
the trap broke and we escaped.
⁸ Our help is the name of the Lord,
maker of heaven and earth.

125 A song of ascents.

Those who trust in the Lord
are like Mount Zion

that cannot be moved,
enduring forever.
2 Jerusalem, hills enfold it,
and the Lord enfolds His people
now and forever.
3 a-The scepter of the wicked shall never rest
upon the land allotted to the righteous,
that the righteous not set their hand to wrongdoing.-a
4 Do good, O Lord, to the good,
to the upright in heart.
5 a-But those who in their crookedness act corruptly,-a
let the Lord make them go the way of evildoers.
May it be well with Israel!

126 A song of ascents.

When the Lord restores the fortunes of Zion
—a-we see it as in a dream-a—
2 our mouths shall be filled with laughter,
our tongues, with songs of joy.
Then shall they say among the nations,
"The Lord has done great things for them!"
3 The Lord will do great things for us
and we shall rejoice.

4 Restore our fortunes, O Lord,
like watercourses in the Negeb.
5 They who sow in tears
shall reap with songs of joy.
6 Though he goes along weeping,
carrying the seed-bag,
he shall come back with songs of joy,
carrying his sheaves.

a-a *Meaning of Heb. uncertain.*
a-a *Lit. "we are veritable dreamers."*

127   A song of ascents. Of Solomon.

Unless the LORD builds the house,
its builders labor in vain on it;
unless the LORD watches over the city,
the watchman keeps vigil in vain.
2 In vain do you rise early
and stay up late,
you who toil for the bread you eat;
a-He provides as much for His loved ones while they
sleep.-*a*

3 Sons are the provision*b* of the LORD;
the fruit of the womb, His reward.
4 Like arrows in the hand of a warrior
are sons born to a man in his youth.
5 Happy is the man who fills his quiver with them;
they shall not be put to shame
when they contend with the enemy in the gate.

128   A song of ascents.

Happy are all who fear the LORD,
who follow His ways.
2 You shall enjoy the fruit of your labors;
you shall be happy and you shall prosper.
3 Your wife shall be like a fruitful vine within your house;
your sons, like olive saplings around your table.
4 So shall the man who fears the LORD be blessed.

5 May the LORD bless you from Zion;
may you share the prosperity of Jerusalem

---

a-a Meaning of Heb. uncertain.
b Lit. "heritage."

all the days of your life,
6 and live to see your children's children.
May all be well with Israel!

129 A song of ascents.

Since my youth they have often assailed me,
let Israel now declare,
2 since my youth they have often assailed me,
but they have never overcome me.
3 Plowmen plowed across my back;
they made long furrows.
4 The LORD, the righteous one,
has snapped the cords of the wicked.

5 Let all who hate Zion
fall back in disgrace.
6 Let them be like grass on roofs
that fades before it can be pulled up,
7 that affords no handful for the reaper,
no armful for the gatherer of sheaves,
8 no exchange with passersby:
"The blessing of the LORD be upon you."
"We bless you by the name of the LORD."

130 A song of ascents.

Out of the depths I call You, O LORD.
2 O Lord, listen to my cry;
let Your ears be attentive
to my plea for mercy.
3 If You keep account of sins, O LORD,
Lord, who will survive?

⁴ Yours is the power to forgive
so that You may be held in awe.

⁵ I look to the LORD;
I look to Him;
I await His word.
⁶ I am more eager for the Lord
than watchmen for the morning,
watchmen for the morning.

⁷ O Israel, wait for the LORD;
for with the LORD is steadfast love
and great power to redeem.
⁸ It is He who will redeem Israel from all their iniquities.

131 A song of ascents. Of David.

O LORD, my heart is not proud
nor my look haughty;
I do not aspire to great things
or to what is beyond me;
2   ᵃ-but I have taught myself to be contented
like a weaned child with its mother;
like a weaned child am I in my mind.⁻ᵃ
³ O Israel, wait for the LORD
now and forever.

132 A song of ascents.

O LORD, remember in David's favor
his extreme self-denial,
2   how he swore to the LORD,
vowed to the Mighty One of Jacob,

ᵃ⁻ᵃ *Meaning of Heb. uncertain.*

3   "I will not enter my house,
    nor will I mount my bed,
4   I will not give sleep to my eyes
    or slumber to my eyelids[a]
5   until I find a place for the LORD,
    an abode for the Mighty One of Jacob."

6 We heard it was in Ephrath;
    we came upon it in the region of Jaar.[b]
7 Let us enter His abode,
    bow at His footstool.
8 Advance, O LORD, to Your resting-place,
    You and Your mighty Ark!
9 Your priests are clothed in triumph;
    Your loyal ones sing for joy.
10 For the sake of Your servant David
    do not reject Your anointed one.

11 The LORD swore to David
    a firm oath that He will not renounce,
    "One of your own issue I will set upon your throne.
12 If your sons keep My covenant
    and My decrees that I teach them,
    then their sons also,
    to the end of time,
    shall sit upon your throne."
13 For the LORD has chosen Zion;
    He has desired it for His seat.
14 "This is my resting-place for all time;
    here I will dwell, for I desire it.
15 I will amply bless its store of food,
    give its needy their fill of bread.
16 I will clothe its priests in victory,
    its loyal ones shall sing for joy.
17 There I will make a horn sprout for David;

[a] *Lit. "eyes."*
[b] *Cf. I Sam. 7.1–2; I Chron. 13.5–6.*

I have prepared a lamp for My anointed one.
¹⁸ I will clothe his enemies in disgrace,
while on him his crown shall sparkle."

133 A song of ascents. Of David.

How good and how pleasant it is
that brothers dwell together.
² It is like fine oil on the head
running down onto the beard,
the beard of Aaron,
that comes down over the collar of his robe;
³ like the dew of Hermon
that falls upon the mountains of Zion.
There the Lord ordained blessing,
everlasting life.

134 A song of ascents.

Now bless the Lord,
all you servants of the Lord
who stand nightly
in the house of the Lord.
² Lift your hands toward the sanctuary
and bless the Lord.
³ May the Lord,
maker of heaven and earth,
bless you from Zion.

135 Hallelujah.
Praise the name of the Lord;
give praise, you servants of the Lord

2 who stand in the house of the LORD,
in the courts of the house of our God.
3 Praise the LORD, for the LORD is good;
sing hymns to His name, for it is pleasant.
4 For the LORD has chosen Jacob for Himself,
Israel, as His treasured possession.

5 For I know that the LORD is great,
that our LORD is greater than all gods.
6 Whatever the LORD desires He does
in heaven and earth,
in the seas and all the depths.
7 He makes clouds rise from the end of the earth;
He makes lightning for the rain;
He releases the wind from His vaults.
8 He struck down the firstborn of Egypt,
man and beast alike;
9 He sent signs and portents against*a* Egypt,
against Pharaoh and all his servants;
10 He struck down many nations
and slew numerous kings—
11 Sihon king of the Amorites,
Og king of Bashan,
and all the royalty of Canaan—
12 and gave their lands as a heritage,
as a heritage to His people Israel.

13 O LORD, Your name endures forever,
Your fame, O LORD, through all generations;
14 for the LORD will champion His people,
and obtain satisfaction for His servants.

15 *b*The idols of the nations are silver and gold,
the work of men's hands.
16 They have mouths, but cannot speak;

a Others "against you."
b With vv. 15–20, cf. Ps. 115.4–11.

they have eyes, but cannot see;
17 they have ears, but cannot hear,
nor is there breath in their mouths.
18 Those who fashion them,
all who trust in them,
shall become like them.

19 O house of Israel, bless the LORD;
O house of Aaron, bless the LORD;
20 O house of Levi, bless the LORD;
you who fear the LORD, bless the LORD.
21 Blessed is the LORD from Zion,
He who dwells in Jerusalem.
Hallelujah.

136 Praise the LORD; for He is good,
His steadfast love is eternal.
2 Praise the God of gods,
His steadfast love is eternal.
3 Praise the Lord of lords,
His steadfast love is eternal;
4 Who alone works great marvels,
His steadfast love is eternal;
5 Who made the heavens with wisdom,
His steadfast love is eternal;
6 Who spread the earth over the water,
His steadfast love is eternal;
7 Who made the great lights,
His steadfast love is eternal;
8 the sun to dominate the day,
His steadfast love is eternal;
9 the moon and the stars to dominate the night,
His steadfast love is eternal;

¹⁰ Who struck Egypt through their firstborn,
His steadfast love is eternal:
¹¹ and brought Israel out of their midst,
His steadfast love is eternal;
¹² with a strong hand and outstretched arm,
His steadfast love is eternal;
¹³ Who split apart the Sea of Reeds,
His steadfast love is eternal;
¹⁴ and made Israel pass through it,
His steadfast love is eternal;
¹⁵ Who hurled Pharaoh and his army into the Sea of Reeds,
His steadfast love is eternal;
¹⁶ Who led His people through the wilderness,
His steadfast love is eternal;
¹⁷ Who struck down great kings,
His steadfast love is eternal;
¹⁸ and slew mighty kings,—
His steadfast love is eternal;
¹⁹ Sihon king of the Amorites,
His steadfast love is eternal;
²⁰ Og king of Bashan—
His steadfast love is eternal;
²¹ and gave their land as a heritage,
His steadfast love is eternal;
²² a heritage to His servant Israel,
His steadfast love is eternal;
²³ Who took note of us in our degradation,
His steadfast love is eternal;
²⁴ and rescued us from our enemies,
His steadfast love is eternal;
²⁵ Who gives food to all flesh,
His steadfast love is eternal.
²⁶ Praise the God of heaven,
His steadfast love is eternal.

137 By the rivers of Babylon,
there we sat,
sat and wept,
as we thought of Zion.
² There on the poplars
we hung up our lyres,
³ for our captors asked us there for songs,
our tormentors,ᵃ for amusement,
"Sing us one of the songs of Zion."
⁴ How can we sing a song of the LORD
on alien soil?
⁵ If I forget you, O Jerusalem,
let my right hand wither;ᵇ
⁶ let my tongue stick to my palate
if I cease to think of you,
if I do not keep Jerusalem in memory
even at my happiest hour.

⁷ Remember, O LORD, against the Edomites
the day of Jerusalem's fall;
how they cried, "Strip her, strip her
to her very foundations!"
⁸ Fair Babylon, you predator,ᶜ
a blessing on him who repays you in kind
what you have inflicted on us;
⁹ a blessing on him who seizes your babies
and dashes them against the rocks!

138 Of David.

I praise You with all my heart,
sing a hymn to You before the divine beings;

ᵃ *Meaning of Heb. uncertain.*
ᵇ *Others "forget its cunning."*
ᶜ *With Targum; others "who are to be destroyed."*

2   I bow toward Your holy temple
    and praise Your name for Your steadfast love and
       faithfulness,
    because You have exalted *a*-Your name, Your word,
       above all.-*a*
3 When I called, You answered me,
    a-You inspired me with courage.-*a*
4 All the kings of the earth shall praise You, O LORD,
    for they have heard the words You spoke.
5 They shall sing of the ways of the LORD,
    "Great is the majesty of the LORD!"
6 High though the LORD is, He sees the lowly;
    lofty, He perceives from afar.
7 Though I walk among enemies,
    You preserve me in the face of my foes;
    You extend Your hand;
    with Your right hand You deliver me.
8 The LORD will settle accounts for me.
    O LORD, Your steadfast love is eternal;
    do not forsake the work of Your hands.

139   For the leader. Of David. A psalm.

   O LORD, You have examined me and know me.
2 When I sit down or stand up You know it;
    You discern my thoughts from afar.
3 *a*-You observe-*a* my walking and reclining,
    and are familiar with all my ways.
4 There is not a word on my tongue
    but that You, O LORD, know it well.
5 You hedge me before and behind;
    You lay Your hand upon me.
6 It is beyond my knowledge;
    it is a mystery; I cannot fathom it.

a-a Meaning of Heb. uncertain.
a-a Meaning of Heb. uncertain.

7 Where can I escape from Your spirit?
Where can I flee from Your presence?
8 If I ascend to heaven, You are there;
if I descend to Sheol, You are there too.
9 If I take wing with the dawn
to come to rest on the western horizon,
10 even there Your hand will be guiding me,
Your right hand will be holding me fast.
11 If I say, "Surely darkness *b*-will conceal me,
night will provide me with cover,"*-b*
12 darkness is not dark for You;
night is as light as day;
darkness and light are the same.
13 It was You who created my conscience;*c*
You fashioned me in my mother's womb.
14 I praise You,
for I am awesomely, wondrously made;
Your work is wonderful;
I know it very well.
15 My frame was not concealed from You
when I was shaped in a hidden place,
knit together in the recesses of the earth.
16 Your eyes saw my unformed limbs;
they were all recorded in Your book;
in due time they were formed,
a-to the very last one of them.*-a*
17 How weighty Your thoughts seem to me, O God,
how great their number!
18 I count them—they exceed the grains of sand;
I end—but am still with You.

19 O God, if You would only slay the wicked—
you murderers, away from me!—
20 *a*-who invoke You for intrigue,
Your enemies who swear by You falsely.*-a*
21 O LORD, You know I hate those who hate You,

b-b *Cf. Rashi, Ibn Ezra; meaning of Heb. uncertain.*
c *Lit. "kidneys."*

and loathe Your adversaries.
22 I feel a perfect hatred toward them;
I count them my enemies.

23 Examine me, O God, and know my mind;
probe me and know my thoughts.
24 See if I have vexatious ways,
and guide me in ways everlasting.

140 For the leader. A psalm of David.

2 Rescue me, O LORD, from evil men;
save me from the lawless,
3 whose minds are full of evil schemes,
who plot war every day.
4 They sharpen their tongues like serpents;
spiders' poison is on their lips.   *Selah.*

5 O LORD, keep me out of the clutches of the wicked;
save me from lawless men
who scheme to *a-*make me fall.*-a*
6 Arrogant men laid traps with ropes for me;
they spread out a net along the way;
they set snares for me.   *Selah.*

7 I said to the LORD: You are my God;
give ear, O LORD, to my pleas for mercy.
8 O GOD, my Lord, the strength of my deliverance,
You protected my head on the day of battle.*b*
9 O LORD, do not grant the desires of the wicked;
do not let their plan succeed,
*c-*else they be exalted.   *Selah.*

---

a-a Lit. "push my feet."
b Lit. "arms."
c-c Meaning of Heb. uncertain.

10 May the heads of those who beset me
   be covered with the mischief of their lips.⁻ᶜ
11 May coals of fire drop down upon them,
   and they be cast into pits, never to rise again.
12 Let slanderers have no place in the land;
   let the evil of the lawless man drive him into corrals.
13 I know that the LORD will champion
   the cause of the poor, the right of the needy.
14 Righteous men shall surely praise Your name;
   the upright shall dwell in Your presence.

141 A psalm of David.

I call You, O LORD, hasten to me;
   give ear to my cry when I call You.
2 Take my prayer as an offering of incense,
   my upraised hands as an evening sacrifice.
3 O LORD, set a guard over my mouth,
   a watch at the door of my lips;
4   let my mind not turn to an evil thing,
   to practice deeds of wickedness
   with men who are evildoers;
   let me not feast on their dainties.
5 ᵃLet the righteous man strike me in loyalty,
   let him reprove me;
   let my head not refuse such choice oil.
My prayers are still against their ᵇ evil deeds.
6 May their judges slip on the rock,
   but let my words be heard, for they are sweet.
7 As when the earth is cleft and broken up
   our bones are scattered at the mouth of Sheol.
8 My eyes are fixed upon You, O GOD my Lord;
   I seek refuge in You, do not put me in jeopardy.
9 Keep me from the trap laid for me,

ᵃ *Meaning of vv. 5–7 uncertain.*
ᵇ *I.e. the evildoers of v. 4.*

and from the snares of evildoers.
¹⁰ Let the wicked fall into their nets
while I alone come through.

142 A *maskil* of David, while he was in the cave.ᵃ A prayer.

² I cry aloud to the LORD;
I appeal to the LORD loudly for mercy.
³ I pour out my complaint before Him;
I lay my trouble before Him
⁴ when my spirit fails within me.
You know my course;
they have laid a trap in the path I walk.
⁵ Look at my right and see—
I have no friend;
there is nowhere I can flee,
no one cares about me.
⁶ So I cry to You, O LORD;
I say, "You are my refuge,
all I have in the land of the living."
⁷ Listen to my cry, for I have been brought very low;
save me from my pursuers,
for they are too strong for me.
⁸ Free me from prison,
that I may praise Your name.
The righteous ᵇ-shall glory in me-ᵇ
for Your gracious dealings with me.

143 A psalm of David.

O LORD, hear my prayer;
give ear to my plea, as You are faithful;

ᵃ *Cf. I Sam. 24.3–4.*
ᵇ⁻ᵇ *Meaning of Heb. uncertain.*

answer me, as You are beneficent.
² Do not enter into judgment with Your servant,
for before You no creature is in the right.

³ My foe hounded me;
he crushed me to the ground;
he made me dwell in darkness
like those long dead.
⁴ My spirit failed within me;
my mind was numbed with horror.
⁵ Then I thought of the days of old;
I rehearsed all Your deeds,
recounted the work of Your hands.
⁶ I stretched out my hands to You,
longing for You like thirsty earth.   *Selah.*

⁷ Answer me quickly, O LORD;
my spirit can endure no more.
Do not hide Your face from me,
or I shall become like those who descend into the Pit.
⁸ Let me learn of Your faithfulness by daybreak,
for in You I trust;
let me know the road I must take,
for on You I have set my hope.
⁹ Save me from my foes, O LORD;
ᵃ-to You I look for cover.-*ᵃ*
¹⁰ Teach me to do Your will,
for You are my God.
Let Your gracious spirit lead me
on level ground.
¹¹ For the sake of Your name, O LORD, preserve me;
as You are beneficent, free me from distress.
¹² As You are faithful, put an end to my foes;
destroy all my mortal enemies,
for I am Your servant.

ᵃ⁻ᵃ *Meaning of Heb. uncertain.*

144 Of David.

Blessed is the LORD, my rock,
who trains my hands for battle,
my fingers for warfare;
2 my faithful one, my fortress,
my haven and my deliverer,
my shield, in whom I take shelter,
who makes peoples[a] subject to me.

3 O LORD, what is man that You should care about him,
mortal man, that You should think of him?
4 Man is like a breath;
his days are like a passing shadow.
5 O LORD, bend Your sky and come down;
touch the mountains and they will smoke.
6 Make lightning flash and scatter them;
shoot Your arrows and rout them.
7 Reach Your hand down from on high;
rescue me, save me from the mighty waters,
from the hands of foreigners,
8 whose mouths speak lies,
and whose oaths[b] are false.

9 O God, I will sing You a new song,
sing a hymn to You with a ten-stringed harp,
10 to You who give victory to kings,
who rescue His servant David from the deadly sword.
11 Rescue me, save me from the hands of foreigners,
whose mouths speak lies,
and whose oaths[b] are false.

---

a *So Targum, Saadia; others "my people."*
b *With Rashi; lit. "right hand."*

12 ᶜFor our sons are like saplings,
   well-tended in their youth;
   our daughters are like cornerstones
   trimmed to give shape to a palace.
13 Our storehouses are full,
   supplying produce of all kinds;
   our flocks number thousands,
   even myriads, in our fields;
14   our cattle are well cared for.
   There is no breaching and no sortie,
   and no wailing in our streets.

15 Happy the people who have it so;
   happy the people whose God is the LORD.

145 A song of praise. Of David.

א   I will extol You, my God and king,
   and bless Your name forever and ever.
ב ² Every day will I bless You
   and praise Your name forever and ever.
ג ³ Great is the LORD and much acclaimed;
   His greatness cannot be fathomed.
ד ⁴ One generation shall laud Your works to another
   and declare Your mighty acts.
ה ⁵ The glorious majesty of Your splendor
   ᵃ-and Your wondrous acts-ᵃ will I recite.
ו ⁶ Men shall talk of the might of Your awesome deeds,
   and I will recount Your greatness.
ז ⁷ They shall celebrate Your abundant goodness,
   and sing joyously of Your beneficence.
ח ⁸ The LORD is gracious and compassionate,
   slow to anger and abounding in kindness.

ᶜ *The meaning of several phrases in vv. 12–14 is uncertain.*

ᵃ⁻ᵃ *A Qumran Pss. scroll reads: "they will speak of, and Your wonders."*

ט   ⁹ The LORD is good to all,
      and His mercy is upon all His works.

י   ¹⁰ All Your works shall praise You, O LORD,
      and Your faithful ones shall bless You.

כ   ¹¹ They shall talk of the majesty of Your kingship,
      and speak of Your might,

ל   ¹²   to make His mighty acts known among men
      and the majestic glory of His kingship.

מ   ¹³ Your kingship is an eternal kingship;
      Your dominion is for all generations.

ס   ¹⁴ The LORD supports all who stumble,
      and makes all who are bent stand straight.

ע   ¹⁵ The eyes of all look to You expectantly,
      and You give them their food when it is due.

פ   ¹⁶ You give it openhandedly,
      feeding every creature to its heart's content.

צ   ¹⁷ The LORD is beneficent in all His ways
      and faithful in all His works.

ק   ¹⁸ The LORD is near to all who call Him,
      to all who call Him with sincerity.

ר   ¹⁹ He fulfills the wishes of those who fear Him;
      He hears their cry and delivers them.

ש   ²⁰ The LORD watches over all who love Him,
      but all the wicked He will destroy.

ת   ²¹ My mouth shall utter the praise of the LORD,
      and all creatures[b] shall bless His holy name forever and
        ever.

146   Hallelujah.
      Praise the LORD, O my soul!
    ² I will praise the LORD all my life,
      sing hymns to my God while I exist.

[b] *Lit. "flesh."*

3 Put not your trust in the great,
in mortal man who cannot save.
4 His breath departs;
he returns to the dust;
on that day his plans come to nothing.

5 Happy is he who has the God of Jacob for his help,
whose hope is in the LORD his God,
6 maker of heaven and earth,
the sea and all that is in them;
who keeps faith forever;
7 who secures justice for those who are wronged,
gives food to the hungry.
The LORD sets prisoners free;
8 The LORD restores sight to the blind;
the LORD makes those who are bent stand straight;
the LORD loves the righteous;
9 The LORD watches over the stranger;
He gives courage to the orphan and widow,
but makes the path of the wicked tortuous.

10 The LORD shall reign forever,
your God, O Zion, for all generations.
Hallelujah.

147 Hallelujah.
It is good to chant hymns to our God;
it is pleasant to sing glorious praise.

2 The LORD rebuilds Jerusalem;
He gathers in the exiles of Israel.
3 He heals their broken hearts,
and binds up their wounds.

⁴ He reckoned the number of the stars;
   to each He gave its name.
⁵ Great is our LORD and full of power;
   His wisdom is beyond reckoning.
⁶ The LORD gives courage to the lowly,
   and brings the wicked down to the dust.

⁷ Sing to the LORD a song of praise,
   chant a hymn with a lyre to our God,
⁸   who covers the heavens with clouds,
   provides rain for the earth,
   makes mountains put forth grass;
⁹   who gives the beasts their food,
   to the raven's brood what they cry for.
¹⁰ He does not prize the strength of horses,
   nor value the fleetness*a* of men;
¹¹   but the LORD values those who fear Him,
   those who depend on His faithful care.

¹² O Jerusalem, glorify the LORD;
   praise your God, O Zion!
¹³ For He made the bars of your gates strong,
   and blessed your children within you.
¹⁴ He endows your realm with well-being,
   and satisfies you with choice wheat.

¹⁵ He sends forth His word to the earth;
   His command runs swiftly.
¹⁶ He lays down snow like fleece,
   scatters frost like ashes.
¹⁷ He tosses down hail like crumbs—
   who can endure His icy cold?
¹⁸ He issues a command—it melts them;
   He breathes—the waters flow.

ᵃ *Lit. "thighs."*

¹⁹ He issued His commands to Jacob,
His statutes and rules to Israel.
²⁰ He did not do so for any other nation;
of such rules they know nothing.
Hallelujah.

148 Hallelujah.

Praise the LORD from the heavens;
praise Him on high.
² Praise Him, all His angels,
praise Him, all His hosts.
³ Praise Him, sun and moon,
praise Him, all bright stars.
⁴ Praise Him, highest heavens,
and you waters that are above the heavens.
⁵ Let them praise the name of the LORD,
for it was He who commanded that they be created.
⁶ He made them endure forever,
establishing an order that shall never change.
⁷ Praise the LORD, O you who are on earth,
all sea monsters and ocean depths,
⁸ fire and hail, snow and smoke,
storm wind that executes His command,
⁹ all mountains and hills,
all fruit trees and cedars,
¹⁰ all wild and tamed beasts,
creeping things and winged birds,
¹¹ all kings and peoples of the earth,
all princes of the earth and its judges,
¹² youths and maidens alike,
old and young together.
¹³ Let them praise the name of the LORD,
for His name, His alone, is sublime;
His splendor covers heaven and earth.

¹⁴ He has exalted the horn of His people
for the glory of all His faithful ones,
Israel, the people close to Him.
Hallelujah.

149 Hallelujah.

Sing to the LORD a new song,
His praises in the congregation of the faithful.
² Let Israel rejoice in its maker;
let the children of Zion exult in their king.
³ Let them praise His name in dance;
with timbrel and lyre let them chant His praises.
⁴ For the LORD delights in His people;
He adorns the lowly with victory.
⁵ Let the faithful exult in glory;
let them shout for joy upon their couches,
⁶ with paeans to God in their throats
and two-edged swords in their hands,
⁷ to impose retribution upon the nations,
punishment upon the peoples,
⁸ binding their kings with shackles,
their nobles with chains of iron,
⁹ executing the doom decreed against them.
This is the glory of all His faithful.
Hallelujah.

150 Hallelujah.

Praise God in His sanctuary;
praise Him in the sky, His stronghold.
² Praise Him for His mighty acts;
praise Him for^a His exceeding greatness.
³ Praise Him with blasts of the horn;
praise Him with harp and lyre.

^a *Or "as befits."*

4 Praise Him with timbrel and dance;
   praise Him with lute and pipe.
5 Praise Him with resounding cymbals;
   praise Him with loud-clashing cymbals.
6 Let all that breathes praise the LORD.
   Hallelujah.

משלי

PROVERBS

משלי

PROVERBS

1 The proverbs of Solomon son of David, king of Israel:

² For learning wisdom and discipline;
For understanding words of discernment;
³ For acquiring the discipline for success,
Righteousness, justice, and equity;
⁴ For endowing the simple with shrewdness,
The young with knowledge and foresight.
⁵ —The wise man, hearing them, will gain more wisdom;
The discerning man will learn to be adroit;
⁶ For understanding proverb and epigram,
The words of the wise and their riddles.

⁷ The fear of the LORD is the beginning*a* of knowledge;
Fools despise wisdom and discipline.

⁸ My son, heed the discipline of your father,
And do not forsake the instruction of your mother;
⁹ For they are a graceful wreath upon your head,
A necklace about your throat.

¹⁰ My son, if sinners entice you, do not yield;
¹¹ If they say, "Come with us,
Let us set an ambush to shed blood,
Let us lie in wait for the innocent
(Without cause!)
¹² Like Sheol, let us swallow them alive;

ᵃ Or "best part."

Whole, like those who go down into the Pit.
¹³ We shall obtain every precious treasure;
We shall fill our homes with loot.
¹⁴ Throw in your lot with us;
We shall all have a common purse."
¹⁵ My son, do not set out with them;
Keep your feet from their path.
¹⁶ For their feet run to evil;
They hurry to shed blood.
¹⁷ In the eyes of every winged creature
The outspread net means nothing.
¹⁸ But they lie in ambush for their own blood;
They lie in wait for their own lives.
¹⁹ Such is the fate of all who pursue unjust gain;
It takes the life of its possessor.

²⁰ Wisdom*ᵇ* cries aloud in the streets,
Raises her voice in the squares.
²¹ At the head of the busy streets she calls;
At the entrance of the gates, in the city, she speaks out:
²² "How long will you simple ones love simplicity,
You scoffers be eager to scoff,
You dullards hate knowledge?
²³ You are indifferent to my rebuke;
I will now speak my mind to you,
And let you know my thoughts.
²⁴ Since you refused me when I called,
And paid no heed when I extended my hand,
²⁵ You spurned all my advice,
And would not hear my rebuke,
²⁶ I will laugh at your calamity,
And mock when terror comes upon you,
²⁷ When terror comes like a disaster,
And calamity arrives like a whirlwind,
When trouble and distress come upon you.

ᵇ *In Proverbs, wisdom is personified as a woman.*

²⁸ Then they shall call me but I will not answer;
They shall seek me but not find me.
²⁹ Because they hated knowledge,
And did not choose fear of the LORD;
³⁰ They refused my advice,
And disdained all my rebukes,
³¹ They shall eat the fruit of their ways,
And have their fill of their own counsels.
³² The tranquillity of the simple will kill them,
And the complacency of dullards will destroy them.
³³ But he who listens to me will dwell in safety,
Untroubled by the terror of misfortune."

2 My son, if you accept my words
And treasure up my commandments;
² If you make your ear attentive to wisdom
And your mind open to discernment;
³ If you call to understanding
And cry aloud to discernment,
⁴ If you seek it as you do silver
And search for it as for treasures,
⁵ Then you will understand the fear of the LORD
And attain knowledge of God.
⁶ For the LORD grants wisdom;
Knowledge and discernment are by His decree.
⁷ He reserves ability for the upright
And is a shield for those who live blamelessly,
⁸ Guarding the paths of justice,
Protecting the way of those loyal to Him.
⁹ You will then understand what is right, just,
And equitable—every good course.
¹⁰ For wisdom will enter your mind
And knowledge will delight you.
¹¹ Foresight will protect you,

And discernment will guard you.
12 It will save you from the way of evil men,
From men who speak duplicity,
13 Who leave the paths of rectitude
To follow the ways of darkness,
14 Who rejoice in doing evil
And exult in the duplicity of evil men,
15 Men whose paths are crooked
And who are devious in their course.
16 It will save you from the forbidden[a] woman,
From the alien woman whose talk is smooth,
17 Who forsakes the companion of her youth
And disregards the covenant of her God.
18 Her house sinks down to Death,
And her course leads to the shades.
19 All who go to her cannot return
And find again the paths of life.

20 So follow the way of the good
And keep to the paths of the just.
21 For the upright will inhabit the earth,
The blameless will remain in it.
22 While the wicked will vanish from the land
And the treacherous will be rooted out of it.

3   My son, do not forget my teaching,
But let your mind retain my commandments;
2 For they will bestow on you length of days,
Years of life and well-being.
3 Let fidelity and steadfastness not leave you;
Bind them about your throat,
Write them on the tablet of your mind,
4 And you will find favor and approbation
In the eyes of God and man.

[a] *Lit. "strange."*

⁵ Trust in the LORD with all your heart,
And do not rely on your own understanding.
⁶ In all your ways acknowledge Him,
And He will make your paths smooth.
⁷ Do not be wise in your own eyes;
Fear the LORD and shun evil.
⁸ It will be a cure for your body,ᵃ
A tonic for your bones.
⁹ Honor the LORD with your wealth,
With the best of all your income,
¹⁰ And your barns will be filled with grain,
Your vats will burst with new wine.
¹¹ Do not reject the discipline of the LORD, my son;
Do not abhor His rebuke.
¹² For whom the LORD loves, He rebukes,
As a father the son whom he favors.

¹³ Happy is the man who finds wisdom,
The man who attains understanding.
¹⁴ Her value in trade is better than silver,
Her yield, greater than gold.
¹⁵ She is more precious than rubies;
All of your goods cannot equal her.
¹⁶ In her right hand is length of days,
In her left, riches and honor.
¹⁷ Her ways are pleasant ways,
And all her paths, peaceful.
¹⁸ She is a tree of life to those who grasp her,
And whoever holds on to her is happy.

¹⁹ The LORD founded the earth by wisdom;
He established the heavens by understanding;
²⁰ By His knowledge the depths burst apart,
And the skies distilled dew.
²¹ My son, do not lose sight of them;

ᵃ Lit. "navel."

Hold on to resourcefulness and foresight.
²² They will give life to your spirit
And grace to your throat.
²³ Then you will go your way safely
And not injure your feet.
²⁴ When you lie down you will be unafraid;
You will lie down and your sleep will be sweet.
²⁵ You will not fear sudden terror
Or the disaster that comes upon the wicked,
²⁶ For the Lord will be your trust;
He will keep your feet from being caught.

²⁷ Do not withhold good from one who deserves it
When you have the power to do it [for him].
²⁸ Do not say to your fellow, "Come back again;
I'll give it to you tomorrow," when you have it with you.
²⁹ Do not devise harm against your fellow
Who lives trustfully with you.
³⁰ Do not quarrel with a man for no cause,
When he has done you no harm.
³¹ Do not envy a lawless man,
Or choose any of his ways;
³² For the devious man is an abomination to the Lord,
But He is intimate with the straightforward.
³³ The curse of the Lord is on the house of the wicked,
But He blesses the abode of the righteous.
³⁴ At scoffers He scoffs,
But to the lowly He shows grace.
³⁵ The wise shall obtain honor,
But dullards get disgrace as their portion.

4 Sons, heed the discipline of a father;
Listen and learn discernment,
² For I give you good instruction;
Do not forsake my teaching.

³ Once I was a son to my father,
The tender darling of my mother.
⁴ He instructed me and said to me,
"Let your mind hold on to my words;
Keep my commandments and you will live.
⁵ Acquire wisdom, acquire discernment;
Do not forget and do not swerve from my words.
⁶ Do not forsake her and she will guard you;
Love her and she will protect you.
⁷ The beginning*a* of wisdom is—acquire wisdom;
With all your acquisitions, acquire discernment.
⁸ Hug her to you and she will exalt you;
She will bring you honor if you embrace her.
⁹ She will adorn your head with a graceful wreath;
Crown you with a glorious diadem."

¹⁰ My son, heed and take in my words,
And you will have many years of life.
¹¹ I instruct you in the way of wisdom;
I guide you in straight courses.
¹² You will walk without breaking stride;
When you run, you will not stumble.
¹³ Hold fast to discipline; do not let go;
Keep it; it is your life.
¹⁴ Do not enter on the path of the wicked;
Do not walk on the way of evil men.
¹⁵ Avoid it; do not pass through it;
Turn away from it; pass it by.
¹⁶ For they cannot sleep unless they have done evil;
Unless they make someone fall they are robbed of
    sleep.
¹⁷ They eat the bread of wickedness
And drink the wine of lawlessness.
¹⁸ The path of the righteous is like radiant sunlight,
Ever brightening until noon.

a Or "best part."

19 The way of the wicked is all darkness;
They do not know what will make them stumble.

20 My son, listen to my speech;
Incline your ear to my words.
21 Do not lose sight of them;
Keep them in your mind.
22 They are life to him who finds them,
Healing for his whole body.
23 More than all that you guard, guard your mind,
For it is the source of life.
24 Put crooked speech away from you;
Keep devious talk far from you.
25 Let your eyes look forward,
Your gaze be straight ahead.
26 Survey the course you take,
And all your ways will prosper.
27 Do not swerve to the right or the left;
Keep your feet from evil.

5   My son, listen to my wisdom;
Incline your ear to my insight,
2 That you may have foresight,
While your lips hold fast to knowledge.
3 For the lips of a forbidden*a* woman drip honey;
Her mouth is smoother than oil;
4 But in the end she is as bitter as wormwood,
Sharp as a two-edged sword.
5 Her feet go down to Death;
Her steps take hold of Sheol.
6 She does not chart a path of life;
Her course meanders for lack of knowledge.
7 So now, sons, pay heed to me,
And do not swerve from the words of my mouth.

a *Lit. "strange."*

⁸ Keep yourself far away from her;
Do not come near the doorway of her house
⁹ Lest you give up your vigor to others,
Your years to a ruthless one;
¹⁰ Lest strangers eat their fill of your strength,
And your toil be for the house of another;
¹¹ And in the end you roar,
When your flesh and body are consumed,
¹² And say,
"O how I hated discipline,
And heartily spurned rebuke.
¹³ I did not pay heed to my teachers,
Or incline my ear to my instructors.
¹⁴ Soon I was in dire trouble
Amidst the assembled congregation."
¹⁵ Drink water from your own cistern,
Running water from your own well.
¹⁶ Your springs will gush forth
In streams in the public squares.
¹⁷ They will be yours alone,
Others having no part with you.
¹⁸ Let your fountain be blessed;
Find joy in the wife of your youth—
¹⁹ A loving doe, a graceful mountain goat.
Let her breasts satisfy you at all times;
Be infatuated with love of her always.
²⁰ Why be infatuated, my son, with a forbidden[a] woman?
Why clasp the bosom of an alien woman?
²¹ For a man's ways are before the eyes of God;
He surveys his entire course.
²² The wicked man will be trapped in his iniquities;
He will be caught up in the ropes of his sin.
²³ He will die for lack of discipline,
Infatuated by his great folly.

6 My son, if you have stood surety for your fellow,
Given your hand for another,[a]
2 You have been trapped by the words of your mouth,
Snared by the words of your mouth.
3 Do this, then, my son, to extricate yourself,
For you have come into the power of your fellow:
Go grovel—and badger your fellow;
4 Give your eyes no sleep,
Your pupils no slumber.
5 Save yourself like a deer out of the hand [of a hunter],
Like a bird out of the hand of a fowler.

6 Lazybones, go to the ant;
Study its ways and learn.
7 Without leaders, officers, or rulers,
8 It lays up its stores during the summer,
Gathers in its food at the harvest.
9 How long will you lie there, lazybones;
When will you wake from your sleep?
10 A bit more sleep, a bit more slumber,
A bit more hugging yourself in bed,
11 And poverty will come [b]calling upon you,[-b]
And want, like a man with a shield.

12 A scoundrel, an evil man
Lives by crooked speech,
13 Winking his eyes,
Shuffling his feet,
Pointing his finger.
14 Duplicity is in his heart;
He plots evil all the time;
He incites quarrels.

[a] *Or "a stranger."*
[b-b] *Meaning of Heb. uncertain.*

¹⁵ Therefore calamity will come upon him without
warning;
Suddenly he will be broken beyond repair.

¹⁶ Six things the Lord hates;
Seven are an abomination to Him:
¹⁷ A haughty bearing,
A lying tongue,
Hands that shed innocent blood,
¹⁸ A mind that hatches evil plots,
Feet quick to run to evil,
¹⁹ A false witness testifying lies,
And one who incites brothers to quarrel.

²⁰ My son, keep your father's commandment;
Do not forsake your mother's teaching.
²¹ Tie them over your heart always;
Bind them around your throat.
²² When you walk it will lead you;
When you lie down it will watch over you;
And when you are awake it will talk with you.
²³ For the commandment is a lamp,
The teaching is a light,
And the way to life is the rebuke that disciplines.
²⁴ It will keep you from an evil woman,
From the smooth tongue of a forbidden^c woman.
²⁵ Do not lust for her beauty
Or let her captivate you with her eyes.
²⁶ The last loaf of bread will go for a harlot;
A married woman will snare a person of honor.
²⁷ Can a man rake embers into his bosom
Without burning his clothes?
²⁸ Can a man walk on live coals
Without scorching his feet?

^c Lit. "alien."

²⁹ It is the same with one who sleeps with his fellow's
wife;
None who touches her will go unpunished.
³⁰ A thief is not held in contempt
For stealing to appease his hunger;
³¹ Yet if caught he must pay sevenfold;
He must give up all he owns.
³² He who commits adultery is devoid of sense;
Only one who would destroy himself does such a thing.
³³ He will meet with disease and disgrace;
His reproach will never be expunged.
³⁴ The fury of the husband will be passionate;
He will show no pity on his day of vengeance.
³⁵ He will not have regard for any ransom;
He will refuse your bribe, however great.

7   My son, heed my words;
And store up my commandments with you.
² Keep my commandments and live,
My teaching, as the apple of your eye.
³ Bind them on your fingers;
Write them on the tablet of your mind.
⁴ Say to Wisdom, "You are my sister,"
And call Understanding a kinswoman.
⁵ She will guard you from a forbidden*a* woman;
From an alien woman whose talk is smooth.

⁶ From the window of my house,
Through my lattice, I looked out
⁷ And saw among the simple,
Noticed among the youths,
A lad devoid of sense.
⁸ He was crossing the street near her corner,
Walking toward her house

ᵃ *Lit. "strange."*

⁹ In the dusk of evening,
In the dark hours of night.
¹⁰ A woman comes toward him
ᵇDressed like a harlot, with set purpose.ᵇ
¹¹ She is bustling and restive;
She is never at home.
¹² Now in the street, now in the square,
She lurks at every corner.
¹³ She lays hold of him and kisses him;
Brazenly she says to him,
¹⁴ "I had to make a sacrifice of well-being;
Today I fulfilled my vows.
¹⁵ Therefore I have come out to you,
Seeking you, and have found you.
¹⁶ I have decked my couch with covers
Of dyed Egyptian linen;
¹⁷ I have sprinkled my bed
With myrrh, aloes, and cinnamon.
¹⁸ Let us drink our fill of love till morning;
Let us delight in amorous embrace.
¹⁹ For the man of the house is away;
He is off on a distant journey.
²⁰ He took his bag of money with him
And will return only at mid-month."

²¹ She sways him with her eloquence,
Turns him aside with her smooth talk.
²² Thoughtlessly he follows her,
Like an ox going to the slaughter,
ᵇLike a fool to the stocks for punishmentᵇ—
²³ Until the arrow pierces his liver.
He is like a bird rushing into a trap,
Not knowing his life is at stake.
²⁴ Now, sons, listen to me;
Pay attention to my words;

ᵇ⁻ᵇ *Meaning of Heb. uncertain.*

25 Let your mind not wander down her ways;
Do not stray onto her paths.
26 For many are those she has struck dead,
And numerous are her victims.
27 Her house is a highway to Sheol
Leading down to Death's inner chambers.

8 It is Wisdom calling,
Understanding raising her voice.
2 She takes her stand at the topmost heights,
By the wayside, at the crossroads,
3 Near the gates at the city entrance;
At the entryways, she shouts,
4 "O men, I call to you;
My cry is to all mankind.
5 O simple ones, learn shrewdness;
O dullards, instruct your minds.
6 Listen, for I speak noble things;
Uprightness comes from my lips;
7 My mouth utters truth;
Wickedness is abhorrent to my lips.
8 All my words are just,
None of them perverse or crooked;
9 All are straightforward to the intelligent man,
And right to those who have attained knowledge.
10 Accept my discipline rather than silver,
Knowledge rather than choice gold.
11 For wisdom is better than rubies;
No goods can equal her.

12 "I, Wisdom, live with Prudence;
I attain knowledge and foresight.
13 To fear the LORD is to hate evil;
I hate pride, arrogance, the evil way,

And duplicity in speech.
14 Mine are counsel and resourcefulness;
I am understanding; courage is mine.
15 Through me kings reign
And rulers decree just laws;
16 Through me princes rule,
Great men and all the *a*-righteous judges.-*a*
17 Those who love me I love,
And those who seek me will find me.
18 Riches and honor belong to me,
Enduring wealth and success.
19 My fruit is better than gold, fine gold,
And my produce better than choice silver.
20 I walk on the way of righteousness,
On the paths of justice.
21 I endow those who love me with substance;
I will fill their treasuries.

22 "The LORD created me at the beginning of His course
As the first of His works of old.
23 In the distant past I was fashioned,
At the beginning, at the origin of earth.
24 There was still no deep when I was brought forth,
No springs rich in water;
25 Before [the foundation of] the mountains were sunk,
Before the hills I was born.
26 He had not yet made earth and fields,
Or the world's first clumps of clay.
27 I was there when He set the heavens into place;
When He fixed the horizon upon the deep;
28 When He made the heavens above firm,
And the fountains of the deep gushed forth;
29 When He assigned the sea its limits,
So that its waters never transgress His command;
When He fixed the foundations of the earth,

a-a *According to some Heb. mss. and printed editions, "judges of the earth."*

³⁰ I was with Him as a confidant,
A source of delight every day,
Rejoicing before Him at all times,
³¹ Rejoicing in His inhabited world,
Finding delight with mankind.
³² Now, sons, listen to me;
Happy are they who keep my ways.
³³ Heed discipline and become wise;
Do not spurn it.
³⁴ Happy is the man who listens to me,
Coming early to my gates each day,
Waiting outside my doors.
³⁵ For he who finds me finds life
And obtains favor from the LORD.
³⁶ But he who misses me destroys himself;
All who hate me love death."

9   Wisdom has built her house,
She has hewn her seven pillars.
² She has prepared the feast,
Mixed the wine,
And also set the table.
³ She has sent out her maids to announce
On the heights of the town,
⁴ "Let the simple enter here";
To those devoid of sense she says,
⁵ "Come, eat my food
And drink the wine that I have mixed;
⁶ Give up simpleness and live,
Walk in the way of understanding."

⁷ To correct a scoffer,
ᵃ⁻Or rebuke a wicked man for his blemish,
Is to call down abuse on oneself.⁻ᵃ
⁸ Do not rebuke a scoffer, for he will hate you;

ᵃ⁻ᵃ *Clauses transposed for clarity.*

Reprove a wise man, and he will love you.
⁹ Instruct a wise man, and he will grow wiser;
Teach a righteous man, and he will gain in learning.
¹⁰ The beginning of wisdom is fear of the LORD,
And knowledge of the Holy One is understanding.
¹¹ For through me your days will increase,
And years be added to your life.
¹² If you are wise, you are wise for yourself;
If you are a scoffer, you bear it alone.
¹³ The stupid woman bustles about;
She is simple and knows nothing.
¹⁴ She sits in the doorway of her house,
Or on a chair at the heights of the town,
¹⁵ Calling to all the wayfarers
Who go about their own affairs,
¹⁶ "Let the simple enter here";
And to those devoid of sense she says,
¹⁷ "Stolen waters are sweet,
And bread eaten furtively is tasty."
¹⁸ He does not know that the shades are there,
That her guests are in the depths of Sheol.

10 The proverbs of Solomon:

A wise son brings joy to his father;
A dull son is his mother's sorrow.
² Ill-gotten wealth is of no avail,
But righteousness saves from death.
³ The LORD will not let the righteous go hungry,
But He denies the wicked what they crave.
⁴ Negligent hands cause poverty,
But diligent hands enrich.
⁵ He who lays in stores during the summer is a capable son,
But he who sleeps during the harvest is an incompetent.
⁶ Blessings light upon the head of the righteous,

But lawlessness covers the mouth of the wicked.
7 The name of the righteous is invoked in blessing,
But the fame of the wicked rots.
8 He whose heart is wise accepts commands,
But he whose speech is foolish comes to grief.
9 He who lives blamelessly lives safely,
But he who walks a crooked path will be found out.
10 He who winks his eye causes sorrow;
He whose speech is foolish comes to grief.
11 The mouth of the righteous is a fountain of life,
But lawlessness covers the mouth of the wicked.
12 Hatred stirs up strife,
But love covers up all faults.
13 Wisdom is to be found on the lips of the intelligent,
But a rod is ready for the back of the senseless.
14 The wise store up knowledge;
The mouth of the fool is an imminent ruin.
15 The wealth of a rich man is his fortress;
The poverty of the poor is his ruin.
16 The labor of the righteous man makes for life;
The produce of the wicked man makes for want.
17 He who follows discipline shows the way to life,
But he who ignores reproof leads astray.
18 He who conceals hatred has lying lips,
While he who speaks forth slander is a dullard.
19 Where there is much talking, there is no lack of trans-
gressing,
But he who curbs his tongue^a shows sense.
20 The tongue of a righteous man is choice silver,
But the mind of the wicked is of little worth.
21 The lips of the righteous sustain many,
But fools die for lack of sense.
22 It is the blessing of the LORD that enriches,
And no toil can increase it.
23 As mischief is sport for the dullard,

a Lit. "lips."

So is wisdom for the man of understanding.
²⁴ What the wicked man plots overtakes him;
What the righteous desire is granted.
²⁵ When the storm passes the wicked man is gone,
But the righteous is an everlasting foundation.
²⁶ Like vinegar to the teeth,
Like smoke to the eyes,
Is a lazy man to those who send him on a mission.
²⁷ The fear of the LORD prolongs life,
While the years of the wicked will be shortened.
²⁸ The righteous can look forward to joy,
But the hope of the wicked is doomed.
²⁹ The way of the LORD is a stronghold for the blameless,
But a ruin for evildoers.
³⁰ The righteous will never be shaken;
The wicked will not inhabit the earth.
³¹ The mouth of the righteous produces wisdom,
But the treacherous tongue shall be cut off.
³² The lips of the righteous know what is pleasing;
The mouth of the wicked [knows] duplicity.

11 False scales are an abomination to the LORD;
An honest[a] weight pleases Him.
² When arrogance appears, disgrace follows,
But wisdom is with those who are unassuming.
³ The integrity of the upright guides them;
The deviousness of the treacherous leads them to ruin.
⁴ Wealth is of no avail on the day of wrath,
But righteousness saves from death.
⁵ The righteousness of the blameless man smooths his way,
But the wicked man is felled by his wickedness.
⁶ The righteousness of the upright saves them,
But the treacherous are trapped by their malice.
⁷ At death the hopes of a wicked man are doomed

---

[a] *Lit. "whole."*

And the ambition of evil men comes to nothing.
8 The righteous man is rescued from trouble
And the wicked man takes his place.
9 The impious man destroys his neighbor through speech,
But through their knowledge the righteous are rescued.
10 When the righteous prosper the city exults;
When the wicked perish there are shouts of joy.
11 A city is built up by the blessing of the upright,
But it is torn down by the speech of the wicked.
12 He who speaks contemptuously of his fellowman is devoid of sense;
A prudent man keeps his peace.
13 A base fellow gives away secrets,
But a trustworthy soul keeps a confidence.
14 For want of strategy an army falls,
But victory comes with much planning.
15 Harm awaits him who stands surety for another;*b*
He who spurns pledging shall be secure.
16 A graceful woman obtains honor;
Ruthless men obtain wealth.
17 A kindly man benefits himself;
A cruel man makes trouble for himself.
18 The wicked man earns illusory wages,
But he who sows righteousness has a true reward.
19 Righteousness is a prop of life,
But to pursue evil leads to death.
20 Men of crooked mind are an abomination to the LORD,
But those whose way is blameless please Him.
21 *c-*Assuredly,*-c* the evil man will not escape,
But the offspring of the righteous will be safe.
22 Like a gold ring in the snout of a pig
Is a beautiful woman bereft of sense.
23 What the righteous desire can only be good;
What the wicked hope for [stirs] wrath.
24 One man gives generously and ends with more;

b *Or "a stranger."*
c-c *Lit. "Hand to hand"; meaning of Heb. uncertain.*

Another stints on doing the right thing and incurs a loss.
25 A generous person enjoys prosperity;
He who satisfies others shall himself be sated.
26 He who withholds grain earns the curses of the people,
But blessings are on the head of the one who dispenses it.
27 He who earnestly seeks what is good pursues what is
    pleasing;
He who is bent on evil, upon him it shall come.
28 He who trusts in his wealth shall fall,
But the righteous shall flourish like foliage.
29 He who makes trouble for his household shall inherit
    the wind;
A fool is a slave to the wise-hearted.
30 The fruit of the righteous is a tree of life;
A wise man captivates people.
31 If the righteous on earth get their deserts,
How much more the wicked man and the sinner.

12 He who loves discipline loves knowledge;
He who spurns reproof is a brutish man.
2 A good man earns the favor of the LORD,
A man of intrigues, His condemnation.
3 A man cannot be established in wickedness,
But the root of the righteous will not be shaken loose.
4 A capable wife is a crown for her husband,
But an incompetent one is like rot in his bones.
5 The purposes of the righteous are justice,
The schemes of the wicked are deceit.
6 The words of the wicked are a deadly ambush,
But the speech of the upright saves them.
7 Overturn the wicked and they are gone,
But the house of the righteous will endure.
8 A man is commended according to his intelligence;

A twisted mind is held up to contempt.
9 Better to be lightly esteemed and have a servant
Than to put on airs and have no food.
10 A righteous man knows the needs of his beast,
But the compassion of the wicked is cruelty.
11 He who tills his land shall have food in plenty,
But he who pursues vanities is devoid of sense.
12 *a*-The wicked covet the catch of evil men;
The root of the righteous yields [fruit].*-a*
13 Sinful speech is a trap for the evil man,
But the righteous escapes from trouble.
14 A man gets his fill of good from the fruit of his speech;
One is repaid in kind for one's deeds.
15 The way of a fool is right in his own eyes;
But the wise man accepts advice.
16 A fool's vexation is known at once,
But a clever man conceals his humiliation.
17 He who testifies faithfully tells the truth,
But a false witness, deceit.
18 There is blunt talk like sword-thrusts,
But the speech of the wise is healing.
19 Truthful speech abides forever,
A lying tongue for but a moment.
20 Deceit is in the minds of those who plot evil;
For those who plan good there is joy.
21 No harm befalls the righteous,
But the wicked have their fill of misfortune.
22 Lying speech is an abomination to the LORD,
But those who act faithfully please Him.
23 A clever man conceals what he knows,
But the mind of a dullard cries out folly.
24 The hand of the diligent wields authority;
The negligent are held in subjection.
25 If there is anxiety in a man's mind let him quash it,
And turn it into joy with a good word.

a-a Meaning of Heb. uncertain.

²⁶ A righteous man ᵃ⁻gives his friend direction,⁻ᵃ
But the way of the wicked leads astray.
²⁷ A negligent man never has game to roast;
ᵃ⁻A diligent man has precious wealth.⁻ᵃ
²⁸ The road of righteousness leads to life;
By way of its path there is no death.

13 A wise son—it is through the discipline of his father;
A scoffer—he never heard reproof.
² A man enjoys good from the fruit of his speech;
But out of the throat of the treacherous comes lawlessness.
³ He who guards his tongueᵃ preserves his life;
He who opens wide his lips, it is his ruin.
⁴ A lazy man craves, but has nothing;
The diligent shall feast on rich fare.
⁵ A righteous man hates lies;
The wicked man is vile and disgraceful.
⁶ Righteousness protects him whose way is blameless;
Wickedness subverts the sinner.
⁷ One man pretends to be rich and has nothing;
Another professes to be poor and has much wealth.
⁸ Riches are ransom for a man's life,
The poor never heard a reproof.
⁹ The light of the righteous is radiant;
The lamp of the wicked is extinguished.
¹⁰ ᵇ⁻Arrogance yields nothing but strife;⁻ᵇ
Wisdom belongs to those who seek advice.
¹¹ Wealth may dwindle to less than nothing,
But he who gathers little by little increases it.
¹² Hope deferred sickens the heart,
But desire realized is a tree of life.
¹³ He who disdains a precept will be injured thereby;
He who respects a command will be rewarded.
¹⁴ The instruction of a wise man is a fountain of life,

ᵃ Lit. "mouth."
ᵇ⁻ᵇ Meaning of Heb. uncertain.

Enabling one to avoid deadly snares.
¹⁵ Good sense wins favor;
The way of treacherous men is unchanging.^c
¹⁶ Every clever man acts knowledgeably,
But a dullard exposes his stupidity.
¹⁷ Harm befalls a wicked messenger;
A faithful courier brings healing.
¹⁸ Poverty and humiliation are for him who spurns discipline;
But he who takes reproof to heart gets honor.
¹⁹ Desire realized is sweet to the soul;
To turn away from evil is abhorrent to the stupid.
²⁰ He who keeps company with the wise becomes wise,
But he who consorts with dullards comes to grief.
²¹ Misfortune pursues sinners,
But the righteous are well rewarded.
²² A good man has what to bequeath to his grandchildren,
For the wealth of sinners is stored up for the righteous.
²³ The tillage of the poor yields much food;
But substance is swept away for lack of moderation.
²⁴ He who spares the rod hates his son,
But he who loves him disciplines him early.
²⁵ The righteous man eats to his heart's content,
But the belly of the wicked is empty.

14 The wisest of women builds her house,
But folly tears it down with its own hands.
² He who maintains his integrity fears the LORD;
A man of devious ways scorns Him.
³ In the mouth of a fool is a rod of haughtiness,
But the lips of the wise protect them.
⁴ If there are no oxen the crib is clean,
But a rich harvest comes through the strength of the ox.
⁵ An honest witness will not lie;

^c Or "harsh."

A false witness testifies lies.
⁶ A scoffer seeks wisdom in vain,
But knowledge comes easily to the intelligent man.
⁷ Keep your distance from a dullard,
For you will not learn wise speech.
⁸ It is the wisdom of a clever man to understand his course;
But the stupidity of the dullard is delusion.
⁹ Reparations mediate between fools,
Between the upright, good will.
¹⁰ The heart alone knows its bitterness,
And no outsider can share in its joy.
¹¹ The house of the wicked will be demolished,
But the tent of the upright will flourish.
¹² A road may seem right to a man,
But in the end it is a road to death.
¹³ The heart may ache even in laughter,
And joy may end in grief.
¹⁴ An unprincipled man reaps the fruits of his ways;
ᵃ⁻A good man, of his deeds.⁻ᵃ
¹⁵ A simple person believes anything;
A clever man ponders his course.
¹⁶ A wise man is diffident and shuns evil,
But a dullard rushes in confidently.
¹⁷ An impatient man commits folly;
A man of intrigues will be hated.
¹⁸ Folly is the lot of the simple,
But clever men ᵇ⁻glory in knowledge.⁻ᵇ
¹⁹ Evil men are brought low before the good,
So are the wicked at the gates of the righteous.
²⁰ A pauper is despised even by his peers,
But a rich man has many friends.
²¹ He who despises his fellow is wrong;
He who shows pity for the lowly is happy.
²² Surely those who plan evil go astray,
While those who plan good earn steadfast love.

ᵃ⁻ᵃ *Taking* 'al *as from* 'll; *cf. Hos. 12.3.*
ᵇ⁻ᵇ *Meaning of Heb. uncertain.*

²³ From all toil there is some gain,
But idle chatter is pure loss.
²⁴ The ornament of the wise is their wealth;
The stupidity of dullards is stupidity.
²⁵ A truthful witness saves lives;
He who testifies lies [spreads] deceit.
²⁶ Fear of the LORD is a stronghold,
A refuge for a man's children.
²⁷ Fear of the LORD is a fountain of life,
Enabling one to avoid deadly snares.
²⁸ A numerous people is the glory of a king;
Without a nation a ruler is ruined.
²⁹ Patience results in much understanding;
Impatience gets folly as its portion.
³⁰ A calm disposition gives bodily health;
Passion is rot to the bones.
³¹ He who withholds what is due to the poor affronts his
Maker;
He who shows pity for the needy honors Him.
³² The wicked man is felled by his own evil;
The righteous man finds security in his death.
³³ Wisdom rests quietly in the mind of a prudent man,
But among dullards it makes itself known.
³⁴ Righteousness exalts a nation;
Sin is a reproach to any people.
³⁵ The king favors a capable servant;
He rages at an incompetent one.

15 A gentle response allays wrath;
A harsh word provokes anger.
² The tongue of the wise produces much knowledge,
But the mouth of dullards pours out folly.
³ The eyes of the LORD are everywhere,
Observing the bad and the good.

⁴ A healing tongue is a tree of life,
But a devious one makes for a broken spirit.
⁵ A fool spurns the discipline of his father,
But one who heeds reproof becomes clever.
⁶ In the house of the righteous there is much treasure,
But in the harvest of the wicked there is trouble.
⁷ The lips of the wise disseminate knowledge;
Not so the minds of dullards.
⁸ The sacrifice of the wicked is an abomination to the
    LORD,
But the prayer of the upright pleases Him.
⁹ The way of the wicked is an abomination to the LORD,
But He loves him who pursues righteousness.
¹⁰ Discipline seems bad to him who forsakes the way;
He who spurns reproof will die.
¹¹ Sheol and Abaddon lie exposed to the LORD,
How much more the minds of men!
¹² The scoffer dislikes being reproved;
He will not resort to the wise.
¹³ A joyful heart makes a cheerful face;
A sad heart makes a despondent mood.
¹⁴ The mind of a prudent man seeks knowledge;
The mouth of the dullard pursues folly.
¹⁵ All the days of a poor man are wretched,
But contentment is a feast without end.
¹⁶ Better a little with fear of the LORD
Than great wealth with confusion.
¹⁷ Better a meal of vegetables where there is love
Than a fattened ox where there is hate.
¹⁸ A hot-tempered man provokes a quarrel;
A patient man calms strife.
¹⁹ The way of a lazy man is like a hedge of thorns,
But the path of the upright is paved.
²⁰ A wise son makes his father happy;
A fool of a man humiliates his mother.

²¹ Folly is joy to one devoid of sense;
A prudent man walks a straight path.
²² Plans are foiled for want of counsel,
But they succeed through many advisers.
²³ A ready response is a joy to a man,
And how good is a word rightly timed!
²⁴ For an intelligent man the path of life leads upward,
In order to avoid Sheol below.
²⁵ The LORD will tear down the house of the proud,
But He will establish the homestead of the widow.
²⁶ Evil thoughts are an abomination to the LORD,
But pleasant words are pure.
²⁷ He who pursues ill-gotten gain makes trouble for his
    household;
He who spurns gifts will live long.
²⁸ The heart[a] of the righteous man rehearses his answer,
But the mouth of the wicked blurts out evil things.
²⁹ The LORD is far from the wicked,
But He hears the prayer of the righteous.
³⁰ What brightens the eye gladdens the heart;
Good news puts fat on the bones.
³¹ He whose ear heeds the discipline of life
Lodges among the wise.
³² He who spurns discipline hates himself;
He who heeds reproof gains understanding.
³³ The fear of the LORD is the discipline of wisdom;
Humility precedes honor.

16 A man may arrange his thoughts,
But what he says depends on the LORD.
² All the ways of a man seem right to him,
But the LORD probes motives.
³ Entrust your affairs to the LORD,
And your plans will succeed.

ᵃ *For* leb *as a source of speech, see note to Eccl. 5.1.*

⁴ The LORD made everything for a purpose,
Even the wicked for an evil day.
⁵ Every haughty person is an abomination to the LORD;
Assuredly,ᵃ he will not go unpunished.
⁶ Iniquity is expiated by loyalty and faithfulness,
And evil is avoided through fear of the LORD.
⁷ When the LORD is pleased with a man's conduct,
He may turn even his enemies into allies.
⁸ Better a little with righteousness
Than a large income with injustice.
⁹ A man may plot out his course,
But it is the LORD who directs his steps.

¹⁰ There is magic on the lips of the king;
He cannot err in judgment.
¹¹ Honest scales and balances are the LORD's;
All the weights in the bag are His work.
¹² Wicked deeds are an abomination to kings,
For the throne is established by righteousness.
¹³ Truthful speech wins the favor of kings;
They love those who speak honestly.
¹⁴ The king's wrath is a messenger of death,
But a wise man can appease it.
¹⁵ The king's smile means life;
His favor is like a rain cloud in spring.

¹⁶ How much better to acquire wisdom than gold;
To acquire understanding is preferable to silver.
¹⁷ The highway of the upright avoids evil;
He who would preserve his life watches his way.
¹⁸ Pride goes before ruin,
Arrogance, before failure.
¹⁹ Better to be humble and among the lowly
Than to share spoils with the proud.
²⁰ He who is adept in a matter will attain success;

ᵃ Lit. "Hand to hand"; meaning of Heb. uncertain.

Happy is he who trusts in the LORD.
²¹ The wise-hearted is called discerning;
One whose speech is pleasing gains wisdom.
²² Good sense is a fountain of life to those who have it,
And folly is the punishment of fools.
²³ The mind of the wise man makes his speech effective
And increases the wisdom on his lips.
²⁴ Pleasant words are like a honeycomb,
Sweet to the palate and a cure for the body.
²⁵ A road may seem right to a man,
But in the end it is a road to death.
²⁶ The appetite of a laborer labors for him,
Because his hunger*b* *c-*forces him on.*-c*

²⁷ A scoundrel plots*c* evil;
What is on his lips is like a scorching fire.
²⁸ A shifty man stirs up strife,
And a querulous one alienates his friend.
²⁹ A lawless man misleads his friend,
Making him take the wrong way.
³⁰ He closes his eyes while meditating deception;
He purses his lips while deciding upon evil.

³¹ Gray hair is a crown of glory;
It is attained by the way of righteousness.
³² Better to be forebearing than mighty,
To have self-control than to conquer a city.
³³ Lots are cast into the lap;
The decision depends on the LORD.

17 Better a dry crust with peace
Than a house full of feasting with strife.
² A capable servant will dominate an incompetent son
And share the inheritance with the brothers.

b Lit. "mouth."
c-c Meaning of Heb. uncertain.

3 For silver—the crucible;
For gold—the furnace,
And the LORD tests the mind.
4 An evildoer listens to mischievous talk;
A liar gives ear to malicious words.
5 He who mocks the poor affronts his Maker;
He who rejoices over another's misfortune will not go
unpunished.
6 Grandchildren are the crown of their elders,
And the glory of children is their parents.
7 Lofty words are not fitting for a villain;
Much less lying words for a great man.
8 A bribe seems like a charm to him who uses it;
He succeeds at every turn.
9 He who seeks love overlooks faults,
But he who harps on a matter alienates his friend.
10 A rebuke works on an intelligent man
More than one hundred blows on a fool.
11 An evil man seeks only to rebel;
A ruthless messenger will be sent against him.
12 Sooner meet a bereaved she-bear
Than a fool with his nonsense.
13 Evil will never depart from the house
Of him who repays good with evil.
14 To start a quarrel is to open a sluice;
Before a dispute *-flares up,-* drop it.
15 To acquit the guilty and convict the innocent—
Both are an abomination to the LORD.
16 What good is money in the hand of a fool
To purchase wisdom, when he has no mind?
17 A friend is devoted at all times;
A brother is born to share adversity.
18 Devoid of sense is he who gives his hand
To stand surety for his fellow.
19 He who loves transgression loves strife;

a-a *Meaning of Heb. uncertain.*

He who builds a high threshold invites broken bones.
²⁰ Man of crooked mind comes to no good,
And he who speaks duplicity falls into trouble.
²¹ One begets a dullard to one's own grief;
The father of a villain has no joy.
²² A joyful heart makes for ᵇ-good health;-ᵇ
Despondency dries up the bones.
²³ The wicked man draws a bribe out of his bosom
To pervert the course of justice.
²⁴ Wisdom lies before the intelligent man;
The eyes of the dullard range to the ends of the earth.
²⁵ A stupid son is vexation for his father
And a heartache for the woman who bore him.
²⁶ To punish the innocent is surely not right,
Or to flog the great for their uprightness.
²⁷ A knowledgeable man is sparing with his words;
A man of understanding is reticent.
²⁸ Even a fool, if he keeps silent, is deemed wise;
Intelligent, if he seals his lips.

18 ᵃ-He who isolates himself pursues his desires;
He disdains all competence.-ᵃ
² The fool does not desire understanding,
But only to air his thoughts.
³ Comes the wicked man comes derision,
And with the rogue, contempt.
⁴ The words a man speaks are deep waters,
A flowing stream, a fountain of wisdom.
⁵ It is not right to be partial to the guilty
And subvert the innocent in judgment.
⁶ The words of a fool lead to strife;
His speech invites blows.
⁷ The fool's speech is his ruin;
His words are a trap for him.
⁸ The words of a querulous man are bruising;ᵃ

ᵇ-ᵇ *Or "a cheerful face"; meaning of Heb. uncertain.*

ᵃ-ᵃ *Meaning of Heb. uncertain.*

They penetrate one's inmost parts.
9 One who is slack in his work
Is a brother to a vandal.
10 The name of the LORD is a tower of strength
To which the righteous man runs and is safe.
11 The wealth of a rich man is his fortress;
a-In his fancy*-a* it is a protective wall.
12 Before ruin a man's heart is proud;
Humility goes before honor.
13 To answer a man before hearing him out
Is foolish and disgraceful.
14 A man's spirit can sustain him through illness;
But low spirits—who can bear them?
15 The mind of an intelligent man acquires knowledge;
The ears of the wise seek out knowledge.
16 A man's gift eases his way
And gives him access to the great.
17 The first to plead his case seems right
Till the other party examines him.
18 The lot puts an end to strife
And separates those locked in dispute.
19 A brother offended is more formidable than a stronghold;
Such strife is like the bars of a fortress.
20 A man's belly is filled by the fruit of his mouth;
He will be filled by the produce of his lips.
21 Death and life are in the power of the tongue;
Those who love it will eat its fruit.
22 He who finds a wife has found happiness
And has won the favor of the LORD.
23 The poor man speaks beseechingly;
The rich man's answer is harsh.
24 There are companions to keep one company,
And there is a friend more devoted than a brother.

19 Better a poor man who lives blamelessly
Than one who speaks perversely and is a dullard.
² A person without knowledge is surely not good;
He who moves hurriedly blunders.
³ A man's folly subverts his way,
And his heart rages against the LORD.
⁴ Wealth makes many friends,
But a poor man loses his last friend.
⁵ A false witness will not go unpunished;
He who testifies lies will not escape.
⁶ Many court the favor of a great man,
And all are the friends of a dispenser of gifts.
⁷ All the brothers of a poor man despise him;
How much more is he shunned by his friends!
ᵃ⁻He who pursues words—they are of no avail.⁻ᵃ
⁸ He who acquires wisdom is his own best friend;
He preserves understanding and attains happiness.
⁹ A false witness will not go unpunished;
He who testifies falsely is doomed.
¹⁰ Luxury is not fitting for a dullard,
Much less that a servant rule over princes.
¹¹ A man shows intelligence by his forebearance;
It is his glory when he overlooks an offense.
¹² The rage of a king is like the roar of a lion;
His favor is like dew upon the grass.
¹³ A stupid son is a calamity to his father;
The nagging of a wife is like the endless dripping of water.
¹⁴ Property and riches are bequeathed by fathers,
But an efficient wife comes from the LORD.
¹⁵ Laziness induces sleep,
And a negligent person will go hungry.
¹⁶ He who has regard for his life pays regard to commandments;

ᵃ⁻ᵃ *Meaning of Heb. uncertain.*

He who is heedless of his ways will die.
¹⁷ He who is generous to the poor makes a loan to the
LORD;
He will repay him his due.
¹⁸ Discipline your son while there is still hope,
And*b* do not *c*-set your heart on his destruction.*-c*
¹⁹ A hot-tempered man incurs punishment;
a-If you try to save him you will only make it worse.*-a*
²⁰ Listen to advice and accept discipline
In order that you may be wise in the end.
²¹ Many designs are in a man's mind,
But it is the LORD's plan that is accomplished.
²² *a*-Greed is a reproach to a man;*-a*
Better be poor than a liar.
²³ He who fears the LORD earns life;
a-He shall abide in contentment,*-a*
Free from misfortune.
²⁴ The lazy man buries his hand in the bowl;
He will not even bring it to his mouth.
²⁵ Beat the scoffer and the simple will become clever;
Reprove an intelligent man and he gains knowledge.
²⁶ A son who causes shame and disgrace
Plunders his father, puts his mother to flight.
²⁷ My son, cease to stray from words of knowledge
And receive discipline.
²⁸ A malicious witness scoffs at justice,
And the speech of the wicked conceals mischief.
²⁹ Punishments are in store for scoffers
And blows for the backs of dullards.

20 Wine is a scoffer, strong drink a roisterer;
He who is muddled by them will not grow wise.
² The terror of a king is like the roar of a lion;
He who provokes his anger risks his life.

b or "But."
c-c or "pay attention to his moaning."

³ It is honorable for a man to desist from strife,
But every fool *a*-becomes embroiled.-*a*
⁴ In winter the lazy man does not plow;
At harvesttime he seeks, and finds nothing.
⁵ The designs in a man's mind are deep waters,
But a man of understanding can draw them out.
⁶ He calls many a man his loyal friend,
But who can find a faithful man?
⁷ The righteous man lives blamelessly;
Happy are his children who come after him.
⁸ The king seated on the throne of judgment
Can winnow out all evil by his glance.
⁹ Who can say, "I have cleansed my heart,
I am purged of my sin"?
¹⁰ False weights and false measures,
Both are an abomination to the LORD.
¹¹ A child may be dissembling in his behavior
Even though his actions are blameless and proper.
¹² The ear that hears, the eye that sees—
The LORD made them both.
¹³ Do not love sleep lest you be impoverished;
Keep your eyes open and you will have plenty of food.
¹⁴ "Bad, bad," says the buyer,
But having moved off, he congratulates himself.
¹⁵ Gold is plentiful, jewels abundant,
But wise speech is a precious object.
¹⁶ Seize his garment, for he stood surety for another;*b*
Take it as a pledge, [for he stood surety] for an unfamiliar
    woman.
¹⁷ Bread gained by fraud may be tasty to a man,
But later his mouth will be filled with gravel.
¹⁸ Plans laid in council will succeed;
Wage war with stratagems.
¹⁹ He who gives away secrets is a base fellow;
Do not take up with a garrulous man.

a-a Meaning of Heb. uncertain.
b Or "a stranger."

234

20 One who reviles his father or mother,
Light will fail him when darkness comes.
21 An estate acquired in haste at the outset
Will not be blessed in the end.
22 Do not say, "I will requite evil";
Put your hope in the LORD and He will deliver you.
23 False weights are an abomination to the LORD;
Dishonest scales are not right.
24 A man's steps are decided by the LORD;
What does a man know about his own way?
25 It is a snare for a man *a*-to pledge a sacred gift rashly*-a*
And to give thought to his vows only after they have been
   made.
26 A wise king winnows out the wicked,
And turns the wheel upon them.
27 The lifebreath of man is the lamp of the LORD
Revealing all his inmost parts.
28 Faithfulness and loyalty protect the king;
He maintains his throne by faithfulness.
29 The glory of youths is their strength;
The majesty of old men is their gray hair.
30 Bruises and wounds are repayment*a* for evil,
Striking at one's inmost parts.

21 Like channeled water is the mind of the king in the LORD's
       hand;
He directs it to whatever He wishes.
2 All the ways of a man seem right to him,
But the LORD probes the mind.
3 To do what is right and just
Is more desired by the LORD than sacrifice.
4 Haughty looks, a proud heart—
The tillage of the wicked is sinful.
5 The plans of the diligent make only for gain;

All rash haste makes only for loss.
⁶ Treasures acquired by a lying tongue
ᵃ⁻Are like driven vapor, heading for extinction.⁻ᵃ
⁷ The violence of the wicked sweeps them away,
For they refuse to act justly.
⁸ The way of a man may be tortuous and strange,
Though his actions are blameless and proper.
⁹ Dwelling in the corner of a roof is better
Than a contentious wife in a ᵃ⁻spacious house.⁻ᵃ
¹⁰ The desire of the wicked is set upon evil;
His fellowman finds no favor in his eyes.
¹¹ When a scoffer is punished, the simple man is edified;
When a wise man is taught, he gains insight.
¹² The Righteous One observes the house of the wicked
   man;
He subverts the wicked to their ruin.
¹³ Who stops his ears at the cry of the wretched,
He too will call and not be answered.
¹⁴ A gift in secret subdues anger,
A present in private, fierce rage.
¹⁵ Justice done is a joy to the righteous,
To evildoers, ruination.
¹⁶ A man who strays from the path of prudence
Will rest in the company of ghosts.
¹⁷ He who loves pleasure comes to want;
He who loves wine and oil does not grow rich.
¹⁸ The wicked are the ransom of the righteous;
The traitor comes in place of the upright.
¹⁹ It is better to live in the desert
Than with a contentious, vexatious wife.
²⁰ Precious treasure and oil are in the house of the wise
   man,
And a fool of a man will run through them.
²¹ He who strives to do good and kind deeds
Attains life, success, and honor.
²² One wise man prevailed over a city of warriors

ᵃ⁻ᵃ *Meaning of Heb. uncertain.*

And brought down its mighty stronghold.
23 He who guards his mouth and tongue
Guards himself from trouble.
24 The proud, insolent man, scoffer is his name,
Acts in a frenzy of insolence.
25 The craving of a lazy man kills him,
For his hands refuse to work.
26 All day long he is seized with craving
While the righteous man gives without stint.
27 The sacrifice of the wicked man is an abomination,
The more so as he offers it in depravity.
28 A false witness is doomed,
But one who really heard will testify with success.
29 The wicked man is brazen-faced;
The upright man discerns his course.
30 No wisdom, no prudence, and no counsel
Can prevail against the LORD.
31 The horse is readied for the day of battle,
But victory comes from the LORD.

22 Repute is preferable to great wealth,
Grace is better than silver and gold.
2 Rich man and poor man meet;
The LORD made them both.
3 The shrewd man saw trouble and took cover;
The simple kept going and paid the penalty.
4 The effect of humility is fear of the LORD,
Wealth, honor, and life.
5 Thorns and snares are in the path of the crooked;
He who values his life will keep far from them.
6 Train a lad in the way he ought to go;
He will not swerve from it even in old age.
7 The rich rule the poor,
And the borrower is a slave to the lender.
8 He who sows injustice shall reap misfortune;

His rod of wrath shall fail.
⁹ The generous man is blessed,
For he gives of his bread to the poor.
¹⁰ Expel the scoffer and contention departs,
Quarrel and contumely cease.
¹¹ A pure-hearted friend,
His speech is gracious;
He has the king for his companion.
¹² The eyes of the LORD watch the wise man;
He subverts the words of the treacherous.
¹³ The lazy man says, "There's a lion in the street;
I shall be killed ᵃ⁻if I step outside."⁻ᵃ
¹⁴ The mouth of a forbiddenᵇ woman is a deep pit;
He who is doomed by the LORD falls into it.
¹⁵ If folly settles in the heart of a lad,
The rod of discipline will remove it.
¹⁶ To profit by withholding what is due to the poor
Is like making gifts to the rich—pure loss.

¹⁷ Incline your ear and listen to the words of the sages;
Pay attention to my wisdom.
¹⁸ It is good that you store them inside you,
And that all of them be constantly on your lips,
¹⁹ That you may put your trust in the LORD.
I let you know today—yes, you—
²⁰ Indeed, I wrote down for you ᶜ⁻a threefold lore,⁻ᶜ
Wise counsel,
²¹ To let you know truly reliable words,
That you may give a faithful reply to him who sent you.
²² Do not rob the wretched because he is wretched;
Do not crush the poor man in the gate;
²³ For the LORD will take up their cause
And despoil those who despoil them of life.
²⁴ Do not associate with an irascible man,
Or go about with one who is hot-tempered,
²⁵ Lest you learn his ways

ᵃ⁻ᵃ Lit. "in the square."
ᵇ Lit. "strange."
ᶜ⁻ᶜ Meaning of Heb. uncertain.

And find yourself ensnared.
²⁶ Do not be one of those who give their hand,
Who stand surety for debts,
²⁷ Lest your bed be taken from under you
When you have no money to pay.
²⁸ Do not remove the ancient boundary stone
That your ancestors set up.
²⁹ See a man skilled at his work—
He shall attend upon kings;
He shall not attend upon ᶜ⁻obscure men.⁻ᶜ

23 When you sit down to dine with a ruler,
Consider well who is before you.
² Thrust a knife into your gullet
If you have a large appetite.
³ Do not crave for his dainties,
For they are counterfeit food.

⁴ Do not toil to gain wealth;
Have the sense to desist.
⁵ You see it, then it is gone;
It grows wings and flies away,
Like an eagle, heavenward.

⁶ Do not eat of a stingy man's food;
Do not crave for his dainties;
⁷ He is like one keeping accounts;
"Eat and drink," he says to you,
But he does not really mean it.
⁸ The morsel you eat you will vomit;
You will waste your courteous words.

⁹ Do not speak to a dullard,
For he will disdain your sensible words.

¹⁰ Do not remove ancient boundary stones;
Do not encroach upon the field of orphans,
¹¹ For they have a mighty kinsman,
And He will surely take up their cause with you.

¹² Apply your mind to discipline
And your ears to wise sayings.
¹³ Do not withhold discipline from a child;
If you beat him with a rod he will not die.
¹⁴ Beat him with a rod
And you will save him from the grave.

¹⁵ My son, if your mind gets wisdom,
My mind, too, will be gladdened.
¹⁶ I shall rejoice with all my heart[a]
When your lips speak right things.
¹⁷ Do not envy sinners in your heart,
But only God-fearing men, at all times,
¹⁸ For then you will have a future,
And your hope will never fail.

¹⁹ Listen, my son, and get wisdom;
Lead your mind in a proper path.
²⁰ Do not be of those who guzzle wine,
Or glut themselves on meat;
²¹ For guzzlers and gluttons will be impoverished,
And drowsing will clothe you in tatters.

²² Listen to your father who begot you;
Do not disdain your mother when she is old.
²³ Buy truth and never sell it,
And wisdom, discipline, and understanding.
²⁴ The father of a righteous man will exult;
He who begets a wise son will rejoice in him.
²⁵ Your father and mother will rejoice;
She who bore you will exult.

[a] *Lit. "kidneys."*

²⁶ Give your mind to me, my son;
Let your eyes watch my ways.
²⁷ A harlot is a deep pit;
A forbidden*b* woman is a narrow well.
²⁸ She too lies in wait as if for prey,
And destroys the unfaithful among men.

²⁹ Who cries, "Woe!" who, "Alas!";
Who has quarrels, who complaints;
Who has wounds without cause;
Who has bleary eyes?
³⁰ Those whom wine keeps till the small hours,
Those who gather to drain the cups.
³¹ Do not ogle that red wine
As it lends its color to the cup,
As it flows on smoothly;
³² In the end, it bites like a snake;
It spits like a basilisk.
³³ Your eyes will see strange sights;
Your heart*c* will speak distorted things.
³⁴ You will be like one lying in bed on high seas,
Like one lying *d*on top of the rigging.*-d*
³⁵ "They struck me, but I felt no hurt;
They beat me, but I was unaware;
As often as I wake,
I go after it again."

24 Do not envy evil men;
Do not desire to be with them;
² For their hearts*a* talk violence,
And their lips speak mischief.

³ A house is built by wisdom,
And is established by understanding;

b Lit. "alien."
c See note to 15.28.
d-d Meaning of Heb. uncertain.

a See note to 15.28.

4 By knowledge are its rooms filled
With all precious and beautiful things.

5 A wise man is strength;
A knowledgeable man exerts power;
6 For by stratagems you wage war,
And victory comes with much planning.

7 Wisdom is too lofty for a fool;
He does not open his mouth in the gate.
8 He who lays plans to do harm
Is called by men a schemer.
9 The schemes of folly are sin,
And a scoffer is an abomination to men.

10 If you showed yourself slack in time of trouble,
Wanting in power,
11 If you refrained from rescuing those taken off to death,
Those condemned to slaughter—
12 If you say, "We knew nothing of it,"
Surely He who fathoms hearts will discern [the truth],
He who watches over your life will know it,
And He will pay each man as he deserves.

13 My son, eat honey, for it is good;
Let its sweet drops be on your palate.
14 Know: such is wisdom for your soul;
If you attain it, there is a future;
Your hope will not be cut off.

15 Wicked man! Do not lurk by the home of the righteous
    man;
Do no violence to his dwelling.
16 Seven times the righteous man falls and gets up,
While the wicked are tripped by one misfortune.

¹⁷ If your enemy falls, do not exult;
If he trips, let your heart not rejoice,
¹⁸ Lest the LORD see it and be displeased,
And avert His wrath from him.

¹⁹ Do not be vexed by evildoers;
Do not be incensed by the wicked;
²⁰ For there is no future for the evil man;
The lamp of the wicked goes out.

²¹ Fear the LORD, my son, and the king,
And do not mix with dissenters,
²² For disaster comes from them suddenly;
The doom both decree who can foreknow?

²³ These also are by the sages:

It is not right to be partial in judgment.
²⁴ He who says to the guilty, "You are innocent,"
Shall be cursed by peoples,
Damned by nations;
²⁵ But it shall go well with them who decide justly;
Blessings of good things will light upon them.

²⁶ Giving a straightforward reply
Is like giving a kiss.
²⁷ Put your external affairs in order,
Get ready what you have in the field,
Then build yourself a home.
²⁸ Do not be a witness against your fellow without
good cause;
Would you mislead with your speech?

²⁹ Do not say, "I will do to him what he did to me;
I will pay the man what he deserves."

³⁰ I passed by the field of a lazy man,
By the vineyard of a man lacking sense.
³¹ It was all overgrown with thorns;
Its surface was covered with chickweed,
And its stone fence lay in ruins.
³² I observed and took it to heart;
I saw it and learned a lesson.
³³ A bit more sleep, a bit more slumber,
A bit more hugging yourself in bed,
³⁴ And poverty will come *b*-calling upon you,-*b*
And want, like a man with a shield.

25 These too are proverbs of Solomon, which the men of King Hezekiah of Judah copied:

² It is the glory of God to conceal a matter,
And the glory of a king to plumb a matter.
³ Like the heavens in their height, like the earth in its
depth,
Is the mind of kings—unfathomable.
⁴ The dross having been separated from the silver,
A vessel emerged for the smith.
⁵ Remove the wicked from the king's presence,
And his throne will be established in justice.
⁶ Do not exalt yourself in the king's presence;
Do not stand in the place of nobles.
⁷ For it is better to be told, "Step up here,"
Than to be degraded in the presence of the great.

Do not let what your eyes have seen
⁸ Be vented rashly in a quarrel;
Think*ᵃ* of what it will effect in the end,

---

b-b *Meaning of Heb. uncertain.*

ᵃ *Lit. "Lest."*

When your fellow puts you to shame.
⁹ Defend your right against your fellow,
But do not give away the secrets of another,
¹⁰ Lest he who hears it reproach you,
And your bad repute never end.

¹¹ Like golden apples in silver showpieces[b]
Is a phrase well turned.
¹² Like a ring of gold, a golden ornament,
Is a wise man's reproof in a receptive ear.
¹³ Like the coldness of snow at harvesttime
Is a trusty messenger to those who send him;
He lifts his master's spirits.
¹⁴ Like clouds, wind—but no rain—
Is one who boasts of gifts not given.
¹⁵ Through forebearance a ruler may be won over;
A gentle tongue can break bones.
¹⁶ If you find honey, eat only what you need,
Lest, surfeiting yourself, you throw it up.
¹⁷ Visit your neighbor sparingly,
Lest he have his surfeit of you and loathe you.
¹⁸ Like a club, a sword, a sharpened arrow,
Is a man who testifies falsely against his fellow.
¹⁹ Like a loose tooth and an unsteady leg
Are a treacherous support in time of trouble.
²⁰ Disrobing on a chilly day,
Like vinegar on natron,
Is one who sings songs to a sorrowful soul.

²¹ If your enemy is hungry, give him bread to eat;
If he is thirsty, give him water to drink.
²² You will be heaping live coals on his head,
And the LORD will reward you.

²³ A north wind produces rain,
And whispered words, a glowering face.

[b] Meaning of Heb. uncertain.

245

²⁴ Dwelling in the corner of a roof is better
Than a contentious woman in ^ba spacious house.^{-b}
²⁵ Like cold water to a parched throat
Is good news from a distant land.
²⁶ Like a muddied spring, a ruined fountain,
Is a righteous man fallen before a wicked one.
²⁷ It is not good to eat much honey,
^bNor is it honorable to search for honor.^{-b}
²⁸ Like an open city without walls
Is a man whose temper is uncurbed.

26 Like snow in summer and rain at harvesttime,
So honor is not fitting for a dullard.
² As a sparrow must flit and a swallow fly,
So a gratuitous curse must backfire.^a
³ A whip for a horse and a bridle for a donkey,
And a rod for the back of dullards.
⁴ Do not answer a dullard in accord with his folly,
Else you will become like him.
⁵ Answer a dullard in accord with his folly,
Else he will think himself wise.
⁶ He who sends a message by a dullard
Will wear out legs and ^bmust put up with^{-b} lawlessness.
⁷ As legs hang limp on a cripple,
So is a proverb in the mouth of dullards.
⁸ Like a pebble in a sling,
So is paying honor to a dullard.
⁹ As a thorn comes to the hand of a drunkard,
So a proverb to the mouth of a dullard.
¹⁰ ^cA master can produce anything,^{-c}
But he who hires a dullard is as one who hires transients.^c
¹¹ As a dog returns to his vomit,
So a dullard repeats his folly.
¹² If you see a man who thinks himself wise,
There is more hope for a dullard than for him.

^a *Kethib, "fail."*
^{b-b} *Lit. "drink."*
^{c-c} *Meaning of Heb. uncertain.*

[13] A lazy man says,
"There's a cub on the road, a lion in the squares."
[14] The door turns on its hinge,
And the lazy man on his bed.
[15] The lazy man buries his hand in the bowl;
He will not even bring it to his mouth.
[16] The lazy man thinks himself wiser
Than seven men who give good advice.

[17] A passerby who gets embroiled in someone else's
quarrel
Is like one who seizes a dog by its ears.
[18] Like a madman[c] scattering deadly firebrands, arrows,
[19] Is one who cheats his fellow and says, "I was only
joking."

[20] For lack of wood a fire goes out,
And without a querulous man contention is stilled.
[21] Charcoal for embers and wood for a fire
And a contentious man for kindling strife.
[22] The words of a querulous man are bruising;[c]
They penetrate one's inmost parts.

[23] Base silver laid over earthenware
Are ardent lips with an evil mind.
[24] An enemy dissembles with his speech,
Inwardly he harbors deceit.
[25] Though he be fair-spoken do not trust him,
For seven abominations are in his mind.
[26] His hatred may be concealed by dissimulation,
But his evil will be exposed to public view.

[27] He who digs a pit will fall in it,
And whoever rolls a stone, it will roll back on him.
[28] A lying tongue hates [c]those crushed by it;[-c]
Smooth speech throws one down.

27 Do not boast of tomorrow,
For you do not know what the day will bring.
2 Let the mouth of another praise you, not yours,
The lips of a stranger, not your own.
3 A stone has weight, sand is heavy,
But a fool's vexation outweighs them both.
4 There is the cruelty of fury, the overflowing of anger,
But who can withstand jealousy?
5 Open reproof is better than concealed love.
6 Wounds by a loved one are long lasting;
The kisses of an enemy are profuse.
7 A sated person disdains honey,
But to a hungry man anything bitter seems sweet.
8 Like a sparrow wandering from its nest
Is a man who wanders from his home.
9 Oil and incense gladden the heart,
And the sweetness of a friend is better than one's own
counsel.
10 Do not desert your friend and your father's friend;
Do not enter your brother's house in your time of
misfortune;
A close neighbor is better than a distant brother.
11 Get wisdom, my son, and gladden my heart,
That I may have what to answer those who taunt me.
12 The shrewd man saw trouble and took cover;
The simple kept going and paid the penalty.
13 Seize his garment, for he stood surety for another;[a]
Take it as a pledge, [for he stood surety] for an unfamiliar
woman.
14 He who greets his fellow loudly early in the morning
Shall have it reckoned to him as a curse.
15 An endless dripping on a rainy day
And a contentious wife are alike;
16 As soon repress her as repress the wind,

[a] Or "a stranger."

Or declare one's right hand to be oil.
[17] As iron sharpens iron
So a man sharpens the wit[b] of his friend.
[18] He who tends a fig tree will enjoy its fruit,
And he who cares for his master will be honored.
[19] As face answers to face in water,
So does one man's heart to another.
[20] Sheol and Abaddon cannot be satisfied,
Nor can the eyes of man be satisfied.
[21] For silver—the crucible, for gold—the furnace,
And a man is tested by his praise.
[22] Even if you pound the fool in a mortar
With a pestle along with grain,
His folly will not leave him.

[23] Mind well the looks of your flock;
Pay attention to your herds;
[24] For property does not last forever,
Or a crown for all generations.
[25] Grass vanishes, new grass appears,
And the herbage of the hills is gathered in.
[26] The lambs will provide you with clothing,
The he-goats, the price of a field.
[27] The goats' milk will suffice for your food,
The food of your household,
And the maintenance of your maids.

28 The wicked flee though no one gives chase,
But the righteous are as confident as a lion.
[2] When there is rebellion in the land, many are its rulers;
[a]-But with a man who has understanding and knowledge,
  stability will last.[-a]
[3] A poor man who withholds what is due to the wretched
Is like a destructive rain that leaves no food.
[4] Those who forsake instruction praise the wicked,

[b] Lit. "face."

[a-a] Meaning of Heb. uncertain.

But those who heed instruction fight them.
5 Evil men cannot discern judgment,
But those who seek the LORD discern all things.
6 Better is a poor man who lives blamelessly
Than a rich man whose ways are crooked.
7 An intelligent son heeds instruction,
But he who keeps company with gluttons disgraces his
father.
8 He who increases his wealth by loans at discount or
interest
Amasses it for one who is generous to the poor.
9 He who turns a deaf ear to instruction—
His prayer is an abomination.
10 He who misleads the upright into an evil course
Will fall into his own pit,
But the blameless will prosper.
11 A rich man is clever in his own eyes,
But a perceptive poor man can see through him.
12 When the righteous exult there is great glory,
But when the wicked rise up men make themselves scarce.
13 He who covers up his faults will not succeed;
He who confesses and gives them up will find mercy.
14 Happy is the man who is anxious always,
But he who hardens his heart falls into misfortune.
15 A roaring lion and a prowling bear
Is a wicked man ruling a helpless people.
16 A prince who lacks understanding is very oppressive;
He who spurns ill-gotten gains will live long.
17 A man oppressed by bloodguilt will flee to a pit;
Let none give him support.
18 He who lives blamelessly will be delivered,
But he who is crooked in his ways will fall all at once.
19 He who tills his land will have food in plenty,
But he who pursues vanities will have poverty in plenty.
20 A dependable man will receive many blessings,

But one in a hurry to get rich will not go unpunished.
²¹ To be partial is not right;
A man may do wrong for a piece of bread.
²² A miserly man runs after wealth;
He does not realize that loss will overtake it.
²³ He who reproves a man will in the end
Find more favor than he who flatters him.
²⁴ He who robs his father and mother and says,
"It is no offense,"
Is a companion to vandals.
²⁵ A greedy man provokes quarrels,
But he who trusts the Lord shall enjoy prosperity.
²⁶ He who trusts his own instinct is a dullard,
But he who lives by wisdom shall escape.
²⁷ He who gives to the poor will not be in want,
But he who shuts his eyes will be roundly cursed.
²⁸ When the wicked rise up, men go into hiding,
But when they perish the righteous increase.

29 One oft reproved may become stiff-necked,
But he will be suddenly broken beyond repair.
² When the righteous become great the people rejoice,
But when the wicked dominate the people groan.
³ A man who loves wisdom brings joy to his father,
But he who keeps company with harlots will lose
his wealth.
⁴ By justice a king sustains the land,
But a fraudulent man tears it down.
⁵ A man who flatters his fellow
Spreads a net for his feet.
⁶ An evil man's offenses are a trap for himself,
But the righteous sing out joyously.
⁷ A righteous man is concerned with the cause of
the wretched;

A wicked man cannot understand such concern.
⁸ Scoffers inflame a city,
But the wise allay anger.
⁹ When a wise man enters into litigation with a fool
There is ranting and ridicule, but no satisfaction.
¹⁰ Bloodthirsty men detest the blameless,
But the upright seek them out.
¹¹ A dullard vents all his rage,
But a wise man calms it down.
¹² A ruler who listens to lies,
All his ministers will be wicked.
¹³ A poor man and a fraudulent man meet;
The Lord gives luster to the eyes of both.
¹⁴ A king who judges the wretched honestly,
His throne will be established forever.
¹⁵ Rod and reproof produce wisdom,
But a lad out of control is a disgrace to his mother.
¹⁶ When the wicked increase, offenses increase,
But the righteous will see their downfall.
¹⁷ Discipline your son and he will give you peace;
He will gratify you with dainties.
¹⁸ For lack of vision a people lose restraint,
But happy is he who heeds instruction.
¹⁹ A slave cannot be disciplined by words;
Though he may comprehend, he does not respond.
²⁰ If you see a man hasty in speech,
There is more hope for a fool than for him.
²¹ A slave pampered from youth
ᵃ⁻Will come to a bad end.⁻ᵃ
²² An angry man provokes a quarrel;
A hot-tempered man commits many offenses
²³ A man's pride will humiliate him,
But a humble man will obtain honor.
²⁴ He who shares with a thief is his own enemy;
He hears the imprecation and does not tell.ᵇ
²⁵ A man's fears become a trap for him,

ᵃ⁻ᵃ *Meaning of Heb. uncertain.*
ᵇ *Cf. Lev. 5.1.*

But he who trusts in the Lord shall be safeguarded.
26 Many seek audience with a ruler,
But it is from the Lord that a man gets justice.
27 The unjust man is an abomination to the righteous,
And he whose way is straight is an abomination to the
  wicked.

30 The words of Agur son of Jakeh, [man of] Massa;
The speech of the man to Ithiel, to Ithiel and Ucal:

2 I am brutish, less than a man;
I lack common sense.
3 I have not learned wisdom,
Nor do I possess knowledge of the Holy One.
4 Who has ascended heaven and come down?
Who has gathered up the wind in the hollow of his hand?
Who has wrapped the waters in his garment?
Who has established all the extremities of the earth?
What is his name or his son's name, if you know it?

5 Every word of God is pure,
A shield to those who take refuge in Him.
6 Do not add to His words,
Lest He indict you and you be proved a liar.

7 Two things I ask of you; do not deny them to me before
  I die:
8 Keep lies and false words far from me;
Give me neither poverty nor riches,
But provide me with my daily bread,
9 Lest, being sated, I renounce, saying,
"Who is the Lord?"
Or, being impoverished, I take to theft
And profane*a* the name of my God.

---

a *Meaning of Heb. uncertain.*

¹⁰ Do not inform on a slave to his master,
Lest he curse you and you incur guilt.

¹¹ There is a breed of men that brings a curse on its fathers
And brings no blessing to its mothers,
¹² A breed that thinks itself pure,
Though it is not washed of its filth;
¹³ A breed so haughty of bearing, so supercilious;
¹⁴ A breed whose teeth are swords,
Whose jaws are knives,
Ready to devour the poor of the land,
The needy among men.

¹⁵ The leech has two daughters, "Give!" and "Give!"
Three things are insatiable;
Four never say, "Enough!":
¹⁶ Sheol, a barren womb,
Earth that cannot get enough water,
And fire which never says, "Enough!"

¹⁷ The eye that mocks a father
And disdains the homage due a mother—
The ravens of the brook will gouge it out,
Young eagles will devour it.

¹⁸ Three things are beyond me;
Four I cannot fathom:
¹⁹ How an eagle makes its way over the sky;
How a snake makes its way over a rock;
How a ship makes its way through the high seas;
How a man has his way with a maiden.
²⁰ Such is the way of an adulteress:
She eats, wipes her mouth,
And says, "I have done no wrong."

²¹ The earth shudders at three things,
At four which it cannot bear:
²² A slave who becomes king;
A scoundrel sated with food;
²³ A loathsome woman who gets married;
A slave-girl who supplants her mistress.

²⁴ Four are among the tiniest on earth,
Yet they are the wisest of the wise:
²⁵ Ants are a folk without power,
Yet they prepare food for themselves in summer;
²⁶ The badger is a folk without strength,
Yet it makes its home in the rock;
²⁷ The locusts have no king,
Yet they all march forth in formation;
²⁸ You can catch the lizard[b] in your hand,
Yet it is found in royal palaces.

²⁹ There are three that are stately of stride,
Four that carry themselves well.
³⁰ The lion is mightiest among the beasts,
And recoils before none;
³¹ ᵃ⁻The greyhound, the he-goat,
The king whom none dares resist.⁻ᵃ

³² If you have been scandalously arrogant,
If you have been a schemer,
Then clap your hand to your mouth.
³³ As milk under pressure produces butter,
And a nose under pressure produces blood,
So patience under pressure produces strife.

ᵇ Or "spider."

31 The words of Lemuel, king of Massa, with which his mother admonished him:

> [2] No, my son!
> No, O son of my womb!
> No, O son of my vows!
> [3] Do not give your strength to women,
> Your vigor,*ᵃ* *ᵇ*to those who destroy kings.*⁻ᵇ*
> [4] Wine is not for kings, O Lemuel;
> Not for kings to drink,
> Nor any strong drink for princes,
> [5] Lest they drink and forget what has been ordained,
> And infringe on the rights of the poor.
> [6] Give strong drink to the hapless
> And wine to the embittered.
> [7] Let them drink and forget their poverty,
> And put their troubles out of mind.
> [8] Speak up for the dumb,
> For the rights of all the unfortunate.
> [9] Speak up, judge righteously,
> Champion the poor and the needy.

> א   [10] What a rare find is a capable wife!
> Her worth is far beyond that of rubies.
> ב   [11] Her husband puts his confidence in her,
> And lacks no good thing.
> ג   [12] She is good to him, never bad,
> All the days of her life.
> ד   [13] She looks for wool and flax,
> And sets her hand to them with a will.
> ה   [14] She is like a merchant fleet,
> Bringing her food from afar.
> ו   [15] She rises while it is still night,
> And supplies provisions for her household,

ᵃ *Lit. "ways."*
ᵇ⁻ᵇ *Meaning of Heb. uncertain.*

The daily fare of her maids.

ז ¹⁶ She sets her mind on an estate and acquires it;
She plants a vineyard by her own labors.

ח ¹⁷ She girds herself with strength,
ᶜ⁻And performs her tasks with vigor.⁻ᶜ

ט ¹⁸ She sees*d* that her business thrives;
Her lamp never goes out at night.

י ¹⁹ She sets her hand to the distaff;
Her fingers work the spindle.

כ ²⁰ She gives generously to the poor;
Her hands are stretched out to the needy.

ל ²¹ She is not worried for her household because of snow,
For her whole household is dressed in crimson.

מ ²² She makes covers for herself;
Her clothing is linen and purple.

נ ²³ Her husband is prominent in the gates,
As he sits among the elders of the land.

ס ²⁴ She makes cloth and sells it,
And offers a girdle to the merchant.

ע ²⁵ She is clothed with strength and splendor;
She looks to the future cheerfully.

פ ²⁶ Her mouth is full of wisdom,
Her tongue with kindly teaching.

צ ²⁷ She oversees the activities of her household
And never eats the bread of idleness.

ק ²⁸ Her children declare her happy;
Her husband praises her,

ר ²⁹ "Many women have done well,
But you surpass them all."

ש ³⁰ Grace is deceptive,
Beauty is illusory;
It is for her fear of the LORD
That a woman is to be praised.

ת ³¹ Extol her for the fruit of her hand,
And let her works praise her in the gates.

ᶜ⁻ᶜ *Lit. "And exerts her arms."*
d *Lit. "tastes."*

איוב

JOB

אִיּוֹב

JOB

1 There was a man in the land of Uz named Job. That man was blameless and upright; he feared God and shunned evil. ² Seven sons and three daughters were born to him; ³ his possessions were seven thousand sheep, three thousand camels, five hundred yoke of oxen and five hundred she-asses, and a very large household. That man was wealthier than anyone in the East.

⁴ It was the custom of his sons to hold feasts, each on his set day in his own home. They would invite their three sisters to eat and drink with them. ⁵ When a round of feast days was over, Job would send word to them to sanctify themselves, and, rising early in the morning, he would make burnt offerings, one for each of them; for Job thought, "Perhaps my children have sinned and blasphemed God in their thoughts." This is what Job always used to do.

⁶ One day the divine beings presented themselves before the LORD, *-and the Adversary-* came along with them. ⁷ The LORD said to the Adversary, "Where have you been?" The Adversary answered the LORD, "I have been roaming all over the earth." ⁸ The LORD said to the Adversary, "Have you noticed My servant Job? There is no one like him on earth, a blameless and upright man who fears God and shuns evil!" ⁹ The Adversary answered the LORD, "Does Job not have good reason to fear God? ¹⁰ Why, it is You who have fenced him round, him and his household and all that he has. You have blessed his efforts so that his possessions spread out in the land. ¹¹ But lay Your hand upon all that he has and he will surely blaspheme You to Your face." ¹² The LORD replied to the Adversary, "See, all that he has is in your power;

ᵃ⁻ᵃ *Heb.* ha-saṭan.

only do not lay a hand on him." The Adversary departed from the presence of the LORD.

¹³ One day, as his sons and daughters were eating and drinking wine in the house of their eldest brother, ¹⁴ a messenger came to Job and said, "The oxen were plowing and the she-asses were grazing alongside them ¹⁵ when Sabeans attacked them and carried them off, and put the boys to the sword; I alone have escaped to tell you." ¹⁶ This one was still speaking when another came and said, "God's fire fell from heaven, took hold of the sheep and the boys, and burned them up; I alone have escaped to tell you." ¹⁷ This one was still speaking when another came and said, "A Chaldean formation of three columns made a raid on the camels and carried them off and put the boys to the sword; I alone have escaped to tell you." ¹⁸ This one was still speaking when another came and said, "Your sons and daughters were eating and drinking wine in the house of their eldest brother ¹⁹ when suddenly a mighty wind came from the wilderness. It struck the four corners of the house so that it collapsed upon the young people and they died; I alone have escaped to tell you."

²⁰ Then Job arose, tore his robe, cut off his hair, and threw himself on the ground and worshiped. ²¹ He said, "Naked came I out of my mother's womb, and naked shall I return there; the LORD has given, and the LORD has taken away; blessed be the name of the LORD."

²² For all that, Job did not sin nor did he cast reproach on God.

2 One day the divine beings presented themselves before the LORD. The Adversary came along with them to present himself before the LORD. ² The LORD said to the Adversary, "Where have you been?" The Adversary answered the LORD, "I have been roaming all over the earth." ³ The LORD said to the Adversary, "Have you noticed My servant Job? There is no one like him on earth, a blameless and upright man who fears God and shuns evil. He still keeps his integrity; so you have incited Me against him

to destroy him for no good reason." ⁴ The Adversary answered the LORD, ᵃ-"Skin for skin-ᵃ—all that a man has he will give up for his life. ⁵ But lay a hand on his bones and his flesh, and he will surely blaspheme You to Your face." ⁶ So the LORD said to the Adversary, "See, he is in your power; only spare his life." ⁷ The Adversary departed from the presence of the LORD and inflicted a severe inflammation on Job from the sole of his foot to the crown of his head. ⁸ He took a potsherd to scratch himself as he sat in ashes. ⁹ His wife said to him, "You still keep your integrity! Blaspheme God and die!" ¹⁰ But he said to her, "You talk as any shameless woman might talk! Should we accept only good from God and not accept evil?" For all that, Job said nothing sinful.

¹¹ When Job's three friends heard about all these calamities that had befallen him, each came from his home—Eliphaz the Temanite, Bildad the Shuhite, and Zophar the Naamathite. They met together to go and console and comfort him. ¹² When they saw him from a distance, they could not recognize him, and they broke into loud weeping; each one tore his robe and threw dust into the air onto his head. ¹³ They sat with him on the ground seven days and seven nights. None spoke a word to him for they saw how very great was his suffering.

3 ᵃAfterward, Job began to speak and cursed the day of his birth. ² Job spoke up and said:

³ Perish the day on which I was born,
And the night it was announced,
"A male has been conceived!"
⁴ May that day be darkness;
May God above have no concern for it;
May light not shine on it;
⁵ May darkness and deep gloom reclaim it;
May a pall lie over it;
May ᵇ-what blackens-ᵇ the day terrify it.

ᵃ⁻ᵃ *Apparently a proverb whose meaning is uncertain.*

ᵃ *There are many difficulties in the poetry of Job, making the interpretation of words, verses, and even chapters uncertain. The rubric "Meaning of Heb. uncertain" in this book indicates only some of the extreme instances.*

ᵇ⁻ᵇ *Meaning of Heb. uncertain.*

⁶ May obscurity carry off that night;
May it not be counted among the days of the year;
May it not appear in any of its months;
⁷ May that night be desolate;
May no sound of joy be heard in it;
⁸ May those who cast spells upon the dayᶜ damn it,
Those prepared to disable Leviathan;
⁹ May its twilight stars remain dark;
May it hope for light and have none;
May it not see the glimmerings of the dawn—
¹⁰ Because it did not block my mother's womb,
And hide trouble from my eyes.

¹¹ Why did I not die at birth,
Expire as I came forth from the womb?
¹² Why were there knees to receive me,
Or breasts for me to suck?
¹³ For now would I be lying in repose, asleep and at rest,
¹⁴ With the world's kings and counselors who rebuild ruins
  for themselves,
¹⁵ Or with nobles who possess gold and who fill their
  houses with silver.
¹⁶ Or why was I not like a buried stillbirth,
Like babies who never saw the light?
¹⁷ There the wicked cease from troubling;
There rest those whose strength is spent.
¹⁸ Prisoners are wholly at ease;
They do not hear the taskmaster's voice.
¹⁹ Small and great alike are there,
And the slave is free of his master.

²⁰ Why does He give light to the sufferer
And life to the bitter in spirit;
²¹ To those who wait for death but it does not come,
Who search for it more than for treasure,

ᶜ Or "sea," taking Heb. yom as equivalent of yam; compare the combination of sea with
Leviathan in Ps. 74.13, 14 and with Dragon in Job 7.12; cf. also Isa. 27.1.

²² Who rejoice to exultation,
And are glad to reach the grave;
²³ To the man who has lost his way,
Whom God has hedged about?

²⁴ My groaning serves as my bread;
My roaring pours forth as water.
²⁵ For what I feared has overtaken me;
What I dreaded has come upon me.
²⁶ I had no repose, no quiet, no rest,
And trouble came.

4 Then Eliphaz the Temanite said in reply:

² If one ventures a word with you, will it be too much?
But who can hold back his words?
³ See, you have encouraged many;
You have strengthened failing hands.
⁴ Your words have kept him who stumbled from falling;
You have braced knees that gave way.
⁵ But now that it overtakes you, it is too much;
It reaches you, and you are unnerved.
⁶ Is not your piety your confidence,
Your integrity your hope?
⁷ Think now, what innocent man ever perished?
Where have the upright been destroyed?
⁸ As I have seen, those who plow evil
And sow mischief reap them.
⁹ They perish by a blast from God,
Are gone at the breath of His nostrils.
¹⁰ The lion may roar, the cub may howl,
But the teeth of the king of beasts ᵃ-are broken.-ᵃ
¹¹ The lion perishes for lack of prey,
And its whelps are scattered.

ᵃ⁻ᵃ *Meaning of Heb. uncertain.*

¹² A word came to me in stealth;
My ear caught a whisper of it.
¹³ In thought-filled visions of the night,
When deep sleep falls on men,
¹⁴ Fear and trembling came upon me,
Causing all my bones to quake with fright.
¹⁵ A wind passed by me,
Making the hair of my flesh bristle.
¹⁶ It halted; its appearance was strange to me;
A form loomed before my eyes;
I heard a murmur, a voice,
¹⁷ "Can mortals be acquitted by God?
Can man be cleared by his Maker?
¹⁸ If He cannot trust His own servants,
And casts reproach*a* on His angels,
¹⁹ How much less those who dwell in houses of clay,
Whose origin is dust,
Who are crushed like the moth,
²⁰ Shattered between daybreak and evening,
Perishing forever, unnoticed.
²¹ Their cord is pulled up
And they die, and not with wisdom."

5   Call now! Will anyone answer you?
To whom among the holy beings will you turn?
² Vexation kills the fool;
Passion slays the simpleton.
³ I myself saw a fool who had struck roots;
Impulsively, I cursed his home:
⁴ May his children be far from success;
May they be oppressed in the gate with none to deliver
    them;
⁵ May the hungry devour his harvest,
a-Carrying it off in baskets;

―――――――

a-a Meaning of Heb. uncertain.

May the thirsty swallow their wealth.[-a]
[6] Evil does not grow out of the soil,
Nor does mischief spring from the ground;
[7] For man is born to [do] mischief,
Just as sparks fly upward.

[8] But I would resort to God;
I would lay my case before God,
[9] Who performs great deeds which cannot be fathomed,
Wondrous things without number;
[10] Who gives rain to the earth,
And sends water over the fields;
[11] Who raises the lowly up high,
So that the dejected are secure in victory;
[12] Who thwarts the designs of the crafty,
So that their hands cannot gain success;
[13] Who traps the clever in their own wiles;
The plans of the crafty go awry.
[14] By day they encounter darkness,
At noon they grope as in the night.
[15] But He saves the needy from the sword of their mouth,
From the clutches of the strong.
[16] So there is hope for the wretched;
The mouth of wrongdoing is stopped.

[17] See how happy is the man whom God reproves;
Do not reject the discipline of the Almighty.
[18] He injures, but He binds up;
He wounds, but His hands heal.
[19] He will deliver you from six troubles;
In seven no harm will reach you:
[20] In famine He will redeem you from death,
In war, from the sword.
[21] You will be sheltered from the scourging tongue;
You will have no fear when violence comes.

²² You will laugh at violence and starvation,
And have no fear of wild beasts.
²³ For you will have a pact with the rocks in the field,
And the beasts of the field will be your allies.
²⁴ You will know that all is well in your tent;
When you visit your wife*ᵇ* you will never fail.
²⁵ You will see that your offspring are many,
Your descendants like the grass of the earth.
²⁶ You will come to the grave *ᵃ*-in ripe old age,-*ᵃ*
As shocks of grain are taken away in their season.
²⁷ See, we have inquired into this and it is so;
Hear it and accept it.

6 Then Job said in reply:

² If my anguish were weighed,
My full calamity laid on the scales,
³ It would be heavier than the sand of the sea;
That is why I spoke recklessly.*ᵃ*
⁴ For the arrows of the Almighty are in me;
My spirit absorbs their poison;
God's terrors are arrayed against me.
⁵ Does a wild ass bray when he has grass?
Does a bull bellow over his fodder?
⁶ Can what is tasteless be eaten without salt?
Does *ᵃ*-mallow juice-*ᵃ* have any flavor?
⁷ I refuse to touch them;
They are like food when I am sick.

⁸ Would that my request were granted,
That God gave me what I wished for;
⁹ Would that God consented to crush me,
Loosed His hand and cut me off.
¹⁰ Then this would be my consolation,

ᵇ *Lit. "home."*

ᵃ *Meaning of Heb. uncertain.*

a-As I writhed in unsparing-*a* pains:
That I did not *b*-suppress my words against the Holy One.-*b*
¹¹ What strength have I, that I should endure?
How long have I to live, that I should be patient?
¹² Is my strength the strength of rock?
Is my flesh bronze?
¹³ Truly, I cannot help myself;
I have been deprived of resourcefulness.

¹⁴ *a*-A friend owes loyalty to one who fails,
Though he forsakes the fear of the Almighty;-*a*
¹⁵ My comrades are fickle, like a wadi,
Like a bed on which streams once ran.
¹⁶ *a*-They are dark with ice;
Snow obscures them;-*a*
¹⁷ But when they thaw, they vanish;
In the heat, they disappear where they are.
¹⁸ Their course twists and turns;
They run into the desert and perish.
¹⁹ Caravans from Tema look to them;
Processions from Sheba count on them.
²⁰ They are disappointed in their hopes;
When they reach the place, they stand aghast.
²¹ So you are as nothing:*c*
At the sight of misfortune, you take fright.
²² Did I say to you, "I need your gift;
Pay a bribe for me out of your wealth;
²³ Deliver me from the clutches of my enemy;
Redeem me from violent men"?
²⁴ Teach me; I shall be silent;
Tell me where I am wrong.
²⁵ *a*-How trenchant honest words are;-*a*
But what sort of reproof comes from you?
²⁶ Do you devise words of reproof,
But count a hopeless man's words as wind?

---

b-b *Meaning of Heb. uncertain; others, "deny the words of the Holy One."*
c *Following* kethib, *with Targum; meaning of Heb. uncertain.*

²⁷ You would even cast lots over an orphan,
Or barter away your friend.
²⁸ Now be so good as to face me;
I will not lie to your face.
²⁹ Relent! Let there not be injustice;
Relent! I am still in the right.
³⁰ Is injustice on my tongue?
Can my palate not discern evil?

7   Truly man has a term of service on earth;
His days are like those of a hireling—
² Like a slave who longs for [evening's] shadows,
Like a hireling who waits for his wage.
³ So have I been allotted months of futility;
Nights of misery have been apportioned to me.
⁴ When I lie down, I think,
"When shall I rise?"
Night ᵃ⁻drags on,⁻ᵃ
And I am sated with tossings till morning twilight.
⁵ My flesh is covered with maggots and clods of earth;
My skin is broken and festering.
⁶ My days fly faster than a weaver's shuttle,
And come to their end ᵇ⁻without hope.⁻ᵇ
⁷ Consider that my life is but wind;
I shall never see happiness again.
⁸ The eye that gazes on me will not see me;
Your eye will seek me, but I shall be gone.
⁹ As a cloud fades away,
So whoever goes down to Sheol does not come up;
¹⁰ He returns no more to his home;
His place does not know him.

¹¹ On my part, I will not speak with restraint;
I will give voice to the anguish of my spirit;

ᵃ⁻ᵃ *Meaning of Heb. uncertain.*
ᵇ⁻ᵇ *Or "when the thread runs out."*

I will complain in the bitterness of my soul.
¹² Am I the sea or the Dragon,ᶜ
That You have set a watch over me?
¹³ When I think, "My bed will comfort me,
My couch will share my sorrow,"
¹⁴ You frighten me with dreams,
And terrify me with visions,
¹⁵ Till I prefer strangulation,
Death, to my wasted frame.
¹⁶ I am sick of it.
I shall not live forever;
Let me be, for my days are a breath.

¹⁷ What is man, that You make much of him,
That You fix Your attention upon him?
¹⁸ You inspect him every morning,
Examine him every minute.
¹⁹ Will You not look away from me for a while,
Let me be, till I swallow my spittle?
²⁰ If I have sinned, what have I done to You,
Watcher of men?
Why make of me Your target,
And a burden to myself?
²¹ Why do You not pardon my transgression
And forgive my iniquity?
For soon I shall lie down in the dust;
When You seek me, I shall be gone.

8 Bildad the Shuhite said in reply:

² How long will you speak such things?
Your utterances are a mighty wind!
³ Will God pervert the right?
Will the Almighty pervert justice?

ᶜ *See note at 3.8.*

⁴ If your sons sinned against Him,
He dispatched them for their transgression.
⁵ But if you seek God
And supplicate the Almighty,
⁶ If you are blameless and upright,
He will protect you,
And grant well-being to your righteous home.
⁷ Though your beginning be small,
In the end you will grow very great.

⁸ Ask the generation past,
Study what their fathers have searched out
⁹ —For we are of yesterday and know nothing;
Our days on earth are a shadow—
¹⁰ Surely they will teach you and tell you,
Speaking out of their understanding.
¹¹ Can papyrus thrive without marsh?
Can rushes grow without water?
¹² While still tender, not yet plucked,
They would wither before any other grass.
¹³ Such is the fate of all who forget God;
The hope of the impious man comes to naught—
¹⁴ Whose confidence is a ᵃ‑thread of gossamer,‑ᵃ
Whose trust is a spider's web.
¹⁵ He leans on his house—it will not stand;
He seizes hold of it, but it will not hold.
¹⁶ He stays fresh even in the sun;
His shoots spring up in his garden;
¹⁷ ᵃ‑His roots are twined around a heap,
They take hold of a house of stones.‑ᵃ
¹⁸ When he is uprooted from his place,
It denies him, [saying,]
"I never saw you."
¹⁹ Such is his happy lot;
And from the earth others will grow.

ᵃ⁻ᵃ *Meaning of Heb. uncertain.*

20 Surely God does not despise the blameless;
He gives no support to evildoers.
21 He will yet fill your mouth with laughter,
And your lips with shouts of joy.
22 Your enemies will be clothed in disgrace;
The tent of the wicked will vanish.

9 Job said in reply:

2 Indeed I know that it is so:
Man cannot win a suit against God.
3 If he insisted on a trial with Him,
He would not answer one charge in a thousand.
4 Wise of heart and mighty in power—
Who ever challenged Him and came out whole?—
5 Him who moves mountains without their knowing it,
Who overturns them in His anger;
6 Who shakes the earth from its place,
Till its pillars quake;
7 Who commands the sun not to shine;
Who seals up the stars;
8 Who by Himself spread out the heavens,
And trod on the back of the sea;
9 Who made the Bear[a] and Orion,
Pleiades, and the chambers of the south wind;
10 Who performs great deeds which cannot be fathomed,
And wondrous things without number.
11 He passes me by—I do not see Him;
He goes by me, but I do not perceive Him.
12 He snatches away—who can stop Him?
Who can say to Him, "What are You doing?"
13 God does not restrain His anger;
Under Him Rahab's[b] helpers sink down.
14 How then can I answer Him,

---

[a] *Meaning of Heb. uncertain.*
[b] *A primeval monster.*

Or choose my arguments against Him?
15 Though I were in the right, I could not speak out,
But I would plead for mercy with my judge.
16 If I summoned Him and He responded,
I do not believe He would lend me His ear.
17 For He crushes me c-for a hair;-c
He wounds me much for no cause.
18 He does not let me catch my breath,
But sates me with bitterness.
19 If a trial of strength—He is the strong one;
If a trial in court—who will summon Him for me?
20 Though I were innocent,
My mouth would condemn me;
Though I were blameless, He would prove me crooked.
21 I am blameless—I am distraught;
I am sick of life.
22 It is all one; therefore I say,
"He destroys the blameless and the guilty."
23 When suddenly a scourge brings death,
He mocks as the innocent fail.
24 The earth is handed over to the wicked one;
He covers the eyes of its judges.
If it is not He, then who?

25 My days fly swifter than a runner;
They flee without seeing happiness;
26 They pass like reed-boats,
Like an eagle swooping onto its prey.
27 If I say, "I will forget my complaint;
Abandon my sorrow^d and be diverted,"
28 I remain in dread of all my suffering;
I know that You will not acquit me.
29 It will be I who am in the wrong;
Why then should I waste effort?
30 If I washed with soap,

c-c With Targum and Peshitta; or "with a storm."
d Lit. "face."

274

Cleansed my hands with lye,
³¹ You would dip me in muck
Till my clothes would abhor me.
³² He is not a man, like me, that I can answer Him,
That we can go to law together.
³³ No arbiter is between us
To lay his hand on us both.
³⁴ If He would only take His rod away from me
And not let His terror frighten me,
³⁵ Then I would speak out without fear of Him;
For I know myself not to be so.

10 I am disgusted with life;
I will give rein to my complaint,
Speak in the bitterness of my soul.
² I say to God, "Do not condemn me;
Let me know what You charge me with.
³ Does it benefit You to defraud,
To despise the toil of Your hands,
While smiling on the counsel of the wicked?
⁴ Do You have the eyes of flesh?
Is Your vision that of mere men?
⁵ Are Your days the days of a mortal,
Are Your years the years of a man,
⁶ That You seek my iniquity
And search out my sin?
⁷ You know that I am not guilty,
And that there is none to deliver from Your hand.

⁸ "Your hands shaped and fashioned me,
Then destroyed every part of me.
⁹ Consider that You fashioned me like clay;
Will You then turn me back into dust?

¹⁰ You poured me out like milk,
Congealed me like cheese;
¹¹ You clothed me with skin and flesh
And wove me of bones and sinews;
¹² You bestowed on me life and care;
Your providence watched over my spirit.
¹³ Yet these things You hid in Your heart;
I know that You had this in mind:
¹⁴ To watch me when I sinned
And not clear me of my iniquity;
¹⁵ Should I be guilty—the worse for me!
And even when innocent, I cannot lift my head;
So sated am I with shame,
And drenched in my misery.
¹⁶ *a*-It is something to be proud of-*a* to hunt me like a lion,
To *b*-show Yourself wondrous through-*b* me time and
again!
¹⁷ You keep sending fresh witnesses against me,
Letting Your vexation with me grow.
a-I serve my term and am my own replacement.-*a*

¹⁸ "Why did You let me come out of the womb?
Better had I expired before any eye saw me,
¹⁹ Had I been as though I never was,
Had I been carried from the womb to the grave.
²⁰ My days are few, so desist!
Leave me alone, let me be diverted awhile
²¹ Before I depart—never to return—
For the land of deepest gloom;
²² A land whose light is darkness,
All gloom and disarray,
Whose light is like darkness."

---

^{a-a} *Meaning of Heb. uncertain.*
^{b-b} *Or "make sport of"; cf. Pal. Aram. 'afli.*

11 Then Zophar the Naamathite said in reply:

² Is a multitude of words unanswerable?
Must a loquacious person be right?
³ Your prattle may silence men;
You may mock without being rebuked,
⁴ And say, "My doctrine is pure,
And I have been innocent in Your sight."
⁵ But would that God might speak,
And talk to you Himself.
⁶ He would tell you the secrets of wisdom,
ᵃ⁻For there are many sides to sagacity;
And know that God has overlooked for you some of your
iniquity.⁻ᵃ

⁷ Would you discover the mystery of God?
Would you discover the limit of the Almighty?
⁸ Higher than heaven—what can you do?
Deeper than Sheol—what can you know?
⁹ Its measure is longer than the earth
And broader than the sea.
¹⁰ ᵃ⁻Should He pass by, or confine,
Or call an assembly, who can stop Him?⁻ᵃ
¹¹ For He knows deceitful men;
When He sees iniquity, does He not discern it?
¹² ᵃ⁻A hollow man will get understanding,
When a wild ass is born a man.⁻ᵃ

¹³ But if you direct your mind,
And spread forth your hands toward Him—
¹⁴ If there is iniquity with you, remove it,
And do not let injustice reside in your tent—
¹⁵ Then, free of blemish, you will hold your head high,

ᵃ⁻ᵃ *Meaning of Heb. uncertain.*

And, *b*-when in straits,-*b* be unafraid.
16 You will then put your misery out of mind,
Consider it as water that has flowed past.
17 *a*-Life will be brighter than noon;-*a*
You will shine, you will be like the morning.
18 You will be secure, for there is hope,
a-And, entrenched,-*a* you will rest secure;
19 You will lie down undisturbed;
The great will court your favor.
20 But the eyes of the wicked pine away;
Escape is cut off from them;
They have only their last breath to look forward to.

12 Then Job said in reply:

2 Indeed, you are the [voice of] the people,
And wisdom will die with you.
3 But I, like you, have a mind,
And am not less than you.
Who does not know such things?
4 I have become a laughingstock to my friend—
"One who calls to God and is answered,
Blamelessly innocent"—a laughingstock.
5 *a*-In the thought of the complacent there is contempt for
    calamity;
It is ready for those whose foot slips.-*a*
6 Robbers live untroubled in their tents,
And those who provoke God are secure,
a-Those whom God's hands have produced.-*a*

7 But ask the beasts, and they will teach you;
The birds of the sky, they will tell you,
8 Or speak to the earth, it will teach you;
The fish of the sea, they will inform you.

b-b *Heb.* muṣaq; *other Heb. editions* muṣṣaq, *"you will be firm."*

a-a *Meaning of Heb. uncertain.*

⁹ Who among all these does not know
That the hand of the LORD has done this?
¹⁰ In His hand is every living soul
And the breath of all mankind.
¹¹ Truly, the ear tests arguments
As the palate tastes foods.
¹² Is wisdom in the aged
And understanding in the long-lived?
¹³ With Him are wisdom and courage;
His are counsel and understanding.
¹⁴ Whatever He tears down cannot be rebuilt;
Whomever He imprisons cannot be set free.
¹⁵ When He holds back the waters, they dry up;
When He lets them loose, they tear up the land.
¹⁶ With Him are strength and resourcefulness;
Erring and causing to err are from Him.
¹⁷ He makes counselors go about naked[b]
And causes judges to go mad.
¹⁸ He undoes the belts of kings,
And fastens loincloths on them.
¹⁹ He makes priests go about naked,[b]
And leads temple-servants[c] astray.
²⁰ He deprives trusty men of speech,
And takes away the reason of elders.
²¹ He pours disgrace upon great men,
And loosens the belt of the mighty.
²² He draws mysteries out of the darkness,
And brings obscurities to light.
²³ He exalts nations, then destroys them;
He expands nations, then leads them away.
²⁴ He deranges the leaders of the people,
And makes them wander in a trackless waste.
²⁵ They grope without light in the darkness;
He makes them wander as if drunk.

[b] *A sign of madness.*
[c] *Cf. Ugaritic* ytnm, *a class of temple servants; others "the mighty."*

13 My eye has seen all this;
My ear has heard and understood it.
² What you know, I know also;
I am not less than you.
³ Indeed, I would speak to the Almighty;
I insist on arguing with God.
⁴ But you invent lies;
All of you are quacks.
⁵ If you would only keep quiet
It would be considered wisdom on your part.
⁶ Hear now my arguments,
Listen to my pleading.
⁷ Will you speak unjustly on God's behalf?
Will you speak deceitfully for Him?
⁸ Will you be partial toward Him?
Will you plead God's cause?
⁹ Will it go well when He examines you?
Will you fool Him as one fools men?
¹⁰ He will surely reprove you
If in *ᵃ-your heart-ᵃ* you are partial toward Him.
¹¹ His threat will terrify you,
And His fear will seize you.
¹² Your briefs are empty*ᵇ* platitudes;
Your responses are unsubstantial.*ᶜ*

¹³ Keep quiet; I will have my say,
Come what may upon me.
¹⁴ How long! I will take my flesh in my teeth;
I will take my life in my hands.
¹⁵ *ᵈ-He may well slay me; I may have no hope;-ᵈ*
Yet I will argue my case before Him.
¹⁶ In this too is my salvation:
That no impious man can come into His presence.

ᵃ⁻ᵃ *Lit. "secret."*
ᵇ *Lit. "ashen."*
ᶜ *Lit. "clayey."*
ᵈ⁻ᵈ *So with* kethib; *others with* qere *"Though He slay me, yet will I trust in Him."*

¹⁷ Listen closely to my words;
Give ear to my discourse.
¹⁸ See now, I have prepared a case;
I know that I will win it.
¹⁹ For who is it that would challenge me?
I should then keep silent and expire.
²⁰ But two things do not do to me,
So that I need not hide from You:
²¹ Remove Your hand from me,
And let not Your terror frighten me.
²² Then summon me and I will respond,
Or I will speak and You reply to me.
²³ How many are my iniquities and sins?
Advise me of my transgression and sin.
²⁴ Why do You hide Your face,
And treat me like an enemy?
²⁵ Will You harass a driven leaf,
Will You pursue dried-up straw,
²⁶ That You decree for me bitter things
And make me ᵉ-answer for-ᵉ the iniquities of my youth,
²⁷ That You put my feet in the stocks
And watch all my ways,
ᶠ-Hemming in my footsteps?-ᶠ
²⁸ Man wastes away like a rotten thing,
Like a garment eaten by moths.

14 Man born of woman is short-lived and sated with trouble.
² He blossoms like a flower and withers;
He vanishes like a shadow and does not endure.
³ Do You fix Your gaze on such a one?
Will You go to law with me?
⁴ ᵃ-Who can produce a clean thing out of an unclean one?
No one!-ᵃ
⁵ His days are determined;

ᵉ⁻ᵉ Lit. "inherit."
ᶠ⁻ᶠ Meaning of Heb. uncertain.

ᵃ⁻ᵃ Meaning of Heb. uncertain.

You know the number of his months;
You have set him limits that he cannot pass.
⁶ Turn away from him, that he may be at ease
Until, like a hireling, he finishes out his day.

⁷ There is hope for a tree;
If it is cut down it will renew itself;
Its shoots will not cease.
⁸ If its roots are old in the earth,
And its stump dies in the ground,
⁹ At the scent of water it will bud
And produce branches like a sapling.
¹⁰ But mortals languish and die;
Man expires; where is he?
¹¹ The waters of the sea fail,
And the river dries up and is parched.
¹² So man lies down never to rise;
He will awake only when the heavens are no more,
Only then be aroused from his sleep.
¹³ O that You would hide me in Sheol,
Conceal me until Your anger passes,
Set me a fixed time to attend to me.
¹⁴ If a man dies, can he live again?
All the time of my service I wait
Until my replacement comes.
¹⁵ You would call and I would answer You;
You would set Your heart on Your handiwork.
¹⁶ Then You would not count my steps,
Or keep watch over my sin.
¹⁷ My transgression would be sealed up in a pouch;
You would coat over my iniquity.

¹⁸ Mountains collapse and crumble;
Rocks are dislodged from their place.
¹⁹ Water wears away stone;

Torrents wash away earth;
So you destroy man's hope,
²⁰ You overpower him for ever and he perishes;
You alter his visage and dispatch him.
²¹ His sons attain honor and he does not know it;
They are humbled and he is not aware of it.
²² He feels only the pain of his flesh,
And his spirit mourns in him.

15 Eliphaz the Temanite said in reply:

² Does a wise man answer with windy opinions,
And fill his belly with the east wind?
³ Should he argue with useless talk,
With words that are of no worth?
⁴ You subvert piety
And restrain prayer to God.
⁵ Your sinfulness dictates your speech,
So you choose crafty language.
⁶ Your own mouth condemns you—not I;
Your lips testify against you.

⁷ Were you the first man born?
Were you created before the hills?
⁸ Have you listened in on the council of God?
Have you sole possession of wisdom?
⁹ What do you know that we do not know,
Or understand that we do not?
¹⁰ Among us are gray-haired old men,
Older by far than your father.
¹¹ Are God's consolations not enough for you,
And His gentle words to you?
¹² How your heart has carried you away,
How your eyes ᵃ-have failed-ᵃ you,

ᵃ⁻ᵃ *Meaning of Heb. uncertain.*

¹³ That you could vent your anger on God,
And let such words out of your mouth!
¹⁴ What is man that he can be cleared of guilt,
One born of woman, that he be in the right?
¹⁵ He puts no trust in His holy ones;
The heavens are not guiltless in His sight;
¹⁶ What then of one loathsome and foul,
Man, who drinks wrongdoing like water!

¹⁷ I will hold forth; listen to me;
What I have seen, I will declare—
¹⁸ That which wise men have transmitted from their
   fathers,
And have not withheld,
¹⁹ To whom alone the land was given,
No stranger passing among them:
²⁰ The wicked man writhes in torment all his days;
Few years are reserved for the ruthless.
²¹ Frightening sounds fill his ears;
When he is at ease a robber falls upon him.
²² He is never sure he will come back from the dark;
A sword stares him in the face.
²³ He wanders about for bread—where is it?
He knows that the day of darkness has been readied
   for him.
²⁴ Troubles terrify him, anxiety overpowers him,
Like a king ᵃ⁻expecting a siege.⁻ᵃ
²⁵ For he has raised his arm against God
And played the hero against the Almighty.
²⁶ He runs at Him defiantlyᵇ
ᵃ⁻With his thickly bossed shield.
²⁷ His face is covered with fat
And his loins with blubber.⁻ᵃ
²⁸ He dwells in cities doomed to ruin,
In houses that shall not be lived in,
That are destined to become heaps of rubble.

ᵇ *Lit. "with neck."*

²⁹ He will not be rich;
His wealth will not endure;
ᵃ⁻His produce shall not bend to the earth.⁻ᵃ
³⁰ He will never get away from the darkness;
Flames will sear his shoots;
ᵃ⁻He will pass away by the breath of His mouth.
³¹ He will not be trusted;
He will be misled by falsehood,
And falsehood will be his recompense.⁻ᵃ
³² He will wither before his time,
His boughs never having flourished.
³³ He will drop his unripe grapes like a vine;
He will shed his blossoms like an olive tree.
³⁴ For the company of the impious is desolate;
Fire consumes the tents of the briber;
³⁵ For they have conceived mischief, given birth to evil,
And their womb has produced deceit.

16 Job said in reply:

² I have often heard such things;
You are all mischievous comforters.
³ Have windy words no limit?
What afflicts you that you speak on?
⁴ I would also talk like you
If you were in my place;
I would barrage you with words,
I would wag my head over you.
⁵ I would encourage you with words,ᵃ
My moving lips would bring relief.
⁶ If I speak, my pain will not be relieved,
And if I do not—what have I lost?
⁷ Now He has truly worn me out;
You have destroyed my whole community.
⁸ You have shriveled me;

ᵃ *Lit. "my mouth."*

My gauntness serves as a witness,
And testifies against me.
⁹ In His anger He tears and persecutes me;
He gnashes His teeth at me;
My foe stabs me with his eyes.
¹⁰ They open wide their mouths at me;
Reviling me, they strike my cheeks;
They inflame themselves against me.
¹¹ God hands me over to an evil man,
Thrusts me into the clutches of the wicked.
¹² I had been untroubled, and He broke me in pieces;
He took me by the scruff and shattered me;
He set me up as His target;
¹³ His bowmen surrounded me;
He pierced my kidneys; He showed no mercy;
He spilled my bile onto the ground.
¹⁴ He breached me, breach after breach;
He rushed at me like a warrior.
¹⁵ I sewed sackcloth over my skin;
I *b*-buried my glory-*b* in the dust.
¹⁶ My face is red with weeping;
Darkness covers my eyes
¹⁷ *c*-For no injustice on my part
And for the purity of my prayer!-*c*

¹⁸ Earth, do not cover my blood;
Let there be no resting place for my outcry!
¹⁹ Surely now my witness is in heaven;
He who can testify for me is on high.
²⁰ O my advocates, my fellows,
Before God my eyes shed tears;
²¹ Let Him arbitrate between a man and God
As between a man and his fellow.

b-b *Lit. "made my horn enter into."*
c-c *Or "Though I did no injustice,*
And my prayer was pure."

17

²² For a few more years will pass,
And I shall go the way of no return.
¹ My spirit is crushed, my days run out;
The graveyard waits for me.

² Surely mocking men keep me company,
And with their provocations I close my eyes.
³ Come now, stand surety for me!
Who will give his hand on my behalf?
⁴ You have hidden understanding from their minds;
Therefore You must not exalt [them].
⁵ He informs on his friends for a share [of their property],
And his children's eyes pine away.

⁶ He made me a byword among people;
I have become like Tophet^a of old.
⁷ My eyes fail from vexation;
All shapes seem to me like shadows.
⁸ The upright are amazed at this;
The pure are aroused against the impious.
⁹ The righteous man holds to his way;
He whose hands are clean grows stronger.
¹⁰ But all of you, come back now;
I shall not find a wise man among you.
¹¹ My days are done, my tendons severed,
The strings of my heart.
¹² They say that night is day,
That light is here—in the face of darkness.
¹³ If I must look forward to Sheol as my home,
And make my bed in the dark place,
¹⁴ Say to the Pit, "You are my father,"
To the maggots, "Mother," "Sister"—
¹⁵ Where, then, is my hope?
Who can see hope for me?
¹⁶ Will it descend to Sheol?
Shall we go down together to the dust?

^a *That consumed children; cf. Jer. 7.31.*

18 Then Bildad the Shuhite said in reply:

² How long? Put an end to talk!
Consider, and then we shall speak.
³ Why are we thought of as brutes,
Regarded by you as stupid?
⁴ You who tear yourself to pieces in anger—
Will ᵃ⁻earth's order be disrupted⁻ᵃ for your sake?
Will rocks be dislodged from their place?
⁵ Indeed, the light of the wicked fails;
The flame of his fire does not shine.
⁶ The light in his tent darkens;
His lamp fails him.
⁷ His iniquitous strides are hobbled;
His schemes overthrow him.
⁸ He is led by his feet into the net;
He walks onto the toils.
⁹ The trap seizes his heel;
The noose tightens on him.
¹⁰ The rope for him lies hidden on the ground;
His snare, on the path.
¹¹ Terrors assault him on all sides
And send his feet flying.
¹² His progeny hunger;
Disaster awaits his wife.ᵇ
¹³ The tendons under his skin are consumed;
Death's firstborn consumes his tendons.
¹⁴ He is torn from the safety of his tent;
Terror marches him to the king.ᶜ
¹⁵ It lodges in his desolate tent;
Sulfur is strewn upon his home.
¹⁶ His roots below dry up,
And above, his branches wither.

ᵃ⁻ᵃ Lit. "the earth be abandoned."
ᵇ Lit. "rib" (cf. Gen. 2.22); or "stumbling."
ᶜ Viz. of the netherworld.

¹⁷ All mention of him vanishes from the earth;
He has no name abroad.
¹⁸ He is thrust from light to darkness,
Driven from the world.
¹⁹ He has no seed or breed among his people,
No survivor where he once lived.
²⁰ Generations to come will be appalled at his fate,
As the previous ones are seized with horror.
²¹ "These were the haunts of the wicked;
Here was the place of him who knew not God."

19 Job said in reply:

² How long will you grieve my spirit,
And crush me with words?
³ ᵃ-Time and again-ᵃ you humiliate me,
And are not ashamed to abuse me.
⁴ If indeed I have erred,
My error remains with me.
⁵ Though you are overbearing toward me,
Reproaching me with my disgrace,
⁶ Yet know that God has wronged me;
He has thrown up siege works around me.
⁷ I cry, "Violence!" but am not answered;
I shout, but can get no justice.
⁸ He has barred my way; I cannot pass;
He has laid darkness upon my path.
⁹ He has stripped me of my glory,
Removed the crown from my head.
¹⁰ He tears down every part of me; I perish;
He uproots my hope like a tree.
¹¹ He kindles His anger against me;
He regards me as one of His foes.
¹² His troops advance together;

ᵃ⁻ᵃ Lit. "Ten times."

They build their road toward me
And encamp around my tent.
¹³ He alienated my kin from me;
My acquaintances disown me.
¹⁴ My relatives are gone;
My friends have forgotten me.
¹⁵ My dependents and maidservants regard me as a stranger;
I am an outsider to them.
¹⁶ I summon my servant but he does not respond;
I must myself entreat him.
¹⁷ My odor is repulsive to my wife;
I am loathsome to my children.
¹⁸ Even youngsters disdain me;
When I rise, they speak against me.
¹⁹ All my bosom friends detest me;
Those I love have turned against me.
²⁰ My bones stick to my skin and flesh;
I escape with the skin of my teeth.

²¹ Pity me, pity me! You are my friends;
For the hand of God has struck me!
²² Why do you pursue me like God,
ᵇ⁻Maligning me insatiably?⁻ᵇ
²³ O that my words were written down;
Would they were inscribed in a record,
²⁴ Incised on a rock forever
With iron stylus and lead!
²⁵ But I know that my Vindicator lives;
In the end He will testify on earth—
²⁶ This, after my skin will have been peeled off.
But I would behold God while still in my flesh,
²⁷ I myself, not another, would behold Him;
Would see with my own eyes:
My heartᶜ pines within me.

ᵇ⁻ᵇ *Lit. "You are not satisfied with my flesh."*
ᶜ *Lit. "kidneys."*

²⁸ You say, "How do we persecute him?
The root of the matter is in him."^d
²⁹ Be in fear of the sword,
For [your] fury is iniquity worthy of the sword;
Know there is a judgment!

20 Zophar the Naamathite said in reply:

² In truth, my thoughts urge me to answer
(It is because of my feelings
³ When I hear reproof that insults me);
A spirit out of my understanding makes me reply:
⁴ Do you not know this, that from time immemorial,
Since man was set on earth,
⁵ The joy of the wicked has been brief,
The happiness of the impious, fleeting?
⁶ Though he grows as high as the sky,
His head reaching the clouds,
⁷ He perishes forever, like his dung;
Those who saw him will say, "Where is he?"
⁸ He flies away like a dream and cannot be found;
He is banished like a night vision.
⁹ Eyes that glimpsed him do so no more;
They cannot see him in his place any longer.
¹⁰ His sons ingratiate themselves with the poor;
His own hands must give back his wealth.
¹¹ His bones, still full of vigor,
Lie down in the dust with him.
¹² Though evil is sweet to his taste,
And he conceals it under his tongue;
¹³ Though he saves it, does not let it go,
Holds it inside his mouth,
¹⁴ His food in his bowels turns
Into asps' venom within him.

^d *With many mss. and versions; printed editions, "me."*

¹⁵ The riches he swallows he vomits;
God empties it out of his stomach.
¹⁶ He sucks the poison of asps;
The tongue of the viper kills him.
¹⁷ Let him not enjoy the streams,
The rivers of honey, the brooks of cream.
¹⁸ He will give back the goods unswallowed;
The value of the riches, undigested.
¹⁹ Because he crushed and tortured the poor,
He will not build up the house he took by force.
²⁰ He will not see his children tranquil;
He will not preserve one of his dear ones.^a
²¹ With no survivor to enjoy it,
His fortune will not prosper.
²² When he has all he wants, trouble will come;
Misfortunes of all kinds will batter him.
²³ Let that fill his belly;
Let Him loose His burning anger at him,
And rain down His weapons upon him.
²⁴ Fleeing from iron arrows,
He is shot through from a bow of bronze.
²⁵ Brandished and run through his body,
The blade, through his gall,
Strikes terror into him.
²⁶ Utter darkness waits for his treasured ones;
A fire fanned by no man will consume him;
Who survives in his tent will be crushed.
²⁷ Heaven will expose his iniquity;
Earth will rise up against him.
²⁸ His household will be cast forth by a flood,
Spilled out on the day of His wrath.
²⁹ This is the wicked man's portion from God,
The lot God has ordained for him.

---

^a *For this meaning of* beṭen *and* ḥamud, *cf. Hos. 9.16.*

21 Job said in reply:

² Listen well to what I say,
And let that be your consolation.
³ Bear with me while I speak,
And after I have spoken, you may mock.
⁴ Is my complaint directed toward a man?
Why should I not lose my patience?
⁵ Look at me and be appalled,
And clap your hand to your mouth.
⁶ When I think of it I am terrified;
My body is seized with shuddering.

⁷ Why do the wicked live on,
Prosper and grow wealthy?
⁸ Their children are with them always,
And they see their children's children.
⁹ Their homes are secure, without fear;
They do not feel the rod of God.
¹⁰ Their bull breeds and does not fail;
Their cow calves and never miscarries;
¹¹ They let their infants run loose like sheep,
And their children skip about.
¹² They sing to the music of timbrel and lute,
And revel to the tune of the pipe;
¹³ They spend their days in happiness,
And go down to Sheol in peace.
¹⁴ They say to God, "Leave us alone,
We do not want to learn Your ways;
¹⁵ What is Shaddai that we should serve Him?
What will we gain by praying to Him?"
¹⁶ Their happiness is not their own doing.
(The thoughts of the wicked are beyond me!)

¹⁷ How seldom does the lamp of the wicked fail,
Does the calamity they deserve befall them,
Does He apportion [their] lot in anger!
¹⁸ Let them become like straw in the wind,
Like chaff carried off by a storm.
¹⁹ [You say,]"God is reserving his punishment for his
sons";
Let it be paid back to him that he may feel it,
²⁰ Let his eyes see his ruin,
And let him drink the wrath of Shaddai!
²¹ For what does he care about the fate of his family,
When his number of months runs out?
²² Can God be instructed in knowledge,
He who judges from such heights?
²³ One man dies in robust health,
All tranquil and untroubled;
²⁴ His pails are full of milk;
The marrow of his bones is juicy.
²⁵ Another dies embittered,
Never having tasted happiness.
²⁶ They both lie in the dust
And are covered with worms.

²⁷ Oh, I know your thoughts,
And the tactics you will devise against me.
²⁸ You will say, "Where is the house of the great man—
And where the tent in which the wicked dwelled?"
²⁹ You must have consulted the wayfarers;
You cannot deny their evidence.
³⁰ For the evil man is spared on the day of calamity,
On the day when wrath is led forth.
³¹ Who will upbraid him to his face?
Who will requite him for what he has done?
³² He is brought to the grave,
While a watch is kept at his tomb.

33 The clods of the wadi are sweet to him,
Everyone follows behind him,
Innumerable are those who precede him.
34 Why then do you offer me empty consolation?
Of your replies only the perfidy remains.

22 Eliphaz the Temanite said in reply:

2 Can a man be of use to God,
A wise man benefit Him?
3 Does Shaddai gain if you are righteous?
Does He profit if your conduct is blameless?
4 Is it because of your piety that He arraigns you,
And enters into judgment with you?
5 You know that your wickedness is great,
And that your iniquities have no limit.
6 You exact pledges from your fellows without reason,
And leave them naked, stripped of their clothes;
7 You do not give the thirsty water to drink;
You deny bread to the hungry.
8 The land belongs to the strong;
The privileged occupy it.
9 You have sent away widows empty-handed;
The strength of the fatherless is broken.
10 Therefore snares are all around you,
And sudden terrors frighten you,
11 Or darkness, so you cannot see;
A flood of waters covers you.

12 God is in the heavenly heights;
See the highest stars, how lofty!
13 You say, "What can God know?
Can He govern through the dense cloud?
14 The clouds screen Him so He cannot see

As He moves about the circuit of heaven."
¹⁵ Have you observed the immemorial path
That evil men have trodden;
¹⁶ How they were shriveled up before their time
And their foundation poured out like a river?
¹⁷ They said to God, "Leave us alone;
What can Shaddai do about it?"
¹⁸ But it was He who filled their houses with good things.
(The thoughts of the wicked are beyond me!)
¹⁹ The righteous, seeing it,ᵃ rejoiced;
The innocent laughed with scorn.
²⁰ Surely their substance was destroyed,
And their remnant consumed by fire.

²¹ Be close to Him and wholehearted;
Good things will come to you thereby.
²² Accept instruction from His mouth;
Lay up His words in your heart.
²³ If you return to Shaddai you will be restored,
If you banish iniquity from your tent;
²⁴ If you regard treasure as dirt,
Ophir-gold as stones of the wadi,
²⁵ And Shaddai be your treasure
And precious silver for you,
²⁶ When you seek the favor of Shaddai,
And lift up your face to God,
²⁷ You will pray to Him, and He will listen to you,
And you will pay your vows.
²⁸ You will decree and it will be fulfilled,
And light will shine upon your affairs.
²⁹ When others sink low, you will say it is pride;
For He saves the humble.
³⁰ He will deliver the guilty;
He will be delivered through the cleanness of your hands.

ᵃ *Referring to v. 16.*

23 Job said in reply:

2 Today again my complaint is bitter;
a-My strength is spent-*a* on account of my groaning.
3 Would that I knew how to reach Him,
How to get to His dwelling-place.
4 I would set out my case before Him
And fill my mouth with arguments.
5 I would learn what answers He had for me
And know how He would reply to me.
6 Would He contend with me overbearingly?
Surely He would not accuse me!
7 There the upright would be cleared by Him,
And I would escape forever from my judge.

8 But if I go East—He is not there;
West—I still do not perceive Him;
9 North—since He is concealed, I do not behold Him;
South—He is hidden, and I cannot see Him.
10 But He knows the way I take;
Would He assay me, I should emerge pure as gold.
11 I have followed in His tracks,
Kept His way without swerving,
12 I have not deviated from what His lips commanded;
I have treasured His words more than my daily bread.
13 He is one; who can dissuade Him?
Whatever He desires, He does.
14 For He will bring my term to an end,
But He has many more such at His disposal.
15 Therefore I am terrified at His presence;
When I consider, I dread Him.
16 God has made me fainthearted;
Shaddai has terrified me.

---

a-a *Lit. "My hand is heavy."*

¹⁷ Yet I am not cut off by the darkness;
He has concealed the thick gloom from me.

24 Why are times for judgment not reserved by Shaddai?
Even those close to Him cannot forsee His actions.^a
² People remove boundary-stones;
They carry off flocks and pasture them;
³ They lead away the donkeys of the fatherless,
And seize the widow's bull as a pledge;
⁴ They chase the needy off the roads;
All the poor of the land are forced into hiding.
⁵ Like the wild asses of the wilderness,
They go about their tasks, seeking food;
The wilderness provides each with food for his lads;
⁶ They harvest fodder in the field,
And glean the late grapes in the vineyards of the wicked.
⁷ They pass the night naked for lack of clothing,
They have no covering against the cold;
⁸ They are drenched by the mountain rains,
And huddle against the rock for lack of shelter.
⁹ ^bThey snatch the fatherless infant from the breast,
And seize the child of the poor as a pledge.
¹⁰ They go about naked for lack of clothing,
And, hungry, carry sheaves;
¹¹ Between rows [of olive trees] they make oil,
And, thirsty, they tread the winepresses.
¹² Men groan in the city;
The souls of the dying cry out;
Yet God does not regard it as a reproach.

¹³ They are rebels against the light;
They are strangers to its ways,
And do not stay in its path.
¹⁴ The murderer arises ^cin the evening^c

---

^a *Lit. "days."*
^b *This verse belongs to the description of the wicked in vv. 2–4a.*
^{c-c} *Cf. Mishnaic Heb. 'or, Aramaic 'orta, "evening"; others "with the light."*

To kill the poor and needy,
And at night he acts the thief.
15 The eyes of the adulterer watch for twilight,
Thinking, "No one will glimpse me then."
He masks his face.
16 In the dark they break into houses;
By day they shut themselves in;
They do not know the light.
17 For all of them morning is darkness;
It is then that they discern the terror of darkness.
18 d May they be flotsam on the face of the water;
May their portion in the land be cursed;
May none turn aside by way of their vineyards.
19 May drought and heat snatch away their snow waters,
And Sheol, those who have sinned.
20 May the womb forget him;
May he be sweet to the worms;
May he be no longer remembered;
May wrongdoers be broken like a tree.
21 May he consort with a barren woman who bears no
child,
Leave his widow deprived of good.
22 Though he has the strength to seize bulls,
May he live with no assurance of survival.
23 Yet [God] gives him the security on which he relies,
And keeps watch over his affairs.
24 Exalted for a while, let them be gone;
Be brought low, and shrivel like mallows,
And wither like the heads of grain.

25 Surely no one can confute me,
Or prove that I am wrong.

---

d From here to the end of the chapter the translation is largely conjectural.

25 Bildad the Shuhite said in reply:

² Dominion and dread are His;
He imposes peace in His heights.
³ Can His troops be numbered?
On whom does His light not shine?
⁴ How can man be in the right before God?
How can one born of woman be cleared of guilt?
⁵ Even the moon is not bright,
And the stars are not pure in His sight.
⁶ How much less man, a worm,
The son-of-man, a maggot.

26 Then Job said in reply:

² You would help without having the strength;
You would deliver with arms that have no power.
³ Without having the wisdom, you offer advice
And freely give your counsel.
⁴ To whom have you addressed words?
Whose breath issued from you?

⁵ The shades tremble
Beneath the waters and their denizens.
⁶ Sheol is naked before Him;
Abaddon has no cover.
⁷ He it is who stretched out Zaphon*ᵃ* over chaos,
Who suspended earth over emptiness.
⁸ He wrapped up the waters in His clouds;
Yet no cloud burst under their weight.
⁹ *ᵇ*He shuts off the view of His throne,
Spreading His cloud over it.*-ᵇ*

ᵃ *Used for heaven; cf. Isa. 14.13 and Ps. 48.3.*
ᵇ⁻ᵇ *Meaning of Heb. uncertain.*

10 He drew a boundary on the surface of the waters,
At the extreme where light and darkness meet.
11 The pillars of heaven tremble,
Astounded at His blast.
12 By His power He stilled the sea;
By His skill He struck down Rahab.
13 By His wind the heavens were calmed;
His hand pierced the *c*-Elusive Serpent.-*c*
14 These are but glimpses of His rule,
The mere whisper that we perceive of Him;
Who can absorb the thunder of His mighty deeds?

27 Job again took up his theme and said:

2 By God who has deprived me of justice!
By Shaddai who has embittered my life!
3 As long as there is life in me,
And God's breath is in my nostrils,
4 My lips will speak no wrong,
Nor my tongue utter deceit.
5 Far be it from me to say you are right;
Until I die I will maintain my integrity.
6 I persist in my righteousness and will not yield;
a-I shall be free of reproach-*a* as long as I live.

7 May my enemy be as the wicked;
My assailant, as the wrongdoer.
8 For what hope has the impious man when he is cut down,
When God takes away his life?
9 Will God hear his cry
When trouble comes upon him,
10 When he seeks the favor of Shaddai,
Calls upon God at all times?
11 I will teach you what is in God's power,

c-c Cf. Isa. 27.1.
a-a Meaning of Heb. uncertain.

And what is with Shaddai I will not conceal.
¹² All of you have seen it,
So why talk nonsense?
¹³ This is the evil man's portion from God,
The lot that the ruthless receive from Shaddai:
¹⁴ Should he have many sons—they are marked for the
sword;
His descendants will never have their fill of bread;
¹⁵ Those who survive him will be buried in a plague,
And their widows will not weep;
¹⁶ Should he pile up silver like dust,
Lay up clothing like dirt—
¹⁷ He may lay it up, but the righteous will wear it,
And the innocent will share the silver.
¹⁸ The house he built is like a bird's nest,
Like the booth a watchman makes.
¹⁹ He lies down, a rich man, with [his wealth] intact;
When he opens his eyes it is gone.
²⁰ Terror overtakes him like a flood;
A storm wind makes off with him by night.
²¹ The east wind carries him far away, and he is gone;
It sweeps him from his place.
²² Then it hurls itself at him without mercy;
He tries to escape from its force.
²³ It claps its hands at him,
And whistles at him from its place.

28 There is a mine for silver,
And a place where gold is refined.
² Iron is taken out of the earth,
And copper smelted from rock.
³ He sets bounds for darkness;
To every limit man probes,
To rocks in deepest darkness.

4 *a*-They open up a shaft far from where men live,
[In places] forgotten by wayfarers,
Destitute of men, far removed.*-a*
5 Earth, out of which food grows,
Is changed below as if into fire.
6 Its rocks are a source of sapphires;
It contains gold dust too.
7 No bird of prey knows the path to it;
The falcon's eye has not gazed upon it.
8 The proud beasts have not reached it;
The lion has not crossed it.
9 Man sets his hand against the flinty rock
And overturns mountains by the roots.
10 He carves out channels through rock;
His eyes behold every precious thing.
11 He dams up the sources of the streams
So that hidden things may be brought to light.

12 But where can wisdom be found;
Where is the source of understanding?
13 No man can set a value on it;
It cannot be found in the land of the living.
14 The deep says, "It is not in me";
The sea says, "I do not have it."
15 It cannot be bartered for gold;
Silver cannot be paid out as its price.
16 The finest gold of Ophir cannot be weighed against it,
Nor precious onyx, nor sapphire.
17 Gold or glass cannot match its value,
Nor vessels of fine gold be exchanged for it.
18 Coral and crystal cannot be mentioned with it;
A pouch of wisdom is better than rubies.
19 Topaz from Nubia cannot match its value;
Pure gold cannot be weighed against it.

---

a-a *Meaning of Heb. uncertain.*

²⁰ But whence does wisdom come?
Where is the source of understanding?
²¹ It is hidden from the eyes of all living,
Concealed from the fowl of heaven.
²² Abaddon and Death say,
"We have only a report of it."
²³ God understands the way to it;
He knows its source;
²⁴ For He sees to the ends of the earth,
Observes all that is beneath the heavens.
²⁵ When He fixed the weight of the winds,
Set the measure of the waters;
²⁶ When He made a rule for the rain
And a course for the thunderstorms,
²⁷ Then He saw it and gauged it;
He measured it and probed it.
²⁸ He said to man,
"See! Fear of the Lord is wisdom;
To shun evil is understanding."

29 Job again took up his theme and said:

² O that I were as in months gone by,
In the days when God watched over me,
³ When His lamp shone over my head,
When I walked in the dark by its light,
⁴ When I was in my prime,
When God's company graced my tent,
⁵ When Shaddai was still with me,
When my lads surrounded me,
⁶ When my feet were bathed in cream,
And rocks poured out streams of oil for me.
⁷ When I passed through the city gates
To take my seat in the square,

⁸ Young men saw me and hid,
Elders rose and stood;
⁹ Nobles held back their words;
They clapped their hands to their mouths.
¹⁰ The voices of princes were hushed;
Their tongues stuck to their palates.
¹¹ The ear that heard me acclaimed me;
The eye that saw, commended me.
¹² For I saved the poor man who cried out,
The orphan who had none to help him.
¹³ I received the blessing of the lost;
I gladdened the heart of the widow.
¹⁴ I clothed myself in righteousness and it robed me;
Justice was my cloak and turban.
¹⁵ I was eyes to the blind
And feet to the lame.
¹⁶ I was a father to the needy,
And I looked into the case of the stranger.
¹⁷ I broke the jaws of the wrongdoer,
And I wrested prey from his teeth.
¹⁸ I thought I would end my days with my family,ᵃ
And ᵇ-be as long-lived as the phoenix,-ᵇ
¹⁹ My roots reaching water,
And dew lying on my branches;
²⁰ My vigor refreshed,
My bow ever new in my hand.
²¹ Men would listen to me expectantly,
And wait for my counsel.
²² After I spoke they had nothing to say;
My words were as drops [of dew] upon them.
²³ They waited for me as for rain,
For the late rain, their mouths open wide.
²⁴ When I smiled at them, they would not believe it;
They never expectedᶜ a sign of my favor.
²⁵ I decided their course and presided over them;

ᵃ Lit. "nest."
ᵇ⁻ᵇ Others "multiply days like sand."
ᶜ Taking yappilun as from pll; cf. Gen. 48.11.

I lived like a king among his troops,
Like one who consoles mourners.

30 But now those younger than I deride me,
[Men] whose fathers I would have disdained to put among
my sheep dogs.
² Of what use to me is the strength of their hands?
All their vigor*a* is gone.
³ Wasted from want and starvation,
They flee to a parched land,
To the gloom of desolate wasteland.
⁴ They pluck saltwort and wormwood;
The roots of broom are their food.
⁵ Driven out *a*-from society,-*a*
They are cried at like a thief.
⁶ They live in the gullies of wadis,
In holes in the ground, and in rocks,
⁷ Braying among the bushes,
Huddling among the nettles,
⁸ Scoundrels, nobodies,
Stricken from the earth.

⁹ Now I am the butt of their gibes;
I have become a byword to them.
¹⁰ They abhor me; they keep their distance from me;
They do not withhold spittle from my face.
¹¹ Because God*b* has disarmed*c* and humbled me,
They have thrown off restraint in my presence.
¹² Mere striplings assail me at my right hand:
They put me to flight;
They build their roads for my ruin.
¹³ They tear up my path;
They promote my fall,
Although it does them no good.

a-a Meaning of Heb. uncertain.
b Lit. "He."
c Lit. "loosened my [bow] string."

¹⁴ They come as through a wide breach;
They roll in *ᵃ*like raging billows.⁻ᵃ
¹⁵ Terror tumbles upon me;
It sweeps away my honor like the wind;
My dignity*ᵈ* vanishes like a cloud.
¹⁶ So now my life runs out;
Days of misery have taken hold of me.
¹⁷ By night my bones feel gnawed;
My sinews never rest.
¹⁸ *ᵃ*With great effort I change clothing;
The neck of my tunic fits my waist.⁻ᵃ
¹⁹ He regarded me as clay,
I have become like dust and ashes.

²⁰ I cry out to You, but You do not answer me;
I wait, but You do [not] consider me.
²¹ You have become cruel to me;
With Your powerful hand You harass me.
²² You lift me up and mount me on the wind;
You make my courage melt.
²³ I know You will bring me to death,
The house assigned for all the living.
²⁴ *ᵃ*Surely He would not strike at a ruin
If, in calamity, one cried out to Him.⁻ᵃ
²⁵ Did I not weep for the unfortunate?
Did I not grieve for the needy?
²⁶ I looked forward to good fortune, but evil came;
I hoped for light, but darkness came.
²⁷ My bowels are in turmoil without respite;
Days of misery confront me.
²⁸ I walk about in sunless gloom;
I rise in the assembly and cry out.
²⁹ I have become a brother to jackals,
A companion to ostriches.
³⁰ My skin, blackened, is peeling off me;

ᵈ *Heb.* yeshu'athi *taken as related to* shoa', *"noble."*

My bones are charred by the heat.
31 So my lyre is given over to mourning,
My pipe, to accompany weepers.

31   I have covenanted with my eyes
Not to gaze on a maiden.
2 What fate is decreed by God above?
What lot, by Shaddai in the heights?
3 Calamity is surely for the iniquitous;
Misfortune, for the worker of mischief.
4 Surely He observes my ways,
Takes account of my every step.

5 Have I walked with worthless men,
Or my feet hurried to deceit?
6 Let Him weigh me on the scale of righteousness;
Let God ascertain my integrity.
7 If my feet have strayed from their course,
My heart followed after my eyes,
And a stain sullied my hands,
8 May I sow, but another reap,
May the growth of my field be uprooted!
9 If my heart was ravished by the wife of my neighbor,
And I lay in wait at his door,
10 May my wife grind for another,
May others kneel over her!
11 For that would have been debauchery,
A criminal offense,
12 A fire burning down to Abaddon,
Consuming the roots of all my increase.
13 Did I ever brush aside the case of my servants, man
   or maid,
When they made a complaint against me?
14 What then should I do when God arises;

When He calls me to account, what should I answer Him?
¹⁵ Did not He who made me in my mother's belly make
him?
Did not One form us both in the womb?
¹⁶ Did I deny the poor their needs,
Or let a*ª* widow pine away,
¹⁷ By eating my food alone,
The fatherless not eating of it also?
¹⁸ Why, from my youth he grew up with me as though I
were his father;
Since I left my mother's womb I was her*ᵇ* guide.
¹⁹ I never saw an unclad wretch,
A needy man without clothing,
²⁰ Whose loins did not bless me
As he warmed himself with the shearings of my sheep.
²¹ If I raised my hand against the fatherless,
Looking to my supporters in the gate,
²² May my arm drop off my shoulder;
My forearm break off *ᶜ*at the elbow.*ᶜ*
²³ For I am in dread of God-sent calamity,
I cannot bear His threat.
²⁴ Did I put my reliance on gold,
Or regard fine gold as my bulwark?
²⁵ Did I rejoice in my great wealth,
In having attained plenty?
²⁶ If ever I saw the light shining,
The moon on its course in full glory,
²⁷ And I secretly succumbed,
And my hand touched my mouth in a kiss,
²⁸ That, too, would have been a criminal offense,
For I would have denied God above.
²⁹ Did I rejoice over my enemy's misfortune?
Did I thrill because evil befell him?
³⁰ I never let my mouth*ᵈ* sin
By wishing his death in a curse.

ª Lit. "the eyes of a."
ᵇ Viz. the widow's.
ᶜ⁻ᶜ Lit. "from its shaft," i.e. the humerus.
ᵈ Lit. "palate."

³¹ (Indeed, the men of my clan said,
"We would consume his flesh insatiably!")
³² No sojourner spent the night in the open;
I opened my doors to the road.
³³ Did I hide my transgressions like Adam,
Bury my wrongdoing in my bosom,
³⁴ That I should [now] fear the great multitude,
And am shattered by the contempt of families,
So that I keep silent and do not step outdoors?

³⁵ O that I had someone to give me a hearing;
O that Shaddai would reply to my writ,
Or my accuser draw up a true bill!
³⁶ I would carry it on my shoulder;
Tie it around me for a wreath.
³⁷ I would give him an account of my steps,
Offer it as to a commander.

³⁸ If my land cries out against me,
Its furrows weep together;
³⁹ If I have eaten its produce without payment,
And made its [rightful] owners despair,
⁴⁰ May nettles grow there instead of wheat;
Instead of barley, stinkweed!

The words of Job are at an end.

32 These three men ceased replying to Job, for he considered himself right. ² Then Elihu son of Barachel the Buzite, of the family of Ram, was angry—angry at Job because he thought himself right against God. ³ He was angry as well at his three friends, because they found no reply, but merely condemned Job. ⁴ Elihu waited out Job's speech, for they were all older than he. ⁵ But

when Elihu saw that the three men had nothing to reply, he was
angry.

⁶ Then Elihu son of Barachel the Buzite said in reply:

> I have but few years, while you are old;
> Therefore I was too awestruck and fearful
> To hold forth among you.
> ⁷ I thought, "Let age speak;
> Let advanced years declare wise things."
> ⁸ But truly it is the spirit in men,
> The breath of Shaddai, that gives them understanding.
> ⁹ It is not the aged who are wise,
> The elders, who understand how to judge.
> ¹⁰ Therefore I say, "Listen to me;
> I too would hold forth."
> ¹¹ Here I have waited out your speeches,
> I have given ear to your insights,
> While you probed the issues;
> ¹² But as I attended to you,
> I saw that none of you could argue with Job,
> Or offer replies to his statements.
> ¹³ I fear you will say, "We have found the wise course;
> God will defeat him, not man."
> ¹⁴ He did not set out his case against me,
> Nor shall I use your reasons to reply to him.
> ¹⁵ They have been broken and can no longer reply;
> Words fail them.
> ¹⁶ I have waited till they stopped speaking,
> Till they ended and no longer replied.
> ¹⁷ Now I also would have my say;
> I too would like to hold forth,
> ¹⁸ For I am full of words;
> The wind in my belly presses me.
> ¹⁹ My belly is like wine not yet opened,

Like jugs of new wine ready to burst.
²⁰ Let me speak, then, and get relief;
Let me open my lips and reply.
²¹ I would not show regard for any man,
Or temper my speech for anyone's sake;
²² For I do not know how to temper my speech—
My Maker would soon carry me off!

33 But now, Job, listen to my words,
Give ear to all that I say.
² Now I open my lips;
My tongue forms words in my mouth.
³ My words bespeak the uprightness of my heart;
My lips utter insight honestly.
⁴ The spirit of God formed me;
The breath of Shaddai sustains me.
⁵ If you can, answer me;
Argue against me, take your stand.
⁶ You and I are the same before God;
I too was nipped from clay.
⁷ You are not overwhelmed by fear of me;
My pressure does not weigh heavily on you.

⁸ Indeed, you have stated in my hearing,
I heard the words spoken,
⁹ "I am guiltless, free from transgression;
I am innocent, without iniquity.
¹⁰ But He finds reasons to oppose me,
Considers me His enemy.
¹¹ He puts my feet in stocks,
Watches all my ways."

¹² In this you are not right;
I will answer you: God is greater than any man.

¹³ Why do you complain against Him
That He does not reply to any of man's charges?
¹⁴ For God speaks ^atime and again^{-a}
—Though man does not perceive it—
¹⁵ In a dream, a night vision,
When deep sleep falls on men,
While they slumber on their beds.
¹⁶ Then He opens men's understanding,
And by disciplining them leaves His signature
¹⁷ To turn man away from an action,
To suppress pride in man.
¹⁸ He spares him from the Pit,
His person, from perishing by the sword.
¹⁹ He is reproved by pains on his bed,
And the trembling in his bones is constant.
²⁰ He detests food;
Fine food [is repulsive] to him.
²¹ His flesh wastes away till it cannot be seen,
And his bones are rubbed away till they are invisible.
²² He comes close to the Pit,
His life [verges] on death.
²³ If he has a representative,
One advocate against a thousand
To declare the man's uprightness,
²⁴ Then He has mercy on him and decrees,
"Redeem him from descending to the Pit,
For I have obtained his ransom;
²⁵ Let his flesh be healthier^b than in his youth;
Let him return to his younger days."
²⁶ He prays to God and is accepted by Him;
He enters His presence with shouts of joy,
For He requites a man for his righteousness.
²⁷ He^c declares^b to men,
"I have sinned; I have perverted what was right;
But I was not paid back for it."

^{a-a} Lit. "once . . . twice."
^b Meaning of Heb. uncertain.
^c I.e. the contrite man.

²⁸ He redeemed ᵈ⁻him from passing into the Pit;
He⁻ᵈ will enjoy the light.
²⁹ Truly, God does all these things
Two or three times to a man,
³⁰ To bring him back from the Pit,
That he may bask in the light of life.

³¹ Pay heed, Job, and hear me;
Be still, and I will speak;
³² If you have what to say, answer me;
Speak, for I am eager to vindicate you.
³³ But if not, you listen to me;
Be still, and I will teach you wisdom.

34 Elihu said in reply:

² Listen, O wise men, to my words;
You who have knowledge, give ear to me.
³ For the ear tests arguments
As the palate tastes food.
⁴ Let us decide for ourselves what is just;
Let us know among ourselves what is good.
⁵ For Job has said, "I am right;
God has deprived me of justice.
⁶ I declare the judgment against me false;
My arrow-wound is deadly, though I am free from trans-
    gression."
⁷ What man is like Job,
Who drinks mockery like water;
⁸ Who makes common cause with evildoers,
And goes with wicked men?
⁹ For he says, "Man gains nothing
When he is in God's favor."

ᵈ⁻ᵈ *Or, with* kethib, *"me . . . I."*

¹⁰ Therefore, men of understanding, listen to me;
Wickedness be far from God,
Wrongdoing, from Shaddai!
¹¹ For He pays a man according to his actions,
And provides for him according to his conduct;
¹² For God surely does not act wickedly;
Shaddai does not pervert justice.
¹³ Who placed the earth in His charge?
Who ordered the entire world?
¹⁴ If He but intends it,
He can call back His spirit and breath;
¹⁵ All flesh would at once expire,
And mankind return to dust.

¹⁶ If you would understand, listen to this;
Give ear to what I say.
¹⁷ Would one who hates justice govern?
Would you condemn the Just Mighty One?
¹⁸ Would you call a king a scoundrel,
Great men, wicked?
¹⁹ He is not partial to princes;
The noble are not preferred to the wretched;
For all of them are the work of His hands.
²⁰ Some die suddenly in the middle of the night;
People are in turmoil and pass on;
Even great men are removed—not by human hands.
²¹ For His eyes are upon a man's ways;
He observes his every step.
²² Neither darkness nor gloom offer
A hiding-place for evildoers.
²³ He has no set time for man
To appear before God in judgment.
²⁴ He shatters mighty men without number
And sets others in their place.
²⁵ Truly, He knows their deeds;

Night is over, and they are crushed.
²⁶ He strikes them down with the wicked
Where people can see,
²⁷ Because they have been disloyal to Him
And have not understood any of His ways;
²⁸ Thus He lets the cry of the poor come before Him;
He listens to the cry of the needy.
²⁹ When He is silent, who will condemn?
If He hides His face, who will see Him,
Be it nation or man?
³⁰ The impious men rule no more,
Nor do those who ensnare the people.
³¹ Has he said to God,
"I will bear [my punishment] and offend no more.
³² What I cannot see You teach me.
If I have done iniquity, I shall not do so again"?
³³ Should He requite as you see fit?
But you have despised [Him]!
You must decide, not I;
Speak what you know.
³⁴ Men of understanding say to me,
Wise men who hear me,
³⁵ "Job does not speak with knowledge;
His words lack understanding."
³⁶ Would that Job were tried to the limit
For answers which befit sinful men.
³⁷ He adds to his sin;
He increases his transgression among us;
He multiplies his statements against God.

35 Elihu said in reply:

² Do you think it just
To say, "I am right against God"?

³ If you ask how it benefits you,
"What have I gained from not sinning?"
⁴ I shall give you a reply,
You, along with your friends.
⁵ Behold the heavens and see;
Look at the skies high above you.
⁶ If you sin, what do you do to Him?
If your transgressions are many,
How do you affect Him?
⁷ If you are righteous,
What do you give Him;
What does He receive from your hand?
⁸ Your wickedness affects men like yourself;
Your righteousness, mortals.

⁹ Because of contention the oppressed cry out;
They shout because of the power of the great.
¹⁰ But none says, "Where is my God, my Maker,
Who gives strength in the night;
¹¹ Who gives us more knowledge than the beasts of
   the earth,
Makes us wiser than the birds of the sky?"
¹² Then they cry out, but He does not respond
Because of the arrogance of evil men.
¹³ Surely it is false that God does not listen,
That Shaddai does not take note of it.
¹⁴ Though you say, "You do not take note of it,"
The case is before Him;
So wait for Him.
¹⁵ ᵃ⁻But since now it does not seem so,
He vents his anger;
He does not realize that it may be long drawn out.⁻ᵃ
¹⁶ Hence Job mouths empty words,
And piles up words without knowledge.

ᵃ⁻ᵃ *Meaning of Heb. uncertain.*

36 Then Elihu spoke once more.

² Wait a little and let me hold forth;
There is still more to say for God.
³ I will make my opinions widely known;
I will justify my Maker.
⁴ In truth, my words are not false;
A man of sound opinions is before you.

⁵ See, God is mighty; He is not contemptuous;
He is mighty in strength and mind.
⁶ He does not let the wicked live;
He grants justice to the lowly.
⁷ He does not withdraw His eyes from the righteous;
With kings on thrones
He seats them forever, and they are exalted.
⁸ If they are bound in shackles
And caught in trammels of affliction,
⁹ He declares to them what they have done,
And that their transgressions are excessive;
¹⁰ He opens their understanding by discipline,
And orders them back from mischief.
¹¹ If they will serve obediently,
They shall spend their days in happiness,
Their years in delight.
¹² But if they are not obedient,
They shall perish by the sword,
Die for lack of understanding.
¹³ But the impious in heart become enraged;
They do not cry for help when He afflicts them.
¹⁴ They die in their youth;
[Expire] among the depraved.
¹⁵ He rescues the lowly from their affliction,

And opens their understanding through distress.
¹⁶ Indeed, He draws you away from the brink of distress
To a broad place where there is no constraint;
Your table is laid out with rich food.
¹⁷ You are obsessed with the case of the wicked man,
But the justice of the case will be upheld.
¹⁸ Let anger at his affluence not mislead you;
Let much bribery not turn you aside.
¹⁹ ^a-Will your limitless wealth avail you,-^a
All your powerful efforts?
²⁰ Do not long for the night
When peoples vanish where they are.
²¹ Beware! Do not turn to mischief;
Because of that you have been tried by affliction.
²² See, God is beyond reach in His power;
Who governs like Him?
²³ Who ever reproached Him for His conduct?
Who ever said, "You have done wrong"?
²⁴ Remember, then, to magnify His work,
Of which men have sung,
²⁵ Which all men have beheld,
Men have seen, from a distance.
²⁶ See, God is greater than we can know;
The number of His years cannot be counted.
²⁷ He forms the droplets of water,
Which cluster into rain, from His mist.
²⁸ The skies rain;
They pour down on all mankind.
²⁹ Can one, indeed, contemplate the expanse of clouds,
The thunderings from His pavilion?
³⁰ See, He spreads His lightning over it;
It fills the bed of the sea.
³¹ By these things He controls peoples;
He gives food in abundance.
³² Lightning fills His hands;

^{a-a} *Meaning of Heb. uncertain.*

He orders it to hit the mark.
³³ Its noise tells of Him.
ᵃ⁻The kindling of anger against iniquity.⁻ᵃ

37 Because of this, too, my heart quakes,
And leaps from its place.
² Just listen to the noise of His rumbling,
To the sound that comes out of His mouth.
³ He lets it loose beneath the entire heavens—
His lightning, to the ends of the earth.
⁴ After it, He lets out a roar;
He thunders in His majestic voice.
No one can find a trace of it by the time His voice is heard.
⁵ God thunders marvelously with His voice;
He works wonders that we cannot understand.
⁶ He commands the snow, "Fall to the ground!"
And the downpour of rain, His mighty downpour of rain,
⁷ Is as a sign on every man's hand,
That all men may know His doings.
⁸ Then the beast enters its lair,
And remains in its den.
⁹ The storm wind comes from its chamber,
And the cold from the constellations.
¹⁰ By the breath of God ice is formed,
And the expanse of water becomes solid.
¹¹ He also loads the clouds with moisture
And scatters His lightning-clouds.
¹² ᵃ⁻He keeps turning events by His stratagems,⁻ᵃ
That they might accomplish all that He commands them
Throughout the inhabited earth,
¹³ Causing each of them to happen to His land,
Whether as a scourge or as a blessing.

¹⁴ Give ear to this, Job;
Stop to consider the marvels of God.

ᵃ⁻ᵃ *Meaning of Heb. uncertain.*

¹⁵ Do you know what charge God lays upon them
When His lightning-clouds shine?
¹⁶ Do you know the marvels worked upon the expanse of
clouds
By Him whose understanding is perfect,
¹⁷ ᵃ-Why your clothes become hot⁻ᵃ
When the land is becalmed by the south wind?
¹⁸ Can you help him stretch out the heavens,
Firm as a mirror of cast metal?
¹⁹ Inform us, then, what we may say to Him;
We cannot argue because [we are in] darkness.
²⁰ Is anything conveyed to Him when I speak?
Can a man say anything when he is confused?
²¹ Now, then, one cannot see the sun,
Though it be bright in the heavens,
Until the wind comes and clears them [of clouds].
²² By the north wind the golden rays emerge;
The splendor about God is awesome.
²³ Shaddai—we cannot attain to Him;
He is great in power and justice
And abundant in righteousness; He does not torment.
²⁴ Therefore, men are in awe of Him
Whom none of the wise can perceive.

38

Then the LORD replied to Job out of the tempest and said:

² Who is this who darkens counsel,
Speaking without knowledge?
³ Gird your loins like a man;
I will ask and you will inform Me.

⁴ Where were you when I laid the earth's foundations?
Speak if you have understanding.
⁵ Do you know who fixed its dimensions
Or who measured it with a line?

⁶ Onto what were its bases sunk?
Who set its cornerstone
⁷ When the morning stars sang together
And all the divine beings shouted for joy?

⁸ Who closed the sea behind doors
When it gushed forth out of the womb,
⁹ When I clothed it in clouds,
Swaddled it in dense clouds,
¹⁰ When I made breakers My limit for it,
And set up its bar and doors,
¹¹ And said, "You may come so far and no farther;
Here your surging waves will stop"?

¹² Have you ever commanded the day to break,
Assigned the dawn its place,
¹³ So that it seizes the corners of the earth
And shakes the wicked out of it?
¹⁴ It changes like clay under the seal
Till [its hues] are fixed like those of a garment.
¹⁵ Their light is withheld from the wicked,
And the upraised arm is broken.

¹⁶ Have you penetrated to the sources of the sea,
Or walked in the recesses of the deep?
¹⁷ Have the gates of death been disclosed to you?
Have you seen the gates of deep darkness?
¹⁸ Have you surveyed the expanses of the earth?
If you know of these—tell Me.

¹⁹ Which path leads to where light dwells,
And where is the place of darkness,
²⁰ That you may take it to its domain
And know the way to its home?

²¹ Surely you know, for you were born then,
And the number of your years is many!

²² Have you penetrated the vaults of snow,
Seen the vaults of hail,
²³ Which I have put aside for a time of adversity,
For a day of war and battle?
²⁴ By what path is the west wind^a dispersed,
The east wind scattered over the earth?
²⁵ Who cut a channel for the torrents
And a path for the thunderstorms,
²⁶ To rain down on uninhabited land,
On the wilderness where no man is,
²⁷ To saturate the desolate wasteland,
And make the crop of grass sprout forth?
²⁸ Does the rain have a father?
Who begot the dewdrops?
²⁹ From whose belly came forth the ice?
Who gave birth to the frost of heaven?
³⁰ Water congeals like stone,
And the surface of the deep compacts.

³¹ Can you tie cords to Pleiades
Or undo the reins of Orion?
³² Can you lead out Mazzaroth^b in its season,
Conduct the Bear with her sons?
³³ Do you know the laws of heaven
Or impose its authority on earth?

³⁴ Can you send up an order to the clouds
For an abundance of water to cover you?
³⁵ Can you dispatch the lightning on a mission
And have it answer you, "I am ready"?
³⁶ Who put wisdom in the hidden parts?

^a *As Aramaic* 'urya.
^b *Evidently a constellation.*

Who gave understanding to the mind?[c]
[37] Who is wise enough to give an account of the heavens?
Who can tilt the bottles of the sky,
[38] Whereupon the earth melts into a mass,
And its clods stick together.

[39] Can you hunt prey for the lion,
And satisfy the appetite of the king of beasts?
[40] They crouch in their dens,
Lie in ambush in their lairs.
[41] Who provides food for the raven
When his young cry out to God
And wander about without food?

39 Do you know the season when the mountain goats give
  birth?
Can you mark the time when the hinds calve?
[2] Can you count the months they must complete?
Do you know the season they give birth,
[3] When they couch to bring forth their offspring,
To deliver their young?
[4] Their young are healthy; they grow up in the open;
They leave and return no more.

[5] Who sets the wild ass free?
Who loosens the bonds of the onager,
[6] Whose home I have made the wilderness,
The salt land his dwelling-place?
[7] He scoffs at the tumult of the city,
Does not hear the shouts of the driver.
[8] He roams the hills for his pasture;
He searches for any green thing.

---

[c] *Or "rooster"; meaning of Heb. uncertain.*

⁹ Would the wild ox agree to serve you?
Would he spend the night at your crib?
¹⁰ Can you hold the wild ox by ropes to the furrow?
Would he plow up the valleys behind you?
¹¹ Would you rely on his great strength
And leave your toil to him?
¹² Would you trust him to bring in the seed
And gather it in from your threshing floor?

¹³ The wing of the ostrich beats joyously;
Are her pinions and plumage like the stork's?
¹⁴ She leaves her eggs on the ground,
Letting them warm in the dirt,
¹⁵ Forgetting they may be crushed underfoot,
Or trampled by a wild beast.
¹⁶ Her young are cruelly abandoned as if they were not
   hers;
Her labor is in vain for lack of concern.
¹⁷ For God deprived her of wisdom,
Gave her no share of understanding,
¹⁸ Else she would soar on high,
Scoffing at the horse and its rider.

¹⁹ Do you give the horse his strength?
Do you clothe his neck with a mane?
²⁰ Do you make him quiver like locusts,
His majestic snorting [spreading] terror?
²¹ He[a] paws with force, he runs with vigor,
Charging into battle.
²² He scoffs at fear; he cannot be frightened;
He does not recoil from the sword.
²³ A quiverful of arrows whizzes by him,
And the flashing spear and the javelin.
²⁴ Trembling with excitement, he swallows[b] the land;
He does not turn aside at the blast of the trumpet.

---

[a] *Lit. "They . . ."*
[b] *Or "digs up."*

²⁵ As the trumpet sounds, he says, "Aha!"
From afar he smells the battle,
The roaring and shouting of the officers.

²⁶ Is it by your wisdom that the hawk grows pinions,
Spreads his wings to the south?
²⁷ Does the eagle soar at your command,
Building his nest high,
²⁸ Dwelling in the rock,
Lodging upon the fastness of a jutting rock?
²⁹ From there he spies out his food;
From afar his eyes see it.
³⁰ His young gulp blood;
Where the slain are, there is he.

40

The LORD said in reply to Job.

² ^{a-}Shall one who should be disciplined complain against
Shaddai?^{-a}
He who arraigns God must respond.

³ Job said in reply to the LORD:

⁴ See, I am of small worth; what can I answer You?
I clap my hand to my mouth.
⁵ I have spoken once, and will not reply;
Twice, and will do so no more.

⁶ Then the LORD replied to Job out of the tempest
and said:

⁷ Gird your loins like a man;
I will ask, and you will inform Me.
⁸ Would you impugn My justice?

^{a-a} Meaning of Heb. uncertain.

Would you condemn Me that you may be right?
9 Have you an arm like God's?
Can you thunder with a voice like His?
10 Deck yourself now with grandeur and eminence;
Clothe yourself in glory and majesty.
11 Scatter wide your raging anger;
See every proud man and bring him low.
12 See every proud man and humble him,
And bring them down where they stand.
13 Bury them all in the earth;
Hide their faces in obscurity.
14 Then even I would praise you
For the triumph your right hand won you.

15 Take now behemoth, whom I made as I did you;
He eats grass, like the cattle.
16 His strength is in his loins,
His might in the muscles of his belly.
17 a-He makes his tail stand up-a like a cedar;
The sinews of his thighs are knit together.
18 His bones are like tubes of bronze,
His limbs like iron rods.
19 He is the first of God's works;
Only his Maker can draw the sword against him.
20 The mountains yield him produce,
Where all the beasts of the field play.
21 He lies down beneath the lotuses,
In the cover of the swamp reeds.
22 The lotuses embower him with shade;
The willows of the brook surround him.
23 He can restrain the river from its rushing;
He is confident the stream^b will gush at his command.
24 Can he be taken by his eyes?
Can his nose be pierced by hooks?
25 Can you draw out Leviathan by a fishhook?

b Lit. "Jordan."

Can you press down his tongue by a rope?
²⁶ Can you put a ring through his nose,
Or pierce his jaw with a barb?
²⁷ Will he plead with you at length?
Will he speak soft words to you?
²⁸ Will he make an agreement with you
To be taken as your lifelong slave?
²⁹ Will you play with him like a bird,
And tie him down for your girls?
³⁰ ᵃ-Shall traders traffic in him?-ᵃ
Will he be divided up among merchants?
³¹ Can you fill his skin with darts
Or his head with fish-spears?
³² Lay a hand on him,
And you will never think of battle again.

41 See, any hope [of capturing] him must be disappointed;
One is prostrated by the very sight of him.
² There is no one so fierce as to rouse him;
Who then can stand up to Me?
³ Whoever confronts Me I will requite,
For everything under the heavens is Mine.
⁴ ᵃ-I will not be silent concerning him
Or the praise of his martial exploits.-ᵃ
⁵ Who can uncover his outer garment?
Who can penetrate the folds of his jowls?
⁶ Who can pry open the doors of his face?
His bared teeth strike terror.
⁷ His protective scales are his pride,
Locked with a binding seal.
⁸ One scale touches the other;
Not even a breath can enter between them.
⁹ Each clings to each;
They are interlocked so they cannot be parted.

ᵃ⁻ᵃ *Meaning of Heb. uncertain.*

10 His sneezings flash lightning,
And his eyes are like the glimmerings of dawn.
11 Firebrands stream from his mouth;
Fiery sparks escape.
12 Out of his nostrils comes smoke
As from a steaming, boiling cauldron.
13 His breath ignites coals;
Flames blaze from his mouth.
14 Strength resides in his neck;
Power leaps before him.
15 The layers of his flesh stick together;
He is as though cast hard; he does not totter.
16 His heart is cast hard as a stone,
Hard as the nether millstone.
17 Divine beings are in dread as he rears up;
As he crashes down, they cringe.
18 No sword that overtakes him can prevail,
Nor spear, nor missile, nor lance.
19 He regards iron as straw,
Bronze, as rotted wood.
20 No arrow can put him to flight;
Slingstones turn into stubble for him.
21 Clubs*a* are regarded as stubble;
He scoffs at the quivering javelin.
22 His underpart is jagged shards;
It spreads a threshing-sledge on the mud.
23 He makes the depths seethe like a cauldron;
He makes the sea [boil] like an ointment-pot.
24 His wake is a luminous path;
He makes the deep seem white-haired.
25 There is no one on land who can dominate him,
Made as he is without fear.
26 He sees all that is haughty;
He is king over all proud beasts.

42 Job said in reply to the LORD:

2 I know that You can do everything,
That nothing you propose is impossible for You.
3 Who is this who obscures counsel without knowledge?
Indeed, I spoke without understanding
Of things beyond me, which I did not know.
4 Hear now, and I will speak;
I will ask, and You will inform me.
5 I had heard You with my ears,
But now I see You with my eyes;
6 Therefore, I recant and relent,
Being but dust and ashes.

7 After the LORD had spoken these words to Job, the LORD said to Eliphaz the Temanite, "I am incensed at you and your two friends, for you have not spoken the truth about Me as did My servant Job. 8 Now take seven bulls and seven rams and go to My servant Job and sacrifice a burnt offering for yourselves. And let Job, My servant, pray for you; for to him I will show favor and not treat you vilely, since you have not spoken the truth about Me as did My servant Job." 9 Eliphaz the Temanite and Bildad the Shuhite and Zophar the Naamathite went and did as the LORD had told them, and the LORD showed favor to Job. 10 The LORD restored Job's fortunes when he prayed on behalf of his friends, and the LORD gave Job twice what he had before.

11 All his brothers and sisters and all his former friends came to him and had a meal with him in his house. They consoled and comforted him for all the misfortune that the LORD had brought upon him. Each gave him one *kesitah*[a] and each one gold ring. 12 Thus the LORD blessed the latter years of Job's life more than the former. He had fourteen thousand sheep, six thousand camels, one thousand yoke of oxen, and one thousand she-asses.

[a] *A unit of unknown value.*

¹³ He also had seven sons and three daughters. ¹⁴ The first he named Jemimah, the second Keziah, and the third Keren-happuch. ¹⁵ Nowhere in the land were women as beautiful as Job's daughters to be found. Their father gave them estates together with their brothers. ¹⁶ Afterward, Job lived one hundred and forty years to see four generations of sons and grandsons. ¹⁷ So Job died old and contented.

שיר השירים

THE SONG OF SONGS

שיר השירים

THE SONG OF SONGS

1 The Song of Songs, by[a] Solomon.

2 [b-]Oh, give me of the kisses of your mouth,[-b]
For your love is more delightful than wine.
3 Your ointments yield a sweet fragrance,
Your name is like finest[c] oil—
Therefore do maidens love you.
4 Draw me after you, let us run!
[d-]The king has brought me to his chambers.[-d]
Let us delight and rejoice in your love,
Savoring it more than wine—
[e-]Like new wine[-e] they love you!

5 I am dark, but comely,
O daughters of Jerusalem—
Like the tents of Kedar,
Like the pavilions of Solomon.
6 Don't stare at me because I am swarthy,
Because the sun has gazed upon me.
My mother's sons quarreled with me,
They made me guard the vineyards;
My own vineyard I did not guard.

7 Tell me, you whom I love so well;
Where do you pasture your sheep?
Where do you rest them at noon?

---

[a] *Or "concerning."*
[b-b] *Heb. "Let him give me of the kisses of his mouth!"*
[c] *Meaning of Heb. uncertain.*
[d-d] *Emendation yields "Bring me, O king, to your chambers."*
[e-e] *Understanding* mesharim *as related to* tirosh; *cf. Aramaic* merath.

Let me not be ᶜˉas one who straysˉᶜ
Beside the flocks of your fellows.
⁸ If you do not know, O fairest of women,
Go follow the tracks of the sheep,
And graze your kids ᶠ
By the tents of the shepherds.

⁹ I have likened you, my darling,
To a mare in Pharaoh's chariots:
¹⁰ Your cheeks are comely with plaited wreaths,
Your neck with strings of jewels.
¹¹ We will add wreaths of gold
To your spangles of silver.

¹² While the king was on his couch,
My nard gave forth its fragrance.
¹³ My beloved to me is a bag of myrrh
Lodged between my breasts.
¹⁴ My beloved to me is a spray of henna blooms
From the vineyards of En-gedi.

¹⁵ Ah, you are fair, my darling,
Ah, you are fair,
With your dove-like eyes!
¹⁶ And you, my beloved, are handsome,
Beautiful indeed!
Our couch is in a bower;
¹⁷ Cedars are the beams of our house,
Cypresses the rafters.

2   I am a roseᵃ of Sharon,
A lily of the valleys.

ᶠ *As a pretext for coming.*
ᵃ *Lit. "crocus."*

² Like a lily among thorns,
So is my darling among the maidens.

³ Like an apple tree among trees of the forest,
So is my beloved among the youths.
I delight to sit in his shade,
And his fruit is sweet to my mouth.

⁴ He brought me to the banquet room
ᵇ⁻And his banner of love was over me.⁻ᵇ
⁵ "Sustain me with raisin cakes,
Refresh me with apples,
For I am faint with love."
⁶ His left hand was under my head,
His right arm embraced me.
⁷ I adjure you, O maidens of Jerusalem,
By gazelles or by hinds of the field:
Do not wake or rouse
Love until it please!

⁸ Hark! My beloved!
There he comes,
Leaping over mountains,
Bounding over hills.
⁹ My beloved is like a gazelle
Or like a young stag.
There he stands behind our wall,
Gazing through the window,
Peering through the lattice.
¹⁰ My beloved spoke thus to me,
"Arise, my darling;
My fair one, come away!
¹¹ For now the winter is past,
The rains are over and gone.

ᵇ⁻ᵇ *Meaning of Heb. uncertain.*

¹² The blossoms have appeared in the land,
The time of pruning*c* has come;
The song of the turtledove
Is heard in our land.
¹³ The green figs form on the fig tree,
The vines in blossom give off fragrance.
Arise, my darling;
My fair one, come away!

¹⁴ "O my dove, in the cranny of the rocks,
Hidden by the cliff,
Let me see your face,
Let me hear your voice;
For your voice is sweet
And your face is comely."
¹⁵ Catch us the foxes,
The little foxes
That ruin the vineyards—
For our vineyard is in blossom.

¹⁶ My beloved is mine
And I am his
Who browses among the lilies.
¹⁷ When the day *ᵈ*-blows gently-*ᵈ*
And the shadows flee,*ᵉ*
Set out, my beloved,
Swift as a gazelle
Or a young stag,
For the hills of spices!*ᶠ*

3   Upon my couch at night*ᵃ*
I sought the one I love—
I sought, but found him not.

ᶜ Or "singing."
ᵈ⁻ᵈ Emendation yields "declines"; cf. Jer. 6.4.
ᵉ Septuagint reads "lengthen"; cf. Jer. 6.4.
ᶠ Heb. bather of uncertain meaning; 8.14 reads besamim, "spices."

ᵃ I.e. in a dream.

338

2 "I must rise and roam the town,
Through the streets and through the squares;
I must seek the one I love."
I sought but found him not.
3 *b*-I met the watchmen-*b*
Who patrol the town.
"Have you seen the one I love?"
4 Scarcely had I passed them
When I found the one I love.
I held him fast, I would not let him go
Till I brought him to my mother's house,
To the chamber of her who conceived me
5 I adjure you, O maidens of Jerusalem,
By gazelles or by hinds of the field:
Do not wake or rouse
Love until it please!

6 Who is she that comes up from the desert
Like columns of smoke,
In clouds of myrrh and frankincense,
Of all the powders of the merchant?
7 There is Solomon's couch,
Encircled by sixty warriors
Of the warriors of Israel,
8 All of them trained*c* in warfare,
Skilled in battle,
Each with sword on thigh
Because of terror by night.

9 King Solomon made him a palanquin
Of wood from Lebanon.
10 He made its posts of silver,
Its back*d* of gold,
Its seat of purple wool.

b-b *Lit. "The watchmen met me."*
c *Cf. Akkadian aḫāzu, "to learn."*
d *Meaning of Heb. uncertain.*

Within, it was decked with *e*love
By the maidens of Jerusalem.-*e*
¹¹ O maidens of Zion, go forth
And gaze upon King Solomon
Wearing the crown that his mother
Gave him on his wedding day,
On his day of bliss.

4   Ah, you are fair, my darling,
Ah, you are fair.
Your eyes are like doves
Behind your veil.
Your hair is like a flock of goats
Streaming down Mount Gilead.
² Your teeth are like a flock of ewes*a*
Climbing up from the washing pool;
All of them bear twins,
And not one loses her young.
³ Your lips are like a crimson thread,
Your mouth is lovely.
Your brow behind your veil
[Gleams] like a pomegranate split open.
⁴ Your neck is like the Tower of David,
Built *b*to hold weapons,-*b*
Hung with a thousand shields—
All the quivers of warriors.
⁵ Your breasts are like two fawns,
Twins of a gazelle,
Browsing among the lilies.
⁶ *c*When the day blows gently
And the shadows flee,
I will betake me to the mount of myrrh,
To the hill of frankincense.
⁷ Every part of you is fair, my darling,

e-e *Emendation yields:*   "ebony.
            O maidens of Jerusalem!"

a *Cf. 6.6; exact nuance of* qeṣuboth *uncertain, perhaps "shorn ones."*
b-b *Apparently a poetic figure for jewelry; meaning of Heb. uncertain.*
c *See notes at 2.17.*

There is no blemish in you
⁸ From Lebanon come with me;
From Lebanon, my bride, with me!
Trip down from Amana's peak,
From the peak of Senir *d* and Hermon,
From the dens of lions,
From the hills *e* of leopards.

⁹ You have captured my heart,
My own, *f* my bride,
You have captured my heart
With one [glance] of your eyes,
With one coil of your necklace.
¹⁰ How sweet is your love,
My own, my bride!
How much more delightful your love than wine,
Your ointments more fragrant
Than any spice!
¹¹ Sweetness drops
From your lips, O bride;
Honey and milk
Are under your tongue;
And the scent of your robes
Is like the scent of Lebanon.
¹² A garden locked
Is my own, my bride,
A fountain locked,
A sealed-up spring.
¹³ Your limbs are an orchard of pomegranates
And of all luscious fruits,
Of henna and of nard—
¹⁴ Nard and saffron,
Fragrant reed and cinnamon,
With all aromatic woods,
Myrrh and aloes—

d Cf. Deut. 3.9.
e Emendation yields "lairs"; cf. Nah. 2.13.
f Lit. "sister"; and so frequently below.

All the choice perfumes.
¹⁵ ^g[You are] a garden spring,
A well of fresh water,^g
A rill of Lebanon.

¹⁶ Awake, O north wind,
Come, O south wind!
Blow upon my garden,
That its perfume may spread.
Let my beloved come to his garden
And enjoy its luscious fruits!

5   I have come to my garden,
My own, my bride;
I have plucked my myrrh and spice,
Eaten my honey and honeycomb,
Drunk my wine and my milk.

Eat, lovers, and drink:
Drink deep of love!

² ^aI was asleep,
But my heart was wakeful.
Hark, my beloved knocks!
"Let me in, my own,
My darling, my faultless dove!
For my head is drenched with dew,
My locks with the damp of night."
³ I had taken off my robe—
Was I to don it again?
I had bathed my feet—
Was I to soil them again?
⁴ My beloved ^btook his hand off the latch,^{-b}
And my heart was stirred ^cfor him.^{-c}

^{g-g} *Emendation yields:*
> *"The spring in my garden*
> *Is a well of fresh water."*

^a *In vv. 2–8 the maiden relates a dream.*
^{b-b} *Meaning of Heb. uncertain.*
^{c-c} *Many manuscripts and editions read "within me" ('alai).*

⁵ I rose to let in my beloved;
My hands dripped myrrh—
My fingers, flowing myrrh—
Upon the handles of the bolt.
⁶ I opened the door for my beloved,
But my beloved had turned and gone.
I was faint ᵈ-because of what he said.-ᵈ
I sought, but found him not;
I called, but he did not answer.
⁷ I met the watchmenᵉ
Who patrol the town;
They struck me, they bruised me.
The guards of the walls
Stripped me of my mantle.
⁸ I adjure you, O maidens of Jerusalem!
If you meet my beloved, tell him this:
That I am faint with love.

⁹ How is your beloved better than another,ᶠ
O fairest of women?
How is your beloved better than anotherᶠ
That you adjure us so?

¹⁰ My beloved is clear-skinned and ruddy,
Preeminent among ten thousand.
¹¹ His head is finest gold,
His locks are curled
And black as a raven.
¹² His eyes are like doves
By watercourses,
Bathed in milk,
ᵇ-Set by a brimming pool.-ᵇ
¹³ His cheeks are like beds of spices,
ᵍ-Banks ofᵍ perfume
His lips are like lilies;

ᵈ⁻ᵈ *Change of vocalization yields "because of him."*
ᵉ *See note at 3.3.*
ᶠ *Or "What sort of beloved is your beloved?"*
ᵍ⁻ᵍ *Septuagint vocalizes as participle, "producing."*

They drip flowing myrrh.
14 His hands are rods of gold,
Studded with beryl;
His belly a tablet of ivory,
Adorned with sapphires.
15 His legs are like marble pillars
Set in sockets of fine gold.
He is majestic as Lebanon,
Stately as the cedars.
16 His mouth is delicious
And all of him is delightful.
Such is my beloved,
Such is my darling,
O maidens of Jerusalem!

6   "Whither has your beloved gone,
O fairest of women?
Whither has your beloved turned?
Let us seek him with you."
2 My beloved has gone down to his garden,
To the beds of spices,
To browse in the gardens
And to pick lilies.
3 I am my beloved's
And my beloved is mine;
He browses among the lilies.

4 You are beautiful, my darling, as Tirzah,
Comely as Jerusalem,
ᵃ-Awesome as bannered hosts.⁻ᵃ
5 Turn your eyes away from me,
For they overwhelm me!
Your hair is like a flock of goats

ᵃ⁻ᵃ *Meaning of Heb. uncertain.*

Streaming down from Gilead.
⁶ Your teeth are like a flock of ewes
Climbing up from the washing pool;
All of them bear twins,
And not one loses her young.
⁷ Your brow behind your veil
[Gleams] like a pomegranate split open.
⁸ There are sixty queens,
And eighty concubines,
And damsels without number.
⁹ Only one is my dove,
My perfect one,
The only one of her mother,
The delight of her who bore her.
Maidens see and acclaim her;
Queens and concubines, and praise her.

¹⁰ Who is she that shines through like the dawn,
Beautiful as the moon,
Radiant as the sun
ᵘ-Awesome as bannered hosts?-ᵃ

¹¹ I went down to the nut grove
To see the budding of the vale;
To see if the vines had blossomed,
If the pomegranates were in bloom.
¹² ᵃ-Before I knew it,
My desire set me
Mid the chariots of Ammi-nadib.-ᵃ

7   Turn back, turn back,
     O maid of Shulem!
     Turn back, turn back,

That we may gaze upon you.
"Why will you gaze at the Shulammite
In*a* the Mahanaim dance?"

² How lovely are your feet in sandals,
O daughter of nobles!
Your rounded thighs are like jewels,
The work of a master's hand.
³ Your navel is like a round goblet—
Let mixed winé not be lacking!—
Your belly like a heap of wheat
Hedged about with lilies.
⁴ Your breasts are like two fawns,
Twins of a gazelle.
⁵ Your neck is like a tower of ivory,
Your eyes like pools in Heshbon
By the gate of Bath-rabbim,
Your nose like the Lebanon tower
That faces toward Damascus.
⁶ The head upon you is like *b*-crimson wool,-*b*
The locks of your head are like purple—
c-A king is held captive in the tresses.-*c*
⁷ How fair you are, how beautiful!
O Love, with all its rapture!
⁸ Your stately form is like the palm,
Your breasts are like clusters.
⁹ I say: Let me climb the palm,
Let me take hold of its branches;
Let your breasts be like clusters of grapes,
Your breath like the fragrance of apples,
¹⁰ And your mouth like choicest wine.
"Let it flow to my beloved as new wine*d*
c-Gliding over the lips of sleepers."-*c*

---

a With many manuscripts and editions; others read "like." Meaning of entire line uncertain.
b-b So Ibn Janah and Ibn Ezra, taking karmel as a by-form of karmil: cf. II Chron. 2:6, 13; 3:14.
c-c Meaning of Heb. uncertain.
d See note at 1.4 end.

¹¹ I am my beloved's,
And his desire is for me.
¹² Come, my beloved,
Let us go into the open;
Let us lodge ^{e-}among the henna shrubs.^{-e}
¹³ Let us go early to the vineyards;
Let us see if the vine has flowered,
If its blossoms have opened,
If the pomegranates are in bloom.
There I will give my love to you.
¹⁴ The mandrakes yield their fragrance,
At our doors are all choice fruits;
Both freshly-picked and long-stored
Have I kept, my beloved, for you.

8   If only it could be as with a brother,
As if you had nursed at my mother's breast:
Then I could kiss you
When I met you in the street,
And no one would despise me.
² I would lead you, I would bring you
To the house of my mother,
Of her who taught^a me—
I would let you drink of the spiced wine,
Of my pomegranate juice.

³ His left hand was under my head,
His right hand caressed me.
⁴ I adjure you, O maidens of Jerusalem:
Do not wake or rouse
Love until it please!

⁵ Who is she that comes up from the desert,
Leaning upon her beloved?

^{e-e} Or "in the villages."
^a Emendation yields "bore"; cf. 6.9; 8.5.

Under the apple tree I roused you;
It was there your mother conceived you,
There she who bore you conceived you.

6 Let me be a seal upon your heart,
Like the seal upon your hand.*b*
For love is fierce as death,
Passion is mighty as Sheol;
Its darts are darts of fire,
A blazing flame.
7 Vast floods cannot quench love,
Nor rivers drown it.
If a man offered all his wealth for love,
He would be laughed to scorn.

8 "We have a little sister,
Whose breasts are not yet formed.
What shall we do for our sister
When she is spoken for?
9 If she be a wall,
We will build upon it a silver battlement;
If she be a door,
We will panel it in cedar."
10 I am a wall,
My breasts are like towers.
So I became in his eyes
As one who finds favor.

11 Solomon had a vineyard
In Baal-hamon.
He had to post guards in the vineyard:
A man would give for its fruit
A thousand pieces of silver.
12 I have my very own vineyard:

b *Lit. "arm."*

348

You may have the thousand, O Solomon,
And the guards of the fruit two hundred!

[13] O you who linger in the garden,[c]
A lover[c] is listening;
Let me hear your voice.
[14] "Hurry, my beloved,
Swift as a gazelle or a young stag,
To the hills of spices!"

[c] *Heb. plural. Meaning of verse uncertain.*

רות

RUTH

רות

RUTH

1 In the days when the chieftains[a] ruled, there was a famine in the land; and a man of Bethlehem in Judah, with his wife and two sons, went to reside in the country of Moab. ² The man's name was Elimelech, his wife's name was Naomi, and his two sons were named Mahlon and Chilion—Ephrathites of Bethlehem in Judah. They came to the country of Moab and remained there.

³ Elimelech, Naomi's husband, died; and she was left with her two sons. ⁴ They married Moabite women, one named Orpah and the other Ruth, and they lived there about ten years. ⁵ Then those two—Mahlon and Chilion—also died; so the woman was left without her two sons and without her husband.

⁶ She started out with her daughters-in-law to return from the country of Moab; for in the country of Moab she had heard that the LORD had taken note of His people and given them food. ⁷ Accompanied by her two daughters-in-law, she left the place where she had been living; and they set out on the road back to the land of Judah.

⁸ But Naomi said to her two daughters-in-law, "Turn back, each of you to her mother's house. May the LORD deal kindly with you, as you have dealt with the dead and with me! ⁹ May the LORD grant that each of you find security in the house of a husband!" And she kissed them farewell. They broke into weeping ¹⁰ and said to her, "No, we will return with you to your people."

¹¹ But Naomi replied, "Turn back, my daughters! Why should you go with me? Have I any more sons in my body who might be husbands for you? ¹² Turn back, my daughters, for I am too old to be married. Even if I thought there was hope for me, even if

---

ᵃ *I.e. the leaders who arose in the period before the monarchy. Others "judges."*

I were married tonight and I also bore sons, [13] should you wait
for them to grow up? Should you on their account debar yourselves from marriage? Oh no, my daughters! My lot is far more
bitter than yours, for the hand of the LORD has struck out against
me."

[14] They broke into weeping again, and Orpah kissed her mother-in-law farewell. But Ruth clung to her. [15] So she said, "See,
your sister-in-law has returned to her people and her gods. Go
follow your sister-in-law." [16] But Ruth replied, "Do not urge me
to leave you, to turn back and not follow you. For wherever you
go, I will go; wherever you lodge, I will lodge; your people shall
be my people, and your God my God. [17] Where you die, I will die,
and there I will be buried. *b*-Thus and more may the LORD do to
me*-b* if anything but death parts me from you." [18] When [Naomi]
saw how determined she was to go with her, she ceased to argue
with her; [19] and the two went on until they reached Bethlehem.

When they arrived in Bethlehem, the whole city buzzed with
excitement over them. The women said, "Can this be Naomi?"
[20] "Do not call me Naomi,*c*" she replied. "Call me Mara,*d* for
Shaddai*e* has made my lot very bitter. [21] I went away full, and the
LORD has brought me back empty. How can you call me Naomi,
when the LORD has *f*-dealt harshly with*-f* me, when Shaddai has
brought misfortune upon me!"

[22] Thus Naomi returned from the country of Moab; she returned with her daughter-in-law Ruth the Moabite. They arrived
in Bethlehem at the beginning of the barley harvest.

2   Now Naomi had a kinsman on her husband's side, a man
of substance, of the family of Elimelech, whose name was Boaz.
[2] Ruth the Moabite said to Naomi, "I would like to go to the
fields and glean among the ears of grain, behind someone who
may show me kindness." "Yes, daughter, go," she replied; [3] and
off she went. She came and gleaned in a field, behind the reapers;

b-b *A formula of imprecation.*
c *I.e. "Pleasantness."*
d *I.e. "Bitterness."*
e *Usually rendered "the Almighty."*
f-f *Others "testified against."*

and, as luck would have it, it was the piece of land belonging to Boaz, who was of Elimelech's family. ⁴ Presently Boaz arrived from Bethlehem. He greeted the reapers, "The LORD be with you!" And they responded, "The LORD bless you!" ⁵ Boaz said to the servant who was in charge of the reapers, "Whose girl is that?" ⁶ The servant in charge of the reapers replied, "She is a Moabite girl who came back with Naomi from the country of Moab. ⁷ She said, 'Please let me glean and gather among the sheaves behind the reapers.' She has been on her feet ever since she came this morning. ᵃ⁻She has rested but little in the hut."⁻ᵃ

⁸ Boaz said to Ruth, ᵇ⁻"Listen to me, daughter.⁻ᵇ Don't go to glean in another field. Don't go elsewhere, but stay here close to my girls. ⁹ Keep your eyes on the field they are reaping, and follow them. I have ordered the men not to molest you. And when you are thirsty, go to the jars and drink some of [the water] that the men have drawn."

¹⁰ She prostrated herself with her face to the ground, and said to him, "Why are you so kind as to single me out, when I am a foreigner?"

¹¹ Boaz said in reply, "I have been told of all that you did for your mother-in-law after the death of your husband, how you left your father and mother and the land of your birth and came to a people you had not known before. ¹² May the LORD reward your deeds. May you have a full recompense from the LORD, the God of Israel, under whose wings you have sought refuge!"

¹³ She answered, "You are most kind, my lord, to comfort me and to speak gently to your maidservant—though I am not so much as one of your maidservants."

¹⁴ At mealtime, Boaz said to her, "Come over here and partake of the meal, and dip your morsel in the vinegar." So she sat down beside the reapers. He handed her roasted grain, and she ate her fill and had some left over.

¹⁵ When she got up again to glean, Boaz gave orders to his workers, "You are not only to let her glean among the sheaves,

ᵃ⁻ᵃ *Meaning of Heb. uncertain.*
ᵇ⁻ᵇ *Lit. "Have you not heard, daughter?"*

without interference, [16] but you must also pull some [stalks] out of the heaps and leave them for her to glean, and not scold her."

[17] She gleaned in the field until evening. Then she beat out what she had gleaned—it was about an *ephah* of barley—[18] and carried it back with her to the town. When her mother-in-law saw what she had gleaned, and when she also took out and gave her what she had left over after eating her fill, [19] her mother-in-law asked her, "Where did you glean today? Where did you work? Blessed be he who took such generous notice of you!" So she told her mother-in-law whom she had worked with, saying, "The name of the man with whom I worked today is Boaz."

[20] Naomi said to her daughter-in-law, "Blessed be he of the LORD, who has not failed in His kindness to the living or to the dead! For," Naomi explained to her daughter-in-law, "the man is related to us; he is one of our redeeming kinsmen.ᶜ" [21] Ruth the Moabite said, "He even told me, 'Stay close by my workers until all my harvest is finished.' " [22] And Naomi answered her daughter-in-law Ruth, "It is best, daughter, that you go out with his girls, and not be annoyed in some other field." [23] So she stayed close to the maidservants of Boaz, and gleaned until the barley harvest and the wheat harvest were finished. Then she stayed at home with her mother-in-law.

3 Naomi, her mother-in-law, said to her, "Daughter, I must seek a home for you, where you may be happy. [2] Now there is our kinsman Boaz, whose girls you were close to. He will be winnowing barley on the threshing floor tonight. [3] So bathe, anoint yourself, dress up, and go down to the threshing floor. But do not disclose yourself to the man until he has finished eating and drinking. [4] When he lies down, note the place where he lies down, and go over and uncover his feet and lie down. He will tell you what you are to do." [5] She replied, "I will do everything you tell me."

[6] She went down to the threshing floor and did just as her

ᶜ *Cf. Lev. 25.25 and note; and Deut. 25.5–6. The fact that Boaz was a kinsman of Ruth's dead husband opened up the possibility of providing an heir for the latter.*

mother-in-law had instructed her. [7] Boaz ate and drank, and in a cheerful mood went to lie down beside the grainpile. Then she went over stealthily and uncovered his feet and lay down. [8] In the middle of the night, the man gave a start and pulled back—there was a woman lying at his feet!

[9] "Who are you?" he asked. And she replied, "I am your handmaid Ruth. [a]-Spread your robe over your handmaid,-[a] for you are a redeeming kinsman."

[10] He exclaimed, "Be blessed of the LORD, daughter! Your latest deed of loyalty is greater than the first, in that you have not turned to younger men, whether poor or rich.[b] [11] And now, daughter, have no fear. I will do in your behalf whatever you ask, for all the [c]-elders of my town-[c] know what a fine woman you are. [12] But while it is true I am a redeeming kinsman, there is another redeemer closer than I. [13] Stay for the night. Then in the morning, if he will act as a redeemer, good! let him redeem. But if he does not want to act as redeemer for you, I will do so myself, as the LORD lives! Lie down until morning."

[14] So she lay at his feet until dawn. She rose before one person could distinguish another, for he thought, "Let it not be known that the woman came to the threshing floor." [15] And he said, "Hold out the shawl you are wearing." She held it while he measured out six measures of barley, and he put it on her back. When she[d] got back to the town, [16] she came to her mother-in-law, who asked, "How is it with you, daughter?" She told her all that the man had done for her; [17] and she added, "He gave me these six measures of barley, saying to me, 'Do not go back to your mother-in-law empty-handed.'" [18] And Naomi said, "Stay here, daughter, till you learn how the matter turns out. For the man will not rest, but will settle the matter today."

4   Meanwhile, Boaz had gone to the gate and sat down there. And now the redeemer whom Boaz had mentioned passed by. He called, "Come over and sit down here, So-and-so!" And he came

---

[a]-[a] *A formal act of espousal; cf. Ezek. 16.8.*
[b] *I.e. she sought out a kinsman of her dead husband; see note at 2.20 above. Her first act of loyalty had been to return with Naomi.*
[c]-[c] *Lit. "gate of my people."*
[d] *So in many Heb. mss. Most mss. read "he."*

over and sat down. ² Then [Boaz] took ten elders of the town and said, "Be seated here"; and they sat down.

³ He said to the redeemer, "Naomi, now returned from the country of Moab, must sell the piece of land which belonged to our kinsman Elimelech. ⁴ I thought I should disclose the matter to you and say: Acquire it in the presence of those seated here and in the presence of the elders of my people. If you are willing to redeem it, redeem! But if you*ᵃ* will not redeem, tell me, that I may know. For there is no one to redeem but you, and I come after you." "I am willing to redeem it," he replied. ⁵ Boaz continued, "When you acquire the property from Naomi *ᵇ*-and from Ruth the Moabite, you must also acquire the wife of the deceased,*-ᵇ* so as to perpetuate the name of the deceased upon his estate." ⁶ The redeemer replied, "Then I cannot redeem it for myself, lest I impair my own estate.*ᶜ* You take over my right of redemption, for I am unable to exercise it."

⁷ Now this was formerly done in Israel in cases of redemption or exchange: to validate any transaction, one man would take off his sandal and hand it to the other. Such was the practice*ᵈ* in Israel. ⁸ So when the redeemer said to Boaz, "Acquire for yourself," he drew off his sandal. ⁹ And Boaz said to the elders and to the rest of the people, "You are witnesses today that I am acquiring from Naomi all that belonged to Elimelech and all that belonged to Chilion and Mahlon. ¹⁰ I am also acquiring Ruth the Moabite, the wife of Mahlon, as my wife, so as to perpetuate the name of the deceased upon his estate, that the name of the deceased may not disappear from among his kinsmen and from the gate of his home town. You are witnesses today."

¹¹ All the people at the gate and the elders answered, "We are. May the LORD make the woman who is coming into your house like Rachel and Leah, both of whom built up the House of Israel! Prosper in Ephrathah*ᵉ* and perpetuate your name in Bethlehem!

ᵃ *So many Heb. mss., Septuagint, and Targum; most mss. read "he."*
ᵇ⁻ᵇ *Emendation yields "you must also acquire Ruth the Moabite, the wife of the deceased"; cf. v.10.*
ᶜ *I.e. by expending capital for property which will go to the son legally regarded as Mahlon's; see Deut. 25.5–6.*
ᵈ *Understanding Heb.* te 'udah *in the sense of the Arabic* 'ādah *and Syriac* 'yādā. *Cf. Ibn Ezra.*
ᵉ *Ephrathah is another name applied to Bethlehem; cf. 1.2; Gen. 35.16, 19; 48.7; Mic. 5.1.*

¹² And may your house be like the house of Perez whom Tamar bore to Judah—through the offspring which the LORD will give you by this young woman."

¹³ So Boaz married Ruth; she became his wife, and he cohabited with her. The LORD let her conceive, and she bore a son. ¹⁴ And the women said to Naomi, "Blessed be the LORD, who has not withheld a redeemer from you today! May his name be perpetuated in Israel! ¹⁵ He will renew your life and sustain your old age; for he is born of your daughter-in-law, who loves you and is better to you than seven sons."

¹⁶ Naomi took the child and held it to her bosom. She became its foster mother, ¹⁷ and the women neighbors gave him a name, saying, "A son is born to Naomi!" They named him Obed; he was the father of Jesse, father of David.

¹⁸ This is the line of Perez: Perez begot Hezron, ¹⁹ Hezron begot Ram, Ram begot Amminadab, ²⁰ Amminadab begot Nahshon, Nahshon begot Salmon,ᶠ ²¹ Salmon begot Boaz, Boaz begot Obed, ²² Obed begot Jesse, and Jesse begot David.

ᶠ *Heb. "Salmah."*

אֵיכָה

LAMENTATIONS

איכה
LAMENTATIONS

1 א   *a*Alas!
   Lonely sits the city
   Once great with people!
   She that was great among nations
   Is become like a widow;
   The princess among states
   Is become a thrall.

ב   ² Bitterly she weeps in the night,
   Her cheek wet with tears.
   There is none to comfort her
   Of all her friends.
   All her allies have betrayed her,
   They have become her foes.

ג   ³ Judah has gone into exile
   Because of misery and harsh oppression;
   When she settled among the nations,
   She found no rest;
   All her pursuers overtook her
   b-In the narrow places.-*b*

ד   ⁴ Zion's roads are in mourning,
   Empty of festival pilgrims;
   All her gates are deserted.
   Her priests sigh,
   Her maidens are unhappy—
   She is utterly disconsolate!

ה   ⁵ Her enemies are now the masters,
   Her foes are at ease,

---

a Chapters 1–4 are alphabetical acrostics, i.e., the verses begin with the successive letters of the Heb. alphabet. Chapter 3 is a triple acrostic. In chapters 2–4 the letter pe precedes the 'ayin.

b-b Meaning of Heb. uncertain.

Because the LORD has afflicted her
For her many transgressions;
Her infants have gone into captivity
Before the enemy.
ו 6 Gone from Fair Zion are all
That were her glory;
Her leaders were like stags
That found no pasture;
They could only walk feebly
Before the pursuer.

ז 7 All the precious things she had
In the days of old
Jerusalem recalled
In her days of woe and sorrow,
When her people fell by enemy hands
With none to help her;
When enemies looked on and gloated
Over her downfall.
ח 8 Jerusalem has greatly sinned,
Therefore she is become a mockery.
All who admired her despise her,
For they have seen her disgraced;
And she can only sigh
And shrink back.
ט 9 Her uncleanness clings to her skirts.
She gave no thought to her future;
She has sunk appallingly,
With none to comfort her.—
See, O LORD, my misery;
How the enemy jeers!
י 10 The foe has laid hands.
On everything dear to her.
She has seen her Sanctuary
Invaded by nations

Which You have denied admission
Into Your community.
 כ ¹¹ All her inhabitants sigh
As they search for bread;
They have bartered their treasures for food,
To keep themselves alive.—
See, O LORD, and behold,
ᶜHow abjectᶜ I have become!

ל ¹² ᵇMay it never befall you,ᵇ
All who pass along the road!
Look about and see:
Is there any agony like mine,
Which was dealt out to me
When the LORD afflicted me
On His day of wrath?
מ ¹³ From above He sent a fire
Down into my bones.
He spread a net for my feet,
He hurled me backward;
He has left me forlorn,
In constant misery.
נ ¹⁴ ᵈThe yoke of my offenses is bound fast,
Lashed tight by His hand;
Imposed upon my neck,
It saps my strength;
The Lord has delivered me into the hands
Of those I cannot withstand.
ס ¹⁵ The Lord in my midst has rejected
All my heroes;
He has proclaimed a set time against me
To crush my young men.
As in a press the Lord has trodden
Fair Maiden Judah.
ע ¹⁶ For these things do I weep,

ᶜ⁻ᶜ Or (ironically) "What a glutton"; cf. Prov. 23.20–21.
ᵈ Meaning of parts of vv. 14 and 15 uncertain.

365

My eyes flow with tears:
Far from me is any comforter
Who might revive my spirit;
My children are forlorn,
For the foe has prevailed.

פ ¹⁷ Zion spreads out her hands,
She has no one to comfort her;
The LORD has summoned against Jacob
His enemies all about him;
Jerusalem has become among them
A thing unclean.

צ ¹⁸ The LORD is in the right,
For I have disobeyed Him.
Hear, all you peoples,
And behold my agony:
My maidens and my youths
Have gone into captivity!

ק ¹⁹ I cried out to my friends,
But they played me false.
My priests and my elders
Have perished in the city
As they searched for food
To keep themselves alive.

ר ²⁰ See, O LORD, the distress I am in!
My heart is in anguish,
ᵉI know how wrong I wasᵉ
To disobey.
Outside the sword deals death;
Indoors, the plague.

ש ²¹ When they heard how I was sighing,
There was none to comfort me;
All my foes heard of my plight and exulted.
For it is Your doing:
ᶠYou have brought on the day that You threatened.

ᵉ⁻ᵉ Lit. "My heart has turned over within me"; cf. Exod. 14.5; Hos. 11.8.
ᶠ⁻ᶠ Emendation yields: "Oh, bring on them what befell me,
        And let them become like me!"

Oh, let them become like me!*ᶠ*

ת ²² Let all their wrongdoing come before You,
And deal with them
As You have dealt with me
For all my transgressions.
For my sighs are many,
And my heart is sick.

2 א Alas!
The Lord in His wrath
Has shamed*ᵃ* Fair Zion,
Has cast down from heaven to earth
The majesty of Israel.
He did not remember His Footstool*ᵇ*
On His day of wrath.

ב ² The Lord has laid waste without pity
All the habitations of Jacob;
He has razed in His anger
Fair Judah's strongholds.
He has brought low in dishonor
The kingdom and its leaders.

ג ³ In blazing anger He has cut down
All the might of Israel;
He has withdrawn His right hand
In the presence of the foe;
He has ravaged Jacob like flaming fire,
Consuming on all sides.

ד ⁴ He bent His bow like an enemy,
Poised His right hand like a foe;
He slew all who delighted the eye.
He poured out His wrath like fire
In the Tent of Fair Zion.

ה ⁵ The Lord has acted like a foe,
He has laid waste Israel,

ᵃ Meaning of Heb. uncertain.
ᵇ I.e. the Temple.

Laid waste all her citadels,
Destroyed her strongholds.
He has increased within Fair Judah
Mourning and moaning.

ו ⁶ He has stripped His Booth[b] like a garden,
He has destroyed His Tabernacle[c];
The LORD has ended in Zion
Festival and sabbath;
In His raging anger He has spurned
King and priest.

ז ⁷ The Lord has rejected His altar,
Disdained His Sanctuary.
He has handed over to the foe
The walls of its citadels;
They raised a shout in the House of the LORD
As on a festival day.

ח ⁸ The LORD resolved to destroy
The wall of Fair Zion;
[d-]He measured with a line,[-d] refrained not
From bringing destruction.
He has made wall and rampart to mourn,
Together they languish.

ט ⁹ Her gates have sunk into the ground,
He has smashed her bars to bits;
Her king and her leaders are [e-]in exile,[-e]
Instruction[f] is no more;
Her prophets, too, receive
No vision from the LORD.

י ¹⁰ Silent sit on the ground
The elders of Fair Zion;
They have strewn dust on their heads
And girded themselves with sackcloth;
The maidens of Jerusalem have bowed
Their heads to the ground.

כ ¹¹ My eyes are spent with tears,

---

[c] Lit. "(Tent of) Meeting."
[d-d] I.e. He made His plans.
[e-e] Lit. "among the nations."
[f] Heb. torah, here priestly instruction; cf. Jer. 18.18; Hag. 2.11; Mal. 2.6.

My heart is in tumult,
g-My being melts away-*g*
Over the ruin of *h*-my poor people,-*h*
As babes and sucklings languish
In the squares of the city.

ל ¹² They keep asking their mothers,
"Where is bread and wine?"
As they languish like battle-wounded
In the squares of the town,
As their life runs out
In their mothers' bosoms.

מ ¹³ What can I *i*-take as witness-*i* or liken
To you, O Fair Jerusalem?
What can I match with you to console you,
O Fair Maiden Zion?
For your ruin is vast as the sea:
Who can heal you?

נ ¹⁴ Your seers prophesied to you
Delusion and folly.
They did not expose your iniquity
So as to restore your fortunes,
But prophesied to you oracles
Of delusion and deception.

ס ¹⁵ All who pass your way
Clap their hands at you;
They hiss and wag their head.
At Fair Jerusalem:*j*
"Is this the city that was called
Perfect in Beauty,
Joy of All the Earth?"

פ ¹⁶ All your enemies
Jeer at you;
They hiss and gnash their teeth,
And cry: "We've ruined her!

---

g-g Lit. *"My liver spills on the ground."*
h-h Lit. *"the daughter of my people"; so elsewhere in poetry.*
i-i *Emendation yields "compare."*
j *These gestures were intended to ward off the calamity from the viewer; cf. e.g. Jer. 18.16 and note; Job 27.23.*

Ah, this is the day we hoped for;
^{k-}We have lived to see it!^{-k}"

ע   ¹⁷ The LORD has done what He purposed,
Has carried out the decree
That He ordained long ago;
He has torn down without pity.
He has let the foe rejoice over you,
Has exalted the might of your enemies.

צ   ¹⁸ ^{l-}Their heart cried out^{-l} to the Lord.
O wall of Fair Zion,
Shed tears like a torrent
Day and night!
Give yourself no respite,
Your eyes no rest.

ק   ¹⁹ Arise, cry out in the night
At the beginning of the watches,
Pour out your heart like water
In the presence of the Lord!
Lift up your hands to Him
For the life of your infants,
Who faint for hunger
At every street corner,

ר   ²⁰ See, O LORD, and behold,
To whom You have done this!
Alas, women eat their own fruit,
Their new-born^m babes!
Alas, priest and prophet are slain
In the Sanctuary of the Lord!

ש   ²¹ Prostrate in the streets lie
Both young and old.
My maidens and youths
Are fallen by the sword;
You slew them on Your day of wrath,

---

^{k-k} *Lit. "We have attained, we have seen."*
^{l-l} *Emendation yields "Cry aloud."*
^m *The root has this meaning in Arabic. Others "dandled."*

You slaughtered without pity.

ת ²² You summoned, as on a festival,
My neighbors from round about.
On the day of the wrath of the LORD,
None survived or escaped;
Those whom I bore*ᵐ* and reared
My foe has consumed.

3 א I am the man *ᵃ*-who has known affliction
Under-*ᵃ* the rod of His wrath;
² Me He drove on and on
In unrelieved darkness;
³ On none but me He brings down His hand
Again and again, without cease.
ב ⁴ He has worn away my flesh and skin;
He has shattered my bones.
⁵ All around me He has built
Misery*ᵇ* and hardship;
⁰ He has made me dwell in darkness,
Like those long dead.
ג ⁷ He has walled me in and I cannot break out;
He has weighed me down with chains.
⁸ And when I cry and plead,
He shuts out my prayer;
⁹ He has walled in my ways with hewn blocks,
He has made my paths a maze.

ד ¹⁰ He is a lurking bear to me,
A lion in hiding;
¹¹ *ᶜ*-He has forced me off my way-*ᶜ* and mangled me,
He has left me numb.
¹² He has bent His bow and made me
The target of His arrows:
ה ¹³ He has shot into my vitals

ᵃ⁻ᵃ Emendation yields "whom the Lord has shepherded with."
ᵇ Taking rosh as equivalent to resh.
ᶜ⁻ᶜ Meaning of Heb. uncertain.

The shafts of His quiver.
¹⁴ I have become a laughingstock to all people,
The butt of their gibes all day long.
¹⁵ He has filled me with bitterness,
Sated me with wormwood.

ו ¹⁶ He has broken my teeth on gravel,
Has ground me into the dust.
¹⁷ My life was bereft of peace,
I forgot what happiness was.
¹⁸ I thought my strength and hope
Had perished before the LORD.
ז ¹⁹ To recall my distress and my misery
Was wormwood and poison;
²⁰ Whenever I thought of them,
I was bowed low.

²¹ But this do I call to mind,
Therefore I have hope:
ח ²² The kindness of the LORD has not ended,
His mercies are not spent.
²³ They are renewed every morning—
Ample is Your grace!
²⁴ "The LORD is my portion," I say with full heart;
Therefore will I hope in Him.
ט ²⁵ The LORD is good to those who trust in Him,
To the one who seeks Him;
²⁶ It is good to wait patiently
Till rescue comes from the LORD.
²⁷ It is good for a man, when young,
To bear a yoke;
י ²⁸ Let him sit alone and be patient,
When He has laid it upon him.
²⁹ Let him put his mouth to the dust—
There may yet be hope.

³⁰ Let him offer his cheek to the smiter;
Let him be surfeited with mockery.
כ ³¹ For the Lord does not
Reject forever,
³² But first afflicts, then pardons
In His abundant kindness.
³³ For He does not willfully bring grief
Or affliction to man,
ל ³⁴ Crushing under His feet
All the prisoners of the earth.
³⁵ To deny a man his rights
In the presence of the Most High,
³⁶ To wrong a man in his cause—
This the Lord does not choose.
מ ³⁷ Whose decree was ever fulfilled,
Unless the Lord willed it?
³⁸ Is it not at the word of the Most High,
That weal and woe befall?
³⁹ Of what shall a living man complain?
Each one of his own sins!

נ ⁴⁰ Let us search and examine our ways,
And turn back to the LORD;
⁴¹ Let us lift up our hearts with^d our hands
To God in heaven:
⁴² We have transgressed and rebelled,
And You have not forgiven.
ס ⁴³ You have clothed Yourself in anger and pursued us,
You have slain without pity.
⁴⁴ You have screened Yourself off with a cloud,
That no prayer may pass through.
⁴⁵ You have made us filth and refuse
In the midst of the peoples.
פ ⁴⁶ All our enemies loudly
Rail against us.

^d Lit. "to"; emendation yields "rather than"; cf. Joel 2.13.

⁴⁷ Panic and pitfall are out lot,
Death and destruction.
⁴⁸ My eyes shed streams of water
Over the ruin of my poorᵉ people.

ע ⁴⁹ My eyes shall flow without cease,
Without respite,
⁵⁰ ᶠ‑Until the LORD looks down
And beholds from heaven.
⁵¹ My eyes have brought me grief‑ᶠ
Over all the maidens of my city.

צ ⁵² My foes have snared me like a bird,
Without any cause.
⁵³ They have ended my life in a pit
And cast stones at me.
⁵⁴ Waters flowed over my head;
I said: I am lost!

ק ⁵⁵ I have called on Your name, O LORD,
From the depths of the Pit.
⁵⁶ Hear my plea;
Do not shut Your ear
To my groan, to my cry!
⁵⁷ You have ever drawn nigh when I called You;
You have said, "Do not fear!"

ר ⁵⁸ You championed my cause, O Lord,
You have redeemed my life.
⁵⁹ You have seen, O LORD, the wrong done me;
Oh, vindicate my right!
⁶⁰ You have seen all their malice,
All their designs against me;

ש ⁶¹ You have heard, O LORD, their taunts,
All their designs against me,
⁶² The mouthings and pratings of my adversaries
Against me all day long.

ᵉ Lit. "the daughter of my"; so frequently in poetry.
ᶠ⁻ᶠ Emendation yields,
   ⁵⁰ "Until the LORD looks down from heaven
       And beholds
   ⁵¹   my affliction.
       The LORD has brought me grief."

374

⁶³ See how, at their ease or at work,
I am the butt of their gibes.
ת ⁶⁴ Give them, O LORD, their deserts
According to their deeds.
⁶⁵ Give them anguish*ᶜ* of heart;
Your curse be upon them!
⁶⁶ Oh, pursue them in wrath and destroy them
From under the heavens of the LORD!

4 א Alas!
The gold is dulled,*ᵃ*
Debased the finest gold!
The sacred*ᵇ* gems are spilled
At every street corner.
ב ² The precious children of Zion;
Once valued as gold—
Alas, they are accounted as earthen pots,
Work of a potter's hands!
ג ³ Even jackals offer the breast
And suckle their young;
But my poor people has turned cruel,
Like ostriches of the desert.
ד ⁴ The tongue of the suckling cleaves
To its palate for thirst.
Little children beg for bread;
None gives them a morsel.
ה ⁵ Those who feasted on dainties
Lie famished in the streets;
Those who were reared in purple
Have embraced refuse heaps.
ו ⁶ The guilt*ᶜ* of my poor*ᵈ* people
Exceeded the iniquity*ᶜ* of Sodom,
Which was overthrown in a moment,
Without a hand striking it.

ᵃ *Meaning of Heb. uncertain.*
ᵇ *Emendation yeilds "precious."*
ᶜ *I.e. punishment.*
ᵈ *See note at 3.48.*

ז   ⁷ Her elect were purer than snow,
Whiter than milk;
Their limbs were ruddier than coral,
Their bodies*a* were like sapphire.

ח   ⁸ Now their faces are blacker than soot,
They are not recognized in the streets;
Their skin has shriveled on their bones,
It has become dry as wood.

ט   ⁹ Better off were the slain of the sword
Than those slain by famine,
a-Who pined away, [as though] wounded,
For lack of-*a* the fruits of the field.

י   ¹⁰ With their own hands, tenderhearted women
Have cooked their children;
Such became their fare,
In the disaster of my poor*d* people.

כ   ¹¹ The LORD vented all His fury,
Poured out His blazing wrath;
He kindled a fire in Zion
Which consumed its foundations.

ל   ¹² The kings of the earth did not believe,
Nor any of the inhabitants of the world,
That foe or adversary could enter
The gates of Jerusalem.

מ   ¹³ It was for the sins of her prophets,
The iniquities of her priests,
Who had shed in her midst
The blood of the just.

נ   ¹⁴ They wandered blindly through the streets,
Defiled with blood,
So that no one was able
To touch their garments.

ס   ¹⁵ "Away! Unclean!" people shouted at them,
"Away! Away! Touch not!"
So they wandered and wandered again;

For the nations had resolved:
"They shall stay here no longer."

פ 16 *e*The Lord's countenance has turned away from them,
He will look on them no more.
They showed no regard for priests,
No favor to elders.

ע 17 Even now our eyes pine away
In vain for deliverance.
As we waited, still we wait
For a nation that cannot help.

צ 18 Our steps were checked,
We could not walk *f*in our squares.*f*
Our doom is near, our days are done—
Alas, our doom has come!

ק 19 Our pursuers were swifter
Than the eagles in the sky;
They chased us in the mountains,
Lay in wait for us in the wilderness.

ר 20 The breath of our life, the Lord's anointed,
Was captured in their traps—
He in whose shade we had thought
To live among the nations.

ש 21 Rejoice and exult, Fair Edom,
Who dwell in the land of Uz!
To you, too, the cup shall pass,
You shall get drunk and expose your nakedness.

ת 22 Your iniquity, Fair Zion, is expiated;
He will exile you no longer.
Your iniquity, Fair Edom, He will note;
He will uncover your sins.

5 Remember, O Lord, what has befallen us;
Behold, and see our disgrace!
2 Our heritage has passed to aliens,
Our homes to strangers.

e *Meaning of line uncertain.*
f-f *Or "With long strides."*

³ We have become orphans, fatherless;
Our mothers are like widows.
⁴ We must pay to drink our own water,
Obtain our own kindling at a price.
⁵ We are hotly^a pursued;
Exhausted, we are given no rest.
⁶ We hold out a hand to Egypt;
To Assyria, for our fill of bread.
⁷ Our fathers sinned and are no more;
And we must bear their guilt.
⁸ Slaves are ruling over us,
With none to rescue us from them.
⁹ We get our bread at the peril of our lives,
Because of the ^b-sword of the wilderness.^{-b}
¹⁰ Our skin glows like an oven,
With the fever of famine.
¹¹ They^c have ravished women in Zion,
Maidens in the towns of Judah.
¹² Princes have been hanged by them;^c
No respect has been shown to elders.
¹³ Young men must carry millstones,
And youths stagger under loads of wood.
¹⁴ The old men are gone from the gate,
The young men from their music.
¹⁵ Gone is the joy of our hearts;
Our dancing is turned into mourning.
¹⁶ The crown has fallen from our head;
Woe to us that we have sinned!

¹⁷ Because of this our hearts are sick,
Because of these our eyes are dimmed:
¹⁸ Because of Mount Zion, which lies desolate;
Jackals prowl over it.

---

^a *Lit. "on our neck"; meaning of Heb. uncertain.*
^{b-b} *Or "heat (cf. Deut. 28.22) of the wilderness"; meaning of Heb. uncertain.*
^c *I.e. the slaves of v.8.*

¹⁹ But You, O LORD, are enthroned forever,
Your throne endures through the ages.
²⁰ Why have You forgotten us utterly,
Forsaken us for all time?
²¹ Take us back, O LORD, to Yourself,
And let us come back;
Renew our days as of old!
²² For truly, you have rejected us,
Bitterly raged against us.

> Take us back, O LORD, to Yourself,
> And let us come back;
> Renew our days as of old!

קהלת

ECCLESIASTES

קהלת
ECCLESIASTES

1 The words of Koheleth[a] son of David, king in Jerusalem.

2 Utter futility!—said Koheleth—
Utter futility! All is futile!
3 What real value is there for a man
In all the gains[b] he makes beneath the sun?

4 One generation goes, another comes,
But the earth remains the same forever.
5 The sun rises, and the sun sets—
And glides[c] back to where it rises.
6 Southward blowing,
Turning northward,
Ever turning blows the wind;
On its rounds the wind returns.
7 All streams flow into the sea,
Yet the sea is never full;
To the place [from] which they flow
The streams flow back again.[d]
8 All such things are wearisome:
No man can ever state them;
The eye never has enough of seeing,
Nor the ear enough of hearing.
9 Only that shall happen
Which has happened,
Only that occur
Which has occurred;

---

[a] Probably "the Assembler," i.e. of hearers or of sayings; cf. 12. 9–11.
[b] So Rashbam. The Heb. 'amal usually has this sense in Ecclesiastes; cf. Ps. 105.44.
[c] So Targum; cf. Bereshith Rabbah on Gen. 1.17.
[d] According to popular belief, through tunnels; so Targum and Rashi.

There is nothing new
Beneath the sun!

¹⁰ Sometimes there is a phenomenon of which they say, "Look, this one is new!"—it occurred long since, in ages that went by before us. ¹¹ The earlier ones are not remembered; so too those that will occur later ᵉ⁻will no more be remembered than⁻ᵉ those that will occur at the very end.

¹² I, Koheleth, was king in Jerusalem over Israel. ¹³ I set my mind to study and to probe with wisdom all that happens under the sun.—An unhappy business, that, which God gave men to be concerned with! ¹⁴ I observed all the happenings beneath the sun, and I found that all is futile and pursuitᶠ of wind:
    ¹⁵ A twisted thing that cannot be made straight,
    A lack that cannot be made good.
    ¹⁶ I said to myself: "Here I have grown richer and wiser than any that ruled before me over Jerusalem, and my mind has zealously absorbed wisdom and learning." ¹⁷ And so I set my mind to appraise wisdom and to appraise madness and folly. And I learned—that this too was pursuit of wind:
    ¹⁸ For as wisdom grows, vexation grows;
    To increase learning is to increase heartache.

2 I said to myself, "Come, I will treat you to merriment. Taste mirth!" That too, I found, was futile.
    ² Of revelry I said, "It's mad!"
    Of merriment, "What good is that?"

³ I ventured to tempt my flesh with wine, and to grasp folly, while letting my mind direct with wisdom, to the end that I might learn which of the two was better for men to practice in their few days of life under heaven. ⁴ I multiplied my possessions. I built myself houses and I planted vineyards. ⁵ I laid out gardens and

---

ᵉ⁻ᵉ Lit. "will not be remembered like . . ." For ʿim meaning "like," cf. 2.16; 7.11; Job 9.26.
ᶠ Lit. "tending," from root raʿah, "to shepherd."

groves, in which I planted every kind of fruit tree. [6] I constructed pools of water, enough to irrigate a forest shooting up with trees. [7] I bought male and female slaves, and I acquired stewards. I also acquired more cattle, both herds and flocks, than all who were before me in Jerusalem. [8] I further amassed silver and gold and treasures of kings and provinces; and I got myself male and female singers, as well as the luxuries of commoners—coffers[a] and coffers of them. [9] Thus, I gained more wealth than anyone before me in Jerusalem. In addition, my wisdom remained with me: [10] I withheld from my eyes nothing they asked for, and denied myself no enjoyment; rather, I got enjoyment out of[b] all my wealth. And that was all I got out of my wealth.

[11] Then my thoughts turned to all the fortune my hands had built up, to the wealth I had acquired and won—and oh, it was all futile and pursuit of wind; there was no real value under the sun! [12] [c]For what will the man be like who will succeed [d]the one who is ruling[d] over what was built up long ago?

My thoughts also turned to appraising wisdom and madness and folly. [13] I found that

Wisdom is superior to folly
As light is superior to darkness;
[14] A wise man has his eyes in his head,
Whereas a fool walks in darkness.

But I also realized that the same fate awaits them both. [15] So I reflected: "The fate of the fool is also destined for me; to what advantage, then, have I been wise?" And I came to the conclusion that that too was futile, [16] because the wise man, just like[e] the fool, is not remembered forever; for, as the succeeding days roll by, both are forgotten. Alas, the wise man dies, just like[e] the fool!

[17] And so I loathed life. For I was distressed by all that goes on under the sun, because everything is futile and pursuit of wind.

[18] So, too, I loathed all the wealth that I was gaining under the sun. For I shall leave it to the man who will succeed me—[19] and

---

[a] *The Heb.* shiddah *occurs only here in the Bible; in the Mishnah it designates a kind of chest.*
[b] *Septuagint and a few Heb. manuscripts have "(in exchange) for"; cf. 2.24; 3.13, 22; 5.17.*
[c] *The order of the two sentences in this verse is reversed in the translation for clarity.*
[d-d] *Change of vocalization yields "me, and who is to rule"; cf. vv. 18–19.*
[e] *See note on 1.11.*

who knows whether he will be wise or foolish?—and he will control all the wealth that I gained by toil and wisdom under the sun. That too is futile. ²⁰ And so I came to view with despair all the gains I had made under the sun. ²¹ For sometimes a person whose fortune was made with wisdom, knowledge, and skill must hand it on to be the portion of somebody who did not toil for it. That too is futile, and a grave evil. ²² For what does a man get for all the toiling and worrying he does under the sun? ²³ All his days his thoughts are grief and heartache, and even at night his mind has no respite. That too is futile!

²⁴ There is nothing worthwhile for a man but to eat and drink and afford himself enjoyment with his means. And even that, I noted, comes from God. ²⁵ For who eats and who enjoys but myself?/ ²⁶ To the man, namely, who pleases Him He has given ^{g-}the wisdom and shrewdness to enjoy himself;^{-g} and to him who displeases, He has given the urge to gather and amass—only for handing on to one who is pleasing to God. That too is futile and pursuit of wind.

3   A season is set for everything, a time for every experience under heaven:^a
  ² A time for ^{b-}being born^{-b} and a time for dying,
  A time for planting and a time for uprooting the planted;
  ³ A time for ^{c-}slaying and a time for healing,^{-c}
  A time for tearing down and a time for building up;
  ⁴ A time for weeping and a time for laughing,
  A time for wailing and a time for dancing;
  ⁵ A time for throwing stones and a time for gathering stones,
  A time for embracing and a time for shunning embraces;
  ⁶ A time for seeking and a time for losing,
  A time for keeping and a time for discarding;
  ⁷ A time for ripping and a time for sewing,
  A time for silence and a time for speaking;

^f *Some mss. and ancient versions read* mimmennu, *"by His doing."*
^{g-g} *Lit. "wisdom and knowledge and enjoyment."*

^a *I.e. all human experiences are preordained by God; see v. 11.*
^{b-b} *Lit. "giving birth."*
^{c-c} *Emendation yields "wrecking . . . repairing"; cf. I Kings 18.30.*

⁸ A time for loving and a time for hating;
A time for war and a time for peace.

⁹ What value, then, can the man of affairs get from what he earns? ¹⁰ I have observed the business that God gave man to be concerned with: ¹¹ He brings everything to pass precisely at its time; He also puts eternity in their mind,*d* but without man ever guessing, from first to last, all the things that God brings to pass. ¹² Thus I realized that the only worthwhile thing there is for them is to enjoy themselves and do what is good*e* in their lifetime; ¹³ also, that whenever a man does eat and drink and get enjoyment out of all his wealth, it is a gift of God.

¹⁴ I realized, too, that whatever God has brought to pass will recur evermore:

Nothing can be added to it
And nothing taken from it—

and God has brought to pass that men revere Him.

¹⁵ ⌐What is occurring occurred long since,
⌐And what is to occur occurred long since:

and God seeks the pursued. ¹⁶ And, indeed, I have observed under the sun:

Alongside justice there is wickedness,
Alongside righteousness there is wickedness.

¹⁷ I mused: "God will doom both righteous and wicked, for ᵍ⁻there isᵍ a time for every experience and for every happening." ¹⁸ ⌐So I decided, as regards men, to dissociate them [from] the divine beings and to face the fact that they are beasts.*h* ¹⁹ For in respect of the fate of man and the fate of beast, they have one and the same fate: as the one dies so dies the other, and both have the same lifebreath; man has no superiority over beast, since both amount to nothing. ²⁰ Both go to the same place; both came from dust and both return to dust. ²¹ Who knows if a man's lifebreath does rise upward and if a beast's breath does sink down into the earth?

²² I saw that there is nothing better for man than to enjoy his possessions, since that is his portion. For who can enable him to see what will happen afterward?

---

d I.e. He preoccupies man with the attempt to discover the times of future events; cf. 8.17.
e I.e. what the author has already concluded (2.24) is good.
f Meaning of parts of verse uncertain.
g-g Shift of a diacritical point yields "He has set."
h Contrast Ps. 8.5–6.

4 I further observed[a] all the oppression that goes on under the sun: the tears of the oppressed, with none to comfort them; and the power of their oppressors—with none to comfort them. [2] Then I accounted those who died long since more fortunate than those who are still living; [3] and happier than either are those who have not yet come into being and have never witnessed the miseries that go on under the sun.

[4] I have also noted that all labor and skillful enterprise come from men's envy of each other—another futility and pursuit of wind!

[5] [True,]
The fool folds his hands together[b]
And has to eat his own flesh.
[6] [But no less truly,]
Better is a handful of gratification
Than two fistfuls of labor which is pursuit of wind.

[7] And I have noted this further futility under the sun: [8] the case of the man who is alone, with no companion, who has neither son nor brother; yet he amasses wealth without limit, and his eye is never sated with riches. For whom, now, [c]is he amassing it while denying himself[c] enjoyment? That too is a futility and an unhappy business.

[9] [d]Two are better off than one, in that they have greater [e]benefit from[e] their earnings. [10] For should they fall, one can raise the other; but woe betide him who is alone and falls with no companion to raise him! [11] Further, when two lie together they are warm; but how can he who is alone get warm? [12] Also, if one attacks, two can stand up to him. A threefold cord is not readily broken!

[a] *Cf. 3.16.*
[b] *I.e. does not work; cf. Prov. 6.10; 24.33.*
[c-c] *Lit. "am I amassing . . . myself."*
[d] *4.9–5.8 consists of a series of observations of which each one is introduced by some slight association with what precedes. The theme of 4.4–8 is not resumed until 5.9.*
[e-e] *Emendation yields "hope for"; cf. 2.20.*

¹³ Better a poor but wise youth than an old but foolish king who no longer has the sense to heed warnings. ¹⁴ For the former can emerge from a dungeon to become king; while the latter, even if born to kingship, can become a pauper./ ¹⁵ [However,] I reflected about ᵍ-all the living who walk under the sun with⁻ᵍ that youthful successor who steps into his place. ¹⁶ Unnumbered are the multitudes of all those who preceded them;ʰ and later generations will not acclaim him either.ⁱ For thatʲ too is futile and pursuit of wind.

¹⁷ ᵏ-Be not overeager to go⁻ᵏ to the House of God: more acceptable is obedience than the offering of fools, for they know nothing [but] to do wrong.

5 Keep your mouth from being rash, and let not your throatᵃ be quick to bring forth speech before God. For God is in heaven and you are on earth; that is why your words should be few. ² Just as dreams come with much brooding, so does foolish utterance come with much speech. ³ When you make a vow to God, do not delay to fulfill it. For He has no pleasure in fools; what you vow, fulfill. ⁴ It is better not to vow at all than to vow and not fulfill. ⁵ Don't let your mouth bring you into disfavor, and don't plead before the messengerᵇ that it was an error, ᶜ-but fear God;⁻ᶜ else God may be angered by your talk and destroy your possessions. ⁶ ᵈFor much dreaming leads to futility and to superfluous talk.

ᶠ *Taking* rash *as a verb; cf. Ps. 34.11.*
ᵍ⁻ᵍ *I.e. "the contemporaries of."*
ʰ *And so never heard of the gifted youth.*
ⁱ *For despite his wisdom, he too will be forgotten; cf. 2.16.*
ʲ *I.e. the advantage of wisdom over folly.*
ᵏ⁻ᵏ *Lit. "Guard your foot when it [or, you] would go."*

ᵃ *Heb.* leb, *lit. "heart," sometimes designates the organ of speech; cf. Isa. 33.18; 59.13; Ps. 19.15; 49.4; Job 8.10.*
ᵇ *Some ancient versions read "God."*
ᶜ⁻ᶜ *Moved up from v. 6 for clarity.*
ᵈ *Meaning of verse uncertain. Emendation yields: "Much brooding results in dreams; and much talk in futilities"; cf. v. 2.*

⁷ If you see in a province oppression of the poor and suppression of right and justice, don't wonder at the fact; for one high official is protected by a higher one, and both of them by still higher ones. ⁸ Thus the greatest advantage in all the land is his: he controls a field that is cultivated.ᵉ

⁹ A lover of money never has his fill of money, nor a lover of wealth his fill of income. That too is futile. ¹⁰ As his substance increases, so do those who consume it; what, then, does the success of its owner amount to but feasting his eyes? ¹¹ A worker'sᶠ sleep is sweet, whether he has much or little to eat; but the rich man's abundance doesn't let him sleep.

¹² Here is a grave evil I have observed under the sun: riches hoarded by their owner to his misfortune, ¹³ in that those riches are lost in some unlucky venture; and if he begets a son, he has nothing in hand.

¹⁴ ᵍ⁻Another grave evil is this: He must depart just as he came.⁻ᵍ As he came out of his mother's womb, so must he depart at last, naked as he came. He can take nothing of his wealth to carry with him. ¹⁵ So what is the good of his toiling for the wind? ¹⁶ Besides, all his days ʰ⁻he eats in darkness,⁻ʰ with much vexation and grief and anger.

¹⁷ Only this, I have found, is a real good: that one should eat and drink and get pleasure with all the gains he makes under the sun, during the numbered days of life that God has given him; for that is his portion. ¹⁸ Also, whenever a man is given riches and property by God, and is also permitted by Him to enjoy them and to take his portion and get pleasure for his gains—that is a gift of God. ¹⁹ For [such a man] will not brood much over the days of his life,ⁱ because God keeps him busy enjoying himself.

ᵉ *I.e. the high official profits from the labor of others; but meaning of verse uncertain.*
ᶠ *Some ancient versions have "slave's."*
ᵍ⁻ᵍ *Moved up from v. 15 for clarity.*
ʰ⁻ʰ *Septuagint reads "are [spent] in darkness and mourning."*
ⁱ *The thought of which is depressing; see v. 16.*

6 There is an evil I have observed under the sun, and a grave one it is for man: ² that God sometimes grants a man riches, property, and wealth, so that he does not want for anything his appetite may crave, but God does not permit him to enjoy it; instead, a stranger will enjoy it. That is futility and a grievous ill. ³ Even if a man should beget a hundred children and live many years—no matter how many the days of his years may come to, if his gullet is not sated through his wealth, I say: The stillbirth, though it was not even accorded a burial,ᵃ is more fortunate than he. ⁴ Though it comes into futility and departs into darkness, and its very name is covered with darkness, ⁵ though it has never seen or experienced the sun, it is better off than he—⁶ yes, even if the other lived a thousand years twice over but never had his fill of enjoyment! For are not both of them bound for the same place? ⁷ ᵇAll of man's earning is for the sake of his mouth, ᶜ⁻yet his gullet is not sated. ⁸ What advantage then has the wise man over the fool, what advantage has the pauper who knows how to get on in life?⁻ᶜ ⁹ ᵈIs the feasting of the eyes more important than the pursuit of desire? That, too, is futility and pursuit of wind.

¹⁰ Whatever happens, it was designated long ago and it was known that it would happen; as for man, he cannot contend with what is stronger than he. ¹¹ Often, much talk means much futility. How does it benefit a man? ¹² Who can possibly know what is best for a man to do in life—the few days of his fleeting life? Forᵉ who can tell him what the future holds for him under the sun?

ᵃ Stillbirths were cast into pits or hidden in the ground in no recognizable graves; cf. v. 4 end.
ᵇ Cf. Prov. 16.26.
ᶜ⁻ᶜ Meaning of Heb. uncertain; emendation yields "And if the gullet is not sated, ⁸what advantage has the wise man over the fool, he who knows how to get on in life over the pauper?"
ᵈ Meaning of first half of verse uncertain.
ᵉ Lit. "according to the shadow that"; cf. Qumran Aramaic betel and Syriac meṭṭol; and see 8.13.

7 [a]A good name is better than fragrant oil, and the day of death than the day of birth.[b]

² It is better to go to a house of mourning than to a house of feasting; for that is the end of every man, and a living one should take it to heart.

³ Vexation is better than revelry;[c] for though the face be sad, the heart may be glad. ⁴ Wise men are drawn to a house of mourning, and fools to a house of merrymaking.

⁵ It is better to listen to a wise man's reproof than to listen to the praise of fools. ⁶ For the levity[d] of the fool is like the crackling of nettles under a kettle.[e] But that too is illusory; ⁷ for cheating[f] may rob the wise man of reason and destroy the prudence of the cautious.[g]

⁸ The end of a matter is better than the beginning
of it.

Better a patient spirit than a haughty spirit.

⁹ Don't let your spirit be quickly vexed, for vexation abides in the breasts of fools.

¹⁰ Don't say, "How has it happened that former times were better than these?" For it is not wise of you to ask that question.

¹¹ Wisdom is as good as a patrimony, and even better, for those who behold the sun. ¹² For to be in the shelter of wisdom is to be also in the shelter of money,[h] and the advantage of intelligence is that wisdom preserves the life of him who possesses it.

¹³ [i]Consider God's doing! Who can straighten what He has

---

[a] *The author now offers a number of practical maxims, which, however, he concludes (vv. 23–24) are of limited value.*
[b] *Until a man dies, there is always danger that he may forfeit his good name.*
[c] *For empty revelry precludes real happiness: cf. 2.2.*
[d] *Emendation yields "praise" (shbḥ).*
[e] *This section, to end of verse 7, is apparently a continuation of the thought in vv. 11–12 and 19.*
[f] *Emendation yields "riches."*
[g] *Lit. "caution"; cf. post-biblical* mathun, *"cautious."*
[h] *Emendation yields "For the possessor of wisdom becomes a possessor of money."*
[i] *Vv. 13–14 continue the thought of v. 10.*

twisted? [14] So in a time of good fortune enjoy the good fortune; and in a time of misfortune, reflect: The one no less than the other was God's doing; consequently, man may find no fault with Him.[j]

[15] In my own brief span of life, I have seen both these things: sometimes a good man perishes in spite of his goodness, and sometimes a wicked one endures in spite of his wickedness. [16] So don't overdo goodness and don't act the wise man to excess, or you may be dumfounded. [17] Don't overdo wickedness and don't be a fool, or you may die before your time. [18] It is best that you grasp the one without letting go of the other, for one who fears God will do his duty[k] by both.

[19] Wisdom is more of a stronghold to a wise man than [l]ten magnates[-l] that a city may contain.

[20] [m]For there is not one good man on earth who does what is best[n] and doesn't err.

[21] Finally, don't pay attention to everything that is said, so that you may not hear your slave reviling you; [22] for well you remember[o] the many times that you yourself have reviled others.

[23] All this I tested with wisdom. I thought I could fathom it,[n] but it eludes me. [24] [The secret of] what happens is elusive and deep, deep down; who can discover it? [25] I put my mind to studying, exploring, and seeking wisdom and the reason of things, and to studying wickedness, stupidity, madness, and folly. [26] Now, I find woman more bitter than death; she is all traps, her hands are fetters and her heart is snares. He who is pleasing to God escapes her, and he who is displeasing is caught by her. [27] See, this is what I found, said Koheleth, item by item in my search for the reason of things. [28] As for what I sought further but did not find, I found only one human being in a thousand, and the one I found among so many was never a woman. [29] But, see, this I did find: God made men plain, but they have engaged in too much reasoning.

[j] *So Rashi; cf. the same thought in Job 1.22; 2.10.*
[k] *Cf. post-biblical* yaṣa yede.
[l-l] *Emendation yields "the riches of the magnates"; cf. Prov. 18.11.*
[m] *Apparently continuing the thought of v. 16.*
[n] *Refers back to 6.12.*
[o] *The same idiom occurs again in 8.5.*

8 *ª-*Who is like the wise man,*-ª* and who knows the meaning of the adage:

"A man's wisdom lights up his face,
So that his deep discontent*ᵇ* is dissembled"?

² I do! "Obey the king's orders—and *ᶜ-*don't rush*-ᶜ* into uttering an oath by God."*ᵈ* ³ *ᵉ-*Leave his presence; do not tarry*-ᵉ* in a dangerous situation, for he can do anything he pleases; ⁴ inasmuch as a king's command is authoritative, and none can say to him, "What are you doing?" ⁵ One who obeys orders will not suffer from the dangerous situation.

A wise man, however, will bear in mind*ᶠ* that there is a time of doom.*ᵍ* ⁶ For there is a time for every experience, including the doom; for a man's calamity*ʰ* overwhelms him. ⁷ Indeed, he does not know what is to happen; even when it is on the point of happening, who can tell him? ⁸ No man has authority over the lifebreath—to hold back the lifebreath;*ⁱ* there is no authority over the day of death. There is no mustering out from that war; wickedness*ʲ* is powerless to save its owner.

⁹ All these things I observed; I noted all that went on under the sun, while men still had authority over men to treat them unjustly. ¹⁰ And then I saw scoundrels *ᵏ-*coming from the Holy Site and being brought to burial,*-ᵏ* while such as had acted righteously were forgotten in the city.

ª-ª Some ancient versions read: "Who here is wise."
ᵇ Lit. "face"; cf. I Sam. 1.18; Job 9.27.
ᶜ-ᶜ Moved up from v. 3 for English word order.
ᵈ The answer to the inquiry about the implications of the proverb in v. 1 is given in the form of another proverb, of which only the first half is relevant and is enlarged upon.
ᵉ-ᵉ Or "Give ground before him; do not resist."
ᶠ The same idiom as in 7.22.
ᵍ Lit. "time and doom"; cf. the synonymous "time of misfortune," lit. "time and misfortune," 9.11.
ʰ Still another term for death; cf. "the time of calamity" for "the hour of death," 9.12.
ⁱ From leaving the body when the time comes; see 12.7; cf. Ps. 104.29; 146.4.
ʲ Emendation yields "riches."
ᵏ-ᵏ Meaning uncertain; emendation yields "approaching [to minister]. They would come and profane the Holy Site."

And here is another frustration: [11] the fact that the sentence imposed for evil deeds is not executed swiftly, which is why men are emboldened to do evil—[12] the fact that a sinner may do evil a hundred times and his [punishment] still be delayed. For although I am aware that "It will be well with those who revere God since they revere Him, [13] and it will not be well with the scoundrel, and he will not live long, because[l] he does not revere God"—[14] here is a frustration that occurs in the world: sometimes an upright man is requited according to the conduct of the scoundrel; and sometimes the scoundrel is requited according to the conduct of the upright. I say all that is frustration.

[15] I therefore praised enjoyment. For the only good a man can have under the sun is to eat and drink and enjoy himself. That much can accompany him, in exchange for his wealth, through the days of life that God has granted him under the sun.

[16] For I have set my mind to learn wisdom and to observe the business that goes on in the world—even to the extent of going without sleep day and night—[17] and I have observed all that God brings to pass. Indeed, man cannot guess the events that occur under the sun. For man tries strenuously, but fails to guess them; and even if a sage should think to discover them he would not be able to guess them.

9 For all this I noted, and I ascertained[a] all this: that the actions of even the righteous and the wise are determined by God. [b-]Even love! Even hate! Man knows none of these in advance[2] —none!-[b] For the same fate is in store for all: for the righteous, and for the wicked; for the good and pure,[c] and for the impure; for him who sacrifices, and for him who does not;[d] for him who is pleasing,[e]

---

[l] *See note on 6.12.*

[a] *Meaning of verb uncertain; construction as in Hos. 12.3; Ezra 3.12.*
[b-b] *Emendation yields: "Even love, even hate, no man can know in advance. All [2] are insignificant."*
[c] *I.e. those who observe the laws of ritual purity.*
[d] *Cf. 4.17.*
[e] *I.e. to God; cf. 2.26; 7.26.*

and for him who is displeasing; and for him who swears, and for him who shuns oaths.*f* 3 That is the sad thing about all that goes on under the sun: that the same fate is in store for all. (Not only that, but men's hearts are full of sadness, and their minds of madness, while they live; and then—to the dead!) 4 For he who is *g*-reckoned among-*g* the living has something to look forward to—even a live dog is better than a dead lion—5 since the living know they will die. But the dead know nothing; they have no more recompense,*h* for even the memory of them has died. 6 Their loves, their hates, their jealousies have long since perished; and they have no more share till the end of time in all that goes on under the sun.

7 Go, eat your bread in gladness, and drink your wine in joy; for your action was long ago approved by God.*i* 8 Let your clothes always be freshly washed, and your head never lack ointment. 9 Enjoy happiness with a woman you love all the fleeting days of life that have been granted to you under the sun—all your fleeting days. For that alone is what you can get out of life and out of the means you acquire under the sun. 10 Whatever it is in your power to do, do with all your might. For there is no action, no reasoning, no learning, no wisdom in Sheol, where you are going.

11 I have further observed under the sun that

The race is not won by the swift,

Nor the battle by the valiant;

Nor is bread won by the wise,

Nor wealth by the intelligent,

Nor favor by the learned.

For the time of mischance*j* comes to all.*k* 12 And a man cannot

f Cf. 8.2.

g-g Lit. "joined to all."

h Emendation yields "hope."

i Cf. 2.24–25; 3.13; 5.18.

j Euphemism for death.

k I.e. the insignificant duration of life renders all successes illusory; cf. 4.15–16.

even know his time. As fishes are enmeshed in a fatal net, and as birds are trapped in a snare, so men are caught at the time of calamity,[j] when it comes upon them without warning.

[13] This thing too I observed under the sun about wisdom, and it affected me profoundly. [14] There was a little city, with few men in it; and to it came a great king, who invested it and built mighty siege works against it. [15] Present in the city was a poor wise man [l]who might have saved[-l] it with his wisdom, but nobody thought of that poor man. [16] So I observed: Wisdom is better than valor; but

> A poor man's wisdom is scorned,
> And his words are not heeded.

[17] [m]Words spoken softly by wise men are heeded [n]sooner than those shouted by a lord in folly.[-n]

[18] Wisdom is more valuable than [o]weapons of war,[-o] but a single error destroys much of value.

10 Dead flies turn the perfumer's ointment fetid and putrid;[a] so a little folly outweighs massive wisdom.

[2] A wise man's mind tends toward the right hand, a fool's toward the left.[b] [3] A fool's mind is also wanting when he travels, and he lets everybody know he is a fool.

[4] If the wrath of a lord flares up against you, don't give up your post;[c] for [d]when wrath abates, grave offenses are pardoned.[-d]

[5] Here is an evil I have seen under the sun as great as an error

---

[l-l] *Others "who saved."*
[m] *9.17–10.19 is a group of loosely connected aphorisms.*
[n-n] *Lit. "than the scream of a lord in [the manner of] the fools."*
[o-o] *Emendation yields "everything precious."*

[a] *Meaning of Heb. uncertain.*
[b] *I.e. a wise man's mind brings him good luck; a fool's brings him bad luck.*
[c] *Emendation yields "hope."*
[d-d] *Lit. "abatement (II Chron. 36.16) remits grave offenses." For* hinniah, *"to remit," cf. Abodah Zarah 13a; cf.* hanahah, *"remission of taxes," Esth. 2.18.*

committed by a ruler: 6 Folly was placed on lofty heights, while rich men sat in low estate. 7 I have seen slaves on horseback, and nobles walking on the ground like slaves.

8 He who digs a pit will fall into it; he who breaches a stone fence will be bitten by a snake. 9 He who quarries stones will *e*-be hurt by them; he who splits wood will be harmed by-*e* it. 10 /If the ax has become dull and he has not whetted the edge, he must exert more strength. Thus the advantage of a skill [depends on the exercise of] prudence. 11 If the snake bites because no spell was uttered, no advantage is gained by the trained charmer.

12 A wise man's talk brings him favor, but a fool's lips are his undoing. 13 His talk begins as silliness and ends as disastrous madness. 14 Yet the fool talks and talks!

*g*A man cannot know what will happen; who can tell him what the future holds?

15 *h*A fool's exertions tire him out, for he doesn't know how to get to a town.

16 Alas for you, O land whose king is a lackey and whose ministers dine in the morning! 17 Happy are you, O land whose king is a master and whose ministers dine at the proper time—with restraint, not with guzzling!

18 Through slothfulness the ceiling sags,
Through lazy hands the house caves in.

19 They*i* make a banquet for revelry; wine makes life merry, and money answers every need.

20 Don't revile a king even among your intimates.*j*
Don't revile a rich man even in your bedchamber;
For a bird of the air may carry the utterance,
And a winged creature may report the word.

---

e-e Emendation yields "profit . . . shall make use of."
f Meaning of verse uncertain.
g The thought of this sentence is resumed at v. 20.
h This verse continues the thought of v. 3.
i I.e. the ministers of v. 16.
j Others "thoughts"; meaning of Heb. uncertain.

11 Send your bread forth upon the waters; for after many days you will find it. [2] Distribute portions to seven or even to eight, for you cannot know what misfortune may occur on earth.

[3] If the clouds are filled, they will pour down rain on the earth; and *a*-if a tree falls to the south or to the north, the tree will stay where it falls.-*a* [4] If one watches the wind, he will never sow; and if one observes the clouds, he will never reap. [5] Just as you do not know how the lifebreath passes into*b* the limbs within the womb of the pregnant woman, so you cannot foresee the actions of God, who causes all things to happen. [6] Sow your seed in the morning, and don't hold back your hand in the evening, since you don't know which is going to succeed, the one or the other, or if both are equally good.

[7] How sweet is the light, what a delight for the eyes to behold the sun! [8] Even if a man lives many years, let him enjoy himself in all of them, remembering how many the days of darkness are going to be. The only future is nothingness!

[9] O youth, enjoy yourself while you are young! Let your heart lead you to enjoyment in the days of your youth. Follow the desires of your heart and the glances of your eyes—but know well that God will call you to account for all such things—[10] and banish care from your mind, and pluck sorrow out of your flesh! For youth and black hair are fleeting.

12 So appreciate your vigor*a* in the days of your youth, before those days of sorrow come and those years arrive of which you will say, "I have no pleasure in them"; [2] before sun and light and moon and stars grow dark, and the clouds come back again after the rain:

a-a Emendation yields, "if a thunderbolt (lit. arrow, cf. e.g. II Sam. 22.15) falls . . . where the thunderbolt falls, only there will it strike."
b So many mss. and Targum; most mss. read "like."

a Cf. post-biblical bori; others "Remember thy Creator."

³ When the guards of the house*b* become shaky,
And the men of valor*c* are bent,
And the maids that grind,*d* grown few, are idle,
And the ladies that peer through the windows*e* grow dim,
⁴ And the doors to the street*f* are shut—
With the noise of the hand mill growing fainter,
And the song of the bird *g*⁻growing feebler,⁻*g*
And all the strains of music dying down;*h*
⁵ When one is afraid of heights
And there is terror on the road.—
For the almond tree may blossom,
i⁻The grasshopper be burdened,⁻*i*
And the caper bush may bud again;*j*
But man sets out for his eternal abode,
With mourners all around in the street.—
⁶ Before the silver cord snaps
And the golden bowl crashes,
The jar is shattered at the spring,
And the jug*k* is smashed at the cistern.*l*
⁷ And the dust returns to the ground
As it was,
And the lifebreath returns to God
Who bestowed it.
⁸ Utter futility—said Koheleth—
All is futile!

b I.e. the arms.
c I.e. the legs.
d I.e. the teeth.
e I.e. the eyes.
f I.e. the ears.
g-g Exact meaning of Heb. uncertain.
h Cf. II Sam. 19.36.
i-i Emendation yields "The squill (post-biblical Heb. ḥaṣab) resume its burden," i.e. its
blossom-stalk and its leaves.
j These plants, after seeming dead for part of the year, revive, unlike man. Cf. Job 14.7–10.
k So in Punic; others "wheel."
l Poetic figure for the end of life.

⁹ A further word: Because Koheleth was a sage, he continued to instruct the people. He listened to and tested the soundness^m of many maxims. ¹⁰ Koheleth sought to discover useful sayings and recorded^n genuinely truthful sayings. ¹¹ The sayings of the wise are like goads, like nails fixed ^o-in prodding sticks.^-o ^p-They were given by one Shepherd.^-p

¹² A further word: ^q-Against them,^-q my son, be warned!
The making of many books is without limit
And much study^r is a wearying of the flesh.

¹³ The sum of the matter, when all is said and done: Revere God and observe His commandments! For this applies to all mankind: ¹⁴ that God will call every creature to account for ^s-everything unknown,^-s be it good or bad.

The sum of the matter, when all is said and done: Revere God and observe His commandments! For this applies to all mankind.

---

^m A noun, like dibber (Jer. 5.13), which occurs in such post-biblical phrases as shanim kethiq(qe)nan, "normal years" (lit. "years according to their propriety").

^n Wekhathub is equivalent to wekhathob, an infinitive employed as in Esth. 9.16 and elsewhere.

^o-o Meaning of Heb. uncertain. Others "are those that are composed in collections."

^p-p Meaning of Heb. uncertain. Emendation yields "They are accounted as a sharp ox goad" (post-biblical marded).

^q-q Emendation yields "Slow, there!" Cf. Arabic mah and mah mah; so also mah (meh) in Prov. 31.2.

^r Meaning of Heb. uncertain.

^s-s Emendation yields "all their conduct."

אסתר

ESTHER

אסתר
ESTHER

1 It happened in the days of Ahasuerus—that Ahasuerus who
reigned over a hundred and twenty-seven provinces from India
to Nubia. ² In those days, when King Ahasuerus occupied the
royal throne in the fortress*ᵃ* Shushan, ³ in the third year of his
reign, he gave a banquet for all the officials and courtiers—the
administration of Persia and Media, the nobles and the governors
of the provinces in his service. ⁴ For no fewer than a hundred and
eighty days he displayed the vast riches of his kingdom and the
splendid glory of his majesty. ⁵ At the end of this period, the king
gave a banquet for seven days in the court of the king's palace
garden for all the people who lived in the fortress Shushan, high
and low alike. ⁶ ᵇ[There were hangings of] white cotton and blue
wool, caught up by cords of fine linen and purple wool to silver
rods and alabaster columns; and there were couches of gold and
silver on a pavement of marble, alabaster, mother-of-pearl, and
mosaics. ⁷ Royal wine was served in abundance, as befits a king,
in golden beakers, beakers of varied design. ⁸ And the rule for the
drinking was, "No restrictions!" For the king had given orders to
every palace steward to comply with each man's wishes. ⁹ In addition, Queen Vashti gave a banquet for women, in the royal palace
of King Ahasuerus.

¹⁰ On the seventh day, when the king was merry with wine, he
ordered Mehuman, Bizzetha, Harbona, Bigtha, Abagtha, Zethar,
and Carcas, the seven eunuchs in attendance on King Ahasuerus,
¹¹ to bring Queen Vashti before the king wearing a royal diadem,
to display her beauty to the peoples and the officials; for she was
a beautiful woman. ¹² But Queen Vashti refused to come at the

---

ᵃ *I.e. the fortified city.*
ᵇ *Meaning of part of this verse uncertain.*

king's command conveyed by the eunuchs. The king was greatly incensed, and his fury burned within him.

¹³ Then the king consulted the sages learned in procedure.^c (For it was the royal practice [to turn] to all who were versed in law and precedent. ¹⁴ His closest advisers were Carshena, Shethar, Admatha, Tarshish, Meres, Marsena, and Memucan, the seven ministers of Persia and Media who had access to the royal presence and occupied the first place in the kingdom.) ¹⁵ "What," [he asked,] "shall be done, according to law, to Queen Vashti for failing to obey the command of King Ahasuerus conveyed by the eunuchs?"

¹⁶ Thereupon Memucan declared in the presence of the king and the ministers: "Queen Vashti has committed an offense not only against Your Majesty but also against all the officials and against all the peoples in all the provinces of King Ahasuerus. ¹⁷ For the queen's behavior will make all wives despise their husbands, as they reflect that King Ahasuerus himself ordered Queen Vashti to be brought before him, but she would not come. ¹⁸ This very day the ladies of Persia and Media, who have heard of the queen's behavior, will cite it to all Your Majesty's officials, and there will be no end of scorn and provocation!

¹⁹ "If it please Your Majesty, let a royal edict be issued by you, and let it be written into the laws of Persia and Media, so that it cannot be abrogated, that Vashti shall never enter the presence of King Ahasuerus. And let Your Majesty bestow her royal state upon another who is more worthy than she. ²⁰ Then will the judgment executed by Your Majesty resound throughout your realm, vast though it is; and all wives will treat their husbands with respect, high and low alike."

²¹ The proposal was approved by the king and the ministers, and the king did as Memucan proposed. ²² Dispatches were sent to all the provinces of the king, to every province in its own script and to every nation in its own language, that every man should wield authority in his home and speak the language of his own people.

^c *Lit. "the times."*

2 Some time afterward, when the anger of King Ahasuerus subsided, he thought of Vashti and what she had done and what had been decreed against her. ² The king's servants who attended him said, "Let beautiful young virgins be sought out for Your Majesty. ³ Let Your Majesty appoint officers in every province of your realm to assemble all the beautiful young virgins at the fortress Shushan, in the harem under the supervision of Hege, the king's eunuch, guardian of the women. Let them be provided with their cosmetics. ⁴ And let the maiden who pleases Your Majesty be queen instead of Vashti." The proposal pleased the king, and he acted upon it.

⁵ In the fortress Shushan lived a Jew by the name of Mordecai, son of Jair son of Shimei son of Kish, a Benjaminite. ⁶ [Kish] had been exiled from Jerusalem in the group that was carried into exile along with King Jeconiah of Judah, which had been driven into exile by King Nebuchadnezzar of Babylon.—⁷ He was foster father to Hadassah—that is, Esther—his uncle's daughter, for she had neither father nor mother. The maiden was shapely and beautiful; and when her father and mother died, Mordecai adopted her as his own daughter.

⁸ When the king's order and edict was proclaimed, and when many girls were assembled in the fortress Shushan under the supervision of Hegai,ᵃ Esther too was taken into the king's palace under the supervision of Hegai, guardian of the women. ⁹ The girl pleased him and won his favor, and he hastened to furnish her with her cosmetics and her rations, as well as with the seven maids who were her due from the king's palace; and he treated her and her maids with special kindness in the harem. ¹⁰ Esther did not reveal her people or her kindred, for Mordecai had told her not to reveal it. ¹¹ Every single day Mordecai would walk about in front of the court of the harem, to learn how Esther was faring and what was happening to her.

¹² When each girl's turn came to go to King Ahasuerus at the

ᵃ Identical with Hege in v. 3.

end of the twelve months' treatment prescribed for women (for that was the period spent on beautifying them: six months with oil of myrrh and six months with perfumes and women's cosmetics, [13] and it was after that that the girl would go to the king), whatever she asked for would be given her to take with her from the harem to the king's palace. [14] She would go in the evening and leave in the morning for a second harem in charge of Shaashgaz, the king's eunuch, guardian of the concubines. She would not go again to the king unless the king wanted her, when she would be summoned by name. [15] When the turn came for Esther daughter of Abihail—the uncle of Mordecai, who had adopted her as his own daughter—to go to the king, she did not ask for anything but what Hegai, the king's eunuch, guardian of the women, advised. Yet Esther won the admiration of all who saw her.

[16] Esther was taken to King Ahasuerus, in his royal palace, in the tenth month, which is the month of Tebeth, in the seventh year of his reign. [17] The king loved Esther more than all the other women, and she won his grace and favor more than all the virgins. So he set a royal diadem on her head and made her queen instead of Vashti. [18] The king gave a great banquet for all his officials and courtiers, "the banquet of Esther." He proclaimed a remission of taxes[b] for the provinces and distributed gifts as befits a king.

[19] [c]When the virgins were assembled a second time, Mordecai sat in the palace gate. [20] But Esther still did not reveal her kindred or her people, as Mordecai had instructed her; for Esther obeyed Mordecai's bidding, as she had done when she was under his tutelage.

[21] At that time, when Mordecai was sitting in the palace gate, Bigthan and Teresh, two of the king's eunuchs who guarded the threshold, became angry, and plotted to do away with King Ahasuerus. [22] Mordecai learned of it and told it to Queen Esther, and Esther reported it to the king in Mordecai's name. [23] The matter was investigated and found to be so, and the two were impaled on stakes. This was recorded in the book of annals at the instance of the king.

b Or "an amnesty."
c Meaning of verse uncertain.

3   Some time afterward, King Ahasuerus promoted Haman son of Hammedatha the Agagite; he advanced him and seated him higher than any of his fellow officials. ² All the king's courtiers in the palace gate knelt and bowed low to Haman, for such was the king's order concerning him; but Mordecai would not kneel or bow low. ³ Then the king's courtiers who were in the palace gate said to Mordecai, "Why do you disobey the king's order?" ⁴ When they spoke to him day after day and he would not listen to them, they told Haman, in order to see whether Mordecai's resolve would prevail; for he had explained to them that he was a Jew.ᵃ ⁵ When Haman saw that Mordecai would not kneel or bow low to him, Haman was filled with rage. ⁶ But he disdained to lay hands on Mordecai alone; having been told who Mordecai's people were, Haman plotted to do away with all the Jews, Mordecai's people, throughout the kingdom of Ahasuerus.

⁷ In the first month, that is, the month of Nisan, in the twelfth year of King Ahasuerus, *pur*—which means "the lot"—was cast before Haman concerning every day and every month, [until it fell on] the twelfth month, that is, the month of Adar. ⁸ Haman then said to King Ahasuerus, "There is a certain people, scattered and dispersed among the other peoples in all the provinces of your realm, whose laws are different from those of any other people and who do not obey the king's laws; and it is not in Your Majesty's interest to tolerate them. ⁹ If it please Your Majesty, let an edict be drawn for their destruction, and I will pay ten thousand talents of silver to the stewards for deposit in the royal treasury." ¹⁰ Thereupon the king removed his signet ring from his hand and gave it to Haman son of Hammedatha the Agagite, the foe of the Jews. ¹¹ And the king said, "The money and the people are yours to do with as you see fit."

¹² On the thirteenth day of the first month, the king's scribes were summoned and a decree was issued, as Haman directed, to the king's satraps, to the governors of every province, and to the officials of every people, to every province in its own script and

---

ᵃ *I.e. that as a Jew he could not bow to a descendant of Agag, the Amalekite king: see I Sam. 15, and cf. Exod. 17.14–16; Deut. 25.17–19.*

to every people in its own language. The orders were issued in
the name of King Ahasuerus and sealed with the king's signet.
¹³ Accordingly, written instructions were dispatched by couriers
to all the king's provinces to destroy, massacre, and exterminate
all the Jews, young and old, children and women, on a single day,
on the thirteenth day of the twelfth month—that is, the month of
Adar—and to plunder their possessions. ¹⁴ The text of the document was to the effect that a law should be proclaimed in every
single province; it was to be publicly displayed to all the peoples,
so that they might be ready for that day.

¹⁵ The couriers went out posthaste on the royal mission, and
the decree was proclaimed in the fortress Shushan. The king and
Haman sat down to drink, but the city of Shushan was dumb-
founded.

4 When Mordecai learned all that had happened, Mordecai
tore his clothes and put on sackcloth and ashes. He went through
the city, crying out loudly and bitterly, ² until he came in front of
the palace gate; for one could not enter the palace gate wearing
sackcloth.—³ Also, in every province that the king's command
and decree reached, there was great mourning among the Jews,
with fasting, weeping, and wailing, and everybody lay in sackcloth
and ashes.—⁴ When Esther's maidens and eunuchs came and
informed her, the queen was greatly agitated. She sent clothing
for Mordecai to wear, so that he might take off his sackcloth; but
he refused.

⁵ Thereupon Esther summoned Hathach, one of the eunuchs
whom the king had appointed to serve her, and sent him to
Mordecai to learn the why and wherefore of it all. ⁶ Hathach went
out to Mordecai in the city square in front of the palace gate;
⁷ and Mordecai told him all that had happened to him, and all
about the money that Haman had offered to pay into the royal
treasury for the destruction of the Jews. ⁸ He also gave him the
written text of the law that had been proclaimed in Shushan for

their destruction. [He bade him] show it to Esther and inform her, and charge her to go to the king and to appeal to him and to plead with him for her people. 9 When Hathach came and delivered Mordecai's message to Esther, 10 Esther told Hathach to take back to Mordecai the following reply: 11 "All the king's courtiers and the people of the king's provinces know that if any person, man or woman, enters the king's presence in the inner court without having been summoned, there is but one law for him—that he be put to death. Only if the king extends the golden scepter to him may he live. Now I have not been summoned to visit the king for the last thirty days."

12 When Mordecai was told what Esther had said, 13 Mordecai had this message delivered to Esther: "Do not imagine that you, of all the Jews, will escape with your life by being in the king's palace. 14 On the contrary, if you keep silent in this crisis, relief and deliverance will come to the Jews from another quarter, while you and your father's house will perish. And who knows, perhaps you have attained to royal position for just such a crisis." 15 Then Esther sent back this answer to Mordecai: 16 "Go, assemble all the Jews who live in Shushan, and fast in my behalf; do not eat or drink for three days, night or day. I and my maidens will observe the same fast. Then I shall go to the king, though it is contrary to the law; and if I am to perish, I shall perish!" 17 So Mordecai went about [the city] and did just as Esther had commanded him.

5 On the third day, Esther put on royal apparel and stood in the inner court of the king's palace, facing the king's palace, while the king was sitting on his royal throne in the throne room facing the entrance of the palace. 2 As soon as the king saw Queen Esther standing in the court, she won his favor. The king extended to Esther the golden scepter which he had in his hand, and Esther approached and touched the tip of the scepter. 3 "What troubles you, Queen Esther?" the king asked her. "And what is your request? Even to half the kingdom, it shall be

granted you." ⁴ "If it please Your Majesty," Esther replied, "let
Your Majesty and Haman come today to the feast that I have
prepared for him." ⁵ The king commanded, "Tell Haman to
hurry and do Esther's bidding." So the king and Haman came to
the feast that Esther had prepared.

⁶ At the wine feast, the king asked Esther, "What is your wish?
It shall be granted you. And what is your request? Even to half
the kingdom, it shall be fulfilled." ⁷ "My wish," replied Esther,
"my request—⁸ if Your Majesty will do me the favor, if it please
Your Majesty to grant my wish and accede to my request—let
Your Majesty and Haman come to the feast which I will prepare
for them; and tomorrow I will do Your Majesty's bidding."

⁹ That day Haman went out happy and lighthearted. But when
Haman saw Mordecai in the palace gate, and Mordecai did not
rise or even stir on his account, Haman was filled with rage at
him. ¹⁰ Nevertheless, Haman controlled himself and went home.
He sent for his friends and his wife Zeresh, ¹¹ and Haman told
them about his great wealth and his many sons, and all about how
the king had promoted him and advanced him above the officials
and the king's courtiers. ¹² "What is more," said Haman, "Queen
Esther gave a feast, and besides the king she did not have anyone
but me. And tomorrow too I am invited by her along with the
king. ¹³ Yet all this means nothing to me every time I see that Jew
Mordecai sitting in the palace gate." ¹⁴ Then his wife Zeresh and
all his friends said to him, "Let a stake be put up, fifty cubits high,
and in the morning ask the king to have Mordecai impaled on it.
Then you can go gaily with the king to the feast." The proposal
pleased Haman, and he had the stake put up.

6 That night, sleep deserted the king, and he ordered the book
of records, the annals, to be brought; and it was read to the king.
² There it was found written that Mordecai had denounced Big-
thana and Teresh, two of the king's eunuchs who guarded the
threshhold, who had plotted to do away with King Ahasuerus.

³ "What honor or advancement has been conferred on Mordecai for this?" the king inquired. "Nothing at all has been done for him," replied the king's servants who were in attendance on him. ⁴ "Who is in the court?" the king asked. For Haman had just entered the outer court of the royal palace, to speak to the king about having Mordecai impaled on the stake he had prepared for him. ⁵ "It is Haman standing in the court," the king's servants answered him. "Let him enter," said the king. ⁶ Haman entered, and the king asked him, "What should be done for a man whom the king desires to honor?" Haman said to himself, "Whom would the king desire to honor more than me?" ⁷ So Haman said to the king, "For the man whom the king desires to honor, ⁸ let royal garb which the king has worn be brought, and a horse on which the king has ridden and on whose head a royal diadem has been set; ⁹ and let the attire and the horse be put in the charge of one of the king's noble courtiers. And let the man whom the king desires to honor be attired and paraded on the horse through the city square, while they proclaim before him: This is what is done for the man whom the king desires to honor!" ¹⁰ "Quick, then!" said the king to Haman. "Get the garb and the horse, as you have said, and do this to Mordecai the Jew, who sits in the king's gate. Omit nothing of all you have proposed." ¹¹ So Haman took the garb and the horse and arrayed Mordecai and paraded him through the city square; and he proclaimed before him: This is what is done for the man whom the king desires to honor!

¹² Then Mordecai returned to the king's gate, while Haman hurried home, his head covered in mourning. ¹³ There Haman told his wife Zeresh and all his friends everything that had befallen him. His advisers and his wife Zeresh said to him, "If Mordecai, before whom you have begun to fall, is of Jewish stock, you will not overcome him; you will fall before him to your ruin."

¹⁴ While they were still speaking with him, the king's eunuchs arrived and hurriedly brought Haman to the banquet which Esther had prepared.

7 So the king and Haman came to feast with Queen Esther. ² On the second day, the king again asked Esther at the banquet, "What is your wish, Queen Esther? It shall be granted you. And what is your request? Even to half the kingdom, it shall be fulfilled." ³ Queen Esther replied: "If Your Majesty will do me the favor, and if it pleases Your Majesty, let my life be granted me as my wish, and my people as my request. ⁴ For we have been sold, my people and I, to be destroyed, massacred, and exterminated. Had we only been sold as bondmen and bondwomen, I would have kept silent; for ᵃ-the adversary-ᵃ is not worthy of the king's trouble."

⁵ Thereupon King Ahasuerus demanded of Queen Esther, "Who is he and where is he who dared to do this?" ⁶ "The adversary and enemy," replied Esther, "is this evil Haman!" And Haman cringed in terror before the king and the queen. ⁷ The king, in his fury, left the wine feast for the palace garden, while Haman remained to plead with Queen Esther for his life; for he saw that the king had resolved to destroy him. ⁸ When the king returned from the palace garden to the banquet room, Haman was lying prostrate on the couch on which Esther reclined. "Does he mean," cried the king, "to ravish the queen in my own palace?" No sooner did these words leave the king's lips than Haman's face ᵇ-was covered.-ᵇ ⁹ Then Harbonah, one of the eunuchs in attendance on the king, said, "What is more, a stake is standing at Haman's house, fifty cubits high, which Haman made for Mordecai—the man whose words saved the king." "Impale him on it!" the king ordered. ¹⁰ So they impaled Haman on the stake which he had put up for Mordecai, and the king's fury abated.

ᵃ⁻ᵃ *Emendation yields "a trifle"* (ḥiṣṣar), *lit. "little finger."*
ᵇ⁻ᵇ *Meaning of Heb. uncertain. Emendation yields "blanched"; cf. Ps. 34.6.*

8 That very day King Ahasuerus gave the property of Haman, the enemy of the Jews, to Queen Esther. Mordecai presented himself to the king, for Esther had revealed how he was related to her. ² The king slipped off his ring, which he had taken back from Haman, and gave it to Mordecai; and Esther put Mordecai in charge of Haman's property.

³ Esther spoke to the king again, falling at his feet and weeping, and beseeching him to avert the evil plotted by Haman the Agagite against the Jews. ⁴ The king extended the golden scepter to Esther, and Esther arose and stood before the king. ⁵ "If it please Your Majesty," she said, "and if I have won your favor and the proposal seems right to Your Majesty, and if I am pleasing to you —let dispatches be written countermanding those which were written by Haman son of Hammedatha the Agagite, embodying his plot to annihilate the Jews throughout the king's provinces. ⁶ For how can I bear to see the disaster which will befall my people! And how can I bear to see the destruction of my kindred!"

⁷ Then King Ahasuerus said to Queen Esther and Mordecai the Jew, "I have given Haman's property to Esther, and he has been impaled on the stake for scheming against the Jews. ⁸ And you may further write with regard to the Jews as you see fit. [Write it] in the king's name and seal it with the king's signet, for an edict that has been written in the king's name and sealed with the king's signet may not be revoked."

⁹ So the king's scribes were summoned at that time, on the twenty-third day of the third month, that is, the month of Sivan; and letters were written, at Mordecai's dictation, to the Jews and to the satraps, the governors and the officials of the one hundred and twenty-seven provinces from India to Ethiopia: to every province in its own script and to every people in its own language, and to the Jews in their own script and language. ¹⁰ He had them written in the name of King Ahasuerus and sealed with the king's

signet. Letters were dispatched by mounted couriers, riding steeds *a*-used in the king's service, bred of the royal stud,-*a* 11 to this effect: The king has permitted the Jews of every city to assemble and fight for their lives; if any people or province attacks them, they may destroy, massacre, and exterminate its armed force together with women and children, and to plunder their possessions—12 on a single day in all the provinces of King Ahasuerus, namely, on the thirteenth day of the twelfth month, that is, the month of Adar. 13 The text of the document was to be issued as a law in every single province: it was to be publicly displayed to all the peoples, so that the Jews should be ready for that day to avenge themselves on their enemies. 14 The couriers, mounted on royal steeds, went out in urgent haste at the king's command; and the decree was proclaimed in the fortress Shushan.

15 Mordecai left the king's presence in royal robes of blue and white, with a magnificent crown of gold and a mantle of fine linen and purple wool. And the city of Shushan rang with joyous cries. 16 The Jews enjoyed light and gladness, happiness and honor. 17 And in every province and in every city, when the king's command and decree arrived, there was gladness and joy among the Jews, a feast and a holiday. And many of the people of the land professed to be Jews, for the fear of the Jews had fallen upon them.

9 And so, on the thirteenth day of the twelfth month—that is, the month of Adar—when the king's command and decree were to be executed, the very day on which the enemies of the Jews had expected to get them in their power, the opposite happened, and the Jews got their enemies in their power. 2 Throughout the provinces of King Ahasuerus, the Jews mustered in their cities to attack those who sought their hurt; and no one could withstand them, for the fear of them had fallen upon all the peoples. 3 Indeed, all the officials of the provinces—the satraps, the gover-

---

a-a *Meaning of Heb. uncertain.*

nors, and the king's stewards—showed deference to the Jews, because the fear of Mordecai had fallen upon them. ⁴ For Mordecai was now powerful in the royal palace, and his fame was spreading through all the provinces; the man Mordecai was growing ever more powerful. ⁵ So the Jews struck at their enemies with the sword, slaying and destroying; they wreaked their will upon their enemies.

⁶ In the fortress Shushan the Jews killed a total of five hundred men. ⁷ They also killed*ᵃ* Parshandatha, Dalphon, Aspatha, ⁸ Poratha, Adalia, Aridatha, ⁹ Parmashta, Arisai, Aridai, and Vaizatha, ¹⁰ the ten sons of Haman son of Hammedatha, the foe of the Jews. But they did not lay hands on the spoil. ¹¹ When the number of those slain in the fortress Shushan was reported on that same day to the king, ¹² the king said to Queen Esther, "In the fortress Shushan alone the Jews have killed a total of five hundred men, as well as the ten sons of Haman. What then must they have done in the provinces of the realm! What is your wish now? It shall be granted you. And what else is your request? It shall be fulfilled." ¹³ "If it please Your Majesty," Esther replied, "let the Jews in Shushan be permitted to act tomorrow also as they did today; and let Haman's ten sons be impaled on the stake." ¹⁴ The king ordered that this should be done, and the decree was proclaimed in Shushan. Haman's ten sons were impaled: ¹⁵ and the Jews in Shushan mustered again on the fourteenth day of Adar and slew three hundred men in Shushan. But they did not lay hands on the spoil.

¹⁶ The rest of the Jews, those in the king's provinces, likewise mustered and fought for their lives. They disposed of their enemies, killing seventy-five thousand of their foes; but they did not lay hands on the spoil. ¹⁷ That was on the thirteenth day of the month of Adar; and they rested on the fourteenth day and made it a day of feasting and merrymaking. (¹⁸ But the Jews in Shushan mustered on both the thirteenth and fourteenth days, and so rested on the fifteenth, and made it a day of feasting and merrymaking.) ¹⁹ That is why village Jews, who live in unwalled

ᵃ *Moved up from v. 10 for greater clarity.*

towns, observe the fourteenth day of the month of Adar and make it a day of merrymaking and feasting, and as a holiday and an occasion for sending gifts to one another.

20 Mordecai recorded these events. And he sent dispatches to all the Jews throughout the provinces of King Ahasuerus, near and far, 21 charging them to observe the fourteenth and fifteenth days of Adar, every year—22 the same days on which the Jews enjoyed relief from their foes and the same month which had been transformed for them from one of grief and mourning to one of festive joy. They were to observe them as days of feasting and merrymaking, and as an occasion for sending gifts to one another and presents to the poor. 23 The Jews accordingly assumed as an obligation that which they had begun to practice and which Mordecai prescribed for them.

24 For Haman son of Hammedatha the Agagite, the foe of all the Jews, had plotted to destroy the Jews, and had cast *pur*—that is, the lot—with intent to crush and exterminate them. 25 But when [Esther] came before the king, he commanded: *b*-"With the promulgation of this decree,-*b* let the evil plot, which he devised against the Jews, recoil on his own head!" So they impaled him and his sons on the stake. 26 For that reason these days were named Purim, after *pur*.

In view, then, of all the instructions in the said letter and of what they had experienced in that matter and what had befallen them, 27 the Jews undertook and irrevocably obligated themselves and their descendants, and all who might join them, to observe these two days in the manner prescribed and at the proper time each year. 28 Consequently, these days are recalled and observed in every generation: by every family, every province, and every city. And these days of Purim shall never cease among the Jews, and the memory of them shall never perish among their descendants.

29 *c*Then Queen Esther daughter of Abihail wrote a second letter of Purim for the purpose of confirming with full authority the aforementioned one of Mordecai the Jew. 30 Dispatches were

---

b-b *Meaning of Heb. uncertain.*
c *Force of vv. 29–31 uncertain in part. V. 29 reads literally, "Then Queen Esther daughter of Abihail, and Mordecai the Jew, wrote with full authority to confirm this second letter of Purim."*

sent to all the Jews in the hundred and twenty-seven provinces of the realm of Ahasuerus with an ordinance of "equity and honesty*d*": ³¹ These days of Purim shall be observed at their proper time, as Mordecai the Jew—and now Queen Esther—has obligated them to do, and just as they have assumed for themselves and their descendants the obligation of the fasts with their lamentations.*e*

³² And Esther's ordinance validating these observances of Purim was recorded in a scroll.

10 King Ahasuerus imposed tribute on the mainland and the islands. ² All his mighty and powerful acts, and a full account of the greatness to which the king advanced Mordecai, are recorded in the Annals of the Kings of Media and Persia. ³ For Mordecai the Jew ranked next to King Ahasuerus and was highly regarded by the Jews and popular with the multitude of his brethren; he sought the good of his people and interceded for the welfare of all his kindred.

---

d I.e. of new holidays, the instituting of which is linked to love of equity and honesty in Zech. 8.19.
e The Jews had long been observing fast days in commemoration of national calamities; see Zech. 7.5; 8.19.

דניאל

DANIEL

דניאל
DANIEL

1 In the third year of the reign of King Jehoiakim of Judah, King Nebuchadnezzar of Babylon came to Jerusalem and laid siege to it. ² The Lord delivered King Jehoiakim of Judah into his power, together with some of the vessels of the House of God, and he brought them to the land of Shinar to the house of his god; he deposited the vessels in the treasury of his god. ³ Then the king ordered Ashpenaz, his chief officer, to bring some Israelites of royal descent and of the nobility—⁴ youths without blemish, handsome, proficient in all wisdom, knowledgeable and intelligent, and capable of serving in the royal palace—and teach them the writings and the language of the Chaldeans. ⁵ The king allotted daily rations to them from the king's food and from the wine he drank. They were to be educated for three years,*-at the end of which they* were to enter the king's service.

⁶ Among them were the Judahites Daniel, Hananiah, Mishael and Azariah. ⁷ The chief officer gave them new names; he named Daniel Belteshazzar, Hananiah Shadrach, Mishael Meshach, and Azariah Abed-nego. ⁸ Daniel resolved not to defile himself with the king's food or the wine he drank, so he sought permission of the chief officer not to defile himself, ⁹ and God disposed the chief officer to be kind and compassionate toward Daniel. ¹⁰ The chief officer said to Daniel, "I fear that my lord the king, who allotted food and drink to you, will notice that you look out of sorts, unlike the other youths of your age—and you will put my life*b* in jeopardy with the king." ¹¹ Daniel replied to the guard whom the chief officer had put in charge of Daniel, Hananiah, Mishael and Azariah, ¹² "Please test your servants for ten days,

---

ᵃ⁻ᵃ *Or "and some of them."*
ᵇ *Lit. "head."*

giving us legumes to eat and water to drink. ¹³ Then compare our appearance with that of the youths who eat of the king's food, and do with your servants as you see fit." ¹⁴ He agreed to this plan of theirs, and tested them for ten days. ¹⁵ When the ten days were over, they looked better and healthier than all the youths who were eating of the king's food. ¹⁶ So the guard kept on removing their food, and the wine they were supposed to drink, and gave them legumes. ¹⁷ God made all four of these young men intelligent and proficient in all writings and wisdom, and Daniel had understanding of visions and dreams of all kinds. ¹⁸ When the time the king had set for their presentation had come, the chief officer presented them to Nebuchadnezzar. ¹⁹ The king spoke with them, and of them all none was equal to Daniel, Hananiah, Mishael and Azariah; so these entered the king's service. ²⁰ Whenever the king put a question to them requiring wisdom and understanding, he found them to be ten times better than all the magicians and exorcists throughout his realm. ²¹ Daniel was there until the first year of King Cyrus.

2 In the second year of the reign of Nebuchadnezzar, Nebuchadnezzar had a dream; his spirit was agitated, yet he ᵃ-was overcome by-ᵃ sleep. ² The king ordered the magicians, exorcists, sorcerers, and Chaldeans to be summoned in order to tell the king what he had dreamed. They came and stood before the king, ³ and the king said to them, "I have had a dream and ᵇ-I am full of anxiety-ᵇ to know what I have dreamed." ⁴ The Chaldeans spoke to the king in Aramaic, "O king, live forever! Relate the dream to your servants, and we will tell its meaning." ⁵ The king said in reply to the Chaldeans, "I hereby decree: If you will not make the dream and its meaning known to me, you shall be torn limb from limb and your houses confiscated.ᶜ ⁶ But if you tell the dream and its meaning, you shall receive from me gifts, presents, and great honor; therefore, tell me the dream and its meaning." ⁷ Once again they answered, "Let the king relate the dream to his

---

ᵃ⁻ᵃ *Meaning of Heb. uncertain; others "could not."*
ᵇ⁻ᵇ *Lit. "My spirit is agitated."*
ᶜ *Meaning uncertain; or "turned into ruins."*

servants, and we will tell its meaning." [8] The king said in reply, "It is clear to me that you are playing for time, since you see that I have decreed [9] that if you do not make the dream known to me, there is but one verdict for you. You have conspired to tell me something false and fraudulent until circumstances change; so relate the dream to me, and I will then know that you can tell its meaning." [10] The Chaldeans said in reply to the king, "There is no one on earth who can [d]-satisfy the king's demand,-[d] for great king or ruler—none has ever asked such a thing of any magician, exorcist, or Chaldean. [11] The thing asked by the king is difficult; there is no one who can tell it to the king except the gods whose abode is not among mortals."[e] [12] Whereupon the king flew into a violent rage, and gave an order to do away with all the wise men of Babylon.

[13] The decree condemning the wise men to death was issued. Daniel and his companions were about to be put to death [14] when Daniel remonstrated with Arioch, the captain of the royal guard who had set out to put the wise men of Babylon to death. [15] He spoke up and said to Arioch, the royal officer, "Why is the decree of the king so urgent?" Thereupon Arioch informed Daniel of the matter. [16] So Daniel went to ask the king for time, that he might tell the meaning to the king. [17] Then Daniel went to his house and informed his companions, Hananiah, Mishael, and Azariah, of the matter, [18] that they might implore the God of Heaven for help regarding this mystery, so that Daniel and his colleagues would not be put to death together with the other wise men of Babylon.

[19] The mystery was revealed to Daniel in a night vision; then Daniel blessed the God of Heaven. [20] Daniel spoke up and said:
"Let the name of God be blessed forever and ever,
For wisdom and power are His.
[21] He changes times and seasons,
Removes kings and installs kings;
He gives the wise their wisdom
And knowledge to those who know.
[22] He reveals deep and hidden things,

[d-d] Lit. "tell the king's matter."
[e] Lit. "flesh."

Knows what is in the darkness,
And light dwells with Him.
23 I acknowledge and praise You,
O God of my fathers,
You who have given me wisdom and power,
For now You have let me know what we asked of You;
You have let us know what concerns the king."

24 Thereupon Daniel went to Arioch, whom the king had appointed to do away with the wise men of Babylon; he came and said to him as follows, "Do not do away with the wise men of Babylon; bring me to the king and I will tell the king the meaning!" 25 So Arioch rushed Daniel into the king's presence and said to him, "I have found among the exiles of Judah a man who can make the meaning known to the king!" 26 The king said in reply to Daniel (who was called Belteshazzar), "Can you really make known to me the dream that I saw and its meaning?" 27 Daniel answered the king and said, "The mystery about which the king has inquired—wise men, exorcists, magicians, and diviners cannot tell to the king. 28 But there is a God in heaven who reveals mysteries, and He has made known to King Nebuchadnezzar what is to be at the end of days. This is your dream and the vision that entered your mind in bed: 29 O king, the thoughts that came to your mind in your bed are about future events; He who reveals mysteries has let you know what is to happen. 30 Not because my wisdom is greater than that of other creatures has this mystery been revealed to me, but in order that the meaning should be made known to the king, and that you may know the thoughts of your mind.

31 "O king, as you looked on, there appeared a great statue. This statue, which was huge and its brightness surpassing, stood before you, and its appearance was awesome. 32 The head of that statue was of fine gold; its breast and arms were of silver; its belly and thighs, of bronze; 33 its legs were of iron, and its feet part iron and part clay. 34 As you looked on, a stone was hewn out, not by hands, and struck the statue on its feet of iron and clay and

crushed them. [35] All at once, the iron, clay, bronze, silver and gold were crushed, and became like chaff of the threshing floors of summer; a wind carried them off until no trace of them was left. But the stone that struck the statue became a great mountain and filled the whole earth.

[36] "Such was the dream, and we will now tell the king its meaning. [37] You, O king—king of kings, to whom the God of Heaven has given kingdom, power, might, and glory; [38] into whose hands He has given men, wild beasts, and the fowl of heaven, wherever they may dwell; and to whom He has given dominion over them all—you are the head of gold. [39] But another kingdom will arise after you, inferior to yours; then yet a third kingdom, of bronze, which will rule over the whole earth. [40] But the fourth kingdom will be as strong as iron; just as iron crushes and shatters everything—and like iron that smashes—so will it crush and smash all these. [41] You saw the feet and the toes, part potter's clay and part iron; that means it will be a divided kingdom; it will have only some of the stability of iron, inasmuch as you saw iron mixed with common clay. [42] And the toes were part iron and part clay; that [means] the kingdom will be in part strong and in part brittle. [43] You saw iron mixed with common clay; that means: f-they shall intermingle with the offspring of men,-f but shall not hold together, just as iron does not mix with clay. [44] And in the time of those kings, the God of Heaven will establish a kingdom that shall never be destroyed, a kingdom that shall not be transferred to another people. It will crush and wipe out all these kingdoms, but shall itself last forever—[45] just as you saw how a stone was hewn from the mountain, not by hands, and crushed the iron, bronze, clay, silver, and gold. The great God has made known to the king what will happen in the future. The dream is sure and its interpretation reliable."

[46] Then King Nebuchadnezzar prostrated himself and paid homage to Daniel and ordered that a meal offering and pleasing offerings be made to him. [47] The king said in reply to Daniel, "Truly your God must be the God of gods and Lord of kings and

f-f Meaning uncertain.

the revealer of mysteries to have enabled you to reveal this mystery." [48] The king then elevated Daniel and gave him very many gifts, and made him governor of the whole province of Babylon and chief prefect of all the wise men of Babylon. [49] At Daniel's request, the king appointed Shadrach, Meshach, and Abed-nego to administer the province of Babylon; while Daniel himself was at the king's court.

3 King Nebuchadnezzar made a statue of gold sixty cubits high and six cubits broad. He set it up in the plain of Dura in the province of Babylon. [2] King Nebuchadnezzar then sent word to gather the satraps, prefects, governors, counselors, treasurers, judges, officers, and all the provincial officials to attend the dedication of the statue that King Nebuchadnezzar had set up. [3] So the satraps, prefects, governors, counselors, treasurers, judges, officers, and all the provincial officials assembled for the dedication of the statue that King Nebuchadnezzar had set up, and stood before the statue that Nebuchadnezzar had set up. [4] The herald proclaimed in a loud voice, "You are commanded, O peoples and nations of every language, [5] when you hear the sound of the horn, pipe, zither, lyre, psaltery, bagpipe, and all other types of instruments, to fall down and worship the statue of gold that King Nebuchadnezzar has set up. [6] Whoever will not fall down and worship shall at once be thrown into a burning fiery furnace." [7] And so, as soon as all the peoples heard the sound of the horn, pipe, zither, lyre, psaltery, and all other types of instruments, all peoples and nations of every language fell down and worshiped the statue of gold that King Nebuchadnezzar had set up.

[8] Seizing the occasion, certain Chaldeans came forward to slander the Jews. [9] They spoke up and said to King Nebuchadnezzar, "O king, live forever! [10] You, O king, gave an order that everyone who hears the horn, pipe, zither, lyre, psaltery, bagpipe, and all types of instruments must fall down and worship the golden statue, [11] and whoever does not fall down and worship shall be

thrown into a burning fiery furnace. [12] There are certain Jews whom you appointed to administer the province of Babylon, Shadrach, Meshach, and Abed-nego; those men pay no heed to you, O king; they do not serve your god or worship the statue of gold that you have set up."

[13] Then Nebuchadnezzar, in raging fury, ordered Shadrach, Meshach, and Abed-nego to be brought; so those men were brought before the king. [14] Nebuchadnezzar spoke to them and said, "Is it true, Shadrach, Meshach, and Abed-nego, that you do not serve my god or worship the statue of gold that I have set up? [15] Now if you are ready to fall down and worship the statue that I have made when you hear the sound of the horn, pipe, zither, lyre, psaltery, and bagpipe, and all other types of instruments, [well and good]; but if you will not worship, you shall at once be thrown into a burning fiery furnace, and what god is there that can save you from my power?" [16] Shadrach, Meshach, and Abed-nego said in reply to the king, "O Nebuchadnezzar, we have no need to answer you in this matter, [17] for if so it must be, our God whom we serve is able to save us from the burning fiery furnace, and He will save us from your power, O king. [18] But even if He does not, be it known to you, O king, that we will not serve your god or worship the statue of gold that you have set up."

[19] Nebuchadnezzar was so filled with rage at Shadrach, Meshach, and Abed-nego that his visage was distorted, and he gave an order to heat up the furnace to seven times its usual heat. [20] He commanded some of the strongest men of his army to bind Shadrach, Meshach, and Abed-nego, and to throw them into the burning fiery furnace. [21] So these men, in their shirts, trousers, hats, and other garments, were bound and thrown into the burning fiery furnace. [22] Because the king's order was urgent, and the furnace was heated to excess, a tongue of flame killed the men who carried up Shadrach, Meshach, and Abed-nego. [23] But those three men, Shadrach, Meshach, and Abed-nego, dropped, bound, into the burning fiery furnace.

[24] Then King Nebuchadnezzar was astonished and, rising in haste, addressed his companions, saying, "Did we not throw

three men, bound, into the fire?" They spoke in reply, "Surely, O king." 25 He answered, "But I see four men walking about unbound and unharmed in the fire and the fourth looks like a divine being." 26 Nebuchadnezzar then approached the hatch of the burning fiery furnace and called, "Shadrach, Meshach, Abed-nego, servants of the Most High God, come out!" So Shadrach, Meshach, and Abed-nego came out of the fire. 27 The satraps, the prefects, the governors, and the royal companions gathered around to look at those men, on whose bodies the fire had had no effect, the hair of whose heads had not been singed, whose shirts looked no different, to whom not even the odor of fire clung. 28 Nebuchadnezzar spoke up and said, "Blessed be the God of Shadrach, Meshach, and Abed-nego, who sent His angel to save His servants who, trusting in Him, flouted the king's decree at the risk of their lives rather than serve or worship any god but their own God. 29 I hereby give an order that [anyone of] any people or nation of whatever language who blasphemes the God of Shadrach, Meshach, and Abed-nego shall be torn limb from limb, and his house confiscated, for there is no other God who is able to save in this way."

30 Thereupon the king promoted Shadrach, Meshach, and Abed-nego in the province of Babylon.

31 "King Nebuchadnezzar to all people and nations of every language that inhabit the whole earth: May your well-being abound! 32 The signs and wonders that the Most High God has worked for me I am pleased to relate. 33 How great are His signs; how mighty His wonders! His kingdom is an everlasting kingdom, and His dominion endures throughout the generations."

4 I, Nebuchadnezzar, was living serenely in my house, flourishing in my palace. 2 I had a dream that frightened me, and my thoughts in bed and the vision of my mind alarmed me. 3 I gave an order to bring all the wise men of Babylon before me to let

me know the meaning of the dream. [4] The magicians, exorcists, Chaldeans, and diviners came, and I related the dream to them, but they could not make its meaning known to me. [5] Finally, Daniel, called Belteshazzar after the name of my god, in whom the spirit of the holy gods was, came to me, and I related the dream to him, [saying], [6] "Belteshazzar, chief magician, in whom I know the spirit of the holy gods to be, and whom no mystery baffles, tell me the meaning of my dream vision that I have seen.
[7] In the visions of my mind in bed

> I saw a tree of great height in the midst of the earth;
> [8] The tree grew and became mighty;
> Its top reached heaven,
> [9] And it was visible to the ends of the earth.
> Its foliage was beautiful
> And its fruit abundant;
> There was food for all in it.
> Beneath it the beasts of the field found shade,
> And the birds of the sky dwelt on its branches;
> All creatures fed on it.

[10] In the vision of my mind in bed, I looked and saw a holy Watcher coming down from heaven. [11] He called loudly and said:

> 'Hew down the tree, lop off its branches,
> Strip off its foliage, scatter its fruit.
> Let the beasts of the field flee from beneath it
> And the birds from its branches,
> [12] But leave the stump with its roots in the ground.
> In fetters of iron and bronze
> In the grass of the field,
> Let him be drenched with the dew of heaven,
> And share earth's verdure with the beasts.
> [13] Let his mind be altered from that of a man,
> And let him be given the mind of a beast,
> And let seven seasons pass over him.
> [14] This sentence is decreed by the Watchers;
> This verdict is commanded by the Holy Ones

So that all creatures may know
That the Most High is sovereign over the realm of man,
And He gives it to whom He wishes
And He may set over it even the lowest of men.'

¹⁵ "I, King Nebuchadnezzar, had this dream; now you, Belteshazzar, tell me its meaning, since all the wise men of my kingdom are not able to make its meaning known to me, but you are able, for the spirit of the holy gods is in you."

¹⁶ Then Daniel, called Belteshazzar, was perplexed for awhile, and alarmed by his thoughts. The king addressed him, "Let the dream and its meaning not alarm you." Belteshazzar replied, "My lord, would that the dream were for your enemy and its meaning for your foe! ¹⁷ The tree that you saw grow and become mighty, whose top reached heaven, which was visible throughout the earth,¹⁸ whose foliage was beautiful, whose fruit was so abundant that there was food for all in it, beneath which the beasts of the field dwelt, and in whose branches the birds of the sky lodged —¹⁹ it is you, O king, you who have grown and become mighty, whose greatness has grown to reach heaven, and whose dominion is to the end of the earth. ²⁰ The holy Watcher whom the king saw descend from heaven and say,

Hew down the tree and destroy it,
But leave the stump with its roots in the ground.
In fetters of iron and bronze
In the grass of the field,
Let him be drenched with the dew of heaven,
And share the lot of the beasts of the field
Until seven seasons pass over him—

²¹ this is its meaning, O king; it is the decree of the Most High which has overtaken my lord the king. ²² You will be driven away from men and have your habitation with the beasts of the field. You will be fed grass like cattle, and be drenched with the dew of heaven; seven seasons will pass over you until you come to know that the Most High is sovereign over the realm of man, and He gives it to whom He wishes. ²³ And the meaning of the command to leave the stump of the tree with its roots is that the

kingdom will remain yours from the time you come to know that Heaven is sovereign. [24] Therefore, O king, may my advice be acceptable to you: Redeem your sins by beneficence and your iniquities by generosity to the poor; then your serenity may be extended."

[25] All this befell King Nebuchadnezzar. [26] Twelve months later, as he was walking on the roof of the royal palace at Babylon, [27] the king exclaimed, "There is great Babylon, which I have built by my vast power to be a royal residence for the glory of my majesty!" [28] The words were still on the king's lips, when a voice fell from heaven, "It has been decreed for you, O King Nebuchadnezzar: The kingdom has passed out of your hands. [29] You are being driven away from men, and your habitation is to be with the beasts of the field. You are to be fed grass like cattle, and seven seasons will pass over you until you come to know that the Most High is sovereign over the realm of man and He gives it to whom He wishes." [30] There and then the sentence was carried out upon Nebuchadnezzar. He was driven away from men, he ate grass like cattle, and his body was drenched with the dew of heaven until his hair grew like eagle's [feathers] and his nails like [the talons of] birds.

[31] "When the time had passed, I, Nebuchadnezzar, lifted my eyes to heaven, and my reason was restored to me. I blessed the Most High, and praised and glorified the Ever-Living One,

Whose dominion is an everlasting dominion
And whose kingdom endures throughout the generations.
[32] All the inhabitants of the earth are of no account.
He does as He wishes with the host of heaven,
And with the inhabitants of the earth.
There is none to stay His hand
Or say to Him, 'What have You done?'

[33] There and then my reason was restored to me, and my majesty and splendor were restored to me for the glory of my kingdom. My companions and nobles sought me out, and I was reestablished over my kingdom, and added greatness was given me. [34] So now I, Nebuchadnezzar, praise, exalt, and glorify the King

of Heaven, all of whose works are just and whose ways are right, and who is able to humble those who behave arrogantly."

5 King Belshazzar gave a great banquet for his thousand nobles, and in the presence of the thousand he drank wine. ² Under the influence of the wine, Belshazzar ordered the gold and silver vessels that his father Nebuchadnezzar had taken out of the temple at Jerusalem to be brought so that the king and his nobles, his consorts, and his concubines could drink from them. ³ The golden vessels that had been taken out of the sanctuary of the House of God in Jerusalem were then brought, and the king, his nobles, his consorts, and his concubines drank from them. ⁴ They drank wine and praised the gods of gold and silver, bronze, iron, wood, and stone. ⁵ Just then, the fingers of a human hand appeared and wrote on the plaster of the wall of the king's palace opposite the lampstand, so that the king could see the hand as it wrote. ⁶ The king's face darkened, and his thoughts alarmed him; the joints of his loins were loosened and his knees knocked together. ⁷ The king called loudly for the exorcists, Chaldeans, and diviners to be brought. The king addressed the wise men of Babylon, "Whoever can read this writing and tell me its meaning shall be clothed in purple and wear a golden chain on his neck, and shall rule as ᵃ-one of three-ᵃ in the kingdom."

⁸ Then all the king's wise men came, but they could not read the writing or make known its meaning to the king. ⁹ King Belshazzar grew exceedingly alarmed and his face darkened, and his nobles were dismayed. ¹⁰ Because of the state of the king and his nobles, the queen came to the banquet hall. The queen spoke up and said, "O king, live forever! Let your thoughts not alarm you or your face darken. ¹¹ There is a man in your kingdom who has the spirit of the holy gods in him; in your father's time, illumination, understanding, and wisdom like that of the gods were to be found in him, and your father, King Nebuchadnezzar, appointed him chief of the magicians, exorcists, Chaldeans, and diviners.

ᵃ⁻ᵃ *Cf. Dan. 6.3; or "third in rank."*

¹² Seeing that there is to be found in Daniel (whom the king called Belteshazzar) extraordinary spirit, knowledge, and understanding to interpret dreams, to explain riddles and solve problems, let Daniel now be called to tell the meaning [of the writing]."

¹³ Daniel was then brought before the king. The king addressed Daniel, "You are Daniel, one of the exiles of Judah whom my father, the king, brought from Judah. ¹⁴ I have heard about you that you have the spirit of the gods in you, and that illumination, knowledge, and extraordinary wisdom are to be found in you. ¹⁵ Now the wise men and exorcists have been brought before me to read this writing and to make known its meaning to me. But they could not tell what it meant. ¹⁶ I have heard about you, that you can give interpretations and solve problems. Now if you can read the writing and make known its meaning to me, you shall be clothed in purple and wear a golden chain on your neck and rule as one of three in the kingdom."

¹⁷ Then Daniel said in reply to the king, "You may keep your gifts for yourself, and give your presents to others. But I will read the writing for the king, and make its meaning known to him. ¹⁸ O king, the Most High God bestowed kingship, grandeur, glory, and majesty upon your father Nebuchadnezzar. ¹⁹ And because of the grandeur that He bestowed upon him, all the peoples and nations of every language trembled in fear of him. He put to death whom he wished, and whom he wished he let live; he raised high whom he wished and whom he wished he brought low. ²⁰ But when he grew haughty and willfully presumptuous, he was deposed from his royal throne and his glory was removed from him. ²¹ He was driven away from men, and his mind made like that of a beast, and his habitation was with wild asses. He was fed grass like cattle, and his body was drenched with the dew of heaven until he came to know that the Most High God is sovereign over the realm of man, and sets over it whom He wishes. ²² But you, Belshazzar his son, did not humble yourself although you knew all this. ²³ You exalted yourself against the Lord of Heaven, and had the vessels of His temple brought to you. You

and your nobles, your consorts, and your concubines drank wine from them and praised the gods of silver and gold, bronze and iron, wood and stone, which do not see, hear, or understand; but the God who controls your lifebreath and every move you make —Him you did not glorify! 24 He therefore made the hand appear, and caused the writing to be inscribed. 25 This is the writing that is inscribed: MENE MENE TEKEL UPHARSIN. 26 And this is its meaning: MENE—God has numbered*a* [the days of] your kingdom and brought it to an end; 27 TEKEL—*-b-* you have been weighed*-b* in the balance and found wanting; 28 PERES—your kingdom *c-*has been divided*-c* and given to the Medes and the Persians." 29 Then, at Belshazzar's command, they clothed Daniel in purple, placed a golden chain on his neck, and proclaimed that he should rule as one of three in the kingdom.

30 That very night, Belshazzar, the Chaldean king, was killed, 6 1 and Darius the Mede received the kingdom, being about sixty-two years old. 2 It pleased Darius to appoint over the kingdom one hundred and twenty satraps to be in charge of the whole kingdom; 3 over them were three ministers, one of them Daniel, to whom these satraps reported, in order that the king not be troubled. 4 This man Daniel surpassed the other ministers and satraps by virtue of his extraordinary spirit, and the king considered setting him over the whole kingdom. 5 The ministers and satraps looked for some fault in Daniel's conduct in matters of state, but they could find neither fault nor corruption, inasmuch as he was trustworthy, and no negligence or corruption was to be found in him. 6 Those men then said, "We are not going to find any fault with this Daniel, unless we find something against him in connection with the laws of his God." 7 Then these ministers and satraps came thronging in to the king and said to him, "O King Darius, live forever! 8 All the ministers of the kingdom, the prefects, satraps, companions, and governors are in agreement that a royal ban should be issued under sanction of an oath that whoever shall address a petition to any god or man, besides you, O king, during the next thirty days shall be thrown into a lions'

---

a Aramaic mena.
b-b Aramaic tekilta.
c-c Aramaic perisat.

den. ⁹ So issue the ban, O king, and put it in writing so that it be unalterable as a law of the Medes and Persians that may not be abrogated." ¹⁰ Thereupon King Darius put the ban in writing.

¹¹ When Daniel learned that it had been put in writing, he went to his house, in whose upper chamber he had had windows made facing Jerusalem, and three times a day he knelt down, prayed, and made confession to his God, as he had always done. ¹² Then those men came thronging in and found Daniel petitioning his God in supplication. ¹³ They then approached the king and reminded him of the royal ban: "Did you not put in writing a ban that whoever addresses a petition to any god or man besides you, O king, during the next thirty days, shall be thrown into a lions' den?" The king said in reply, "The order stands firm, as a law of the Medes and Persians that may not be abrogated." ¹⁴ Thereupon they said to the king, "Daniel, one of the exiles of Judah, pays no heed to you, O king, or to the ban that you put in writing; three times a day he offers his petitions [to his God]." ¹⁵ Upon hearing that, the king was very disturbed, and he set his heart upon saving Daniel, and until the sun set made every effort to rescue him. ¹⁶ Then those men came thronging in to the king and said to the king, "Know, O king, that it is a law of the Medes and Persians that any ban that the king issues under sanction of oath is unalterable." ¹⁷ By the king's order, Daniel was then brought and thrown into the lions' den. The king spoke to Daniel and said, "Your God, whom you serve so regularly, will deliver you." ¹⁸ A rock was brought and placed over the mouth of the den; the king sealed it with his signet and with the signet of his nobles, so that nothing might be altered concerning Daniel.

¹⁹ The king then went to his palace and spent the night fasting; no diversions were brought to him, and his sleep fled from him. ²⁰ Then, at the first light of dawn, the king arose and rushed to the lions' den. ²¹ As he approached the den, he cried to Daniel in a mournful voice; the king said to Daniel, "Daniel, servant of the living God, was the God whom you served so regularly able to deliver you from the lions?" ²² Daniel then talked with the king,

"O king, live forever! 23 My God sent His angel, who shut the mouths of the lions so that they did not injure me, inasmuch as I was found innocent by Him, nor have I, O king, done you any injury." 24 The king was very glad, and ordered Daniel to be brought up out of the den. Daniel was brought up out of the den, and no injury was found on him, for he had trusted in his God. 25 Then, by order of the king, those men who had slandered Daniel were brought and, together with their children and wives, were thrown into the lions' den. They had hardly reached the bottom of the den when the lions overpowered them and crushed all their bones.

26 Then King Darius wrote to all peoples and nations of every language that inhabit the earth, "May your well-being abound! 27 I have hereby given an order that throughout my royal domain men must tremble in fear before the God of Daniel, for He is the living God who endures forever; His kingdom is indestructible, and His dominion is to the end of time; 28 He delivers and saves, and performs signs and wonders in heaven and on earth, for He delivered Daniel from the power of the lions." 29 Thus Daniel prospered during the reign of Darius and during the reign of Cyrus the Persian.

7 In the first year of King Belshazzar of Babylon, Daniel saw a dream and a vision of his mind in bed; afterward he wrote down the dream. Beginning the account, 2 Daniel related the following: "In my vision at night, I saw the four winds of heaven stirring up the great sea. 3 Four mighty beasts different from each other emerged from the sea. 4 The first was like a lion but had eagles' wings. As I looked on, its wings were plucked off, and it was lifted off the ground and set on its feet like a man and given the mind of a man. 5 Then I saw a second, different beast, which was like a bear but raised on one side, and with three fangs in its mouth among its teeth; it was told, 'Arise, eat much meat!'6 After that,

as I looked on, there was another one, like a leopard, and it had on its back four wings like those of a bird; the beast had four heads, and dominion was given to it. ⁷ After that, as I looked on in the night vision, there was a fourth beast—fearsome, dreadful, and very powerful, with great iron teeth—that devoured and crushed, and stamped the remains with its feet. It was different from all the other beasts which had gone before it; and it had ten horns. ⁸ While I was gazing upon these horns, a new little horn sprouted up among them; three of the older horns were uprooted to make room for it. There were eyes in this horn like those of a man, and a mouth that spoke arrogantly. ⁹ As I looked on,

> Thrones were set in place,
> And the Ancient of Days took His seat.
> His garment was like white snow,
> And the hair of His head was like lamb's^a wool.
> His throne was tongues of flame;
> Its wheels were blazing fire.
> ¹⁰ A river of fire streamed forth before Him;
> Thousands upon thousands served Him;
> Myriads upon myriads attended Him;
> The court sat and the books were opened.

¹¹ I looked on. Then, because of the arrogant words that the horn spoke, the beast was killed as I looked on; its body was destroyed and it was consigned to the flames. ¹² The dominion of the other beasts was taken away, but an extension of life was given to them for a time and season. ¹³ As I looked on, in the night vision,

> One like a human being
> Came with the clouds of heaven;
> He reached the Ancient of Days
> And was presented to Him.
> ¹⁴ Dominion, glory, and kingship were given to him;
> All peoples and nations of every language must serve him.

^a Or "clean."

His dominion is an everlasting dominion that shall not
pass away,
And his kingship, one that shall not be destroyed.

¹⁵ As for me, Daniel, my spirit was disturbed within me and the
vision of my mind alarmed me. ¹⁶ I approached one of the attendants and asked him the true meaning of all this. He gave me this
interpretation of the matter: ¹⁷ 'These great beasts, four in number [mean] four kingdomsᵃ will arise out of the earth; ¹⁸ then holy
ones of the Most High will receive the kingdom, and will possess
the kingdom forever—forever and ever.' ¹⁹ Then I wanted to
ascertain the true meaning of the fourth beast, which was different from them all, very fearsome, with teeth of iron, claws of
bronze, that devoured and crushed, and stamped the remains;
²⁰ and of the ten horns on its head; and of the new one that
sprouted, to make room for which three fell—the horn that had
eyes, and a mouth that spoke arrogantly, and which was more
conspicuous than its fellows. ²¹ (I looked on as that horn made
war with the holy ones and overcame them, ²² until the Ancient
of Days came and judgment was rendered in favor of the holy
ones of the Most High, for the time had come, and the holy ones
took possession of the kingdom.) ²³ This is what he said: 'The
fourth beast [means]—there will be a fourth kingdom upon the
earth which will be different from all the kingdoms; it will devour
the whole earth, tread it down, and crush it. ²⁴ And the ten horns
[mean]—from that kingdom, ten kings will arise, and after them
another will arise. He will be different from the former ones, and
will bring low three kings. ²⁵ He will speak words against the Most
High, and will harass the holy ones of the Most High. He will
think of changing times and laws, and they will be delivered into
his power for a ᵇ-time, times, and half a time.⁻ᵇ ²⁶ Then the court
will sit and his dominion will be taken away, to be destroyed and
abolished for all time. ²⁷ The kingship and dominion and grandeur belonging to all the kingdoms under heaven will be given
to the people of the holy ones of the Most High. Their kingdom

ᵃ *Lit. "kings."*
ᵇ⁻ᵇ *I.e. a year, two years, and half a year.*

shall be an everlasting kingdom, and all dominions shall serve and obey them.' " 28 Here the account ends.

I, Daniel, was very alarmed by my thoughts, and my face darkened; and I could not put the matter out of my mind.

8 In the third year of the reign of King Belshazzar, a vision appeared to me, to me, Daniel, after the one that had appeared to me earlier. 2 I saw in the vision—at the time I saw it I was in the fortress of Shushan, in the province of Elam—I saw in the vision that I was beside the Ulai River. 3 I looked and saw a ram standing between me and the river; he had two horns; the horns were high, with one higher than the other, and the higher sprouting last. 4 I saw the ram butting westward, northward, and southward. No beast could withstand him, and there was none to deliver from his power. He did as he pleased and grew great. 5 As I looked on, a he-goat came from the west, passing over the entire earth without touching the ground. The goat had a conspicuous horn on its forehead. 6 He came up to the two-horned ram that I had seen standing between me and the river and charged at him with furious force. 7 I saw him reach the ram and rage at him; he struck the ram and broke its two horns, and the ram was powerless to withstand him. He threw him to the ground and trampled him, and there was none to deliver the ram from his power. 8 Then the he-goat grew very great, but at the peak of his power his big horn was broken. In its place, four conspicuous horns sprouted toward the four winds of heaven. 9 From one of them emerged a small horn, which extended itself greatly toward the south, toward the east, and toward the beautiful land. 10 It grew as high as the host of heaven and it hurled some stars of the [heavenly] host to the ground and trampled them. 11 It vaunted itself against the very chief of the host; on its account the regular offering was suspended, and His holy place was abandoned. 12 a-An army was arrayed iniquitously against the regular offer-

---

a-a Meaning of Heb. uncertain.

ing;-*a* it hurled truth to the ground and prospered in what it did.

¹³ Then I heard a holy being speaking, and another holy being said to whomever it was who was speaking, "How long will [what was seen in] the vision last—*a*-the regular offering be forsaken because of transgression; the Sanctuary be surrendered and the [heavenly] host be trampled?"-*a* ¹⁴ He answered me,*b* "For twenty-three hundred evenings and mornings; then the sanctuary shall be cleansed." ¹⁵ While I, Daniel, was seeing the vision, and trying to understand it, there appeared before me one who looked like a man. ¹⁶ I heard a human voice from the middle of Ulai calling out, "Gabriel, make that man understand the vision." ·¹⁷ He came near to where I was standing, and as he came I was terrified, and fell prostrate. He said to me, "Understand, O man, that the vision refers to the time of the end." ¹⁸ When he spoke with me, I was overcome by a deep sleep as I lay prostrate on the ground. Then he touched me and made me stand up, ¹⁹ and said, "I am going to inform you of what will happen when wrath is at an end, for [it refers] to the time appointed for the end.

²⁰ "The two-horned ram that you saw [signifies] the kings of Media and Persia; ²¹ and the buck, the he-goat—the king of Greece; and the large horn on his forehead, that is the first king. ²² One was broken and four came in its stead—that [means]: four kingdoms will arise out of a nation, but without its power. ²³ When their kingdoms are at an end, when the measure of transgression*c* has been filled, then a king will arise, impudent and versed in intrigue. ²⁴ He will have great strength, but not through his own strength. He will be extraordinarily destructive; he will prosper in what he does, and destroy the mighty and the people of holy ones. ²⁵ By his cunning, he will use deceit successfully. He will make great plans, will destroy many, taking them unawares, and will rise up against the chief of chiefs, but will be broken, not by [human] hands. ²⁶ What was said in the vision about evenings and mornings is true. Now you keep the vision a secret, for it pertains to far-off days." ²⁷ So I, Daniel, was stricken,*a* and languished many days. Then I arose and attended

b Several ancient versions "him."
c Lit. "transgressors."

to the king's business, but I was dismayed by the vision and no one could explain it.

9 In the first year of Darius son of Ahasuerus, of Median descent, who was made king over the kingdom of the Chaldeans— ² in the first year of his reign, I, Daniel, consulted the books concerning the number of years that, according to the word of the LORD that had come to Jeremiah the prophet, were to be the term of Jerusalem's desolation—seventy years. ³ I turned my face to the Lord God, devoting myself to prayer and supplication, in fasting, in sackcloth and ashes. ⁴ I prayed to the LORD my God, making confession thus: "O Lord, great and awesome God, who stays faithful to His covenant with those who love Him and keep His commandments! ⁵ We have sinned; we have gone astray; we have acted wickedly; we have been rebellious and have deviated from Your commandments and Your rules, ⁶ and have not obeyed Your servants the prophets who spoke in Your name to our kings, our officers, our fathers, and all the people of the land. ⁷ With you, O Lord, is the right, and the shame is on us to this very day, on the men of Judah and the inhabitants of Jerusalem, all Israel, near and far, in all the lands where You have banished them, for the trespass they committed against You. ⁸ The shame, O LORD, is on us, on our kings, our officers, and our fathers, because we have sinned against You. ⁹ To the Lord our God belong mercy and forgiveness, for we rebelled against Him, ¹⁰ and did not obey the LORD our God by following His teachings which He set before us through His servants the prophets. ¹¹ All Israel has violated Your teaching and gone astray, disobeying You; so the curse and the oath written in the Teaching of Moses, the servant of God, have been poured down upon us, for we have sinned against Him. ¹² He carried out the threat that He made against us, and against our rulers who ruled us, to bring upon us great misfortune; under the whole heaven there has never been done the like of what was done to Jerusalem. ¹³ All that calamity,

just as is written in the Teaching of Moses, came upon us, yet we did not supplicate the LORD our God, did not repent of our iniquity or become wise through Your truth. [14] Hence the LORD was intent upon bringing calamity upon us, for the LORD our God is in the right in all that He has done, but we have not obeyed Him.

[15] "Now, O Lord our God—You who brought Your people out of the land of Egypt with a mighty hand, winning fame for Yourself to this very day—we have sinned, we have acted wickedly. [16] O Lord, as befits Your abundant benevolence, let Your wrathful fury turn back from Your city Jerusalem, Your holy mountain; for because of our sins and the iniquities of our fathers, Jerusalem and Your people have become a mockery among all who are around us.

[17] "O our God, hear now the prayer of Your servant and his plea, and show Your favor to Your desolate sanctuary, for the Lord's sake. [18] Incline Your ear, O my God, and hear; open Your eyes and see our desolation and the city to which Your name is attached. Not because of any merit of ours do we lay our plea before You but because of Your abundant mercies. [19] O Lord, hear! O Lord, forgive! O Lord, listen, and act without delay for Your own sake, O my God; for Your name is attached to Your city and Your people!"

[20] While I was speaking, praying, and confessing my sin and the sin of my people Israel, and laying my supplication before the LORD my God on behalf of the holy mountain of my God— [21] while I was uttering my prayer, the man Gabriel, whom I had previously seen in the vision, was sent forth in flight and reached me about the time of the evening offering. [22] He made me understand by speaking to me and saying, "Daniel, I have just come forth to give you understanding. [23] A word went forth as you began your plea, and I have come to tell it, for you are precious; so mark the word and understand the vision.

²⁴ "Seventy weeks^a have been decreed for your people and your holy city until the measure of transgression is filled and that of sin complete, until iniquity is expiated, and eternal righteousness ushered in; and prophetic vision ratified,^b and the holy of holies anointed. ²⁵ You must know and understand: From the issuance of the word to restore and rebuild Jerusalem until the [time of the] anointed leader is seven weeks; and for sixty-two weeks it will be rebuilt, square and moat, but in a time of distress. ²⁶ And after those sixty-two weeks, the anointed one will disappear and vanish.^c The army of a leader who is to come will destroy the city and the sanctuary, but its end will come through a flood. Desolation is decreed until the end of war. ²⁷ During one week he will make a firm covenant with many. For half a week he will put a stop to the sacrifice and the meal offering. At the ^{c-}corner [of the altar]^{-c} will be an appalling abomination until the decreed destruction will be poured down upon the appalling thing."

10 In the third year of King Cyrus of Persia, an oracle was revealed to Daniel, who was called Belteshazzar. That oracle was true, ^{a-}but it was a great task to understand the prophecy; understanding came to him through the vision.^{-a}

² At that time, I, Daniel, kept three full weeks of mourning. ³ I ate no tasty food, nor did any meat or wine enter my mouth. I did not anoint myself until the three weeks were over. ⁴ It was on the twenty-fourth day of the first month, when I was on the bank of the great river—the Tigris—⁵ that I looked and saw a man dressed in linen, his loins girt in ^{b-}fine gold.^{-b} ⁶ His body was like beryl, his face had the appearance of lightning, his eyes were like flaming torches, his arms and legs had the color of burnished bronze, and the sound of his speech was like the noise of a multitude.

⁷ I, Daniel, alone saw the vision; the men who were with me did not see the vision, yet they were seized with a great terror and fled

---

^a *Viz. of years.*
^b *Lit. "sealed."*
^c *Meaning of Heb. uncertain.*

^{a-a} *Meaning of Heb. uncertain.*
^{b-b} *Or "gold of Uphaz."*

into hiding. [8] So I was left alone to see this great vision. I was drained of strength, my vigor was destroyed, and I could not summon up strength. [9] I heard him speaking; and when I heard him speaking, overcome by a deep sleep, I lay prostrate on the ground. [10] Then a hand touched me, and shook me onto my hands and knees. [11] He said to me, "O Daniel, precious man, mark what I say to you and stand up, for I have been sent to you." After he said this to me, I stood up, trembling. [12] He then said to me, "Have no fear, Daniel, for from the first day that you set your mind to get understanding, practicing abstinence before your God, your prayer was heard, and I have come because of your prayer. [13] However, the prince of the Persian kingdom opposed me for twenty-one days; now Michael, a prince of the first rank, has come to my aid, after I was detained there with the kings of Persia. [14] So I have come to make you understand what is to befall your people in the days to come, for there is yet a vision for those days."

[15] While he was saying these things to me, I looked down and kept silent. [16] Then one who looked like a man touched my lips, and I opened my mouth and spoke, saying to him who stood before me, "My lord, because of the vision, I have been seized with pangs and cannot summon strength. [17] How can this servant of my lord speak with my lord, seeing that my strength has failed and no spirit is left in me?" [18] He who looked like a man touched me again, and strengthened me. [19] He said, "Have no fear, precious man, all will be well with you; be strong, be strong!" As he spoke with me, I was strengthened, and said, "Speak on, my lord, for you have strengthened me!" [20] Then he said, "Do you know why I have come to you? Now I must go back to fight the prince of Persia. When I go off, the prince of Greece will come in. [21] c-No one is helping me against them except your prince, Michael. However, I will tell you what is recorded in the book of truth.-c

c-c *Order of clauses inverted for clarity.*

11 "In the first year of Darius the Mede, I took my stand to strengthen and fortify him. ² And now I will tell you the truth: Persia will have three more kings, and the fourth will be wealthier than them all; by the power he obtains through his wealth, he will stir everyone up against the kingdom of Greece. ³ Then a warrior king will appear who will have an extensive dominion and do as he pleases. ⁴ But after his appearance, his kingdom will be broken up and scattered to the four winds of heaven, but not for any of his posterity, nor with dominion like that which he had; for his kingdom will be uprooted and belong to others beside these.

⁵ "The king of the south will grow powerful; however, one of his officers will overpower him and rule, having an extensive dominion. ⁶ After some years, an alliance will be made, and the daughter of the king of the south will come to the king of the north to effect the agreement, but she will not maintain her strength, nor will his strength endure. She will be surrendered together with those who escorted her and the one who begot her and helped her during those times. ⁷ A shoot from her stock will appear in his place, will come against the army and enter the fortress of the king of the north; he will fight and overpower them. ⁸ He will also take their gods with their molten images and their precious vessels of silver and gold back to Egypt as booty. For some years he will leave the king of the north alone, ⁹ who will [later] invade the realm of the king of the south, but will go back to his land.

¹⁰ "His sons will wage war, collecting a multitude of great armies; he will advance and sweep through as a flood, and will again wage war as far as his stronghold. ¹¹ Then the king of the south, in a rage, will go out to do battle with him, with the king of the north. He will muster a great multitude, but the multitude will be delivered into his [foe's] power. ¹² But when the multitude is carried off, he will grow arrogant; he will cause myriads to perish, but will not prevail. ¹³ Then the king of the north will again

muster a multitude even greater than the first. After a time, a matter of years, he will advance with a great army and much baggage. ¹⁴ In those times, many will resist the king of the south, and the lawless sons of your people will assert themselves to confirm the vision, but they will fail. ¹⁵ The king of the north will advance and throw up siege ramps and capture a fortress city, and the forces of the south will not hold out; even the elite of his army will be powerless to resist. ¹⁶ His opponent will do as he pleases, for none will hold out against him; he will install himself in the beautiful land with destruction within his reach. ¹⁷ He will set his mind upon invading the strongholds throughout his [foe's] kingdom, but in order to destroy it he will effect an agreement with him and give him a daughter in marriage; he will not succeed at it and it will not come about. ¹⁸ He will turn to the coastlands and capture many; but a consul will put an end to his insults, nay pay him back for his insults. ¹⁹ He will head back to the strongholds of his own land, but will stumble, and fall, and vanish. ²⁰ His place will be taken by one who will dispatch an officer to exact tribute for royal glory, but he will be broken in a few days, not by wrath or by war. ²¹ His place will be taken by a contemptible man, on whom royal majesty was not conferred; he will come in unawares and seize the kingdom through trickery. ²² The forces of the flood will be overwhelmed by him and will be broken, and so too the covenant leader. ²³ And, from the time an alliance is made with him, he will practice deceit; and he will rise to power with a small band. ²⁴ He will invade the richest of provinces unawares, and will do what his father and forefathers never did, lavishing on them^a spoil, booty, and wealth; he will have designs upon strongholds, but only for a time.

²⁵ "He will muster his strength and courage against the king of the south with a great army. The king of the south will wage war with a very great and powerful army but will not stand fast, for they will devise plans against him. ²⁶ Those who eat of his food will ruin him. His army will be overwhelmed, and many will fall slain. ²⁷ The minds of both kings will be bent on evil; while sitting

^a *I.e. his followers.*

at the table together, they will lie to each other, but to no avail, for there is yet an appointed term. ²⁸ He will return to his land with great wealth, his mind set against the holy covenant. Having done his pleasure, he will return to his land. ²⁹ At the appointed time, he will again invade the south, but the second time will not be like the first. ³⁰ Ships from Kittim will come against him. He will be checked, and will turn back, raging against the holy covenant. Having done his pleasure, he will then attend to those who forsake the holy covenant. ³¹ Forces will be levied by him; they will desecrate the temple, the fortress; they will abolish the regular offering and set up the appalling abomination. ³² He will flatter with smooth words those who act wickedly toward the covenant, but the people devoted to their God will stand firm. ³³ The knowledgeable among the people will make the many understand; and for a while they shall fall by sword and flame, suffer captivity and spoliation. ³⁴ In defeat, they will receive a little help, and many will join them insincerely. ³⁵ Some of the knowledgeable will fall, that they may be refined and purged and whitened until the time of the end, for an interval still remains until the appointed time.

³⁶ "The king will do as he pleases; he will exalt and magnify himself above every god, and he will speak awful things against the God of gods. He will prosper until wrath is spent, and what has been decreed is accomplished. ³⁷ He will not have regard for the god of his ancestors or for the one dear to women; he will not have regard for any god, but will magnify himself above all. ³⁸ He will honor the god of fortresses on his stand; he will honor with gold and silver, with precious stones and costly things, a god that his ancestors never knew. ³⁹ He will deal with fortified strongholds with the help of an alien god. He will heap honor on those who acknowledge him, and will make them master over many; he will distribute land for a price. ⁴⁰ At the time of the end, the king of the south will lock horns with him, but the king of the north will attack him with chariots and riders and many ships. He will invade lands, sweeping through them like a flood; ⁴¹ he will in-

vade the beautiful land, too, and many will fall, but these will escape his clutches: Edom, Moab, and the chief part of the Ammonites. ⁴² He will lay his hands on lands; not even the land of Egypt will escape. ⁴³ He will gain control over treasures of gold and silver and over all the precious things of Egypt, and the Libyans and Cushites will follow at his heel. ⁴⁴ But reports from east and north will alarm him, and he will march forth in a great fury to destroy and annihilate many. ⁴⁵ He will pitch his royal pavilion between the sea and the beautiful holy mountain, and he will meet his doom with no one to help him.

12 "At that time, the great prince, Michael, who stands beside the sons of your people, will appear. It will be a time of trouble, the like of which has never been since the nation came into being. At that time, your people will be rescued, all who are found inscribed in the book. ² Many of those that sleep in the dust of the earth will awake, some to eternal life, others to reproaches, to everlasting abhorrence. ³ And the knowledgeable will be radiant like the bright expanse of sky, and those who lead the many to righteousness will be like the stars forever and ever.

⁴ "But you, Daniel, keep the words secret, and seal the book until the time of the end. Many will range far and wide and knowledge will increase."

⁵ Then I, Daniel, looked and saw two others standing, one on one bank of the river, the other on the other bank of the river. ⁶ One said to the man clothed in linen, who was above the water of the river, "How long until the end of these awful things?" ⁷ Then I heard the man dressed in linen, who was above the water of the river, swear by the Ever-Living One as he lifted his right hand and his left hand to heaven: "For a ᵃ-time, times, and half a time;⁻ᵃ and when the breaking of the power of the holy people comes to an end, then shall all these things be fulfilled."

⁸ I heard and did not understand, so I said, "My lord, what will be the outcome of these things?" ⁹ He said, "Go, Daniel, for these words are secret and sealed to the time of the end. ¹⁰ Many will be purified and purged and refined; the wicked will act wickedly

ᵃ⁻ᵃ *See note at 7:25.*

and none of the wicked will understand; but the knowledgeable will understand. (¹¹ From the time the regular offering is abolished, and an appalling abomination is set up—it will be a thousand two hundred and ninety days. Happy the one who waits and reaches one thousand three hundred and thirty-five days.) ¹² But you, go on to the end; you shall rest, and arise to your destiny at the end of the days."

עזרא
EZRA

עזרא
EZRA

1 In the first year of King Cyrus of Persia, when the word of the LORD spoken by Jeremiah was fulfilled,ᵃ the LORD roused the spirit of King Cyrus of Persia to issue a proclamation throughout his realm by word of mouth and in writing as follows:
2 "Thus said King Cyrus of Persia: The LORD God of Heaven has given me all the kingdoms of the earth and has charged me with building Him a house in Jerusalem, which is in Judah. 3 Anyone of you of all His people—may his God be with him, and let him go up to Jerusalem that is in Judah and build the House of the LORD God of Israel, the God that is in Jerusalem; 4 and all who stay behind, wherever he may be living, let the people of his place assist him with silver, gold, goods, and livestock, beside the freewill offering to the House of God that is in Jerusalem."

5 So the chiefs of the clans of Judah and Benjamin, and the priests and Levites, all whose spirit had been roused by God, got ready to go up to build the House of the LORD that is in Jerusalem. 6 All their neighbors supported them with silver vessels, with gold, with goods, with livestock, and with precious objects, besides what had been given as a freewill offering. 7 King Cyrus of Persia released the vessels of the LORD's house which Nebuchadnezzar had taken away from Jerusalem and had put in the house of his god. 8 These King Cyrus of Persia released through the office of Mithredath the treasurer, who gave an inventory of them to Sheshbazzar the prince of Judah. 9 This is the inventory: 30 gold basins, 1000 silver basins, 29 knives, 10 30 gold bowls, 410 silver ᵇ⁻double bowls,⁻ᵇ 1000 other vessels; 11 in all, 5400 gold

---

ᵃ Cf. Jer. 29.10.
ᵇ⁻ᵇ Meaning of Heb. uncertain.

and silver vessels. Sheshbazzar brought all these back when the exiles came back from Babylon to Jerusalem.

2 *These are the people of the province who came up from among the captive exiles whom King Nebuchadnezzar of Babylon had carried into exile to Babylon, who returned to Jerusalem and Judah, each to his own city, 2 who came with Zerubbabel, Jeshua, Nehemiah, Seraiah, Reelaiah, Mordecai, Bilshan, Mispar, Bigvai, Rehum, Baanah:

The list of the men of the people of Israel: 3 the sons of Parosh —2172; 4 the sons of Shephatiah—372; 5 the sons of Arah—775; 6 the sons of Pahath-moab: the sons of Jeshua and Joab—2812; 7 the sons of Elam—1254; 8 the sons of Zattu—945; 9 the sons of Zaccai—760; 10 the sons of Bani—642; 11 the sons of Bebai—623; 12 the sons of Azgad—1222; 13 the sons of Adonikam—666; 14 the sons of Bigvai—2056; 15 the sons of Adin—454; 16 the sons of Ater: Hezekiah—98; 17 the sons of Bezai—323; 18 the sons of Jorah—112; 19 the sons of Hashum—223; 20 the sons of Gibbar— 95; 21 the sons of Bethlehem—123; 22 the sons of Netophah—56; 23 the sons of Anathoth—128; 24 the sons of Azmaveth—42; 25 the sons of Kiriath-arim: Chephirah and Beeroth—743; 26 the sons of Ramah and Geba—621; 27 the men of Michmas—122; 28 the men of Beth-el and Ai—223; 29 the men of Nebo—52; 30 the sons of Magbish—156; 31 the sons of the other Elam—1254; 32 the sons of Harim—320; 33 the sons of Lod, Hadid, and Ono—725; 34 the sons of Jericho—345; 35 the sons of Senaah—3630.

36 The priests: the sons of Jedaiah: the house of Jeshua—973; 37 the sons of Immer—1052; 38 the sons of Pashhur—1247; 39 the sons of Harim—1017.

40 The Levites: the sons of Jeshua and Kadmiel: the sons of Hodaviah—74.

41 The singers: the sons of Asaph—128.

42 The gatekeepers: the sons of Shallum, the sons of Ater, the

---

ª *This chapter appears as Neh. 7.6–73 with variations in the names and numbers.*

sons of Talmon, the sons of Akkub, the sons of Hatita, the sons of Shobai, all told—139.

⁴³ The temple servants: the sons of Ziha, the sons of Hasupha, the sons of Tabbaoth, ⁴⁴ the sons of Keros, the sons of Siaha, the sons of Padon, ⁴⁵ the sons of Lebanah, the sons of Hagabah, the sons of Akkub, ⁴⁶ the sons of Hagab, the sons of Salmai, the sons of Hanan, ⁴⁷ the sons of Giddel, the sons of Gahar, the sons of Reaiah, ⁴⁸ the sons of Rezin, the sons of Nekoda, the sons of Gazzam, ⁴⁹ the sons of Uzza, the sons of Paseah, the sons of Besai, ⁵⁰ the sons of Asnah, the sons of Meunim, the sons of Nephusim, ⁵¹ the sons of Bakbuk, the sons of Hakupha, the sons of Harhur, ⁵² the sons of Bazluth, the sons of Mehida, the sons of Harsha, ⁵³ the sons of Barkos, the sons of Sisera, the sons of Temah, ⁵⁴ the sons of Neziah, the sons of Hatipha.

⁵⁵ The sons of Solomon's servants: the sons of Sotai, the sons of Hassophereth, the sons of Peruda, ⁵⁶ the sons of Jaalah, the sons of Darkon, the sons of Giddel, ⁵⁷ the sons of Shephatiah, the sons of Hattil, the sons of Pochereth-hazzebaim, the sons of Ami.

⁵⁸ The total of temple servants and the sons of Solomon's servants—392.

⁵⁹ The following were those who came up from Tel-melah, Tel-harsha, Cherub, Addan and Immer—they were unable to tell whether their father's house and descent were Israelite: ⁶⁰ the sons of Delaiah, the sons of Tobiah, the sons of Nekoda—652.

⁶¹ Of the sons of the priests, the sons of Habaiah, the sons of Hakkoz, the sons of Barzillai who had married a daughter of Barzillai and had taken his*b* name—⁶² these searched for their genealogical records, but they could not be found, so they were disqualified for the priesthood. ⁶³ The Tirshatha*c* ordered them not to eat of the most holy things until a priest with Urim and Thummim should appear.

⁶⁴ The sum of the entire community was 42,360, ⁶⁵ not counting their male and female servants, those being 7337; they also had 200 male and female singers. ⁶⁶ Their horses—736; their mules—245; ⁶⁷ their camels—435; their asses—6720.

b Lit. "their."
c A Persian title.

⁶⁸ Some of the chiefs of the clans, on arriving at the House of the LORD in Jerusalem, gave a freewill offering to erect the House of God on its site. ⁶⁹ In accord with their means, they donated to the treasury of the work: gold—6100 drachmas, silver—5000 minas, and priestly robes—100.

⁷⁰ The priests, the Levites and some of the people, and the singers, gatekeepers, and the temple servants took up residence in their towns and all Israel in their towns.

3 When the seventh month arrived—the Israelites being settled in their towns—the entire people assembled as one man in Jerusalem. ² Then Jeshua son of Jozadak and his brother priests, and Zerubbabel son of Shealtiel and his brothers set to and built the altar of the God of Israel to offer burnt offerings upon it as is written in the Teaching of Moses, the man of God. ³ They set up the altar on its site because they were in fear of the peoples of the land, and they offered burnt offerings on it to the LORD, burnt offerings each morning and evening. ⁴ Then they celebrated the festival of Tabernacles as is written, with its daily burnt offerings in the proper quantities, on each day as is prescribed for it, ⁵ followed by the regular burnt offering and the offerings for the new moons and for all the sacred fixed times of the LORD, and whatever freewill offerings were made to the LORD. ⁶ From the first day of the seventh month they began to make burnt offerings to the LORD, though the foundation of the Temple of the LORD had not been laid. ⁷ They paid the hewers and craftsmen with money, and the Sidonians and Tyrians with food, drink, and oil to bring cedarwood from Lebanon by sea to Joppa, in accord with the authorization granted them by King Cyrus of Persia.

⁸ In the second year after their arrival at the House of God, at Jerusalem, in the second month, Zerubbabel son of Shealtiel and Jeshua son of Jozadak, and the rest of their brother priests and Levites, and all who had come from the captivity to Jerusalem, as

their first step appointed Levites from the age of twenty and upward to supervise the work of the House of the Lord. [9] Jeshua, his sons and brothers, Kadmiel and his sons, [a-]the sons of Judah,[-a] together were appointed in charge of those who did the work in the House of God; also the sons of Henadad, their sons and brother Levites.

[10] When the builders had laid the foundation of the Temple of the Lord, priests in their vestments with trumpets, and Levites sons of Asaph with cymbals were stationed to give praise to the Lord, as King David of Israel had ordained. [11] They sang songs extolling and praising the Lord, [b-]"For He is good, His steadfast love for Israel is eternal."[-b] All the people raised a great shout extolling the Lord because the foundation of the House of the Lord had been laid. [12] Many of the priests and Levites and the chiefs of the clans, the old men who had seen the first house, wept loudly at the sight of the founding of this house. Many others shouted joyously at the top of their voices. [13] The people could not distinguish the shouts of joy from the people's weeping, for the people raised a great shout, the sound of which could be heard from afar.

4 When the adversaries of Judah and Benjamin heard that the returned exiles were building a temple to the Lord God of Israel, [2] they approached Zerubbabel and the chiefs of the clans and said to them, "Let us build with you, since we too worship your God, having offered sacrifices to Him since the time of King Esarhaddon of Assyria, who brought us here." [3] Zerubbabel, Jeshua, and the rest of the chiefs of the clans of Israel answered them, "It is not for you and us to build a House to our God, but we alone will build it to the Lord God of Israel, in accord with the charge that the king, King Cyrus of Persia, laid upon us." [4] Thereupon the people of the land undermined the resolve of the people of Judah, and made them afraid to build. [5] They

[a-a] *I.e. Hodaviah of 2.40.*
[b-b] *Cf. Ps. 106.1; 136.*

bribed ministers in order to thwart their plans all the years of King Cyrus of Persia and until the reign of King Darius of Persia.

6 And in the reign of Ahasuerus, at the start of his reign, they drew up an accusation against the inhabitants of Judah and Jerusalem.

7 And in the time of Artaxerxes, Bishlam, Mithredath, Tabeel, and the rest of their colleagues wrote to King Artaxerxes of Persia, a letter written in Aramaic and translated.[a]

Aramaic:[b] 8 Rehum the commissioner and Shimshai the scribe wrote a letter concerning Jerusalem to King Artaxerxes as follows: (9 [c] Then Rehum the commissioner and Shimshai the scribe, and the rest of their colleagues, the judges, officials, officers, and overseers, the men of Erech, and of Babylon, and of Susa—that is the Elamites—10 and other peoples whom the great and glorious Osnappar deported and settled in the city of Samaria and the rest of the province of Beyond the River [wrote]—and now 11 this is the text of the letter which they sent to him:)—"To King Artaxerxes [from] your servants, men of the province of Beyond the River. And now 12 be it known to the king that the Jews who came up from you to us have reached Jerusalem and are rebuilding that rebellious and wicked city; they are completing the walls and repairing the foundation. 13 Now be it known to the king that if this city is rebuilt and the walls completed, they will not pay tribute, poll-tax, or land-tax, and in the end it will harm the kingdom. 14 Now since we eat the salt of the palace, and it is not right that we should see the king dishonored, we have written to advise the king [of this] 15 so that you may search the records of your fathers and find in the records and know that this city is a rebellious city, harmful to kings and states. Sedition has been rife in it from early times; on that account this city was destroyed. 16 We advise the king that if this city is rebuilt and its walls are completed, you will no longer have any portion in the province of Beyond the River."

[a] *Cf. below v. 18 and note d.*
[b] *A note indicating that what follows is in the Aramaic language.*
[c] *Vv. 9–11 amplify v. 8.*

¹⁷ The king sent back the following message: "To Rehum the commissioner and Shimshai the scribe, and the rest of their colleagues, who dwell in Samaria and in the rest of the province of Beyond the River, greetings. ¹⁸ Now the letter that you wrote me has been read to me in translation.*d* ¹⁹ At my order a search has been made, and it has been found that this city has from earliest times risen against kings, and that rebellion and sedition have been rife in it. ²⁰ Powerful kings have ruled over Jerusalem and exercised authority over the whole province of Beyond the River, and tribute, poll-tax, and land-tax were paid to them. ²¹ Now issue an order to stop these men; this city is not to be rebuilt until I so order. ²² Take care not to be lax in this matter or there will be much damage and harm to the kingdom."

²³ When the text of the letter of King Artaxerxes was read before Rehum and Shimshai the scribe and their colleagues, they hurried to Jerusalem, to the Jews, and stopped them by main force. ²⁴ At that time, work on the House of God in Jerusalem stopped and remained in abeyance until the second year of the reign of King Darius of Persia.

5 Then the prophets, Haggai the prophet and Zechariah son of Iddo, prophesied to the Jews in Judah and Jerusalem, *a* inspired by the God of Israel.*-a* ² Thereupon Zerubbabel son of Shealtiel and Jeshua son of Jozadak began rebuilding the House of God in Jerusalem, with the full support of the prophets of God. ³ At once Tattenai, governor of the province of Beyond the River, Shethar-bozenai, and their colleagues descended upon them and said this to them, "Who issued orders to you to rebuild this house and complete its furnishing?" ⁴ Then we*b* said to them, "What are the names of the men who are engaged in the building?" ⁵ But God watched over the elders of the Jews and they were not stopped while a report went to Darius and a letter was sent back in reply to it.

d I.e. from Aramaic to Persian.
a-a Lit. "with the name of the God of Israel upon them."
b The officials of v. 3; cf. v. 10. Greek and Syriac read "they."

⁶ This is the text of the letter that Tattenai, governor of the province of Beyond the River, and Shethar-bozenai and his colleagues, the officials of Beyond the River, sent to King Darius. ⁷ They sent a message to him and this is what was written in it: "To King Darius, greetings, and so forth. ⁸ Be it known to the king, that we went to the province of Judah, to the house of the great God. It is being rebuilt of hewn stone, and wood is being laid in the walls. The work is being done with dispatch and is going well. ⁹ Thereupon we directed this question to these elders, 'Who issued orders to you to rebuild this house and to complete its furnishings?' ¹⁰ We also asked their names so that we could write down the names of their leaders for your information. ¹¹ This is what they answered us: 'We are the servants of the God of heaven and earth; we are rebuilding the house that was originally built many years ago; a great king of Israel built it and completed it. ¹² But because our fathers angered the God of Heaven, He handed them over to Nebuchadnezzar the Chaldean, king of Babylon, who demolished this house and exiled the people to Babylon. ¹³ But in the first year of King Cyrus of Babylon, King Cyrus issued an order to rebuild this House of God. ¹⁴ Also the silver and gold vessels of the House of God that Nebuchadnezzar had taken away from the temple in Jerusalem and brought to the temple in Babylon—King Cyrus released them from the temple in Babylon to be given to the one called Sheshbazzar whom he had appointed governor. ¹⁵ He said to him, "Take these vessels, go, deposit them in the temple in Jerusalem, and let the House of God be rebuilt on its original site." ¹⁶ That same Sheshbazzar then came and laid the foundations for the House of God in Jerusalem; and ever since then it has been under construction, but is not yet finished.' ¹⁷ And now, if it please the king, let the royal archives there in Babylon be searched to see whether indeed an order had been issued by King Cyrus to rebuild this House of God in Jerusalem. May the king convey to us his pleasure in this matter."

6 Thereupon, at the order of King Darius, they searched the archives where the treasures were stored in Babylon. ² But it was in the citadel of Ecbatana, in the province of Media, that a scroll was found in which the following was written: "Memorandum: ³ In the first year of King Cyrus, King Cyrus issued an order concerning the House of God in Jerusalem: 'Let the house be rebuilt, a place for offering sacrifices, with a base built up high. Let it be sixty cubits high and sixty cubits wide, ⁴ with a course of unused timber for each three courses of hewn stone. The expenses shall be paid by the palace. ⁵ And the gold and silver vessels of the House of God which Nebuchadnezzar had taken away from the temple in Jerusalem and transported to Babylon shall be returned, and let each go back to the temple in Jerusalem where it belongs; you shall deposit it in the House of God.'

⁶ "Now*ᵃ* you, Tattenai, governor of the province of Beyond the River, Shethar-bozenai and colleagues, the officials of the province of Beyond the River, stay away from that place. ⁷ Allow the work of this House of God to go on; let the governor of the Jews and the elders of the Jews rebuild this House of God on its site. ⁸ And I hereby issue an order concerning what you must do to help these elders of the Jews rebuild this House of God: the expenses are to be paid to these men with dispatch out of the resources of the king, derived from the taxes of the province of Beyond the River, so that the work not be stopped. ⁹ They are to be given daily, without fail, whatever they need of young bulls, rams, or lambs as burnt offerings for the God of Heaven, and wheat, salt, wine, and oil, at the order of the priests in Jerusalem, ¹⁰ so that they may offer pleasing sacrifices to the God of heaven and pray for the life of the king and his sons. ¹¹ I also issue an order that whoever alters this decree shall have a beam removed from his house, and he shall be impaled on it and his house confiscated.*ᵇ* ¹² And may the God who established His name there

---

ᵃ *This introduces the text of the reply of Darius that would have contained the preceding narrative (vv. 1–5) as a preliminary.*
ᵇ *Meaning uncertain; or "turned into ruins."*

cause the downfall of any king or nation that undertakes to alter or damage that House of God in Jerusalem. I, Darius, have issued the decree; let it be carried out with dispatch."

13 Then Tattenai, governor of the province of Beyond the River, Shethar-bozenai, and their colleagues carried out with dispatch what King Darius had written. 14 So the elders of the Jews progressed in the building, urged on by the prophesying of Haggai the prophet and Zechariah son of Iddo, and they brought the building to completion under the aegis of the God of Israel and by the order of Cyrus and Darius and King Artaxerxes of Persia. 15 The house was finished on the third of the month of Adar in the sixth year of the reign of King Darius. 16 The Israelites, the priests, and the Levites, and all the other exiles celebrated the dedication of the House of God with joy. 17 And they sacrificed for the dedication of this House of God one hundred bulls, two hundred rams, four hundred lambs, and twelve goats as a purification offering for all of Israel, according to the number of the tribes of Israel. 18 They appointed the priests in their courses and the Levites in their divisions for the service of God in Jerusalem, according to the prescription in the Book of Moses.

19 c The returned exiles celebrated the Passover on the fourteenth day of the first month, 20 for the priests and Levites had purified themselves to a man; they were all pure. They slaughtered the passover offering for all the returned exiles, and for their brother priests and for themselves. 21 The children of Israel who had returned from the exile, together with all who joined them in separating themselves from the uncleanliness of the nations of the lands to worship the LORD God of Israel, ate of it. 22 They joyfully celebrated the Feast of Unleavened Bread for seven days, for the LORD had given them cause for joy by inclining the heart of the Assyrian king toward them so as to give them support in the work of the House of God, the God of Israel.

c Hebrew resumes here.

7 After these events, during the reign of King Artaxerxes of Persia, Ezra son of Seraiah son of Azariah son of Hilkiah ² son of Shallum son of Zadok son of Ahitub ³ son of Amariah son of Azariah son of Meraioth ⁴ son of Zerahiah son of Uzzi son of Bukki ⁵ son of Abishua son of Phinehas son of Eleazar son of Aaron the chief priest—⁶ that Ezra came up from Babylon, a scribe expert in the Teaching of Moses which the LORD God of Israel had given, whose request the king had granted in its entirety, thanks to the benevolence of the LORD toward him.

(⁷ Some of the Israelites, the priests and Levites, the singers, the gatekeepers, and the temple servants set out for Jerusalem in the seventh year of King Artaxerxes, ⁸ arriving in Jerusalem in the fifth month in the seventh year of the king.) ⁹ On the first day of the first month the journey up from Babylon was started, and on the first day of the fifth month he arrived in Jerusalem, thanks to the benevolent care of his God for him. ¹⁰ For Ezra had dedicated himself to study the Teaching of the LORD so as to observe it, and to teach laws and rules to Israel.

¹¹ The following is the text of the letter which King Artaxerxes gave Ezra the priest-scribe, a scholar in matters concerning the commandments of the LORD and His laws to Israel:

¹² ᵃ "Artaxerxes king of kings, to Ezra the priest, scholar in the law of the God of heaven, ᵇ⁻and so forth.ᵃ⁻ᵇ And now, ¹³ I hereby issue an order that anyone in my kingdom who is of the people of Israel and its priests and Levites who feels impelled to go to Jerusalem may go with you. ¹⁴ For you are commissioned by the king and his seven advisers to regulate Judah and Jerusalem according to the law of your God, which is in your care, ¹⁵ and to bring the freewill offering of silver and gold, which the king and his advisers made to the God of Israel, whose dwelling is in Jerusalem, ¹⁶ and whatever silver and gold that you find throughout the province of Babylon, together with the freewill offerings which the people and the priests will give for the House of their

ᵃ *Aramaic resumes here through v. 26.*
ᵇ⁻ᵇ *Meaning uncertain.*

God which is in Jerusalem. [17] You shall, therefore, with dispatch acquire with this money bulls, rams, and lambs, with their meal offerings and libations, and offer them on the altar of the House of your God in Jerusalem. [18] And whatever you wish to do with the leftover silver and gold, you and your kinsmen may do, in accord with the will of your God. [19] The vessels for the service of the House of your God which are given to you, deliver to God in Jerusalem, [20] and any other needs of the House of your God which it falls to you to supply, do so from the royal treasury. [21] I, King Artaxerxes, for my part, hereby issue an order to all the treasurers in the province of Beyond the River that whatever request Ezra the priest, scholar in the law of the God of Heaven, makes of you is to be fulfilled with dispatch [22] up to the sum of one hundred talents of silver, one hundred kor of wheat, one hundred bath of oil, and salt without limit. [23] Whatever is by order of the God of Heaven must be carried out diligently for the House of the God of Heaven, else wrath will come upon the king and his sons. [24] We further advise you that it is not permissible to impose tribute, poll tax, or land tax on any priest, Levite, singer, gatekeeper, temple servant, or other servant of this House of God. [25] And you, Ezra, by the divine wisdom you possess, appoint magistrates and judges to judge all the people in the province of Beyond the River who know the laws of your God, and to teach those who do not know them. [26] Let anyone who does not obey the law of your God and the law of the king be punished with dispatch, whether by death, corporal punishment, confiscation of possessions, or imprisonment."

[27] [c]Blessed is the Lord God of our fathers, who put it into the mind of the king to glorify the House of the Lord in Jerusalem, [28] and who inclined the king and his counselors and the king's military officers to be favorably disposed toward me. For my part, thanks to the care of the Lord for me, I summoned up courage and assembled leading men in Israel to go with me.

[c] *Hebrew resumes here.*

466

8 These are the chiefs of the clans and the register of the genealogy of those who came up with me from Babylon in the reign of King Artaxerxes: ² Of the sons of Phinehas, Gershom; of the sons of Ithamar, Daniel; of the sons of David, Hattush. ³ Of the sons of Shecaniah: of the sons of Parosh, Zechariah; through him the genealogy of 150 males was registered. ⁴ Eliehoenai son of Zerahiah, of the sons of Pahath-moab, and with him 200 males. ⁵ Of the sons of Shecaniah son of Jahaziel; and with him 300 males. ⁶ And of the sons of Adin, Ebed son of Jonathan; and with him 50 males. ⁷ And of the sons of Elam, Jeshaiah son of Athaliah; and with him 70 males. ⁸ And of the sons of Shephatiah, Zebadiah son of Michael; and with him 80 males. ⁹ Of the sons of Joab, Obadiah son of Jehiel; and with him 218 males. ¹⁰ And of the sons of Shelomith, the son of Josiphiah; and with him 160 males. ¹¹ And of the sons of Bebai, Zechariah son of Bebai; and with him 28 males. ¹² And of the sons of Azgad, Johanan son of Hakkatan; and with him 110 males. ¹³ And of the sons of Adonikam, who were the last; and these are their names: Eliphelet, Jeiel, and Shemaiah; and with them 60 males. ¹⁴ And of the sons of Bigvai, Uthai and Zaccur; and with them 70 males.

¹⁵ These I assembled by the river that enters Ahava, and we encamped there for three days. I reviewed the people and the priests, but I did not find any Levites there. ¹⁶ I sent for Eliezer, Ariel, Shemaiah, Elnathan, Jarib, Elnathan, Nathan, Zechariah, and Meshullam, the leading men, and also for Joiarib and Elnathan, the instructors, ¹⁷ and I gave them an order for Iddo, the leader at the place [called] Casiphia. I gave them a message to convey to Iddo [and] his brother temple servants at the place [called] Casiphia, that they should bring us attendants for the House of our God. ¹⁸ Thanks to the benevolent care of our God for us, they brought us a capable man of the family of Mahli son of Levi son of Israel, and Sherebiah and his sons and brothers,

eighteen in all, ¹⁹ and Hashabiah, and with him Jeshaiah of the family of Merari, his brothers and their sons, twenty in all; ²⁰ and of the temple servants whom David and the officers had appointed for the service of the Levites—220 temple servants, all of them listed by name.

²¹ I proclaimed a fast there by the Ahava River to afflict ourselves before our God to beseech Him for a smooth journey for us and for our children and for all our possessions; ²² for I was ashamed to ask the king for soldiers and horsemen to protect us against any enemy on the way, since we had told the king, "The benevolent care of our God is for all who seek Him, while His fierce anger is against all who forsake Him." ²³ So we fasted and besought our God for this, and He responded to our plea. ²⁴ Then I selected twelve of the chiefs of the priests, namely Sherebiah and Hashabiah with ten of their brothers, ²⁵ and I weighed out to them the silver, the gold, and the vessels, the contribution to the House of our God which the king, his counselors and officers, and all Israel who were present had made. ²⁶ I entrusted to their safekeeping the weight of six hundred and fifty talents of silver, one hundred silver vessels of one talent each, one hundred talents of gold; ²⁷ also, twenty gold bowls worth one thousand darics and two vessels of good, shining bronze, as precious as gold. ²⁸ I said to them, "You are consecrated to the LORD, and the vessels are consecrated, and the silver and gold are a freewill offering to the LORD God of your fathers. ²⁹ Guard them diligently until such time as you weigh them out in the presence of the officers of the priests and the Levites and the officers of the clans of Israel in Jerusalem in the chambers of the House of the LORD."

³⁰ So the priests and the Levites received the cargo of silver and gold and vessels by weight, to bring them to Jerusalem to the House of our God. ³¹ We set out for Jerusalem from the Ahava River on the twelfth of the first month. We enjoyed the care of our God who saved us from enemy ambush on the journey.

³² We arrived in Jerusalem and stayed there three days. ³³ On the fourth day the silver, gold, and vessels were weighed out in the House of our God into the keeping of Meremoth son of Uriah the priest, with whom was Eleazar son of Phinehas. Jozabad son of Jeshua, and Noadiah son of Binnui, the Levites, were with them. ³⁴ Everything accorded as to number and weight, the entire cargo being recorded at that time.

³⁵ The returning exiles who arrived from captivity made burnt offerings to the God of Israel: twelve bulls for all Israel, ninety-six rams, seventy-seven lambs and twelve he-goats as a purification offering, all this a burnt offering to the LORD. ³⁶ They handed the royal orders to the king's satraps and the governors of the province of Beyond the River who gave support to the people and the House of God.

9 When this was over, the officers approached me, saying, "The people of Israel and the priests and Levites have not separated themselves from the peoples of the land whose abhorrent practices are like those of the Canaanites, the Hittites, the Perizzites, the Jebusites, the Ammonites, the Moabites, the Egyptians, and the Amorites. ² They have taken their daughters as wives for themselves and for their sons, so that the holy seed has become intermingled with the peoples of the land; and it is the officers and prefects who have taken the lead in this trespass."

³ When I heard this, I rent my garment and robe, I tore hair out of my head and beard, and I sat desolate. ⁴ Around me gathered all who were concerned over the words of the God of Israel because of the returning exiles' trespass, while I sat desolate until the evening offering. ⁵ At the time of the evening offering I ended my self-affliction; still in my torn garment and robe, I got down on my knees and spread out my hands to the LORD my God, ⁶ and said, "O my God, I am too ashamed and mortified to lift my face to You, O my God, for our iniquities ᵃ⁻are overwhelming⁻ᵃ

ᵃ⁻ᵃ *Lit. "are numerous above the head."*

and our guilt has grown high as heaven. [7] From the time of our fathers to this very day we have been deep in guilt. Because of our iniquities, we, our kings, and our priests have been handed over to foreign kings, to the sword, to captivity, to pillage, and to humiliation, as is now the case.

[8] "But now, for a short while, there has been a reprieve from the LORD our God, who has granted us a surviving remnant and given us a stake in His holy place; our God has restored the luster to our eyes and furnished us with a little sustenance in our bondage. [9] For bondsmen we are, though even in our bondage God has not forsaken us, but has disposed the king of Persia favorably toward us, to furnish us with sustenance and to raise again the House of our God, repairing its ruins and giving us a hold[b] in Judah and Jerusalem.

[10] "Now, what can we say in the face of this, O our God, for we have forsaken Your commandments, [11] which You gave us through Your servants the prophets when You said, 'The land which you are about to possess is a land unclean through the uncleanness of the peoples of the land, through their abhorrent practices with which they, in their impurity, have filled it from one end to the other. [12] Now then, do not give your daughters in marriage to their sons or let their daughters marry your sons; do nothing for their well-being or advantage, then you will be strong and enjoy the bounty of the land and bequeath it to your children forever.' [13] After all that has happened to us because of our evil deeds and our deep guilt—though You, our God, have been forebearing, [punishing us] less than our iniquity [deserves] in that You have granted us such a remnant as this—[14] shall we once again violate Your commandments by intermarrying with these peoples who follow such abhorrent practices? Will You not rage against us till we are destroyed without remnant or survivor? [15] O LORD, God of Israel, You are benevolent,[c] for we have survived as a remnant, as is now the case. We stand before You in all our guilt, for we cannot face You on this account."

[b] Lit. "fence."
[c] Or "in the right."

10 While Ezra was praying and making confession, weeping and prostrating himself before the House of God, a very great crowd of Israelites gathered about him, men, women, and children; the people were weeping bitterly. ² Then Shecaniah son of Jehiel of the family of Elam spoke up and said to Ezra, "We have trespassed against our God by bringing into our homes foreign women from the peoples of the land; *a*-but there is still hope for Israel despite this.*-a* ³ Now then, let us make a covenant with our God to expel all these women and those who have been born to them, in accordance with the bidding of the LORD and of all who are concerned over the commandment of our God, and let the Teaching be obeyed. ⁴ Take action, for the responsibility is yours and we are with you. Act with resolve!"

⁵ So Ezra at once put the officers of the priests and the Levites and all Israel under oath to act accordingly, and they took the oath. ⁶ Then Ezra rose from his place in front of the House of God and went into the chamber of Jehohanan son of Eliashib; there, he ate no bread and drank no water, for he was in mourning over the trespass of those who had returned from exile. ⁷ Then a proclamation was issued in Judah and Jerusalem that all who had returned from the exile should assemble in Jerusalem, ⁸ and that anyone who did not come in three days would, by decision of the officers and elders, have his property confiscated and himself excluded from the congregation of the returning exiles.

⁹ All the men of Judah and Benjamin assembled in Jerusalem in three days; it was the ninth month, the twentieth of the month. All the people sat in the square of the House of God, trembling on account of the event and because of the rains. ¹⁰ Then Ezra the priest got up and said to them, "You have trespassed by bringing home foreign women, thus aggravating the guilt of Israel. ¹¹ So now, make confession to the LORD, God of your fathers, and do

---

ᵃ⁻ᵃ *Or "Is there . . . ?"*

His will, and separate yourselves from the peoples of the land and from the foreign women."

¹² The entire congregation responded in a loud voice, "We must surely do just as you say. ¹³ However, many people are involved, and it is the rainy season; it is not possible to remain out in the open, nor is this the work of a day or two, because we have transgressed extensively in this matter. ¹⁴ Let our officers remain on behalf of the entire congregation, and all our towns-people who have brought home foreign women shall appear before them at scheduled times, together with the elders and judges of each town, in order to avert the burning anger of our God from us on this account." ¹⁵ Only Jonathan son of Asahel and Jahzeiah son of Tikvah remained for this purpose, assisted by Meshullam and Shabbethai, the Levites. ¹⁶ The returning exiles did so. Ezra the priest and the men who were the chiefs of the ancestral clans—all listed by name—sequestered themselves on the first day of the tenth month to study the matter. ¹⁷ By the first day of the first month they were done with all the men who had brought home foreign women. ¹⁸ Among the priestly families who were found to have brought foreign women were Jeshua son of Jozadak and his brothers Maaseiah, Eliezer, Jarib, and Gedaliah. ¹⁹ They gave their word*ᵇ* to expel their wives and, acknowledging their guilt, offered a ram from the flock to expiate it. ²⁰ Of the sons of Immer: Hanani and Zebadiah; ²¹ of the sons of Harim: Maaseiah, Elijah, Shemaiah, Jehiel, and Uzziah; ²² of the sons of Pashhur: Elioenai, Maaseiah, Ishmael, Nethanel, Jozabad, and Elasah; ²³ of the Levites: Jozabad, Shimei, Kelaiah who is Kelita, Pethahiah, Judah and Eliezer. ²⁴ Of the singers: Eliashib. Of the gatekeepers: Shallum, Telem, and Uri. ²⁵ Of the Israelites: of the sons of Parosh: Ramiah, Izziah, Malchijah, Mijamin, Eleazar, Malchijah and Benaiah; ²⁶ of the sons of Elam: Mattaniah, Zechariah, Jehiel, Abdi, Jeremoth, and Elijah; ²⁷ of the sons of Zattu: Elioenai, Eliashib, Mattaniah, Jeremoth, Zabad, and Aziza; ²⁸ of the sons of Bebai: Jehohanan, Hananiah, Zabbai, and Athlai; ²⁹ of the sons of Bani: Meshullam, Malluch, Adaiah, Jashub,

ᵇ *Lit. "hand."*

Sheal, and Ramoth; ³⁰ of the sons of Pahath-moab: Adna, Chelal, Benaiah, Maaseiah, Mattaniah, Bezalel, Binnui, and Manasseh; ³¹ of the sons of Harim: Eliezer, Isshijah, Malchijah, Shemaiah, and Shimeon; ³² also Benjamin, Malluch, and Shemariah; ³³ of the sons of Hashum: Mattenai, Mattattah, Zabad, Eliphelet, Jeremai, Manasseh and Shimei; ³⁴ of the sons of Bani: Maadai, Amram, and Uel; ³⁵ also Benaiah, Bedeiah, Cheluhu, ³⁶ Vaniah, Meremoth, Eliashib, ³⁷ Mattaniah, Mattenai, Jaasai, ³⁸ Bani, Binnui, Shimei, ³⁹ Shelemiah, Nathan, Adaiah, ⁴⁰ Machnadebai, Shashai, Sharai, ⁴¹ Azarel, Shelemiah, Shemariah, ⁴² Shallum, Amariah, and Joseph; ⁴³ of the sons of Nebo: Jeiel, Mattithiah, Zabad, Zebina, Jaddai, Joel, and Benaiah.

⁴⁴ All these had married foreign women, among whom were some women ᶜ⁻who had borne children.⁻ᶜ

ᶜ⁻ᶜ *Meaning of Heb. uncertain.*

נחמיה

NEHEMIAH

נחמיה

NEHEMIAH

1 The narrative of Nehemiah son of Hacaliah:

In the month of Kislev of the twentieth year,[a] when I was in the fortress of Shushan, [2] Hanani, one of my brothers, together with some men of Judah, arrived, and I asked them about the Jews, the remnant who had survived the captivity, and about Jerusalem. [3] They replied, "The survivors who have survived the captivity there in the province are in dire trouble and disgrace; Jerusalem's wall is full of breaches, and its gates have been destroyed by fire."

[4] When I heard that, I sat and wept, and was in mourning for days, fasting and praying to the God of heaven. [5] I said, "O LORD, God of heaven, great and awesome God, who stays faithful to His covenant with those who love Him and keep His commandments! [6] Let Your ear be attentive and Your eyes open to receive the prayer of Your servant that I am praying to You now, day and night, on behalf of the Israelites, Your servants, confessing the sins that we Israelites have committed against You, sins that I and my father's house have committed. [7] We have offended You by not keeping the commandments, the laws, and the rules that You gave to Your servant Moses. [8] Be mindful of the promise You gave to Your servant Moses: 'If you are unfaithful, I will scatter you among the peoples; [9] but if you turn back to Me, faithfully keep My commandments, even if your dispersed are at the ends of the earth,[b] I will gather them from there and bring them to the place where I have chosen to establish My name.' [10] For they are Your servants and Your people whom You redeemed by Your great power and Your mighty hand. [11] O Lord! Let Your ear be attentive to the prayer of Your servant, and to the prayer of Your

---

[a] *I.e. of King Artaxerxes; cf. 2.1.*
[b] *Lit. "sky."*

477

servants who desire to hold Your name in awe. Grant Your servant success today, and dispose that man to be compassionate toward him!"

I was the king's cupbearer at the time.

2 In the month of Nisan, in the twentieth year of King Artaxerxes, wine was set before him; I took the wine and gave it to the king—I had never been out of sorts in his presence. ² The king said to me, "How is it that you look bad, though you are not ill? It must be bad thoughts." I was very frightened, ³ but I answered the king, "May the king live forever! How should I not look bad when the city of the graveyard of my ancestors lies in ruins, and its gates have been consumed by fire?" ⁴ The king said to me, "What is your request?" With a prayer to the God of heaven, ⁵ I answered the king, "If it please the king, and if your servant has found favor with you, send me to Judah, to the city of my ancestors' graves, to rebuild it." ⁶ With the consort seated at his side, the king said to me, "How long will you be gone and when will you return?" So it was agreeable to the king to send me, and I gave him a date. ⁷ Then I said to the king, "If it please the king, let me have letters to the governors of the province of Beyond the River, directing them to grant me passage until I reach Judah; ⁸ likewise, a letter to Asaph, the keeper of the King's Park, directing him to give me timber for roofing the gatehouses of the temple fortress and the city walls and for the house I shall occupy." The king gave me these, thanks to my God's benevolent care for me. ⁹ When I came to the governors of the province of Beyond the River I gave them the king's letters. The king also sent army officers and cavalry with me.

¹⁰ When Sanballat the Horonite and Tobiah the Ammonite servant heard, it displeased them greatly that someone had come, intent on improving the condition of the Israelites.

¹¹ I arrived in Jerusalem. After I was there three days ¹² I got up at night, I and a few men with me, and telling no one what my

God had put into my mind to do for Jerusalem, and taking no other beast than the one on which I was riding, [13] I went out by the Valley Gate, at night, toward the Jackals' Spring and the Dung Gate; and I surveyed the walls of Jerusalem that were breached, and its gates, consumed by fire. [14] I proceeded to the Fountain Gate and to the King's Pool, where there was no room for the beast under me to continue. [15] So I went up the wadi by night, surveying the wall, and, entering again by the Valley Gate, I returned. [16] The prefects knew nothing of where I had gone or what I had done, since I had not yet divulged it to the Jews—the priests, the nobles, the prefects, or the rest of the officials.

[17] Then I said to them, "You see the bad state we are in— Jerusalem lying in ruins and its gates destroyed by fire. Come, let us rebuild the wall of Jerusalem and suffer no more disgrace." [18] I told them of my God's benevolent care for me, also of the things that the king had said to me, and they said, "Let us start building!" They were encouraged by [His] benevolence.

[19] When Sanballat the Horonite and Tobiah the Ammonite servant and Geshem the Arab heard, they mocked us and held us in contempt and said, "What is this that you are doing? Are you rebelling against the king?" [20] I said to them in reply, "The God of heaven will grant us success, and we, His servants, will start building. But you have no share or claim or stake[a] in Jerusalem!"

3 Then Eliashib the high priest and his fellow priests set to and rebuilt the Sheep Gate; they consecrated it and set up its doors, consecrating it as far as the Hundred's Tower, as far as the Tower of Hananel. [2] Next to him, the men of Jericho built. Next to them,[a] Zaccur son of Imri. [3] The sons of Hassenaah rebuilt the Fish Gate; they roofed it and set up its doors, locks, and bars. [4] Next to them, Meremoth son of Uriah son of Hakkoz repaired; and next to him,[b] Meshullam son of Berechiah son of Meshezabel. Next to him,[b] Zadok son of Baana repaired. [5] Next to him,[b] the Tekoites repaired, though their nobles would not take upon their shoul-

---

[a] Lit. "record."

[a] Lit. "him."
[b] Lit. "them."

ders-ᶜ the work of their lord. ⁶ Joiada son of Paseah and Meshullam son of Besodeiah repaired the Jeshanah Gate; they roofed it and set up its doors, locks, and bars. ᶜ⁻⁷ Next to them, Melatiah the Gibeonite and Jadon the Meronothite repaired, [with] the men of Gibeon and Mizpah, ᵈ⁻under the jurisdiction-ᵈ of the governor of the province of Beyond the River. ⁸ Next to them,ᵃ Uzziel son of Harhaiah, [of the] smiths, repaired. Next to him, Hananiah, ofᵉ the perfumers. They restored Jerusalem as far as the Broad Wall. ⁹ Next to them, Rephaiah son of Hur, chief of half the district of Jerusalem, repaired. ¹⁰ Next to him,ᵇ Jedaiah son of Harumaph repaired in front of his house. Next to him, Hattush son of Hashabneiah repaired. ¹¹ Malchijah son of Harim and Hasshub son of Pahath-moab repaired a second stretch, including the Tower of Ovens. ¹² Next to them,ᵃ Shallum son of Hallohesh, ᶠ chief of half the district of Jerusalem, repaired—he and his daughters. ¹³ Hanun and the inhabitants of Zanoah repaired the Valley Gate; they rebuilt it and set up its doors, locks, and bars. And [they also repaired] a thousand cubits of wall to the Dung Gate. ¹⁴ Malchijah son of Rechab, chief of the district of Beth-haccherem, repaired the Dung Gate; he rebuilt it and set up its doors, locks, and bars. ¹⁵ Shallun son of Col-hozeh, chief of the district of Mizpah, repaired the Fountain Gate; he rebuilt it and covered it, and set up its doors, locks, and bars, as well as the wall of the irrigationᵍ pool of the King's Garden as far as the steps going down from the City of David. ¹⁶ After him, Nehemiah son of Azbuk, chief of half the district of Beth-zur, repaired, from in front of the graves of David as far as the artificial pool, and as far as the House of the Warriors. ¹⁷ After him, the Levites repaired: Rehum son of Bani. Next to him, Hashabiah, chief of half the district of Keilah, repaired for his district. ¹⁸ After him, their brothers repaired: Bavvai son of Henadad, chief of half the district of Keilah. ¹⁹ Next to him, Ezer son of Jeshua, the chief of Mizpah, repaired a second stretch, from in front of the ascent to the armory [at] the angle [of the wall]. ²⁰ After him, Baruch son of Zaccai zealously repaired a second stretch, from the angle to the entrance to the house of Eliashib, the high priest. ²¹ After him, Meremoth son of Uriah son

ᶜ⁻ᶜ Lit. "bring their neck into."
ᵈ⁻ᵈ Lit. "of the throne"; meaning of Heb. uncertain.
ᵉ Lit. "son of," i.e. member of the guild of.
ᶠ I.e. the charmer.
ᵍ Following Kimhi; cf. Mishnaic Heb. bet hashelahin, irrigated field.

of Hakkoz repaired a second stretch, from the entrance to Eliashib's house to the end of Eliashib's house. 22 After him, the
priests, inhabitants of the plain, repaired. 23 After them,*a* Benjamin and Hasshub repaired in front of their houses. After them,*a*
Azariah son of Maaseiah son of Ananiah repaired beside his
house. 24 After him, Binnui son of Henadad repaired a second
stretch, from the house of Azariah to the angle, to the corner.
25 Palal son of Uzai—from in front of the angle and the tower that
juts out of the house of the king, the upper [tower] of the prison
compound. After him, Pedaiah son of Parosh. (26 The temple
servants were living on the Ophel, as far as a point in front of
the Water Gate in the east, and the jutting tower.) 27 After him,
the Tekoites repaired a second stretch, from in front of the
great jutting tower to the wall of the Ophel. 28 Above the Horse
Gate, the priests repaired, each in front of his house. 29 After
them,*a* Zadok son of Immer repaired in front of his house.
After him, Shemaiah son of Shechaniah, keeper of the East
Gate, repaired. 30 After him, Hananiah son of Shelemiah and
Hanun, the sixth son of Zalaph, repaired a second stretch. After
them,*a* Meshullam son of Berechiah repaired in front of his
chamber. 31 After him, Malchijah of the smiths repaired as far as
the house of the temple servants and the merchants, [from] in
front of the Muster Gate to the corner loft. 32 And between
the corner loft to the Sheep Gate the smiths and the merchants
repaired.

33 When Sanballat heard that we were rebuilding the wall, it
angered him, and he was extremely vexed. He mocked the Jews,
34 saying in the presence of his brothers and the Samarian force,
"What are the miserable Jews doing? Will they restore, offer
sacrifice, and finish one day? Can they revive those stones out of
the dust heaps, burned as they are?" 35 Tobiah the Ammonite,
alongside him, said, "That stone wall they are building—if a fox
climbed it he would breach it!"

36 Hear, our God, how we have become a mockery, and return
their taunts upon their heads! Let them be taken as spoil to a land

of captivity! ³⁷ Do not cover up their iniquity or let their sin be blotted out before You, for they hurled provocations at the builders.

³⁸ We rebuilt the wall till it was continuous all around to half its height; for the people's heart was in the work.

4 When Sanballat and Tobiah, and the Arabs, the Ammonites, and the Ashdodites heard that healing had come to the walls of Jerusalem, that the breached parts had begun to be filled, it angered them very much, ² and they all conspired together to come and fight against Jerusalem and to throw it into confusion. ³ Because of them we prayed to our God, and set up a watch over them*ᵃ* day and night.

⁴ Judah was saying,

"The strength of the basket-carrier has failed,
And there is so much rubble;
We are not able ourselves
To rebuild the wall."

⁵ And our foes were saying, "Before they know or see it, we shall be in among them and kill them, and put a stop to the work." ⁶ When the Jews living near them*ᵇ* would arrive, they would tell us ᶜ⁻time and again⁻ᶜ ᵈ⁻" . . . from all the places where . . . you shall come back to us. . . ."⁻ᵈ ⁷ I stationed, on the lower levels of the place, behind the walls, on the bare rock—I stationed the people by families with their swords, their lances, and their bows. ⁸ Then I decided to exhort the nobles, the prefects, and the rest of the people, "Do not be afraid of them! Think of the great and awesome Lord, and fight for your brothers, your sons and daughters, your wives and homes!"

⁹ When our enemies learned that it had become known to us, since God had thus frustrated their plan, we could all return to the wall, each to his work. ¹⁰ From that day on, half my servants did work and half held lances and shields, bows and armor. And the officers stood behind the whole house of Judah ¹¹ who were

---

ᵃ *I.e. the workers on the walls.*
ᵇ *I.e. the foes.*
ᶜ⁻ᶜ *Lit. "ten times."*
ᵈ⁻ᵈ *Heb. seems to be abbreviated; a possible restoration of the sentence, with the missing elements enclosed in brackets, is: [of their evil plan; and we would say to them,] "From all the places where [you get such information] you shall come back to us [and convey it]."*

rebuilding the wall. The basket-carriers were burdened, doing work with one hand while the other held a weapon. ¹² As for the builders, each had his sword girded at his side as he was building. The trumpeter stood beside me. ¹³ I said to the nobles, the prefects, and the rest of the people, "There is much work and it is spread out; we are scattered over the wall, far from one another. ¹⁴ When you hear a trumpet call, gather yourselves to me at that place; our God will fight for us!" ¹⁵ And so we worked on, while half were holding lances, from the break of day until the stars appeared.

¹⁶ I further said to the people at that time, "Let every man with his servant lodge in Jerusalem, that we may use the night to stand guard and the day to work." ¹⁷ Nor did I, my brothers, my servants, or the guards following me ever take off our clothes,ᵉ-[or] each his weapon, even at the water.⁻ᵉ

5 There was a great outcry by the common folk and their wives against their brother Jews. ² Some said, "Our sons and daughters are numerous; we must get grain to eat in order that we may live!" ³ Others said, "We must pawn our fields, our vineyards, and our homes to get grain to stave off hunger." ⁴ Yet others said, "We have borrowed money against our fields and vineyards to pay the king's tax. ⁵ Now ᵃ-we are as good as-ᵃ our brothers, and our children as good as theirs; yet here we are subjecting our sons and daughters to slavery—some of our daughters are already subjected—and we are powerless, while our fields and vineyards belong to others."

⁶ It angered me very much to hear their outcry and these complaints. ⁷ After pondering the matter carefully, I censured the nobles and the prefects, saying, "Are you pressing claims on loans made to your brothers?" Then I raised a large crowd against them ⁸ and said to them, "We have done our best to buy back our Jewish brothers who were sold to the nations; will you now sell your brothers so that they must be sold [back] to us?"

ᵉ⁻ᵉ *Meaning of Heb. uncertain.*

ᵃ⁻ᵃ *Lit. "our flesh is as good as the flesh of."*

483

They kept silent, for they found nothing to answer. [9] So I continued, "What you are doing is not right. You ought to act in a God-fearing way so as not to give our enemies, the nations, room to reproach us. [10] I, my brothers, and my servants also have claims of money and grain against them; let us now abandon those claims! [11] Give back at once their fields, their vineyards, their olive trees, and their homes, and [abandon] the claims for the hundred pieces of silver, the grain, the wine, and the oil that you have been pressing against them!" [12] They replied, "We shall give them back, and not demand anything of them; we shall do just as you say." Summoning the priests, I put them under oath to keep this promise. [13] I also shook out the bosom of my garment and said, "So may God shake free of his household and property any man who fails to keep this promise; may he be thus shaken out and stripped." All the assembled answered, "Amen," and praised the LORD.

The people kept this promise.

[14] Furthermore, from the day I was commissioned to be governor in the land of Judah—from the twentieth year of King Artaxerxes until his thirty-second year, twelve years in all—neither I nor my brothers ever ate of the governor's food allowance. [15] The former governors who preceded me laid heavy burdens on the people, and took from them for bread and wine more than[b] forty shekels of silver. Their servants also tyrannized over the people. But I, out of the fear of God, did not do so. [16] I also supported the work on this wall; we did not buy any land, and all my servants were gathered there at the work. [17] Although there were at my table, between Jews and prefects, one hundred and fifty men in all, beside those who came to us from surrounding nations; [18] and although what was prepared for each day came to one ox, six select sheep, and fowl, all prepared for me, and at ten-day intervals all sorts of wine in abundance—yet I did not resort to the governor's food allowance, for the [king's] service lay heavily on the people.

b *Lit. "after"; meaning of Heb. uncertain.*

¹⁹ O my God, remember to my credit all that I have done for this people!

6 When word reached Sanballat, Tobiah, Geshem the Arab, and the rest of our enemies that I had rebuilt the wall and not a breach remained in it—though at that time I had not yet set up doors in the gateways—² Sanballat and Geshem sent a message to me, saying, "Come, let us get together in Kephirim in the Ono valley"; they planned to do me harm. ³ I sent them messengers, saying, "I am engaged in a great work and cannot come down, for the work will stop if I leave it in order to come down to you." ⁴ They sent me the same message four times, and I gave them the same answer. ⁵ Sanballat sent me the same message a fifth time by his servant, who had an open letter with him. ⁶ Its text was: "Word has reached the nations, and Geshem*ᵃ* too says that you and the Jews are planning to rebel—for which reason you are building the wall—and that you are to be their king. *ᵇ* Such is the word.*⁻ᵇ* ⁷ You have also set up prophets in Jerusalem to proclaim about you, 'There is a king in Judah!' Word of these things will surely reach the king; so come, let us confer together."

⁸ I sent back a message to him, saying, "None of these things you mention has occurred; they are figments of your imagination"—⁹ for they all wished to intimidate us, thinking, "They will desist from the work, and it will not get done." Now strengthen my hands!

¹⁰ Then I visited Shemaiah son of Delaiah son of Mehetabel when he was housebound, and he said,

"Let us meet in the House of God, inside the sanctuary,
And let us shut the doors of the sanctuary, for they are
coming to kill you,
By night they are coming to kill you."

¹¹ I replied, "Will a man like me take flight? Besides, who such as I can go into the sanctuary and live? I will not go in." ¹² Then I

ᵃ *Heb.* Gashmu.
ᵇ⁻ᵇ *Meaning of Heb. uncertain.*

realized that it was not God who sent him, but that he uttered that prophecy about me—Tobiah and Sanballat having hired him— ¹³ because he was a hireling, that I might be intimidated and act thus and commit a sin, and so provide them a scandal with which to reproach me.

¹⁴ "O my God, remember against Tobiah and Sanballat these deeds of theirs,ᶜ and against Noadiah the prophetess, and against the other prophets that they wished to intimidate me!"

¹⁵ The wall was finished on the twenty-fifth of Elul, after fifty-two days. ¹⁶ When all our enemies heard it, all the nations round about us were intimidated, and fell very low in their own estimation; they realized that this work had been accomplished by the help of our God.

¹⁷ Also in those days, the nobles of Judah kept up a brisk correspondence with Tobiah, and Tobiah with them. ¹⁸ Many in Judah were his confederates, for he was a son-in-law of Shecaniah son of Arah, and his son Jehohanan had married the daughter of Meshullam son of Berechiah. ¹⁹ They would also speak well of him to me, and would divulge my affairs to him. Tobiah sent letters to intimidate me.

7 When the wall was rebuilt and I had set up the doors, tasks were assigned to the gatekeepers, the singers, and the Levites. ² I put Hanani my brother and Hananiah, the captain of the fortress, in charge of Jerusalem, for he was a more trustworthy and God-fearing man than most. ³ I said to them, "The gates of Jerusalem are not to be opened until the heat of the day,ᵃ and ᵇ-before you leave your posts-ᵇ let the doors be closed and barred. And assign the inhabitants of Jerusalem to watches, each man to his watch, and each in front of his own house."

⁴ The city was broad and large, the people in it were few, and houses were not yet built. ⁵ My God put it into my mind to assemble the nobles, the prefects, and the people, in order to register them by families. I found the genealogical register of

ᶜ *Lit. "his."*

ᵃ *Lit. "sun."*
ᵇ⁻ᵇ *Lit. "while they are still standing."*

those who were the first to come up, and there I found written:
⁶ᶜ These are the people of the province who came up from among the captive exiles that Nebuchadnezzar, king of Babylon, had deported, and who returned to Jerusalem and to Judah, each to his own city, ⁷ who came with Zerubbabel, Jeshua, Nehemiah, Azariah, Raamiah, Nahamani, Mordecai, Bilshan, Mispereth, Bigvai, Nehum, Baanah.

The number of the men of the people of Israel: ⁸ the sons of Parosh—2172; ⁹ the sons of Shephatiah—372; ¹⁰ the sons of Arah —652; ¹¹ the sons of Pahath-moab: the sons of Jeshua and Joab —2818; ¹² the sons of Elam—1254; ¹³ the sons of Zattu—845; ¹⁴ the sons of Zaccai—760; ¹⁵ the sons of Binnui—648; ¹⁶ the sons of Bebai—628; ¹⁷ the sons of Azgad—2322; ¹⁸ the sons of Adonikam—667; ¹⁹ the sons of Bigvai—2067; ²⁰ the sons of Adin—655; ²¹ the sons of Ater: Hezekiah—98; ²² the sons of Hashum—328; ²³ the sons of Bezai—324; ²⁴ the sons of Hariph—112; ²⁵ the sons of Gibeon—95; ²⁶ the men of Bethlehem and Netophah—188; ²⁷ the men of Anathoth—128; ²⁸ the men of Beth-azmaveth— 42;²⁹ the men of Kiriath-jearim, Chephirah, and Beeroth—743; ³⁰ the men of Ramah and Geba—621; ³¹ the men of Michmas— 122; ³² the men of Bethel and Ai—123; ³³ the men of the other Nebo—52; ³⁴ the sons of the other Elam—1254; ³⁵ the sons of Harim—320; ³⁶ the sons of Jericho—345; ³⁷ the sons of Lod, Hadid, and Ono—721; ³⁸ the sons of Senaah—3930.

³⁹ The priests: the sons of Jedaiah: the house of Jeshua—973; ⁴⁰ the sons of Immer—1052; ⁴¹ the sons of Pashhur—1247; ⁴² the sons of Harim—1017.

⁴³ The Levites: the sons of Jeshua: Kadmiel, the sons of Hodeiah—74.

⁴⁴ The singers: the sons of Asaph—148.

⁴⁵ The gatekeepers: the sons of Shallum, the sons of Ater, the

ᶜ *Vv. 6–43 appear as Ezra 2 with variations in the names and numbers.*

sons of Talmon, the sons of Akkub, the sons of Hatita, the sons of Shobai—138.

[46] The temple servants: the sons of Ziha, the sons of Hasupha, the sons of Tabbaoth, [47] the sons of Keros, the sons of Siah, the sons of Padon, [48] the sons of Lebanah, the sons of Hagabah, the sons of Shalmai, [49] the sons of Hanan, the sons of Giddel, the sons of Gahar, [50] the sons of Reaiah, the sons of Rezin, the sons of Nekoda, [51] the sons of Gazzam, the sons of Uzza, the sons of Paseah, [52] the sons of Besai, the sons of Meunim, the sons of Nephishesim, [53] the sons of Bakbuk, the sons of Hakupha, the sons of Harhur, [54] the sons of Bazlith, the sons of Mehida, the sons of Harsha, [55] the sons of Barkos, the sons of Sisera, the sons of Temah, [56] the sons of Neziah, the sons of Hatipha.

[57] The sons of Solomon's servants: the sons of Sotai, the sons of Sophereth, the sons of Perida, [58] the sons of Jala, the sons of Darkon, the sons of Giddel, [59] the sons of Shephatiah, the sons of Hattil, the sons of Pochereth-hazzebaim, the sons of Amon.

[60] The total of temple servants and the sons of Solomon's servants—392.

[61] The following were those who came up from Tel-melah, Tel-harsha, Cherub, Addon, and Immer—they were unable to tell whether their father's house and descent were Israelite: [62] the sons of Delaiah, the sons of Tobiah, the sons of Nekoda—642.

[63] Of the priests: the sons of Habaiah, the sons of Hakkoz, the sons of Barzillai who had married a daughter of Barzillai the Gileadite and had taken his[d] name—[64] these searched for their genealogical records, but they could not be found, so they were disqualified for the priesthood. [65] The Tirshatha[e] ordered them not to eat of the most holy things until a priest with Urim and Thummim should appear.

[66] The sum of the entire community was 42,360, [67] not counting their male and female servants, these being 7337; they also had 245 male and female singers. [68] [f][Their horses—736, their mules—245,][f] camels—435, asses—6720.

[d] Lit. "their."
[e] A Persian title.
[f-f] These words are missing in some mss. and editions; but cf. Ezra 2.66.

69 Some of the heads of the clans made donations for the work. The Tirshatha donated to the treasury: gold—1000 drachmas, basins—50, priestly robes—530.

70 Some of the heads of the clans donated to the work treasury: gold—20,000 drachmas, and silver—2200 minas.

71 The rest of the people donated: gold—20,000 drachmas, silver—2000, and priestly robes—67.

72 The priests, the Levites, the gatekeepers, the singers, some of the people, the temple servants, and all Israel took up residence in their towns.

8 When the seventh month arrived—the Israelites being [settled] in their towns—1 the entire people assembled as one man in the square before the Water Gate, and they asked Ezra the scribe to bring the scroll of the Teaching of Moses with which the LORD had charged Israel. 2 On the first day of the seventh month, Ezra the priest brought the Teaching before the congregation, men and women and all who could listen with understanding. 3 He read from it, facing the square before the Water Gate, from the first light until midday, to the men and the women and those who could understand; the ears of all the people were given to the scroll of the Teaching.

4 Ezra the scribe stood upon a wooden tower made for the purpose, and beside him stood Mattithiah, Shema, Anaiah, Uriah, Hilkiah, and Maaseiah at his right, and at his left Pedaiah, Mishael, Malchijah, Hashum, Hashbaddanah, Zechariah, Meshullam. 5 Ezra opened the scroll in the sight of all the people, for he was above all the people; as he opened it, all the people stood up. 6 Ezra blessed the LORD, the great God, and all the people answered, "Amen, Amen," with hands upraised. Then they bowed their heads and prostrated themselves before the LORD with their faces to the ground. 7 Jeshua, Bani, Sherebiah, Jamin, Akkub, Shabbethai, Hodiah, Maaseiah, Kelita, Azariah, Jozabad, Hanan, Pelaiah, and the Levites explained the Teaching to the people,

while the people stood in their places. [8] They read from the scroll of the Teaching of God, translating it and giving the sense; so they understood the reading.

[9] Nehemiah the Tirshatha, Ezra the priest and scribe, and the Levites who were explaining to the people said to all the people, "This day is holy to the LORD your God: you must not mourn or weep," for all the people were weeping as they listened to the words of the Teaching. [10] He further said to them, "Go, eat choice foods and drink sweet drinks and send portions to whoever has nothing prepared, for the day is holy to our Lord. Do not be sad, for your rejoicing in the LORD is the source of your strength." [11] The Levites were quieting the people, saying, "Hush, for the day is holy; do not be sad." [12] Then all the people went to eat and drink and send portions and make great merriment, for they understood the things they were told.

[13] On the second day, the heads of the clans of all the people and the priests and Levites gathered to Ezra the scribe to study the words of the Teaching. [14] They found written in the Teaching that the LORD had commanded Moses that the Israelites must dwell in booths during the festival of the seventh month, [15] and that they must announce and proclaim throughout all their towns and Jerusalem as follows, "Go out to the mountains and bring leafy branches of olive trees, pine[a] trees, myrtles, palms and [other] leafy[a] trees to make booths, as it is written." [16] So the people went out and brought them, and made themselves booths on their roofs, in their courtyards, in the courtyards of the House of God, in the square of the Water Gate and in the square of the Ephraim Gate. [17] The whole community that returned from the captivity made booths and dwelt in the booths—the Israelites had not done so from the days of Joshua[b] son of Nun to that day—and there was very great rejoicing. [18] He read from the scroll of the Teaching of God each day, from the first to the last day. They celebrated the festival seven days, and there was a solemn gathering on the eighth, as prescribed.

[a] *Meaning of Heb. uncertain.*
[b] *Heb.* Jeshua.

9 On the twenty-fourth day of this month, the Israelites assembled, fasting, in sackcloth, and with earth upon them. [2] Those of the stock of Israel separated themselves from all foreigners, and stood and confessed their sins and the iniquities of their fathers. [3] Standing in their places, they read from the scroll of the Teaching of the LORD their God for one-fourth of the day, and for another fourth they confessed and prostrated themselves before the LORD their God. [4] On the raised platform of the Levites stood Jeshua and Bani, Kadmiel, Shebaniah, Bunni, Sherebiah, Bani, and Chenani, and cried in a loud voice to the LORD their God. [5] The Levites Jeshua, Kadmiel, Bani, Hashabniah, Sherebiah, Hodiah, and Pethahiah said, "Rise, bless the LORD your God who is from eternity to eternity: 'May Your glorious name be blessed, exalted though it is above every blessing and praise!'

[6] "You alone are the LORD. You made the heavens, the highest[a] heavens, and all their host, the earth and everything upon it, the seas and everything in them. You keep them all alive, and the host of heaven prostrate themselves before You. [7] You are the LORD God, who chose Abram, who brought him out of Ur of the Chaldeans and changed his name to Abraham. [8] Finding his heart true to You, You made a covenant with him to give the land of the Canaanite, the Hittite, the Amorite, the Perizzite, the Jebusite and the Girgashite—to give it to his descendants. And You kept Your word, for You are righteous. [9] You took note of our fathers' affliction in Egypt, and heard their cry at the Sea of Reeds. [10] You performed signs and wonders against Pharaoh, all his servants, and all the people of his land, for You knew that they acted presumptuously toward them. You made a name for Yourself that endures to this day. [11] You split the sea before them; they passed through the sea on dry land, but You threw their pursuers into the depths, like a stone into the raging waters.

[12] "You led them by day with a pillar of cloud, and by night with a pillar of fire, to give them light in the way they were to go.

[a] Lit. "the heavens of the."

491

¹³ You came down on Mount Sinai and spoke to them from heaven; You gave them right rules and true teachings, good laws and commandments. ¹⁴ You made known to them Your holy sabbath, and You ordained for them laws, commandments and Teaching, through Moses Your servant. ¹⁵ You gave them bread from heaven when they were hungry, and produced water from a rock when they were thirsty. You told them to go and possess the land that You swore to give them. ¹⁶ But they—our fathers—acted presumptuously; they stiffened their necks and did not obey Your commandments. ¹⁷ Refusing to obey, unmindful of Your wonders that You did for them, they stiffened their necks, and in their defiance resolved to return to their slavery. But You, being a forgiving God, gracious and compassionate, long-suffering and abounding in faithfulness, did not abandon them. ¹⁸ Even though they made themselves a molten calf and said, 'This is your God who brought you out of Egypt,' thus committing great impieties, ¹⁹ You, in Your abundant compassion, did not abandon them in the wilderness. The pillar of cloud did not depart from them to lead them on the way by day, nor the pillar of fire by night to give them light in the way they were to go. ²⁰ You endowed them with Your good spirit to instruct them. You did not withhold Your manna from their mouth; You gave them water when they were thirsty. ²¹ Forty years You sustained them in the wilderness so that they lacked nothing; their clothes did not wear out, and their feet did not swell.

²² "You gave them kingdoms and peoples, and *ᵇ*allotted them territory.*ᵇ* They took possession of the land of Sihon, the land of the king of Heshbon, and the land of Og, king of Bashan. ²³ You made their children as numerous as the stars of heaven, and brought them to the land which You told their fathers to go and possess. ²⁴ The sons came and took possession of the land; You subdued the Canaanite inhabitants of the land before them; You delivered them into their power, both their kings and the peoples of the land, to do with them as they pleased. ²⁵ They captured fortified cities and rich lands; they took possession of

ᵇ⁻ᵇ *Meaning of Heb. uncertain.*

houses filled with every good thing, of hewn cisterns, vineyards, olive trees, and fruit trees in abundance. They ate, they were filled, they grew fat; they luxuriated in Your great bounty. 26 Then, defying You, they rebelled; they cast Your Teaching behind their back. They killed Your prophets who admonished them to turn them back to You; they committed great impieties.

27 "You delivered them into the power of their adversaries who oppressed them. In their time of trouble they cried to You; You in heaven heard them, and in Your abundant compassion gave them saviors who saved them from the power of their adversaries. 28 But when they had relief, they again did what was evil in Your sight, so You abandoned them to the power of their enemies, who subjugated them. Again they cried to You, and You in heaven heard and rescued them in Your compassion, time after time. 29 You admonished them in order to turn them back to Your Teaching, but they acted presumptuously and disobeyed Your commandments, and sinned against Your rules, by following which a man shall live. They turned a defiant shoulder, stiffened their neck, and would not obey. 30 You bore with them for many years, admonished them by Your spirit through Your prophets, but they would not give ear, so You delivered them into the power of the peoples of the lands. 31 Still, in Your great compassion You did not make an end of them or abandon them, for You are a gracious and compassionate God.

32 "And now, our God, great, mighty, and awesome God, who stays faithful to His covenant, do not treat lightly all the suffering that has overtaken us—our kings, our officers, our priests, our prophets, our fathers, and all Your people—from the time of the Assyrian kings to this day. 33 Surely You are in the right with respect to all that has come upon us, for You have acted faithfully, and we have been wicked. 34 Our kings, officers, priests, and fathers did not follow Your Teaching, and did not listen to Your commandments or to the warnings that You gave them. 35 When they had their own kings and enjoyed the good that You lavished upon them, and the broad and rich land that You put at their

disposal, they would not serve You, and did not turn from their wicked deeds. [36] Today we are slaves, and the land that You gave our fathers to enjoy its fruit and bounty—here we are slaves on it! [37] On account of our sins it yields its abundant crops to kings whom You have set over us. They rule over our bodies and our beasts as they please, and we are in great distress.

10 "In view of all this, we make this pledge and put it in writing; and on the sealed copy [are subscribed] our officials, our Levites, and our priests.

[2] "On the sealed copy[a] [are subscribed]: Nehemiah the Tirshatha son of Hacaliah and Zedekiah, [3] Seraiah, Azariah, Jeremiah, [4] Pashhur, Amariah, Malchijah, [5] Hattush, Shebaniah, Malluch, [6] Harim, Meremoth, Obadiah, [7] Daniel, Ginnethon, Baruch, [8] Meshullam, Abijah, Mijamin, [9] Maaziah, Bilgai, Shemaiah; these are the priests.

[10] "And the Levites: Jeshua son of Azaniah, Binnui of the sons of Henadad, and Kadmiel. [11] And their brothers: Shebaniah, Hodiah, Kelita, Pelaiah, Hanan, [12] Mica, Rehob, Hashabiah, [13] Zaccur, Sherebiah, Shebaniah, [14] Hodiah, Bani, and Beninu.

[15] "The heads of the people: Parosh, Pahath-moab, Elam, Zattu, Bani, [16] Bunni, Azgad, Bebai, [17] Adonijah, Bigvai, Adin, [18] Ater, Hezekiah, Azzur, [19] Hodiah, Hashum, Bezai, [20] Hariph, Anathoth, Nebai, [21] Magpiash, Meshullam, Hezir, [22] Meshezabel, Zadok, Jaddua, [23] Pelatiah, Hanan, Anaiah, [24] Hoshea, Hananiah, Hasshub, [25] Hallohesh, Pilha, Shobek, [26] Rehum, Hashabnah, Maaseiah, [27] and Ahiah, Hanan, Anan, [28] Malluch, Harim, Baanah.

[29] "And the rest of the people, the priests, the Levites, the gatekeepers, the singers, the temple servants, and all who separated themselves from the peoples of the lands to [follow] the Teaching of God, their wives, sons and daughters, all who know enough to understand, [30] join with their noble brothers, and take

a *Heb. plural.*

an oath with sanctions to follow the Teaching of God, given through Moses the servant of God, and to observe carefully all the commandments of the LORD our Lord, His rules and laws.

31 "Namely: We will not give our daughters in marriage to the peoples of the land, or take their daughters for our sons.

32 "The peoples of the land who bring their wares and all sorts of foodstuff for sale on the sabbath day—we will not buy from them on the sabbath or a holy day.

"We will forgo [the produce of] the seventh year, and every outstanding debt.

33 "We have laid upon ourselves obligations: To charge ourselves one-third of a shekel yearly for the service of the House of our God—34 for the rows of bread, for the regular meal offering and for the regular burnt offering, [for those of the] sabbaths, new moons, festivals, for consecrations, for sin offerings to atone for Israel, and for all the work in the House of our God.

35 "We have cast lots [among] the priests, the Levites, and the people, to bring the wood offering to the House of our God by clans annually at set times in order to provide fuel for the altar of the LORD our God, as is written in the Teaching.

36 "And [we undertake] to bring to the House of the LORD annually the firstfruits of our soil, and of every fruit of every tree; 37 also, the firstborn of our sons and our beasts, as is written in the Teaching; and to bring the firstlings of our cattle and flocks to the House of our God for the priests who minister in the House of our God.

38 "We will bring to the storerooms of the House of our God the first part of our dough, and our gifts [of grain], and of the fruit of every tree, wine and oil for the priests, and the tithes of our land for the Levites—the Levites who collect the tithe in all our towns *b*-subject to royal service.*-b* 39 An Aaronite priest must be with the Levites when they collect the tithe, and the Levites must bring up a tithe of the tithe to the House of our God, to the storerooms of the treasury. 40 For it is to the storerooms that the Israelites and the Levites must bring the gifts of grain, wine, and

b-b *For this sense of* 'abodah, *"service," cf. 5.18.*

oil. The equipment of the sanctuary and of the ministering priests and the gatekeepers and the singers is also there. "We will not neglect the House of our God."

11 The officers of the people settled in Jerusalem; the rest of the people cast lots for one out of ten to come and settle in the holy city of Jerusalem, and the other nine-tenths to stay in the towns. ² The people gave their blessing to all the men who willingly settled in Jerusalem.

³ These are the heads of the province who lived in Jerusalem —in the countryside*a* of Judah, the people lived in their towns, each on his own property, Israelites, priests, Levites, temple servants, and the sons of Solomon's servants, ⁴ while in Jerusalem some of the Judahites and some of the Benjaminites lived:

Of the Judahites: Athaiah son of Uzziah son of Zechariah son of Amariah son of Shephatiah son of Mahalalel, of the clan of Perez, ⁵ and Maaseiah son of Baruch son of Col-hozeh son of Hazaiah son of Adaiah son of Joiarib son of Zechariah son of the Shilonite. ⁶ All the clan of Perez who were living in Jerusalem— 468 valorous men.

⁷ These are the Benjaminites: Sallu son of Meshullam son of Joed son of Pedaiah son of Kolaiah son of Maaseiah son of Ithiel son of Jeshaiah. ⁸ After him, Gabbai and Sallai—928.

⁹ Joel son of Zichri was the official in charge of them, and Judah son of Hassenuah was the second-in-command of the city.

¹⁰ Of the priests: Jedaiah son of Joiarib, Jachin, ¹¹ Seraiah son of Hilkiah son of Meshullam son of Zadok son of Meraioth son of Ahitub, chief officer of the House of God, ¹² and their brothers, who did the work of the House—822; and Adaiah son of Jeroham son of Pelaliah son of Amzi son of Zechariah son of Pashhur son of Malchijah, ¹³ and his brothers, heads of clans—242; and Amashsai son of Azarel son of Ahzai son of Meshillemoth son of Immer, ¹⁴ and their brothers, valorous warriors—128. Zabdiel son of Haggedolim was the official in charge of them.

ª *Lit. "towns."*

¹⁵ Of the Levites: Shemaiah son of Hasshub son of Azrikam son of Hashabiah son of Bunni, ¹⁶ and Shabbethai and Jozabad of the heads of the Levites were in charge of the external work of the House of God. ¹⁷ Mattaniah son of Micha son of Zabdi son of Asaph was the head; at prayer, he would lead off with praise; and Bakbukiah, one of his brothers, was his second-in-command; and Abda son of Shammua son of Galal son of Jeduthun. ¹⁸ All the Levites in the holy city—284.

¹⁹ And the gatekeepers: Akkub, Talmon, and their brothers, who stood watch at the gates—172.

²⁰ And the rest of the Israelites, the priests, and the Levites in all the towns of Judah [lived] each on his estate.

²¹ The temple servants lived on the Ophel; Ziha and Gishpa were in charge of the temple servants.

²² The overseer of the Levites in Jerusalem was Uzzi son of Bani son of Hashabiah son of Mattaniah son of Micha, of the Asaphite singers, over the work of the House of God. ²³ There was a royal order concerning them, a stipulation concerning the daily duties of the singers.

²⁴ Petahiah son of Meshezabel, of the sons of Zerah son of Judah, advised the king concerning all the affairs of the people.

²⁵ As concerns the villages with their fields: Some of the Judahites lived in Kiriath-arba and its outlying hamlets, in Dibon and its outlying hamlets, and in Jekabzeel and its villages; ²⁶ in Jeshua, in Moladah, and in Beth-pelet; ²⁷ in Hazar-shual, in Beer-sheba and its outlying hamlets; ²⁸ and in Ziklag and in Meconah and its outlying hamlets; ²⁹ in En-rimmon, in Zorah and in Jarmuth; ³⁰ Zanoah, Adullam, and their villages; Lachish and its fields; Azekah and its outlying hamlets. They settled from Beer-sheba to the Valley of Hinnom.

³¹ The Benjaminites: from Geba, Michmash, Aija, and Bethel and its outlying hamlets; ³² Anathoth, Nob, Ananiah, ³³ Hazor, Ramah, Gittaim, ³⁴ Hadid, Zeboim, Neballat, ³⁵ Lod, Ono, Geharashim. ³⁶ Some of the Judahite divisions of Levites were [shifted] to Benjamin.

12 These are the priests and the Levites who came up with Zerubbabel son of Shealtiel and Jeshua:

Seraiah, Jeremiah, Ezra, ² Amariah, Malluch, Hattush, ³ Shecaniah, Rehum, Meramoth, ⁴ Iddo, Ginnethoi, Abijah, ⁵ Mijamin, Maadiah, Bilgah, ⁶ Shemaiah, Joiarib, Jedaiah, ⁷ Sallu, Amok, Hilkiah, Jedaiah. These were the heads of the priests and their brothers in the time of Jeshua.

⁸ The Levites: Jeshua, Binnui, Kadmiel, Sherebiah, Judah, and Mattaniah, in charge of thanksgiving songs,ᵃ he and his brothers; ⁹ and Bakbukiah and Unni [and] their brothers served opposite them by shifts.

¹⁰ Jeshua begot Joiakim; Joiakim begot Eliashib; Eliashib begot Joiada; ¹¹ Joiada begot Jonathan; Jonathan begot Jaddua.

¹² In the time of Joiakim, the heads of the priestly clans were: Meriaiah—of the Seraiah clan; Hananiah—of the Jeremiah clan; ¹³ Meshullam—of the Ezra clan; Jehohanan—of the Amariah clan; ¹⁴ Jonathan—of the Melicu clan; Joseph—of the Shebaniah clan; ¹⁵ Adna—of the Harim clan; Helkai—of the Meraioth clan; ¹⁶ Zechariah—of the Iddo clan; Meshullam—of the Ginnethon clan; ¹⁷ Zichri—of the Abijah clan . . . of the Miniamin clan; Piltai —of the Moadiah clan; ¹⁸ Shammua—of the Bilgah clan; Jehonathan—of the Shemaiah clan; ¹⁹ Mattenai—of the Joiarib clan; Uzzi —of the Jedaiah clan; ²⁰ Kallai—of the Sallai clan; Eber—of the Amok clan; ²¹ Hashabiah—of the Hilkiah clan; Nethanel—of the Jedaiah clan.

²² The Levites and the priests were listed by heads of clans in the days of Eliashib, Joiada, Johanan, and Jaddua, down to the reign of Darius the Persian. ²³ But the Levite heads of clans are listed in the book of the chronicles to the time of Johanan son of Eliashib.

²⁴ The heads of the Levites: Hashabiah, Sherebiah, Jeshua son of Kadmiel, and their brothers served opposite them, singing praise and thanksgiving hymns by the ordinance of David the

ᵃ *Meaning of Heb. uncertain.*

man of God—served opposite them in shifts; ²⁵ Mattaniah, Bakbukiah, Obadiah, Meshullam, Talmon, and Akkub, guarding as gatekeepers by shifts at the vestibules of the gates.

²⁶ These were in the time of Joiakim son of Jeshua son of Jozadak, and in the time of Nehemiah the governor, and of Ezra the priest, the scribe.

²⁷ At the dedication of the wall of Jerusalem, the Levites, wherever they lived, were sought out and brought to Jerusalem to celebrate a joyful dedication with thanksgiving and with song, accompanied by cymbals, harps, and lyres. ²⁸ The companies of singers assembled from the [Jordan] plain, the environs of Jerusalem, and from the Netophathite villages; ²⁹ from Bethhagilgal, from the countryside of Geba and Azmaveth, for the singers built themselves villages in the environs of Jerusalem.

³⁰ The priests and Levites purified themselves; then they purified the people, and the gates, and the wall.

³¹ I had the officers of Judah go up onto the wall, and I appointed two large thanksgiving [choirs] and processions. [One marched] south on the wall, to the Dung Gate; ³² behind them were Hoshaiah and half the officers of Judah, ³³ and Azariah, Ezra, Meshullam, ³⁴ Judah, Benjamin, Shemaiah, and Jeremiah, ³⁵ and some of the young priests, with trumpets; Zechariah son of Jonathan son of Shemaiah son of Mattaniah son of Micaiah son of Zaccur son of Asaph, ³⁶ and his brothers Shemaiah, and Azarel, Milalai, Gilalai, Maai, Nethanel, Judah, and Hanani, with the musical instruments of David, the man of God; and Ezra the scribe went ahead of them. ³⁷ From there to the Fountain Gate, where they ascended the steps of the City of David directly before them, by the ascent on the wall, above the house of David, [and onward] to the Water Gate on the east.

³⁸ The other thanksgiving [choir] marched on the wall in the opposite direction, with me and half the people behind it, above the Tower of Ovens to the Broad Wall; ³⁹ and above the Gate of Ephraim, the Jeshanah Gate, the Fish Gate, the Tower of Hananel, the Tower of the Hundred, to the Sheep Gate; and they

halted at the Gate of the Prison Compound. [40] Both thanksgiving choirs halted at the House of God, and I and half the prefects with me, [41] and the priests Eliakim, Maaseiah, Miniamin, Micaiah, Elioenai, Zechariah, Hananiah, with trumpets, [42] and Maaseiah and Shemaiah, Eleazar, Uzzi, Jehohanan, Malchijah, Elam, and Ezer. Then the singers sounded forth, with Jezrahiah in charge.

[43] On that day, they offered great sacrifices and rejoiced, for God made them rejoice greatly; the women and children also rejoiced, and the rejoicing in Jerusalem could be heard from afar.

[44] At that time men were appointed over the chambers that served as treasuries for the gifts, the firstfruits, and the tithes, into which the portions prescribed by the Teaching for the priests and Levites were gathered from the fields of the towns; for the people of Judah were grateful to the priests and Levites who were in attendance, [45] who kept the charge of their God and the charge of purity, as well as to the singers and gatekeepers [serving] in accord with the ordinance of David and Solomon his son—[46] for the chiefs of the singers and songs of praise and thanksgiving to God already existed in the time of David and Asaph. [47] And in the time of Zerubbabel, and in the time of Nehemiah, all Israel contributed the daily portions of the singers and the gatekeepers, and made sacred contributions for the Levites, and the Levites made sacred contributions for the Aaronites.

13 At that time they read to the people from the Book of Moses, and it was found written that no Ammonite or Moabite might ever enter the congregation of God, [2] since they did not meet Israel with bread and water, and hired Balaam against them to curse them; but our God turned the curse into a blessing. [3] When they heard the Teaching, they separated all the alien admixture from Israel.

[4] Earlier, the priest Eliashib, a relative of Tobiah, who had been appointed over the rooms in the House of our God, [5] had as-

signed to him[a] a large room where they used to store the meal offering, the frankincense, the equipment, the tithes of grain, wine, and oil, the dues of the Levites, singers and gatekeepers, and the gifts for the priests. [6] During all this time, I was not in Jerusalem, for in the thirty-second year of King Artaxerxes of Babylon, I went to the king, and only after a while did I ask leave of the king [to return]. [7] When I arrived in Jerusalem, I learned of the outrage perpetrated by Eliashib on behalf of Tobiah in assigning him a room in the courts of the House of God. [8] I was greatly displeased, and had all the household gear of Tobiah thrown out of the room; [9] I gave orders to purify the rooms, and had the equipment of the House of God and the meal offering and the frankincense put back.

[10] I then discovered that the portions of the Levites had not been contributed, and that the Levites and the singers who performed the [temple] service had made off, each to his fields. [11] I censured the prefects, saying, "How is it that the House of God has been neglected?" Then I recalled [the Levites] and installed them again in their posts; [12] and all Judah brought the tithes of grain, wine, and oil into the treasuries. [13] I put the treasuries in the charge of the priest Shelemiah, the scribe Zadok, and Pedaiah of the Levites; and assisting them was Hanan son of Zaccur son of Mattaniah—for they were regarded as trustworthy persons, and it was their duty to distribute the portions to their brothers.

[14] O my God, remember me favorably for this, and do not blot out the devotion I showed toward the House of my God and its attendants.

[15] At that time I saw men in Judah treading winepresses on the sabbath, and others bringing heaps of grain and loading them onto asses, also wine, grapes, figs, and all sorts of goods, and bringing them into Jerusalem on the sabbath. I admonished them there and then for selling provisions. [16] Tyrians who lived there brought fish and all sorts of wares and sold them on the sabbath

---

[a] *I.e. Tobiah.*

to the Judahites in Jerusalem. [17] I censured the nobles of Judah, saying to them, "What evil thing is this that you are doing, profaning the sabbath day! [18] This is just what your ancestors did, and for it God brought all this misfortune on this city; and now you give cause for further wrath against Israel by profaning the sabbath!"

[19] When shadows filled the gateways of Jerusalem at the approach of the sabbath, I gave orders that the doors be closed, and ordered them not to be opened until after the sabbath. I stationed some of my servants at the gates, so that no goods should enter on the sabbath. [20] Once or twice the merchants and the vendors of all sorts of wares spent the night outside Jerusalem, [21] but I warned them, saying, "What do you mean by spending the night alongside the wall? If you do so again, I will lay hands upon you!" From then on they did not come on the sabbath. [22] I gave orders to the Levites to purify themselves and come and guard the gates, to preserve the sanctity of the sabbath.

This too, O my God, remember to my credit, and spare me in accord with your abundant faithfulness.

[23] Also at that time, I saw that Jews had married Ashdodite, Ammonite, and Moabite women; [24] a good number of their children spoke the language of Ashdod and the language of those various peoples, and did not know how to speak Judean. [25] I censured them, cursed them, flogged them, tore out their hair, and adjured them by God, saying, "You shall not give your daughters in marriage to their sons, or take any of their daughters for your sons or yourselves. [26] It was just in such things that King Solomon of Israel sinned! Among the many nations there was not a king like him, and so well loved was he by his God that God made him king of all Israel, yet foreign wives caused even him to sin. [27] How, then, can we acquiesce in your doing this great wrong, breaking faith with our God by marrying foreign women?" [28] One of the sons of Joiada son of the high priest Eliashib was a son-in-law of Sanballat the Horonite; I drove him away from me.

[29] Remember to their discredit, O my God, how they polluted the priesthood, the covenant of the priests and Levites. [30] I purged them of every foreign element, and arranged for the priests and the Levites to work each at his task by shifts, [31] and for the wood offering [to be brought] at fixed times and for the firstfruits.

O my God, remember it to my credit!

דברי הימים א

I CHRONICLES

דברי הימים א
I CHRONICLES

1 Adam, Seth, Enosh; [2] Kenan, Mahalalel, Jared; [3] Enoch, Methuselah, Lamech; [4] Noah, Shem, Ham, and Japheth.

[5] [a] The sons of Japheth: Gomer, Magog, Madai, Javan, Tubal, Meshech, and Tiras. [6] The sons of Gomer: Ashkenaz, Diphath, and Togarmah. [7] The sons of Javan: Elishah, Tarshish, Kittim, and Rodanim.

[8] The sons of Ham: Cush, Mizraim, Put, and Canaan. [9] The sons of Cush: Seba, Havilah, Sabta, Raama, and Sabteca. The sons of Raamah: Sheba and Dedan. [10] Cush begot Nimrod; he was the first mighty one on earth.

[11] Mizraim begot the Ludim, the Anamim, the Lehabim, the Naphtuhim, [12] the Pathrusim, the Casluhim (whence the Philistines came forth), and the Caphtorim.

[13] Canaan begot Sidon his firstborn, and Heth, [14] and the Jebusites, the Amorites, the Girgashites, [15] the Hivites, the Arkites, the Sinites, [16] the Arvadites, the Zemarites, and the Hamathites.

[17] The sons of Shem: Elam, Asshur, Arpachshad, Lud, Aram, Uz, Hul, Gether, and Meshech. [18] Arpachshad begot Shelah; and Shelah begot Eber. [19] Two sons were born to Eber: the name of the one was Peleg (for in his days the earth was divided), and the name of his brother Joktan. [20] Joktan begot Almodad, Sheleph, Hazarmaveth, Jerah, [21] Hadoram, Uzal, Diklah, [22] Ebal, Abimael, Sheba, [23] Ophir, Havilah, and Jobab; all these were the sons of Joktan.

[24] Shem, Arpachshad, Shelah; [25] Eber, Peleg, Reu; [26] Serug, Nahor, Terah; [27] Abram, that is, Abraham.

[28] [b] The sons of Abraham: Isaac and Ishmael. [29] This is their

[a] With vv. 5–23, cf. Gen. 10. 1–30.
[b] With vv. 28–33, cf. Gen. 25. 1–16.

line: The firstborn of Ishmael, Nebaioth; and Kedar, Abdeel, Mibsam, ³⁰ Mishma, Dumah, Massa, Hadad, Tema, ³¹ Jetur, Naphish, and Kedmah. These are the sons of Ishmael. ³² The sons of Keturah, Abraham's concubine: she bore Zimran, Jokshan, Medan, Midian, Ishbak, and Shuah. The sons of Jokshan: Sheba and Dedan. ³³ The sons of Midian: Ephah, Epher, Enoch, Abida, and Eldaah. All these were the descendants of Keturah.

³⁴ Abraham begot Isaac. The sons of Isaac: Esau and Israel. ³⁵ The sons of Esau: Eliphaz, Reuel, Jeush, Jalam, and Korah. ³⁶ The sons of Eliphaz: Teman, Omar, Zephi, Gatam, Kenaz, Timna, and Amalek. ³⁷ The sons of Reuel: Nahath, Zerah, Shammah, and Mizzah.

³⁸ The sons of Seir: Lotan, Shobal, Zibeon, Anah, Dishon, Ezer, and Dishan. ³⁹ The sons of Lotan: Hori and Homam; and Lotan's sister was Timna. ⁴⁰ The sons of Shobal: Alian, Manahath, Ebal, Shephi, and Onam. The sons of Zibeon: Aiah and Anah. ⁴¹ The sons of Anah: Dishon. The sons of Dishon: Hamran, Eshban, Ithran, and Cheran. ⁴² The sons of Ezer: Bilhan, Zaavan, and Jaakan. The sons of Dishan: Uz and Aran.

⁴³ ᶜ These are the kings who reigned in the land of Edom before any king reigned over the Israelites: Bela son of Beor, and the name of his city was Dinhabah. ⁴⁴ When Bela died, Jobab son of Zerah from Bozrah succeeded him as king. ⁴⁵ When Jobab died, Husham of the land of the Temanites succeeded him as king. ⁴⁶ When Husham died, Hadad son of Bedad, who defeated the Midianites in the country of Moab, succeeded him as king, and the name of his city was Avith. ⁴⁷ When Hadad died, Samlah of Masrekah succeeded him as king. ⁴⁸ When Samlah died, Saul of Rehoboth-on-the-River succeeded him as king. ⁴⁹ When Saul died, Baal-hanan son of Achbor succeeded him as king. ⁵⁰ When Baal-hanan died, Hadad succeeded him as king; and the name of his city was Pai, and his wife's name Mehetabel daughter of Matred daughter of Me-zahab. ⁵¹ And Hadad died.

The clans of Edom were the clans of Timna, Alvah, Jetheth,

ᶜ With vv. 43–50, cf. Gen. 36. 31–43.

⁵²Oholibamah, Elah, Pinon, ⁵³Kenaz, Teman, Mibzar, ⁵⁴Magdiel, and Iram; these are the clans of Edom.

2 These are the sons of Israel: Reuben, Simeon, Levi, Judah, Issachar, Zebulun, ²Dan, Joseph, Benjamin, Naphtali, Gad, and Asher. ³The sons of Judah: Er, Onan, and Shelah; these three, Bath-shua the Canaanite woman bore to him. But Er, Judah's firstborn, was displeasing to the LORD, and He took his life. ⁴His daughter-in-law Tamar also bore him Perez and Zerah. Judah's sons were five in all.

⁵The sons of Perez: Hezron and Hamul. ⁶The sons of Zerah: Zimri, Ethan, Heman, Calcol, and Dara, five in all. ⁷The sons of Carmi: Achar, the troubler of Israel, who committed a trespass against the proscribed thing; ⁸and Ethan's son was Azariah.

⁹The sons of Hezron, that were born to him: Jerahmeel, Ram, and Chelubai. ¹⁰Ram begot Amminadab, and Amminadab begot Nahshon, prince of the sons of Judah. ¹¹Nahshon was the father of Salma, Salma of Boaz, ¹²Boaz of Obed, Obed of Jesse. ¹³Jesse begot Eliab his firstborn, Abinadab the second, Shimea the third, ¹⁴Nethanel the fourth, Raddai the fifth, ¹⁵Ozem the sixth, David the seventh; ¹⁶their sisters were Zeruiah and Abigail. The sons of Zeruiah: Abishai, Joab, and Asahel, three. ¹⁷Abigail bore Amasa, and the father of Amasa was Jether the Ishmaelite.

¹⁸Caleb son of Hezron had children by his wife Azubah, and by Jerioth; these were her sons: Jesher, Shobab, and Ardon. ¹⁹When Azubah died, Caleb married Ephrath, who bore him Hur. ²⁰Hur begot Uri, and Uri begot Bezalel.

²¹Afterward Hezron had relations with the daughter of Machir father of Gilead—he had married her when he was sixty years old —and she bore him Segub; ²²and Segub begot Jair; he had twenty-three cities in the land of Gilead. ²³But Geshur and Aram took from them Havvoth-jair, Kenath and its dependencies, sixty towns. All these were the sons of Machir, the father of Gilead.

²⁴ After the death of Hezron, in Caleb-ephrathah, Abijah, wife of Hezron, bore Ashhur, the father of Tekoa.

²⁵ The sons of Jerahmeel the firstborn of Hezron: Ram his firstborn, Bunah, Oren, Ozem, and Ahijah. ²⁶ Jerahmeel had another wife, whose name was Atarah; she was the mother of Onam. ²⁷ The sons of Ram the firstborn of Jerahmeel: Maaz, Jamin, and Eker. ²⁸ The sons of Onam: Shammai and Jada. The sons of Shammai: Nadab and Abishur. ²⁹ The name of Abishur's wife was Abihail, and she bore him Ahban and Molid. ³⁰ The sons of Nadab: Seled and Appaim; Seled died childless. ³¹ The sons of Appaim: Ishi. The sons of Ishi: Sheshan. The sons of Sheshan: Ahlai. ³² The sons of Jada, Shammai's brother: Jether and Jonathan; Jether died childless. ³³ The sons of Jonathan: Peleth and Zaza. These were the descendants of Jerahmeel. ³⁴ Sheshan had no sons, only daughters; Sheshan had an Egyptian slave, whose name was Jarha. ³⁵ So Sheshan gave his daughter in marriage to Jarha his slave; and she bore him Attai. ³⁶ Attai begot Nathan and Nathan begot Zabad. ³⁷ Zabad begot Ephlal, and Ephlal begot Obed. ³⁸ Obed begot Jehu, and Jehu begot Azariah. ³⁹ Azariah begot Helez, and Helez begot Eleasah. ⁴⁰ Eleasah begot Sisamai, and Sisamai begot Shallum. ⁴¹ Shallum begot Jekamiah, and Jekamiah begot Elishama.

⁴² The sons of Caleb brother of Jerahmeel: Meshah his firstborn, who was the father of Ziph. The sons of Mareshah father of Hebron. ⁴³ The sons of Hebron: Korah, Tappuah, Rekem, and Shema. ⁴⁴ Shema begot Raham the father of Jorkeam, and Rekem begot Shammai. ⁴⁵ The son of Shammai: Maon, and Maon begot Bethzur. ⁴⁶ Ephah, Caleb's concubine, bore Haran, Moza, and Gazez; Haran begot Gazez. ⁴⁷ The sons of Jahdai: Regem, Jotham, Geshan, Pelet, Ephah, and Shaaph. ⁴⁸ Maacah, Caleb's concubine, bore Sheber and Tirhanah. ⁴⁹ She also bore Shaaph father of Madmannah, Sheva father of Machbenah and father of Gibea; the daughter of Caleb was Achsah. ⁵⁰ These were the descendants of Caleb.

The sons of Hur the firstborn of Ephrathah: Shobal father of

Kiriath-jearim, [51] Salma father of Bethlehem, Hareph father of Beth-gader. [52] Shobal father of Kiriath-jearim had sons: Haroeh, half of the Monuhoth. [53] And the families of Kiriath-jearim: the Ithrites, the Puthites, the Shumathites, and the Mishraites; from these came the Zorathites and the Eshtaolites. [54] The sons of Salma: Bethlehem, the Netophathites, Atroth-beth-joab, and half of the Manahathites, the Zorites. [55] The families of the scribes that dwelt at Jabez: the Tirathites, the Shimeathites, the Sucathites; these are the Kenites who came from Hammath, father of the house of Rechab.

3 These are the sons of David who were born to him in Hebron: the firstborn Amnon, by Ahinoam the Jezreelite; the second Daniel, by Abigail the Carmelite; [2] the third Absalom, son of Maacah daughter of King Talmai of Geshur; the fourth Adonijah, son of Haggith; [3] the fifth Shephatiah, by Abital; the sixth Ithream, by his wife Eglah; [4] six were born to him in Hebron. He reigned there seven years and six months, and in Jerusalem he reigned thirty-three years. [5] These were born to him in Jerusalem: Shimea, Shobab, Nathan, and Solomon, four by Bath-shua daughter of Ammiel; [6] then Ibhar, Elishama, Eliphelet, [7] Nogah, Nepheg, Japhia, [8] Elishama, Eliada, and Eliphelet—nine. [9] All were David's sons, besides the sons of the concubines; and Tamar was their sister.

[10] The son of Solomon: Rehoboam; his son Abijah, his son Asa, his son Jehoshaphat, [11] his son Joram, his son Ahaziah, his son Joash, [12] his son Amaziah, his son Azariah, his son Jotham, [13] his son Ahaz, his son Hezekiah, his son Manasseh, [14] his son Amon, and his son Josiah. [15] The sons of Josiah: Johanan the firstborn, the second Jehoiakim, the third Zedekiah, the fourth Shallum. [16] The descendants of Jehoiakim: his son Jeconiah, his son Zedekiah; [17] and the sons of Jeconiah, the captive: Shealtiel his son, [18] Malchiram, Pedaiah, Shenazzar, Jekamiah, Hoshana, and Nedabiah; [19] the sons of Pedaiah: Zerubbabel and Shimei; the

sons of Zerubbabel: Meshullam and Hananiah, and Shelomith was their sister; ²⁰ Hashubah, Ohel, Berechiah, Hasadiah, and Jushab-hesed—five. ²¹ And the sons of Hananiah: Pelatiah and Jeshaiah; the sons of [Jeshaiah]: Rephaiah; the sons of [Rephaiah]: Arnan; the sons of [Arnan]: Obadiah; the sons of [Obadiah]: Shecaniah. ²² And the sons of Shecaniah: Shemaiah; and the sons of Shemaiah: Hattush, and Igal, and Bariah, and Neariah, and Shaphat—six. ²³ And the sons of Neariah: Elioenai, and Hizkiah, and Azrikam—three. ²⁴ And the sons of Elioenai: Hodaviah, and Eliashib, and Pelaiah, and Akkub, and Johanan, and Delaiah, and Anani—seven.

4 The sons of Judah: Perez, Hezron, Carmi, Hur, and Shobal. ² Reaiah son of Shobal begot Jahath, and Jahath begot Ahumai and Lahad. These were the families of the Zorathites. ³ These were [the sons of] the father of Etam: Jezreel, Ishma, and Idbash; and the name of their sister was Hazlelponi, ⁴ and Penuel was the father of Gedor, and Ezer the father of Hushah. These were the sons of Hur, the firstborn of Ephrathah, the father of Bethlehem. ⁵ Ashhur the father of Tekoa had two wives, Helah and Naarah; ⁶ Naarah bore him Ahuzam, Hepher, Temeni, and Ahashtari. These were the sons of Naarah. ⁷ The sons of Helah: Zereth, Zohar, and Ethnan. ⁸ Koz was the father of Anub, Zobebah, and the families of Aharhel son of Harum. ⁹ Jabez was more esteemed than his brothers; and his mother named him Jabez, "Because," she said, "I bore him in pain."^a ¹⁰ Jabez invoked the God of Israel, saying, "Oh, bless me, enlarge my territory, stand by me, and make me not suffer pain from misfortune!" And God granted what he asked. ¹¹ Chelub the brother of Shuhah begot Mehir, who was the father of Eshton. ¹² Eshton begot Bethrapha, Paseah, and Tehinnah father of Ir-nahash. These were the men of Recah. ¹³ The sons of Kenaz: Othniel and Seraiah; and the sons of Othniel: ¹⁴ Hathath and Meonothai. He begot Ophrah. Seraiah begot Joab father of Ge-harashim,^b so-called because they were crafts-

---

^a Heb. 'oṣeb, connected with "Jabez."
^b Lit. "the valley of the craftsmen."

men. ¹⁵ The sons of Caleb son of Jephunneh: Iru, Elah, and Naam; and the sons of Elah: Kenaz. ¹⁶ The sons of Jehallelel: Ziph, Ziphah, Tiria, and Asarel. ¹⁷ The sons of Ezrah: Jether, Mered, Epher, and Jalon. She*c* conceived and bore Miriam, Shammai, and Ishbah father of Eshtemoa. ¹⁸ And his Judahite wife bore Jered father of Gedor, Heber father of Soco, and Jekuthiel father of Zanoah. These were the sons of Bithiah daughter of Pharaoh, whom Mered married. ¹⁹ The sons of the wife of Hodiah sister of Naham were the fathers of Keilah the Garmite and Eshtemoa the Maacathite. ²⁰ The sons of Shimon: Amnon, Rinnah, Ben-hanan, and Tilon. The sons of Ishi: Zoheth and Ben-zoheth. ²¹ The sons of Shelah son of Judah: Er father of Lecah, Laadah father of Mareshah, and the families of the linen factory at Beth-ashbea; ²² and Jokim, and the men of Cozeba and Joash, and Saraph, who married into Moab and Jahubi Lehem (the records are ancient). ²³ These were the potters who dwelt at Netaim and Gederah; they dwelt there in the king's service.

²⁴ The sons of Simeon: Nemuel, Jamin, Jarib, Zerah, Shaul; ²⁵ his son Shallum, his son Mibsam, his son Mishma. ²⁶ The sons of Mishma: his son Hammuel, his son Zaccur, his son Shimei. ²⁷ Shimei had sixteen sons and six daughters; but his brothers had not many children; in all, their families were not as prolific as the Judahites. ²⁸ They dwelt in Beersheba, Moladah, Hazar-shual, ²⁹ Bilhah, Ezem, Tolad, ³⁰ Bethuel, Hormah, Ziklag, ³¹ Beth-marcaboth, Hazar-susim, Beth-biri, and Shaaraim. These were their towns until David became king, ³² together with their villages, Etam, Ain, Rimmon, Tochen, and Ashan—five towns, ³³ along with all their villages that were around these towns as far as Baal; such were their settlements.

Registered in their genealogy were: ³⁴ Meshobab, Jamlech, Joshash son of Amaziah, ³⁵ Joel, Jehu son of Joshibiah son of Seraiah son of Asiel. ³⁶ Elioenai, Jaakobah, Jeshohaiah, Asaiah, Adiel, Jesimiel, Benaiah, ³⁷ Ziza son of Shiphi son of Allon son of Jedaiah son of Shimri son of Shemaiah—³⁸ these mentioned by name were chiefs in their families, and their clans increased

c Apparently Bithiah; cf. v. 18.

513

greatly. [39] They went to the approaches to Gedor, to the eastern side of the valley, in search of pasture for their flocks. [40] They found rich, good pasture, and the land was ample, quiet, and peaceful. The former inhabitants were of Ham; [41] those recorded by name came in the days of King Hezekiah of Judah, and attacked their encampments and the Meunim who were found there, and wiped them out forever, and settled in their place, because there was pasture there for their flocks. [42] And some of them, five hundred of the Simeonites, went to Mount Seir, with Pelatiah, Neariah, Rephaiah, and Uzziel, sons of Ishi, at their head, [43] and they destroyed the last surviving Amalekites, and they live there to this day.

5 The sons of Reuben the firstborn of Israel. (He was the firstborn; but when he defiled his father's bed, his birthright was given to the sons of Joseph son of Israel, so he is not reckoned as firstborn in the genealogy; [2] though Judah became more powerful than his brothers and a leader came from him, yet the birthright belonged to Joseph.) [3] The sons of Reuben, the firstborn of Israel: Enoch, Pallu, Hezron, and Carmi. [4] The sons of Joel: his son Shemaiah, his son Gog, his son Shimei, [5] his son Micah, his son Reaiah, his son Baal, [6] his son Beerah—whom King Tillegath-pilneser of Assyria exiled—was chieftain of the Reubenites. [7] And his kinsmen, by their families, according to their lines in the genealogy: the head, Jeiel, and Zechariah, [8] and Bela son of Azaz son of Shema son of Joel; he dwelt in Aroer as far as Nebo and Baal-meon. [9] He also dwelt to the east as far as the fringe of the wilderness this side of the Euphrates, because their cattle had increased in the land of Gilead. [10] And in the days of Saul they made war on the Hagrites, who fell by their hand; and they occupied their tents throughout all the region east of Gilead.

[11] The sons of Gad dwelt facing them in the land of Bashan as far as Salcah: [12] Joel the chief, Shapham the second, Janai, and

Shaphat in Bashan. [13] And by clans: Michael, Meshullam, Sheba, Jorai, Jacan, Zia, and Eber—seven. [14] These were the sons of Abihail son of Huri son of Jaroah son of Gilead son of Michael son of Jeshishai son of Jahdo son of Buz; [15] Ahi son of Abdiel son of Guni was chief of their clan, [16] and they dwelt in Gilead, in Bashan, and in its dependencies, and in all the pasturelands of Sharon, to their limits. [17] All of them were registered by genealogies in the days of King Jotham of Judah, and in the days of King Jeroboam of Israel.

[18] The Reubenites, the Gadites, and the half-tribe of Manasseh had warriors who carried shield and sword, drew the bow, and were experienced at war—44,760, ready for service. [19] They made war on the Hagrites—Jetur, Naphish, and Nodab. [20] They prevailed against them; the Hagrites and all who were with them were delivered into their hands, for they cried to God in the battle, and He responded to their entreaty because they trusted in Him. [21] They carried off their livestock: 50,000 of their camels, 250,000 sheep, 2,000 asses, and 100,000 people. [22] For many fell slain, because it was God's battle. And they dwelt in their place until the exile.

[23] The members of the half-tribe of Manasseh dwelt in the land; they were very numerous from Bashan to Baal-hermon, Senir, and Mount Hermon. [24] These were the chiefs of their clans: Epher, Ishi, Eliel, Azriel, Jeremiah, Hodaviah, and Jahdiel, men of substance, famous men, chiefs of their clans. [25] But they trespassed against the God of their fathers by going astray after the gods of the peoples of the land, whom God had destroyed before them. [26] So the God of Israel roused the spirit of King Pul of Assyria—the spirit of King Tillegath-pilneser of Assyria—and he carried them away, namely, the Reubenites, the Gadites, and the half-tribe of Manasseh, and brought them to Halah, Habor, Hara, and the river Gozan, to this day.

[27] [a] The sons of Levi: Gershom, Kohath, and Merari. [28] The sons of Kohath: Amram, Izhar, Hebron, and Uzziel. [29] The children of Amram: Aaron, Moses, and Miriam. The sons of Aaron: Nadab,

[a] In some editions, ch. 6 begins here.

Abihu, Eleazar, and Ithamar. ³⁰ Eleazar begot Phinehas, Phinehas begot Abishua, ³¹ Abishua begot Bukki, Bukki begot Uzzi, ³² Uzzi begot Zerahiah, Zerahiah begot Meraioth, ³³ Meraioth begot Amariah, Amariah begot Ahitub, ³⁴ Ahitub begot Zadok, Zadok begot Ahimaaz, ³⁵ Ahimaaz begot Azariah, Azariah begot Johanan, ³⁶ and Johanan begot Azariah (it was he who served as priest in the House that Solomon built in Jerusalem). ³⁷ Azariah begot Amariah, Amariah begot Ahitub, ³⁸ Ahitub begot Zadok, Zadok begot Shallum, ³⁹ Shallum begot Hilkiah, Hilkiah begot Azariah, ⁴⁰ Azariah begot Seraiah, Seraiah begot Jehozadak; ⁴¹ and Jehozadak went into exile when the LORD exiled Judah and Jerusalem by the hand of Nebuchadnezzar.

6 The sons of Levi: Gershom, Kohath, and Merari. ² And these are the names of the sons of Gershom: Libni and Shimei. ³ The sons of Kohath: Amram, Izhar, Hebron, and Uzziel. ⁴ The sons of Merari: Mahli and Mushi. These were the families of the Levites according to their clans. ⁵ Of Gershom: his son Libni, his son Jahath, his son Zimmah, ⁶ his son Joah, his son Iddo, his son Zerah, his son Jeatherai. ⁷ The sons of Kohath: his son Amminadab, his son Korah, his son Assir, ⁸ his son Elkanah, his son Ebiasaph, his son Assir, ⁹ his son Tahath, his son Uriel, his son Uzziah, and his son Shaul. ¹⁰ The sons of Elkanah: Amasai and Ahimoth, ¹¹ his son Elkanah, his son Zophai, his son Nahath, ¹² his son Eliab, his son Jeroham, his son Elkanah. ¹³ The sons of Samuel: his firstborn ᵃ-Vashni, and-ᵃ Abijah. ¹⁴ The sons of Merari: Mahli, his son Libni, his son Shimei, his son Uzzah, ¹⁵ his son Shimea, his son Haggiah, and his son Asaiah.

¹⁶ These were appointed by David to be in charge of song in the House of the LORD, from the time the Ark came to rest. ¹⁷ They served at the Tabernacle of the Tent of Meeting with song until Solomon built the House of the LORD in Jerusalem; and they carried out their duties as prescribed for them. ¹⁸ Those were the appointed men; and their sons were: the Kohathites: Heman the singer, son of Joel son of Samuel ¹⁹ son of Elkanah

ᵃ⁻ᵃ *Some ancient vv. read, "Joel, and the second"; cf. I Sam. 8.2.*

son of Jeroham son of Eliel son of Toah ²⁰ son of Zuph son of Elkanah son of Mahath son of Amasai ²¹ son of Elkanah son of Joel son of Azariah son of Zephaniah ²² son of Tahath son of Assir son of Ebiasaph son of Korah ²³ son of Izhar son of Kohath son of Levi son of Israel; ²⁴ and his kinsmen Asaph, who stood on his right, namely, Asaph son of Berechiah son of Shimea ²⁵ son of Michael son of Baaseiah son of Malchijah ²⁶ son of Ethni son of Zerah son of Adaiah ²⁷ son of Ethan son of Zimmah son of Shimei ²⁸ son of Jahath son of Gershom son of Levi. ²⁹ On the left were their kinsmen: the sons of Merari: Ethan son of Kishi son of Abdi son of Malluch ³⁰ son of Hashabiah son of Amaziah son of Hilkiah ³¹ son of Amzi son of Bani son of Shemer ³² son of Mahli son of Mushi son of Merari son of Levi; ³³ and their kinsmen the Levites were appointed for all the service of the Tabernacle of the House of God.

³⁴ But Aaron and his sons made offerings upon the altar of burnt offering and upon the altar of incense, performing all the tasks of the most holy place, to make atonement for Israel, according to all that Moses the servant of God had commanded. ³⁵ These are the sons of Aaron: his son Eleazar, his son Phinehas, his son Abishua, ³⁶ his son Bukki, his son Uzzi, his son Zerahiah, ³⁷ his son Meraioth, his son Amariah, his son Ahitub, ³⁸ his son Zadok, his son Ahimaaz. ³⁹ ^bThese are their dwelling-places according to their settlements within their borders: to the sons of Aaron of the families of Kohathites, for theirs was the [first] lot; ⁴⁰ they gave them Hebron in the land of Judah and its surrounding pasturelands, ⁴¹ but the fields of the city and its villages they gave to Caleb son of Jephunneh. ⁴² To the sons of Aaron they gave the cities^c of refuge: Hebron and Libnah with its pasturelands, Jattir and Eshtemoa with its pasturelands, ⁴³ Hilen with its pasturelands, Debir with its pasturelands, ⁴⁴ Ashan with its pasturelands, and Beth-shemesh with its pasturelands. ⁴⁵ From the tribe of Benjamin, Geba with its pasturelands, Alemeth with its pasturelands, and Anathoth with its pasturelands. All their cities throughout their families were thirteen.

⁴⁶ To the remaining Kohathites were given by lot out of the

^b With vv. 24–51, cf. Josh. 21.3–42.
^c Josh. 21.13, "city."

family of the tribe, out of the half-tribe, the half of Manasseh, ten cities. [47] To the Gershomites according to their families were allotted thirteen cities out of the tribes of Issachar, Asher, Naphtali, and Manasseh in Bashan. [48] To the Merarites according to their families were allotted twelve cities out of the tribes of Reuben, Gad, and Zebulun. [49] So the people of Israel gave the Levites the cities with their pasturelands. [50] They gave them by lot out of the tribe of the Judahites these cities which are mentioned by name, and out of the tribe of the Simeonites, and out of the tribe of the Benjaminites.

[51] And some of the families of the sons of Kohath had cities of their territory out of the tribe of Ephraim. [52] They gave them the cities of refuge: Shechem with its pasturelands in the hill country of Ephraim, Gezer with its pasturelands, [53] Jokmeam with its pasturelands, Beth-horon with its pasturelands, [54] Aijalon with its pasturelands, Gath-rimmon with its pasturelands; [55] and out of the half-tribe of Manasseh: Aner with its pasturelands, and Bileam with its pasturelands, for the rest of the families of the Kohathites.

[56] To the Gershomites; out of the half-tribe of Manasseh: Golan in Bashan with its pasturelands and Ashtaroth with its pasturelands; [57] and out of the tribe of Issachar: Kedesh with its pasturelands, Dobrath with its pasturelands, [58] Ramoth with its pasturelands, and Anem with its pasturelands; [59] out of the tribe of Asher: Mashal with its pasturelands, Abdon with its pasturelands, [60] Hukok with its pasturelands, and Rehob with its pasturelands; [61] and out of the tribe of Naphtali: Kedesh in Galilee with its pasturelands; Hammon with its pasturelands, and Kiriathaim with its pasturelands. [62] To the rest of the Merarites, out of the tribe of Zebulun: Rimmono with its pasturelands, Tabor with its pasturelands; [63] and beyond the Jordan at Jericho, on the east side of the Jordan, out of the tribe of Reuben: Bezer in the wilderness with its pasturelands, Jahaz with its pasturelands, [64] Kedemoth with its pasturelands, and Mephaath with its pasturelands; [65] and out of the tribe of Gad: Ramoth in Gilead with

its pasturelands, Mahanaim with its pasturelands, ⁶⁶ Heshbon with its pasturelands, and Jazer with its pasturelands.

7 The sons of Issachar: Tola, Puah, Jashub, and Shimron—four. ² The sons of Tola: Uzzi, Rephaiah, Jeriel, Jahmai, Ibsam, Shemuel, chiefs of their clans, men of substance according to their lines; their number in the days of David was 22,600. ³ The sons of Uzzi: Izrahiah. And the sons of Izrahiah: Michael, Obadiah, Joel, and Isshiah—five. All of them were chiefs. ⁴ And together with them, by their lines, according to their clans, were units of the fighting force, 36,000, for they had many wives and sons. ⁵ Their kinsmen belonging to all the families of Issachar were in all 87,000 men of substance; they were all registered by genealogy.

⁶ [The sons of] Benjamin: Bela, Becher, and Jediael—three. ⁷ The sons of Bela: Ezbon, Uzzi, Uzziel, Jerimoth, and Iri—five, chiefs of clans, men of substance, registered by genealogy—22,034 and thirty four. ⁸ The sons of Becher: Zemirah, Joash, Eliezer, Elioenai, Omri, Jeremoth, Abijah, Anathoth, and Alemeth. All these were the sons of Becher; ⁹ and they were registered by genealogy according to their lines, as chiefs of their clans, men of substance—20,200. ¹⁰ The sons of Jediael: Bilhan. And the sons of Bilhan: Jeush, Benjamin, Ehud, Chenaanah, Zethan, Tarshish, and Ahishahar. ¹¹ All these were the sons of Jediael, chiefs of the clans, men of substance—17,200, who made up the fighting force. ¹² And Shuppim and Huppim were the sons of Ir; Hushim the sons of Aher.

¹³ The sons of Naphtali: Jahziel, Guni, Jezer, and Shallum, the descendants of Bilhah.

¹⁴ The sons of Manasseh: Asriel, whom his Aramean concubine bore; she bore Machir the father of Gilead. ¹⁵ And Machir took wives for Huppim and for Shuppim. The name of his sister was Maacah. And the name of the second was Zelophehad; and Zelophehad had daughters. ¹⁶ And Maacah the wife of Machir bore a

son, and she named him Peresh; and the name of his brother was Sheresh; and his sons were Ulam and Rekem. ¹⁷ The sons of Ulam: Bedan. These were the sons of Gilead son of Machir son of Manasseh. ¹⁸ And his sister Hammolecheth bore Ishhod, Abiezer, and Mahlah. ¹⁹ The sons of Shemida were Ahian, Shechem, Likhi, and Aniam.

²⁰ The sons of Ephraim: Shuthelah, his son Bered, his son Tahath, his son Eleadah, his son Tahath, ²¹ his son Zabad, his son Shuthelah, also Ezer and Elead. The men of Gath, born in the land, killed them because they had gone down to take their cattle. ²² And Ephraim their father mourned many days, and his brothers came to comfort him. ²³ He cohabited with his wife, who conceived and bore a son; and she named him Beriah, because it occurred when there was misfortune*a* in his house. ²⁴ His daughter was Sheerah, who built both Lower and Upper Bethhoron, and Uzzen-sheerah. ²⁵ His son Rephah, his son Resheph, his son Telah, his son Tahan, ²⁶ his son Ladan, his son Ammihud, his son Elishama, ²⁷ his son Non, his son Joshua. ²⁸ Their possessions and settlements were Bethel and its dependencies, and on the east Naaran, and on the west Gezer and its dependencies, Shechem and its dependencies, and Aiah and its dependencies; ²⁹ also along the borders of the Manassites, Beth-shean and its dependencies, Taanach and its dependencies, Megiddo and its dependencies, Dor and its dependencies. In these dwelt the sons of Joseph son of Israel.

³⁰ The sons of Asher: Imnah, Ishvah, Ishvi, Beriah, and their sister Serah. ³¹ The sons of Beriah: Ḥeber and Malchiel, who was the father of Birzaith. ³² Heber begot Japhlet, Shomer, Hotham, and their sister Shua. ³³ The sons of Japhlet: Pasach, Bimhal, and Ashvath. These were the sons of Japhlet. ³⁴ The sons of Shemer: Ahi, Rohgah, Hubbah, and Aram. ³⁵ The sons of Helem his brother: Zophah, Imna, Shelesh, and Amal. ³⁶ The sons of Zophah: Suah, Harnepher, Shual, Beri, Imrah, ³⁷ Bezer, Hod, Shamma, Shilshah, Ithran, and Beera. ³⁸ The sons of Jether: Jephunneh, Pispa, and Ara. ³⁹ The sons of Ulla: Arah, Hanniel, and

---

ª *Heb* beraʻah.

Rizia. [40] All of these men of Asher, chiefs of the clans, select men, men of substance, heads of the chieftains. And they were registered by genealogy according to fighting force; the number of the men was 26,000 men.

8 Benjamin begot Bela his firstborn, Ashbel the second, Aharah the third, [2] Nohah the fourth, and Rapha the fifth. [3] And Bela had sons: Addar, Gera, Abihud, [4] Abishua, Naaman, Ahoah, [5] Gera, Shephuphan, and Huram. [6] These were the sons of Ehud —they were chiefs of clans of the inhabitants of Geba, and they were exiled to Manahath: [7] Naaman, Ahijah, and Gera—he exiled them and begot Uzza and Ahihud. [8] And Shaharaim had sons in the country of Moab after he had sent away Hushim and Baara his wives. [9] He had sons by Hodesh his wife: Jobab, Zibia, Mesha, Malcam, [10] Jeuz, Sachiah, and Mirmah. These were his sons, chiefs of clans. [11] He also begot by Hushim: Abitub and Elpaal. [12] The sons of Elpaal: Eber, Misham, and Shemed, who built Ono and Lod with its dependencies, [13] and Beriah and Shema—they were chiefs of clans of the inhabitants of Aijalon, who put to flight the inhabitants of Gath; [14] and Ahio, Shashak, and Jeremoth. [15] Zebadiah, Arad, Eder, [16] Michael, Ishpah, and Joha were sons of Beriah. [17] Zebadiah, Meshullam, Hizki, Heber, [18] Ishmerai, Izliah, and Jobab were the sons of Elpaal. [19] Jakim, Zichri, Zabdi, [20] Elienai, Zillethai, Eliel, [21] Adaiah, Beraiah, and Shimrath were the sons of Shimei. [22] Ishpan, Eber, Eliel, [23] Abdon, Zichri, Hanan, [24] Hananiah, Elam, Anthothiah, [25] Iphdeiah, and Penuel were the sons of Shashak. [26] Shamsherai, Shehariah, Athaliah, [27] Jaareshiah, Elijah, and Zichri were the sons of Jeroham. [28] These were the chiefs of the clans, according to their lines. These chiefs dwelt in Jerusalem.

[29] The father of Gibeon dwelt in Gibeon, and the name of his wife was Maacah. [30] His firstborn son: Abdon; then Zur, Kish, Baal, Nadab, [31] Gedor, Ahio, Zecher. [32] Mikloth begot Shimeah. And they dwelt in Jerusalem opposite their kinsmen, with their

kinsmen. [33] Ner begot Kish, Kish begot Saul, Saul begot Jonathan, Malchi-shua, Abinadab, and Eshbaal; [34] and the son of Jonathan was Merib-baal; and Merib-baal begot Micah. [35] The sons of Micah: Pithon, Melech, Taarea, and Ahaz. [36] Ahaz begot Jehoaddah; and Jehoaddah begot Alemeth, Azmaveth, and Zimri; Zimri begot Moza. [37] Moza begot Binea; his son Eleasah, his son Azel. [38] Azel had six sons, and these are their names: Azrikam, Bocheru, Ishmael, Sheariah, Obadiah, and Hanan. All these were the sons of Azel. [39] The sons of Eshek his brother: Ulam his firstborn, Jeush the second, and Eliphelet the third. [40] The descendants of Ulam—men of substance, who drew the bow, had many children and grandchildren—one hundred and fifty; all these were Benjaminites.

9 All Israel was registered by genealogies; and these are in the book of the kings of Israel. And Judah was taken into exile in Babylon because of their trespass. [2] [a] The first to settle in their towns, on their property, were Israelites, priests, Levites, and temple servants, [3] while some of the Judahites and some of the Benjaminites and some of the Ephraimites and Manassehites settled in Jerusalem; [4] Uthai son of Ammihud son of Omri son of Imri son of Bani, from the sons of Perez son of Judah; [5] and of the Shilonites: Asaiah the firstborn and his sons. [6] Of the sons of Zerah: Jeuel and their kinsmen—690. [7] Of the Benjaminites: Sallu son of Meshullam son of Hodaviah son of Hassenuah, [8] Ibneiah son of Jeroham, Elah son of Uzzi son of Michri, and Meshullam son of Shephatiah son of Reuel son of Ibneiah; [9] and their kinsmen, according to their lines—956. All these were chiefs of their ancestral clans.

[10] Of the priests: Jedaiah, Jehoiarib, Jachin, [11] and Azariah son of Hilkiah son of Meshullam son of Zadok son of Meraioth son of Ahitub, chief officer of the House of God; [12] and Adaiah son of Jeroham son of Pashhur son of Malchijah, and Maasai son of Adiel son of Jahzerah son of Meshullam son of Meshillemith son

[a] With vv. 2–17, cf. Neh. 11.3–19.

of Immer, [13] together with their kinsmen, chiefs of their clans—1760, men of substance for the work of the service of the House of God.

[14] Of the Levites: Shemaiah son of Hasshub son of Azrikam son of Hashabiah, of the sons of Merari; [15] and Bakbakkar, Heresh, Galal, and Mattaniah son of Mica son of Zichri son of Asaph; [16] and Obadiah son of Shemaiah son of Galal son of Jeduthun, and Berechiah son of Asa son of Elkanah, who dwelt in the villages of the Netophathites.

[17] The gatekeepers were: Shallum, Akkub, Talmon, Ahiman; and their kinsman Shallum was the chief [18] hitherto in the King's Gate on the east. They were the keepers belonging to the Levite camp. [19] Shallum son of Kore son of Ebiasaph son of Korah, and his kinsmen of his clan, the Korahites, were in charge of the work of the service, guards of the threshold of the Tent; their fathers had been guards of the entrance to the camp of the LORD. [20] And Phinehas son of Eleazar was the chief officer over them in time past; the LORD was with him. [21] Zechariah the son of Meshelemiah was gatekeeper at the entrance of the Tent of Meeting. [22] All these, who were selected as gatekeepers at the thresholds, were 212. They were selected by genealogies in their villages. David and Samuel the seer established them in their office of trust. [23] They and their descendants were in charge of the gates of the House of the LORD, that is, the House of the Tent, as guards. [24] The gatekeepers were on the four sides, east, west, north, and south; [25] and their kinsmen in their villages were obliged to join them every seven days, according to a fixed schedule. [26] The four chief gatekeepers, who were Levites, were entrusted to be over the chambers and the treasuries of the House of God. [27] They spent the night near the House of God; for they had to do guard duty, and they were in charge of opening it every morning.

[28] Some of them had charge of the service vessels, for they were counted when they were brought back and taken out. [29] Some of them were in charge of the vessels and all the holy vessels, and of the flour, wine, oil, incense, and spices. [30] Some of the priests

blended the compound of spices. ³¹ Mattithiah, one of the Levites, the firstborn of Shallum the Korahite, was entrusted with making the flat cakes. ³² Also some of their Kohathite kinsmen had charge of the rows of bread, to prepare them for each sabbath.

³³ Now these are the singers, the chiefs of Levitical clans who remained in the chambers free of other service, for they were on duty day and night. ³⁴ These were chiefs of Levitical clans, according to their lines; these chiefs lived in Jerusalem.

³⁵ The father of Gibeon, Jeiel, lived in Gibeon, and the name of his wife was Maacah. ³⁶ His firstborn son, Abdon; then Zur, Kish, Baal, Ner, Nadab, ³⁷ Gedor, Ahio, Zechariah, and Mikloth; ³⁸ Mikloth begot Shimeam; and they lived in Jerusalem opposite their kinsmen, with their kinsmen. ³⁹ Ner begot Kish, Kish begot Saul, Saul begot Jonathan, Malchi-shua, Abinadab, and Eshbaal; ⁴⁰ and the son of Jonathan was Merib-baal; and Merib-baal begot Micah. ⁴¹ The sons of Micah: Pithon, Melech, Taharea; ⁴² Ahaz begot Jarah, and Jarah begot Alemeth, Azmaveth, and Zimri; Zimri begot Moza. ⁴³ Moza begot Binea; his son was Rephaiah, his son Eleasah, his son Azel. ⁴⁴ Azel had six sons and these were their names: Azrikam, Bocheru, Ishmael, Sheariah, Obadiah, and Hanan. These were the sons of Azel.

10 ᵃ The Philistines attacked Israel, and the men of Israel fled before the Philistines and [many] fell on Mount Gilboa. ² The Philistines pursued Saul and his sons, and the Philistines struck down Jonathan, Abinadab, and Malchi-shua, sons of Saul. ³ The battle raged around Saul, and the archers hit him, and he ᵇ⁻was wounded⁻ᵇ by the archers. ⁴ Saul said to his arms-bearer, "Draw your sword and run me through, so that these uncircumcised may not come and make sport of me." But his arms-bearer, out of great awe, refused; whereupon Saul grasped the sword and fell upon it. ⁵ When the arms-bearer saw that Saul was dead, he too fell on his sword and died. ⁶ Thus Saul and his three sons and his

ᵃ *With vv. 1–12, cf. I Sam. 31.1–13.*
ᵇ⁻ᵇ *Meaning of Heb. uncertain.*

entire house died together. 7 And when all the men of Israel who were in the valley saw that they^c had fled and that Saul and his sons were dead, they abandoned their towns and fled; the Philistines then came and occupied them.

8 The next day the Philistines came to strip the slain, and they found Saul and his sons lying on Mount Gilboa. 9 They stripped him, and carried off his head and his armor, and sent them throughout the land of the Philistines to spread the news to their idols and among the people. 10 They placed his armor in the temple of their god, and they impaled his head in the temple of Dagan. 11 When all Jabesh-gilead heard everything that the Philistines had done to Saul, 12 all their stalwart men set out, removed the bodies of Saul and his sons, and brought them to Jabesh. They buried the bones under the oak tree in Jabesh, and they fasted for seven days. 13 Saul died for the trespass which he had committed against the LORD in not having fulfilled the command of the LORD; moreover, he had consulted a ghost to seek advice, 14 and did not seek advice of the LORD; so He had him slain and the kingdom transferred to David son of Jesse.

11 ^aAll Israel gathered to David at Hebron and said, "We are your own flesh and blood. 2 Long before now, even when Saul was king, you were the leader of Israel; and the LORD your God said to you: You shall shepherd My people Israel; you shall be ruler of My people Israel." 3 All the elders of Israel came to the king at Hebron, and David made a pact with them in Hebron before the LORD. And they anointed David king over Israel, according to the word of the LORD through Samuel.

4 David and all Israel set out for Jerusalem, that is Jebus, where the Jebusite inhabitants of the land lived. 5 David was told by the inhabitants of Jebus, "You will never get in here!" But David captured the stronghold of Zion; it is now the City of David. 6 David said, "Whoever attacks the Jebusites first will be the chief officer"; Joab son of Zeruiah attacked first, and became the chief.

^c *I.e. Israel.*

^a *With vv. 1–9, cf. II Sam. 5.1–10, and with vv. 11–41, cf. II Sam. 23.8–39.*

⁷ David occupied the stronghold; therefore it was renamed the City of David. ⁸ David also fortified the surrounding area, from the Millo round about, and Joab rebuilt the rest of the city. ⁹ David kept growing stronger, for the LORD of Hosts was with him.

¹⁰ And these were David's chief warriors who strongly supported him in his kingdom, together with all Israel, to make him king, according to the word of the LORD concerning Israel.

¹¹ This is the list of David's warriors: Jashobeam son of Hachmoni, the chief officer; he wielded his spear against three hundred and slew them all on one occasion. ¹² Next to him was Eleazar son of Dodo, the Ahohite; he was one of the three warriors. ¹³ He was with David at Pas Dammim when the Philistines gathered there for battle. There was a plot of ground full of barley there; the troops had fled from the Philistines, ¹⁴ but they took their stand in the middle of the plot and defended it, and they routed the Philistines. Thus the LORD wrought a great victory.

¹⁵ Three of the thirty chiefs went down to the rock to David, at the cave of Adullam, while a force of Philistines was encamped in the Valley of Rephaim. ¹⁶ David was then in the stronghold, and a Philistine garrison was then at Bethlehem. ¹⁷ David felt a craving and said, "If only I could get a drink of water from the cistern which is by the gate of Bethlehem!" ¹⁸ So the three got through the Philistine camp, and drew water from the cistern which is by the gate of Bethlehem, and they carried it back to David. But David would not drink it, and he poured it out as a libation to the LORD. ¹⁹ For he said, "God forbid that I should do this! Can I drink the blood of these men who risked their lives?" —for they had brought it at the risk of their lives, and he would not drink it. Such were the exploits of the three warriors.

²⁰ Abshai, the brother of Joab, was head of another three. He once wielded his spear against three hundred and slew them. He won a name among the three; ²¹ among the three he was more

highly regarded than the other two, and so he became their commander. However, he did not attain to the other three. ²² Benaiah son of Jehoiada from Kabzeel was a brave soldier who performed great deeds. He killed the two [sons] of Ariel of Moab. Once, on a snowy day, he went down into a pit and killed a lion. ²³ He also killed an Egyptian, a giant of a man five cubits tall. The Egyptian had a spear in his hand, like a weaver's beam, yet [Benaiah] went down against him with a club, wrenched the spear out of the Egyptian's hand, and killed him with his own spear. ²⁴ Such were the exploits of Benaiah son of Jehoiada; and he won a name among the three warriors. ²⁵ He was highly regarded among the thirty, but he did not attain to the three. David put him in charge of his bodyguard.^b

²⁶ The valiant warriors: Asahel brother of Joab, Elhanan son of Dodo from Bethlehem, ²⁷ Shammoth the Harorite, Helez the Pelonite, ²⁸ Ira son of Ikkesh from Tekoa, Abiezer of Anathoth, ²⁹ Sibbecai the Hushathite, Ilai the Ahohite, ³⁰ Mahrai the Netophathite, Heled son of Baanah the Netophathite, ³¹ Ittai son of Ribai from Gibeah of the Benjaminites, Benaiah of Pirathon, ³² Hurai of Nahale-gaash, Abiel the Arbathite, ³³ Azmaveth the Bahrumite, Eliahba of Shaalbon, ³⁴ the sons of Hashem the Gizonite, Jonathan son of Shageh the Hararite, ³⁵ Ahiam son of Sacar the Hararite, Eliphal son of Ur, ³⁶ Hepher the Mecherathite, Ahijah the Pelonite, ³⁷ Hezro the Carmelite, Naarai son of Ezbai, ³⁸ Joel brother of Nathan, Mibhar son of Hagri, ³⁹ Zelek the Ammonite, Naharai the Berothite—the arms-bearer of Joab son of Zeruiah—⁴⁰ Ira the Ithrite, Gareb the Ithrite, ⁴¹ Uriah the Hittite, Zabad son of Ahlai. ⁴² Adina son of Shiza the Reubenite, a chief of the Reubenites, and thirty with him; ⁴³ Hanan son of Maacah, and Joshaphat the Mithnite; ⁴⁴ Uzziah the Ashterathite, Shama and Jeiel sons of Hotham the Aroerite; ⁴⁵ Jedaiael son of Shimri, and Joha his brother, the Tizite; ⁴⁶ Eliel the Mahavite, and Jeribai and Joshaviah sons of Elnaam, and Ithmah the Moabite; ⁴⁷ Eliel, Obed, and Jaassiel the Mezobaite.

^b *Meaning of Heb. uncertain.*

12 The following joined David at Ziklag while he was still in hiding from Saul son of Kish; these were the warriors who gave support in battle; 2 they were armed with the bow and could use both right hand and left hand to sling stones or shoot arrows with the bow; they were kinsmen of Saul from Benjamin. 3 At the head were Ahiezer and Joash, sons of Shemaah of Gibeah; and Jeziel and Pelet, sons of Azmaveth; and Beracah and Jehu of Anathoth; 4 Ishmaiah of Gibeon, a warrior among the thirty, leading the thirty; 5 Jeremiah, Jahaziel, Johanan, and Jozabad of Gederah; 6 Eluzai, Jerimoth, Bealiah, Shemariah, and Shephatiah the Hariphite; 7 Elkanah, Isshiah, Azarel, Joezer, and Jashobeam the Korahites; 8 Joelah and Zebadiah, sons of Jeroham of Gedor.ᵃ 9 Of the Gadites, there withdrew to follow David to the wilderness stronghold valiant men, fighters fit for battle, armed with shield and spear; they had the appearance of lions, and were as swift as gazelles upon the mountains: 10 Ezer the chief, Obadiah the second, Eliab the third, 11 Mashmannah the fourth, Jeremiah the fifth, 12 Attai the sixth, Eliel the seventh, 13 Johanan the eighth, Elzabad the ninth, 14 Jeremiah the tenth, Machbannai the eleventh. 15 Those were the Gadites, heads of the army. The least was equal to a hundred, the greatest to a thousand. 16 These were the ones who crossed the Jordan in the first month, when it was at its crest, and they put to flight all the lowlanders to the east and west. 17 Some of the Benjaminites and Judahites came to the stronghold to David, 18 and David went out to meet them, saying to them, "If you come on a peaceful errand, to support me, then I will make common cause with you, but if to betray me to my foes, for no injustice on my part, then let the God of our fathers take notice and give judgment." 19 Then the spirit seized Amasai, chief of the captains:

"We are yours, David,
On your side, son of Jesse;
At peace, at peace with you,

ᵃ Or, "the troop," reading Heb. gedud with several mss.

And at peace with him who supports you,
For your God supports you."
So David accepted them, and placed them at the head of his band.

²⁰ Some Manassites went over to David's side when he came with the Philistines to make war against Saul, but they were of no help to them, because the lords of the Philistines in council dismissed him, saying, "He will go over to the side of his lord, Saul, and it will cost us our heads"; ²¹ when he went to Ziklag, these Manassites went over to his side—Adnah, Jozabad, Jediael, Michael, Jozabad, Elihu, and Zillethai, chiefs of the clans of Manasseh.

²² It was they who gave support to David against the band,^b for all were valiant men; and they were officers of the force.

²³ Day in day out, people came to David to give him support, until there was an army as vast as the army of God.

²⁴ These are the numbers of the [men of the] armed bands who joined David at Hebron to transfer Saul's kingdom to him, in accordance with the word of the LORD:

²⁵ Judahites, equipped with shield and spear—6800 armed men; ²⁶ Simeonites, valiant men, fighting troops—7100; ²⁷ of the Levites—4600; ²⁸ Jehoiada, chief officer of the Aaronides; with him, 3700; ²⁹ Zadok, a young valiant man, with his clan—22 officers; ³⁰ of the Benjaminites, kinsmen of Saul, 3000 in their great numbers, hitherto protecting the interests of the house of Saul; ³¹ of the Ephraimites, 20,800 valiant men, famous in their clans; ³² of the half-tribe of Manasseh, 18,000, who were designated by name to come and make David king; ³³ of the Issacharites, men who knew how to interpret the signs of the times, to determine how Israel should act; their chiefs were 200, and all their kinsmen followed them; ³⁴ of Zebulun, those ready for service, able to man a battle line with all kinds of weapons, 50,000, giving support wholeheartedly; ³⁵ of Naphtali, 1000 chieftains with their shields and lances—37,000; ³⁶ Of the Danites, able to man the battle line —28,600; ³⁷ of Asher, those ready for service to man the battle line—40,000; ³⁸ from beyond the Jordan, of the Reubenites, the

^b *I.e. the band of Amalekite raiders; cf. I Sam. 30.8,15.*

Gadites, and the half-tribe of Manasseh, together with all kinds of military weapons—120,000.

³⁹ All these, fighting men, manning the battle line with whole heart, came to Hebron to make David king over all Israel. Likewise, all the rest of Israel was of one mind to make David king.

⁴⁰ They were there with David three days, eating and drinking, for their kinsmen had provided for them.

⁴¹ And also, their relatives as far away as Issachar, Zebulun, and Naphtali brought food by ass, camel, mule, and ox—provisions of flour, cakes of figs, raisin-cakes, wine, oil, cattle, and sheep in abundance, for there was joy in Israel.

13 Then David consulted with the officers of the thousands and the hundreds, with every chief officer. ² David said to the entire assembly of Israel, "If you approve, and if the LORD our God concurs,^a let us send far and wide to our remaining kinsmen throughout the territories of Israel, including the priests and Levites in the towns where they have pasturelands, that they should gather together to us ³ in order to transfer the Ark of our God to us, for throughout the days of Saul we paid no regard to it." ⁴ The entire assembly agreed to do so, for the proposal pleased all the people. ⁵ David then assembled all Israel from Shihor of Egypt to Lebo-hamath, in order to bring the Ark of God from Kiriath-jearim. ⁶ ^bDavid and all Israel went up to Baalah, Kiriath-jearim of Judah, to bring up from there the Ark of God, the LORD, Enthroned on the Cherubim, to which the Name was attached. ⁷ They transported the Ark of God on a new cart from the house of Abinadab; Uzza and Ahio guided the cart, ⁸ and David and all Israel danced before God with all their might—with songs, lyres, harps, timbrels, cymbals, and trumpets. ⁹ But when they came to the threshing floor of Chidon, Uzza put out his hand to hold the Ark of God because the oxen had stumbled.^a ¹⁰ The LORD was incensed at Uzza, and struck him down, because he laid a hand on the Ark; and so he died there before God.

^a *Meaning of Heb. uncertain.*
^b *With vv. 6–14, cf. II Sam. 6.2–11.*

¹¹ David was distressed because the LORD ᶜ⁻had burst out⁻ᶜ against Uzza; and that place was named Perez-uzzah, as it is still called. ¹² David was afraid of God that day; he said, "How can I bring the Ark of God here?" ¹³ So David did not remove the Ark to his place in the City of David; instead, he diverted it to the house of Obed-edom the Gittite. ¹⁴ The Ark of God remained in the house of Obed-edom, in its own abode, three months, and the LORD blessed the house of Obed-edom and all he had.

14 ᵃKing Hiram of Tyre sent envoys to David with cedar logs, stonemasons, and carpenters to build a palace for him. ² Thus David knew that the LORD had established him as king over Israel, and that his kingship was highly exalted for the sake of His people Israel.

³ David took more wives in Jerusalem, and David begot more sons and daughters. ⁴ These are the names of the children born to him in Jerusalem:ᵇ Shammua, Shobab, Nathan, and Solomon; ⁵ Ibhar, Elishua, and Elpelet; ⁶ Nogah, Nepheg, and Japhia; ⁷ Elishama, Beeliada, and Eliphelet.

⁸ When the Philistines heard that David had been anointed king over all Israel, all the Philistines went up in search of David; but David heard of it, and he went out to them. ⁹ The Philistines came and raided the Valley of Rephaim. ¹⁰ David inquired of God, "Shall I go up against the Philistines? Will You deliver them into my hands?" And the LORD answered him, "Go up, and I will deliver them into your hands." ¹¹ Thereupon David ascended Baal-perazim, and David defeated them there. David said, "God ᶜ⁻burst out⁻ᶜ against my enemies by my hands as waters burst out." That is why that place was named Baal-perazim. ¹² They abandoned their gods there, and David ordered these to be burned.

¹³ Once again the Philistines raided the valley. ¹⁴ David inquired of God once more, and God answered, "Do not go up after them, but circle around them and confront them at the bacaᵈ

ᶜ⁻ᶜ *Heb.* paraṣ . . . pereṣ.
ᵃ *With vv. 1–16, cf. II Sam. 5.11–25.*
ᵇ *With the list in vv. 4–7, cf. also I Chron. 3.5–8.*
ᶜ⁻ᶜ *Heb.* paraṣ . . . pereṣ.
ᵈ *Meaning of Heb. uncertain.*

trees. [15] And when you hear the sound of marching in the tops of the *baca* trees, then go out to battle, for God will be going in front of you to attack the Philistine forces." [16] David did as God had commanded him; and they routed the Philistines from Gibeon all the way to Gezer. [17] David became famous throughout the lands, and the LORD put the fear of him in all the nations.

15 He had houses made for himself in the City of David, and he prepared a place for the Ark of God, and pitched a tent for it. [2] Then David gave orders that none but the Levites were to carry the Ark of God, for the LORD had chosen them to carry the Ark of the LORD and to minister to Him forever. [3] David assembled all Israel in Jerusalem to bring up the Ark of the LORD to its place, which he had prepared for it. [4] Then David gathered together the Aaronides and the Levites: [5] the sons of Kohath: Uriel the officer and his kinsmen—120; [6] the sons of Merari: Asaiah the officer and his kinsmen—220; [7] the sons of Gershom: Joel the officer and his kinsmen—130; [8] the sons of Elizaphan: Shemaiah the officer and his kinsmen—200; [9] the sons of Hebron: Eliel the officer and his kinsmen—80; [10] the sons of Uzziel: Amminadab the officer and his kinsmen—112.

[11] David sent for Zadok and Abiathar the priests, and for the Levites: Uriel, Asaiah, Joel, Shemaiah, Eliel, and Amminadab. [12] He said to them, "You are the heads of the clans of the Levites; sanctify yourselves, you and your kinsmen, and bring up the Ark of the LORD God of Israel to [the place] I have prepared for it. [13] *a-*Because you were not there the first time,*-a* the LORD our God burst out against us, for we did not show due regard for Him."

[14] The priests and Levites sanctified themselves in order to bring up the Ark of the LORD God of Israel. [15] The Levites carried the Ark of God by means of poles on their shoulders, as Moses had commanded in accordance with the word of the LORD. [16] David ordered the officers of the Levites to install their kins-

---

[a-a] *Meaning of Heb. uncertain.*

men, the singers, with musical instruments, harps, lyres, and cymbals, joyfully making their voices heard. ¹⁷ So the Levites installed Heman son of Joel and, of his kinsmen, Asaph son of Berachiah; and, of the sons of Merari their kinsmen, Ethan son of Kushaiah. ¹⁸ Together with them were their kinsmen of second rank, Zechariah, Ben, Jaaziel, Shemiramoth, Jehiel, Unni, Eliab, Benaiah, Maaseiah, Mattithiah, Eliphalehu, Mikneiah, Obed-edom and Jeiel the gatekeepers. ¹⁹ Also the singers Heman, Asaph, and Ethan to sound the bronze cymbals, ²⁰ and Zechariah, Aziel, Shemiramoth, Jehiel, Unni, Eliab, Maaseiah, and Benaiah with harps *ᵃ-on alamoth;-ᵃ ²¹ also Mattithiah, Eliphalehu, Mikneiah, Obed-edom, Jeiel, and Azaziah, with lyres to lead *ᵃ-on the *sheminith;-ᵃ ²² also Chenaniah, officer of the Levites in song;ᵃ he was in charge of the songᵃ because he was a master. ²³ Berechiah and Elkanah were gatekeepers for the Ark. ²⁴ Shebaniah, Joshaphat, Nethanel, Amasai, Zechariah, Benaiah, and Eliezer the priests sounded the trumpets before the Ark of God, and Obed-edom and Jehiah were gatekeepers for the Ark. ²⁵ ᵇ Then David and the elders of Israel and the officers of the thousands who were going to bring up the Ark of the Covenant of the Lord from the house of Obed-edom were joyful. ²⁶ Since God helped the Levites who were carrying the Ark of the Covenant of the Lord, they sacrificed seven bulls and seven rams. ²⁷ Now David and all the Levites who were carrying the Ark, and the singers and Chenaniah, officer of song of the singers, ᵃ-were wrapped-ᵃ in robes of fine linen, and David wore a linen ephod. ²⁸ All Israel brought up the Ark of the Covenant of the Lord with shouts and with blasts of the horn, with trumpets and cymbals, playing on harps and lyres. ²⁹ As the Ark of the Covenant of the Lord arrived at the City of David, Michal daughter of Saul looked out of the window and saw King David leaping and dancing, and she despised him for it.

ᵇ *Vv. 25–29 are found also in II Sam. 6.12–16.*

16 *a*They brought in the Ark of God and set it up inside the tent which David had pitched for it, and they sacrificed burnt offerings and offerings of well-being before God. ² When David finished sacrificing the burnt offerings and the offerings of well-being, he blessed the people in the name of the LORD. ³ And he distributed to every person in Israel—man and woman alike—to each a loaf of bread, *b*-a cake made in a pan, and a raisin cake.*-b* ⁴ He appointed Levites to minister before the Ark of the LORD, to invoke, to praise, and to extol the LORD God of Israel: ⁵ Asaph the chief, Zechariah second in rank, Jeiel, Shemiramoth, Jehiel, Mattithiah, Eliab, Benaiah, Obed-edom, and Jeiel, with harps and lyres, and Asaph sounding the cymbals, ⁶ and Benaiah and Jehaziel the priests, with trumpets, regularly before the Ark of the Covenant of God. ⁷ Then, on that day, David first commissioned Asaph and his kinsmen to give praise to the LORD:

⁸ "*c*Praise the LORD;
call on His name;
proclaim His deeds among the peoples.
⁹ Sing praises unto Him;
speak of all His wondrous acts.
¹⁰ Exult in His holy name;
let all who seek the LORD rejoice.
¹¹ Turn to the LORD, to His might;*d*
seek His presence constantly.
¹² Remember the wonders He has done;
His portents and the judgments He has pronounced,
¹³ O offspring of Israel, His servant,
O descendants of Jacob, His chosen ones.
¹⁴ He is the LORD our God;
His judgments are throughout the earth.
¹⁵ Be ever mindful of His covenant,
the promise He gave for a thousand generations,
¹⁶ that He made with Abraham,

ª *With vv. 1–3, cf. II Sam. 6.17–19.*
b-b *Meaning of Heb. uncertain.*
ᶜ *With vv. 8–22, cf. Ps. 105.1–15.*
ᵈ *I.e. the Ark; cf. Ps. 78.61; 132.8.*

swore to Isaac,
¹⁷ and confirmed in a decree for Jacob,
for Israel, as an eternal covenant,
¹⁸ saying, 'To you I will give the land of Canaan
as your allotted heritage.'
¹⁹ You were then few in number,
a handful, merely sojourning there,
²⁰ wandering from nation to nation,
from one kingdom to another.
²¹ He allowed no one to oppress them;
He reproved kings on their account,
²² 'Do not touch My anointed ones;
do not harm My prophets.'

²³ ᵉ"Sing to the LORD, all the earth.
proclaim His victory day after day.
²⁴ Tell of His glory among the nations,
His wondrous deeds among all peoples.
²⁵ For the LORD is great and much acclaimed,
He is held in awe by all divine beings.
²⁶ All the gods of the peoples are mere idols,
but the LORD made the heavens.
²⁷ Glory and majesty are before Him;
strength and joy are in His place.

²⁸ "Ascribe to the LORD, O families of the peoples,
ascribe to the LORD glory and strength.
²⁹ Ascribe to the LORD the glory of His name,
bring tribute and enter before Him,
bow down to the LORD majestic in holiness.
³⁰ Tremble in His presence, all the earth!
The world stands firm; it cannot be shaken.
³¹ Let the heavens rejoice and the earth exult;
³² let the sea and all within it thunder,
the fields and everything in them exult;

ᵉ With vv. 23-33, cf. Ps. 96.1-13.

535

³³ then shall all the trees of the forest shout for joy
at the presence of the LORD,
for He is coming to rule the earth.
³⁴ Praise the LORD for He is good;
His steadfast love is eternal.
³⁵ ⸠Declare:
Deliver us, O God, our deliverer,
and gather us and save us from the nations,
to acclaim Your holy name,
to glory in Your praise.
³⁶ Blessed is the LORD, God of Israel, from eternity to eternity."
And all the people said, "Amen" and "Praise the LORD."⸠

³⁷ He left Asaph and his kinsmen there before the Ark of the
Covenant of the LORD to minister before the Ark regularly as
each day required, ³⁸ as well as Obed-edom with their kinsmen—
68; also Obed-edom son of Jedithun and Hosah as gatekeepers;
³⁹ also Zadok the priest and his fellow priests before the Tabernacle of the LORD at the shrine which was in Gibeon; ⁴⁰ to sacrifice
burnt offerings to the LORD on the altar of the burnt offering
regularly, morning and evening, in accordance with what was
prescribed in the Teaching of the LORD with which He charged
Israel. ⁴¹ With them were Heman and Jeduthun and the other
selected men designated by name to give praise to the LORD,
"For His steadfast love is eternal." ⁴² Heman and Jeduthun had
with them trumpets and cymbals to sound, and instruments for
the songs of God; and the sons of Jeduthun were to be at the gate.
⁴³ Then all the people went everyone to his home, and David
returned to greet his household.

17 ᵃWhen David settled in his palace, David said to the prophet
Nathan, "Here I am dwelling in a house of cedar, while the Ark
of the Covenant of the LORD is under tent-cloths." ² Nathan said
to David, "Do whatever you have in mind, for God is with you."
³ But that same night the word of God came to Nathan: ⁴ "Go

f-f Cf. Ps. 106.47–48.
ᵃ With this chapter, cf. II Sam. 7.

and say to My servant David: Thus said the LORD: You are not the one to build a house for Me to dwell in. ⁵ From the day that I brought out Israel to this day, I have not dwelt in a house, but have [gone] from tent to tent and from one Tabernacle [to another]. ⁶ As I moved about wherever Israel went, did I ever reproach any of the judges of Israel whom I appointed to care for My people Israel: Why have you not built Me a house of cedar?

⁷ "Further, say thus to My servant David: Thus said the LORD of Hosts: I took you from the pasture, from following the flock, to be ruler of My people Israel, ⁸ and I have been with you wherever you went, and have cut down all your enemies before you. Moreover, I will give you renown like that of the greatest men on earth. ⁹ I will establish a home for My people Israel and will plant them firm, so that they shall dwell secure and shall tremble no more. Evil men shall not wear them down any more as in the past, ¹⁰ ever since I appointed judges over My people Israel. I will subdue all your enemies.

And I declare to you: The LORD will build a house*ᵇ* for you. ¹¹ When your days are done and you follow your fathers, I will raise up your offspring after you, one of your own sons, and I will establish his kingship. ¹² He shall build a house for Me, and I will establish his throne forever. ¹³ I will be a father to him, and he shall be a son to Me, but I will never withdraw My favor from him as I withdrew it from your predecessor. ¹⁴ I will install him in My house and in My kingship forever, and his throne shall be established forever."

¹⁵ Nathan spoke to David in accordance with all these words and all this prophecy. ¹⁶ Then King David came and sat before the LORD, and he said, "What am I, O LORD God, and what is my family, that You have brought me thus far? ¹⁷ Yet even this, O God, has seemed too little to You; for You have spoken of Your servant's house for the future. *ᶜ*You regard me as a man of distinction,*ᶜ* O LORD God. ¹⁸ What more can David add regarding the honoring of Your servant? You know Your servant. ¹⁹ O LORD, *ᶜ*for Your servant's sake, and of Your own accord,*ᶜ* You

---

ᵇ *I.e. a dynasty; play on "house" (i.e. Temple) in v. 4.*
ᶜ⁻ᶜ *Meaning of Heb. uncertain.*

have wrought this great thing, and made known all these great things. [20] O LORD, there is none like You, and there is no other God but You, as we have always heard. [21] And who is like Your people Israel, a unique nation on earth, whom God went and redeemed as His people, winning renown for Yourself for great and marvelous deeds, driving out nations before Your people whom You redeemed from Egypt. [22] You have established Your people Israel as Your very own people forever; and You, O LORD, have become their God.

[23] "And now, O LORD, let Your promise concerning Your servant and his house be fulfilled forever; and do as You have promised. [24] Let it be fulfilled that Your name be glorified forever, in that men will say, 'The LORD of Hosts, God of Israel, is Israel's God'; and may the house of Your servant David be established before You. [25] Because You, my God, have revealed to Your servant that You will build a house for him, Your servant has ventured to pray to You. [26] And now, O LORD, You are God and You have made this gracious promise to Your servant. [27] Now, it has pleased You to bless Your servant's house, that it abide before You forever; for You, O LORD, have blessed and are blessed forever."

18 [a]Some time afterward, David attacked the Philistines and subdued them; and David took Gath and its dependencies from the Philistines. [2] He also defeated the Moabites; the Moabites became tributary vassals of David.

[3] David defeated Hadadezer, king of Zobah-hamath, who was on his way to set up his monument at the Euphrates River. [4] David captured 1000 chariots and 7000 horsemen and 20,000 foot soldiers of his force; and David hamstrung all the chariot horses except for 100, which he retained. [5] And when the Arameans of Damascus came to the aid of King Hadadezer of Zobah-hamath, David struck down 22,000 of the Arameans. [6] David stationed [garrisons] in Aram of Damascus, and the Arameans became

[a] With this chapter, cf. II Sam. 8.

tributary vassals of David. The LORD gave David victory wherever he went. [7] David took the gold shields[b] carried by Hadadezer's retinue and brought them to Jerusalem; [8] and from Tibbath and Cun, towns of Hadadezer, David took a vast amount of copper, from which Solomon made the bronze tank, the columns, and the bronze vessels.

[9] When King Tou of Hamath heard that David had defeated the entire army of King Hadadezer of Zobah, [10] he sent his son Hadoram to King David to greet him and to congratulate him on his military victory over Hadadezer—for Hadadezer had been at war with Tou; [he brought with him] all manner of gold, silver, and copper objects. [11] King David dedicated these to the LORD, along with the other silver and gold that he had taken from all the nations: from Edom, Moab, and Ammon; from the Philistines and the Amalekites.

[12] Abshai son of Zeruiah struck down Edom in the Valley of Salt, 18,000 in all. [13] He stationed garrisons in Edom, and all the Edomites became vassals of David. The LORD gave David victory wherever he went.

[14] David reigned over all Israel, and David executed true justice among all his people. [15] Joab son of Zeruiah was commander of the army; Jehoshaphat son of Ahilud was recorder; [16] Zadok son of Ahitub and Abimelech son of Abiathar were priests; Shavsha was scribe; [17] Benaiah son of Jehoiada was commander of the Cherethites and the Pelethites; and David's sons were first ministers of the king.

19 [a]Some time afterward, Nahash the king of the Ammonites died, and his son succeeded him as king. [2] David said, "I will keep faith with Hanun son of Nahash, since his father kept faith with me." David sent messengers with condolences to him over his father. But when David's courtiers came to the land of Ammon to Hanun, with condolences, [3] the Ammonite officials said to Hanun, "Do you think David is really honoring your father just

[b] Or "quivers."

[a] With this chapter, cf. II Sam. 10.

because he sent you men with condolences? Why, it is to explore, to subvert, and to spy out the land that his courtiers have come to you." ⁴ So Hanun seized David's courtiers, shaved them, and cut away half of their garments up to the buttocks, and sent them off. ⁵ When David was told about the men, he dispatched others to meet them, for the men were greatly embarrassed. And the king gave orders, "Stay in Jericho until your beards grow back; then you can return."

⁶ The Ammonites realized that they had incurred the wrath of David; so Hanun and the Ammonites sent 1000 silver talents to hire chariots and horsemen from Aram-naharaim, Aram-maacah and Zobah. ⁷ They hired 32,000 chariots, the king of Maacah, and his army, who came and encamped before Medeba. The Ammonites were mobilized from their cities and came to do battle.

⁸ On learning this, David sent out Joab and the whole army, [including] the professional fighters. ⁹ The Ammonites marched out and took up their battle position at the entrance of the city, while the kings who came [took their stand] separately in the open. ¹⁰ Joab saw that there was a battle line against him both front and rear. So he made a selection from all the picked men of Israel and arrayed them against the Arameans, ¹¹ and the rest of the troops he put under the command of his brother Abishai and arrayed them against the Ammonites. ¹² Joab said, "If the Arameans prove too strong for me, you come to my aid; and if the Ammonites prove too strong for you, I will come to your aid. ¹³ Let us be strong and resolute for the sake of our people and the towns of our God; and the LORD will do what He deems right."

¹⁴ Joab and the troops with him marched into battle against the Arameans, who fled before him. ¹⁵ And when the Ammonites saw that the Arameans had fled, they too fled before his brother Abishai, and withdrew into the city. So Joab went to Jerusalem.

¹⁶ When the Arameans saw that they had been routed by Israel, they sent messengers to bring out the Arameans from across the Euphrates; Shophach, Hadadezer's army commander, led them.

¹⁷ David was informed of it; he assembled all Israel, crossed the Jordan, and came and took up positions against them. David drew up his forces against Aram; and they fought with him. ¹⁸ But the Arameans were put to flight by Israel. David killed 7000 Aramean charioteers and 40,000 footmen; he also killed Shophach, the army commander. ¹⁹ And when all the vassals of Hadadezer saw that they had been routed by Israel, they submitted to David and became his vassals. And the Arameans would not help the Ammonites anymore.

20 ^aAt the turn of the year, the season when kings go out [to battle], Joab led out the army force and devastated the land of Ammon, and then besieged Rabbah, while David remained in Jerusalem; Joab reduced Rabbah and left it in ruins. ² David took the crown from the head of their king; he found that it weighed a talent of gold, and in it were precious stones. It was placed on David's head. He also carried off a vast amount of booty from the city. ³ He led out the people who lived there and ^{b-}he hacked them^{-b} with saws and iron threshing boards and axes;^c David did thus to all the towns of Ammon. Then David and all the troops returned to Jerusalem. ⁴ After this, fighting broke out with the Philistines at Gezer; that was when Sibbecai the Hushathite killed Sippai, a descendant of the Rephaim, and they were humbled.

⁵ Again there was fighting with the Philistines, and Elhanan son of Jair killed Lahmi, the brother of Goliath the Gittite; his spear had a shaft like a weaver's beam. ⁶ Once again there was fighting at Gath. There was a giant of a man who had twenty-four fingers [and toes], six [on each hand] and six [on each foot]; he too was descended from the Raphah. ⁷ When he taunted Israel, Jonathan son of David's brother Shimea killed him. ⁸ These were descended from the Raphah in Gath, and they fell by the hands of David and his men.

---

^a With vv. 1–3, cf. II Sam. 11.1; 12.30–31.
^{b-b} Meaning of Heb. uncertain. II Sam. 12.31 has "set them to work."
^c Heb. megeroth; cf. II Sam. 12.31 magzeroth, "axes."

21 ^aSatan arose against Israel and incited David to number Israel. ² David said to Joab and to the commanders of the army, "Go and count Israel from Beer-sheba to Dan and bring me information as to their number." ³ Joab answered, "May the Lord increase His people a hundredfold; my lord king, are they not all subjects of my lord? Why should my lord require this? Why should it be a cause of guilt for Israel?"

⁴ However, the king's command to Joab remained firm, so Joab set out and traversed all Israel; he then came to Jerusalem. ⁵ Joab reported to David the number of the people that had been recorded. All Israel comprised 1,100,000 ready to draw the sword, while in Judah there were 470,000 men ready to draw the sword. ⁶ He did not record among them Levi and Benjamin, because the king's command had become repugnant to Joab. ⁷ God was displeased about this matter and He struck Israel.

⁸ David said to God, "I have sinned grievously in having done this thing; please remit the guilt of Your servant, for I have acted foolishly." ⁹ The Lord ordered Gad, David's seer: ¹⁰ "Go and tell David: Thus said the Lord: I offer you three things; choose one of them and I will bring it upon you." ¹¹ Gad came to David and told him, "Thus said the Lord: Select for yourself ¹² a three-year famine; or that you be swept away three months before your adversaries with the sword of your enemies overtaking you; or three days of the sword of the Lord, pestilence in the land, the angel of the Lord wreaking destruction throughout the territory of Israel. Now consider what reply I shall take back to Him who sent me." ¹³ David said to Gad, "I am in great distress. Let me fall into the hands of the Lord, for His compassion is very great; and let me not fall into the hands of men."

¹⁴ The Lord sent a pestilence upon Israel, and 70,000 men fell in Israel. ¹⁵ God sent an angel to Jerusalem to destroy it, but as he was about to wreak destruction, the Lord saw and renounced further punishment and said to the destroying angel, "Enough!

ª With vv. 1–26, cf. II Sam. 24.

Stay your hand!" The angel of the LORD was then standing by the threshing floor of Ornan the Jebusite. [16] David looked up and saw the angel of the LORD standing between heaven and earth, with a drawn sword in his hand directed against Jerusalem. David and the elders, covered in sackcloth, threw themselves on their faces. [17] David said to God, "Was it not I alone who ordered the numbering of the people? I alone am guilty, and have caused severe harm; but these sheep, what have they done? O LORD my God, let Your hand fall upon me and my father's house, and let not Your people be plagued!" [18] The angel of the LORD told Gad to inform David that David should go and set up an altar to the LORD on the threshing floor of Ornan the Jebusite. [19] David went up, following Gad's instructions which he had delivered in the name of the LORD. [20] Ornan too saw the angel; his four sons who were with him hid themselves while Ornan kept on threshing wheat. [21] David came to Ornan; when Ornan looked up, he saw David and came off the threshing floor and bowed low to David, with his face to the ground. [22] David said to Ornan, "Sell me the site of the threshing floor, that I may build on it an altar to the LORD. Sell it to me at the full price, that the plague against the people will be checked." [23] Ornan said to David, "Take it and let my lord the king do whatever he sees fit. See, I donate oxen for burnt offerings, and the threshing boards for wood, as well as wheat for a meal offering—I donate all of it." [24] But King David replied to Ornan, "No, I will buy them at the full price. I cannot make a present to the LORD of what belongs to you, or sacrifice a burnt offering that has cost me nothing." [25] So David paid Ornan for the site 600 shekels' worth of gold. [26] And David built there an altar to the LORD and sacrificed burnt offerings and offerings of well-being. He invoked the LORD, who answered him with fire from heaven on the altar of burnt offerings. [27] The LORD ordered the angel to return his sword to its sheath. [28] At that time, when David saw that the LORD answered him at the threshing floor of Ornan the Jebusite, then he sacrificed there—[29] for the Tabernacle of the LORD, which Moses had made in the wilderness, and the altar of burnt offerings, were at that time in the shrine at Gibeon, [30] and David was unable to go to it to worship the LORD because he was terrified by the sword of the angel of the LORD.[1] David said, "Here will be the House of the LORD and here the altar of burnt offerings for Israel."

22

[2] David gave orders to assemble the aliens living in the land of Israel, and assigned them to be hewers, to quarry and dress stones for building the House of God. [3] Much iron for nails for the doors of the gates and for clasps did David lay aside, and so much copper it could not be weighed, [4] and cedar logs without number—for the Sidonians and the Tyrians brought many cedar logs to David.

[5] For David thought, "My son Solomon is an untried youth, and the House to be built for the LORD is to be made exceedingly great to win fame and glory throughout all the lands; let me then lay aside material for him." So David laid aside much material before he died. [6] Then he summoned his son Solomon and charged him with building the House for the LORD God of Israel.

[7] David said to Solomon, "My son, I wanted to build a House for the name of the LORD my God. [8] But the word of the LORD came to me, saying, 'You have shed much blood and fought great battles; you shall not build a House for My name for you have shed much blood on the earth in My sight. [9] But you will have a son who will be a man at rest, for I will give him rest from all his enemies on all sides; Solomon[a] will be his name and I shall confer peace[b] and quiet on Israel in his time. [10] He will build a House for My name; he shall be a son to Me and I to him a father, and I will establish his throne of kingship over Israel forever.' [11] Now, my son, may the LORD be with you, and may you succeed in building the House of the LORD your God as He promised you would. [12] Only let God give you sense and understanding and put you in charge of Israel and the observance of the Teaching of the LORD your God. [13] Then you shall succeed, if you observantly carry out the laws and the rules which the LORD charged Moses to lay upon Israel. Be strong and of good courage; do not be

[a] *Heb.* Shelomoh.
[b] *Heb.* shalom.

544

afraid or dismayed. [14] See, ᶜ-by denying myself,-ᶜ I have laid aside for the House of the LORD one hundred thousand talents of gold and one thousand talents of silver, and so much copper and iron it cannot be weighed; I have also laid aside wood and stone, and you shall add to them. [15] An abundance of workmen is at your disposal—hewers, workers in stone and wood, and every kind of craftsman in every kind of material—[16] gold, silver, copper, and iron without limit. Go and do it, and may the LORD be with you."

[17] David charged all the officers of Israel to support his son Solomon, [18] "See, the LORD your God is with you, and He will give you rest on every side, for He delivered the inhabitants of the land into my hand so that the land lies conquered before the LORD and before His people. [19] Now, set your minds and hearts on worshiping the LORD your God, and go build the Sanctuary of the LORD your God so that you may bring the Ark of the Covenant of the LORD and the holy vessels of God to the house that is built for the name of the LORD."

23 When David reached a ripe old age, he made his son Solomon king over Israel. [2] Then David assembled all the officers of Israel and the priests and the Levites. [3] The Levites, from the age of thirty and upward, were counted; the head-count of their males was 38,000: [4] of these there were 24,000 in charge of the work of the House of the LORD, 6000 officers and magistrates, [5] 4000 gatekeepers, and 4000 for praising the LORD "with instruments I devised for singing praises." [6] David formed them into divisions:

The sons of Levi: Gershon, Kohath, and Merari. [7] The Gershonites: Ladan and Shimei. [8] The sons of Ladan: Jehiel the chief, Zetham, and Joel—3. [9] The sons of Shimei: Shelomith, Haziel, and Haran—3. These were the chiefs of the clans of the Ladanites. [10] And the sons of Shimei: Jahath, Zina, Jeush, and Beriah; these were the sons of Shimei—4. [11] Jahath was the chief and Zizah the second, but Jeush and Beriah did not have many chil-

ᶜ-ᶜ *With Targum; or "in my poverty."*

dren, so they were enrolled together as a single clan. [12] The sons of Kohath: Amram, Izhar, Hebron, and Uzziel—4. [13] The sons of Amram: Aaron and Moses. Aaron was set apart, he and his sons, forever, to be consecrated as most holy, to make burnt offerings to the LORD and serve Him and pronounce blessings in His name forever. [14] As for Moses, the man of God, his sons were named after the tribe of Levi. [15] The sons of Moses: Gershom and Eliezer. [16] The sons of Gershom: Shebuel the chief. [17] And the sons of Eliezer were: Rehabiah the chief. Eliezer had no other sons, but the sons of Rehabiah were very numerous. [18] The sons of Izhar: Shelomith the chief. [19] The sons of Hebron: Jeriah the chief, Amariah the second, Jahaziel the third, and Jekameam the fourth. [20] The sons of Uzziel: Micah the chief and Isshiah the second. [21] The sons of Merari: Mahli and Mushi. The sons of Mahli: Eleazar and Kish. [22] Eleazar died having no sons but only daughters; the sons of Kish, their kinsmen, married them. [23] The sons of Mushi: Mahli, Eder, and Jeremoth—3.

[24] These are the sons of Levi by clans, with their clan-chiefs as they were enrolled, with a list of their names by heads, who did the work of the service of the House of the LORD from the age of twenty and upward. [25] For David said, "The LORD God of Israel has given rest to His people and made His dwelling in Jerusalem forever. [26] Therefore the Levites need not carry the Tabernacle and all its various service vessels." [27] Among the last acts of David was the counting of the Levites from the age of twenty and upward. [28] For their appointment was alongside the Aaronites for the service of the House of the LORD, to look after the courts and the chambers, and the purity of all the holy things, and the performance of the service of the House of God, [29] and the rows of bread, and the fine flour for the meal offering, and the unleavened wafers, and the cakes made on the griddle and soaked, and every measure of capacity and length; [30] and to be present every morning to praise and extol the LORD, and at evening too, [31] and whenever offerings were made to the LORD, according to the quantities prescribed for them, on sabbaths, new moons and

holidays, regularly, before the LORD; [32] and so to keep watch over the Tent of Meeting, over the holy things, and over the Aaronites their kinsmen, for the service of the House of the LORD.

24 The divisions of the Aaronites were:

The sons of Aaron: Nadab and Abihu, Eleazar and Ithamar. [2] Nadab and Abihu died in the lifetime of their father, and they had no children, so Eleazar and Ithamar served as priests. [3] David, Zadok of the sons of Eleazar, and Ahimelech of the sons of Ithamar divided them into offices by their tasks. [4] The sons of Eleazar turned out to be more numerous by male heads than the sons of Ithamar, so they divided the sons of Eleazar into sixteen chiefs of clans and the sons of Ithamar into eight clans. [5] They divided them by lot, both on an equal footing, since they were all Sanctuary officers and officers of God—the sons of Eleazar and the sons of Ithamar. [6] Shemaiah son of Nathanel, the scribe, who was of the Levites, registered them under the eye of the king, the officers, and Zadok the priest, and Ahimelech son of Abiathar, and the chiefs of clans of the priests and Levites— [a]one clan more taken for Eleazar for each one taken of Ithamar.[a]

[7] The first lot fell on Jehoiarib; the second on Jedaiah; [8] the third on Harim; the fourth on Seorim; [9] the fifth on Malchijah; the sixth on Mijamin; [10] the seventh on Hakkoz; the eighth on Abijah; [11] the ninth on Jeshua; the tenth on Shecaniah; [12] the eleventh on Eliashib; the twelfth on Jakim; [13] the thirteenth on Huppah; the fourteenth on Jeshebeab; [14] the fifteenth on Bilgah; the sixteenth on Immer; [15] the seventeenth on Hezir; the eighteenth on Happizzez; [16] the nineteenth on Pethahiah; the twentieth on Jehezkel; [17] the twenty-first on Jachin; the twenty-second on Gamul [18] the twenty-third on Delaiah; the twenty-fourth on Maaziah.

[19] According to this allocation of offices by tasks, they were to enter the House of the LORD as was laid down for them by Aaron their father, as the LORD God of Israel had commanded him.

[20] The remaining Levites: the sons of Amram: Shubael; the

[a-a] *Meaning of Heb. uncertain.*

sons of Shubael: Jehdeiah; ²¹ Rehabiah. The sons of Rehabiah: Isshiah, the chief. ²² Izharites: Shelomoth. The sons of Shelomoth: Jahath ²³ and Benai, Jeriah; the second, Amariah; the third, Jahaziel; the fourth, Jekamean. ²⁴ The sons of Uzziel: Micah. The sons of Micah: Shamir. ²⁵ The brother of Micah: Isshiah. The sons of Isshiah: Zechariah. ²⁶ The sons of Merari: Mahli and Mushi. The sons of Jaazaiah, his son ²⁷ —the sons of Merari by Jaazaiah his son: Shoham, Zakkur, and Ibri. ²⁸ Mahli: Eleazar; he had no sons. ²⁹ Kish: the sons of Kish: Jerahmeel. ³⁰ The sons of Mushi: Mahli, Eder, and Jerimoth. These were the sons of the Levites by their clans.

³¹ These too cast lots corresponding to their kinsmen, the sons of Aaron, under the eye of King David and Zadok and Ahimelech and the chiefs of the clans of the priests and Levites, on the principle of "chief and youngest brother alike."

25 David and the officers of the army set apart for service the sons of Asaph, of Heman, and of Jeduthun, who prophesied to the accompaniment of lyres, harps, and cymbals. The list of men who performed this work, according to their service, was:

² Sons of Asaph: Zaccur, Joseph, Nethaniah, and Asarelah—sons of Asaph under the charge of Asaph, who prophesied by order of the king. ³ Jeduthun—the sons of Jeduthun: Gedaliah, Zeri, Jeshaiah, Hashabiah, Mattithiah—6, under the charge of their father Jeduthun, who, accompanied on the harp, prophesied, praising and extolling the LORD. ⁴ Heman—the sons of Heman: Bukkiah, Mattaniah, Uzziel, Shebuel, Jerimoth, Hananiah, Hanani, Eliathah, Giddalti, Romamti-ezer, Joshbekashah, Mallothi, Hothir, and Mahazioth; ⁵ all these were sons of Heman, the seer of the king, [who uttered] prophecies of God for His greater glory. God gave Heman fourteen sons and three daughters; ⁶ all these were under the charge of their father for the singing in the House of the LORD, to the accompaniment of cymbals, harps, and lyres, for the service of the House of God by

order of the king. Asaph, Jeduthun, and Heman—⁷ their total number with their kinsmen, trained singers of the LORD—all the masters, 288.

⁸ They cast lots for shifts on the principle of "small and great alike, like master like apprentice."

⁹ The first lot fell to Asaph—to Joseph; the second, to Gedaliah, he and his brothers and his sons—12; ¹⁰ the third, to Zaccur: his sons and his brothers—12; ¹¹ the fourth, to Izri: his sons and his brothers—12; ¹² the fifth, to Nethaniah: his sons and his brothers—12; ¹³ the sixth, to Bukkiah: his sons and his brothers—12; ¹⁴ the seventh, to Jesarelah: his sons and his brothers—12; ¹⁵ the eighth, to Jeshaiah: his sons and his brothers—12; ¹⁶ the ninth, to Mattaniah: his sons and his brothers—12; ¹⁷ the tenth, to Shimei: his sons and his brothers—12; ¹⁸ the eleventh to Azarel; his sons and his brothers—12; ¹⁹ the twelfth, to Hashabiah: his sons and his brothers—12; ²⁰ the thirteenth, to Shubael: his sons and his brothers—12; ²¹ the fourteenth, to Mattithiah: his sons and his brothers—12; ²² the fifteenth, to Jeremoth: his sons and his brothers—12; ²³ the sixteenth, to Hananiah: his sons and his brothers—12; ²⁴ the seventeenth, to Joshbekashah: his sons and his brothers—12; ²⁵ the eighteenth, to Hanani: his sons and his brothers—12; ²⁶ the nineteenth, to Mallothi: his sons and his brothers—12; ²⁷ the twentieth, to Eliathah; his sons and his brothers—12; ²⁸ the twenty-first, to Hothir: his sons and his brothers—12; ²⁹ the twenty-second, to Giddalti: his sons and his brothers—12; ³⁰ the twenty-third, to Mahazioth: his sons and his brothers—12; ³¹ the twenty-fourth, to Romamti-ezer: his sons and his brothers—12.

26 The divisions of the gatekeepers: Korahites: Meshelemiah son of Kore, of the sons of Asaph. ² Sons of Meshelemiah: Zechariah the firstborn, Jediael the second, Zebediah the third, Jathniel the fourth, ³ Elam the fifth, Jehohanan the sixth, Eliehoenai the seventh. ⁴ Sons of Obed-edom: Shemaiah the firstborn,

Jehozabad the second, Joah the third, Sacar the fourth, Nethanel the fifth, ⁵ Ammiel the sixth, Issachar the seventh, Peullethai the eighth—for God had blessed him. ⁶ To his son Shemaiah were born sons who exercised authority in their clans because they were men of substance. ⁷ The sons of Shemaiah: Othni, Rephael, Obed, Elzabad—his brothers, men of ability, were Elihu and Semachiah. ⁸ All these, sons of Obed-edom; they and their sons and brothers, strong and able men for the service—62 of Obed-edom. ⁹ Meshelemiah had sons and brothers, able men—18. ¹⁰ Hosah of the Merarites had sons: Shimri the chief (he was not the firstborn, but his father designated him chief), ¹¹ Hilkiah the second, Tebaliah the third, Zechariah the fourth. All the sons and brothers of Hosah—13.

¹² These are the divisions of the gatekeepers, by their chief men, [who worked in] shifts corresponding to their kinsmen, ministering in the House of the LORD. ¹³ They cast lots, small and great alike, by clans, for each gate.

¹⁴ The lot for the east [gate] fell to Shelemiah. Then they cast lots [for] Zechariah his son, a prudent counselor, and his lot came out to·be the north [gate]. ¹⁵ For Obed-edom, the south [gate], and for his sons, the vestibule. ¹⁶ For Shuppim and for Hosah, the west [gate], with the Shallecheth gate on the ascending highway. Watch corresponded to watch: ¹⁷ At the east—six Levites; at the north—four daily; at the south—four daily; at the vestibule—two by two; ¹⁸ at the colonnade on the west—four at the causeway and two at the colonnade. ¹⁹ These were the divisions of the gatekeepers of the sons of Korah and the sons of Merari.

²⁰ And the Levites: Ahijah over the treasuries of the House of God and the treasuries of the dedicated things. ²¹ The sons of Ladan: the sons of the Gershonites belonging to Ladan; the chiefs of the clans of Ladan, the Gershonite—Jehieli. ²² The sons of Jehieli: Zetham and Joel; his brother was over the treasuries of the House of the LORD.

²³ Of the Amramites, the Izharites, the Hebronites, the Uzzielites: ²⁴ Shebuel son of Gershom son of Moses was the chief officer

over the treasuries. [25] And his brothers: Eliezer, his son Rehabiah, his son Jeshaiah, his son Joram, his son Zichri, his son
Shelomith—[26] that Shelomith and his brothers were over all the
treasuries of dedicated things that were dedicated by King David
and the chiefs of the clans, and the officers of thousands and
hundreds and the other army officers; [27] they dedicated some of
the booty of the wars to maintain the House of the LORD. [28] All
that Samuel the seer had dedicated, and Saul son of Kish, and
Abner son of Ner, and Joab son of Zeruiah—or [what] any other
man had dedicated, was under the charge of Shelomith and his
brothers.

[29] The Izharites: Chenaniah and his sons were over Israel as
clerks and magistrates for affairs outside [the Sanctuary]. [30] The
Hebronites: Hashabiah and his brothers, capable men, 1700,
supervising Israel on the west side of the Jordan in all matters of
the LORD and the service of the king. [31] The Hebronites: Jeriah,
the chief of the Hebronites—they were investigated in the forti-
eth year of David's reign by clans of all their lines, and men of
substance were found among them in Jazer-gilead. [32] His brothers, able men, 2700, chiefs of clans—David put them in charge
of the Reubenites, the Gadites and the half-tribe of Manasseh in
all matters of God and matters of the king.

27 The number of Israelites—chiefs of clans, officers of thousands and hundreds and their clerks, who served the king in all
matters of the divisions, who worked in monthly shifts during all
the months of the year—each division, 24,000. [2] Over the first
division for the first month—Jashobeam son of Zabdiel; his division had 24,000. [3] Of the sons of Perez, he, the chief of all the
officers of the army, [served] for the first month. [4] Over the division of the second month—Dodai the Ahohite; Mikloth was chief
officer of his division; his division had 24,000. [5] The third army
officer for the third month—Benaiah son of Jehoiada, the chief
priest; his division had 24,000. [6] That was Benaiah, one of the

warriors of the thirty and over the thirty; and [over] his division was Ammizabad his son. ⁷ The fourth, for the fourth month, Asahel brother of Joab, and his son Zebadiah after him; his division had 24,000. ⁸ The fifth, for the fifth month, the officer Shamhut the Izrahite; his division had 24,000. ⁹ The sixth, for the sixth month, Ira son of Ikkesh the Tekoite; his division had 24,000. ¹⁰ The seventh, for the seventh month, Helez the Pelonite, of the Ephraimites; his division had 24,000. ¹¹ The eighth, for the eighth month, Sibbecai the Hushathite, of Zerah; his division had 24,000. ¹² The ninth, for the ninth month, Abiezer the Anathothite, of Benjamin; his division had 24,000. ¹³ The tenth, for the tenth month, Mahrai the Netophathite, of Zerah; his division had 24,000. ¹⁴ The eleventh, for the eleventh month, Menaiah the Pirathonite, of the Ephraimites; his division had 24,000. ¹⁵ The twelfth, for the twelfth month, Heldai the Netophathite, of Othniel; his division had 24,000.

¹⁶ Over the tribes of Israel: Reuben: the chief officer, Eliezer son of Zichri. Simeon: Shephatiah son of Maaca. ¹⁷ Levi: Hashabiah son of Kemuel. Aaron: Zadok. ¹⁸ Judah: Elijah, of the brothers of David. Issachar: Omri son of Michael. ¹⁹ Zebulun: Ishmaiah son of Obadiah. Naphtali: Jerimoth son of Azriel. ²⁰ Ephraimites: Hoshea son of Azaziah. The half-tribe of Manasseh: Joel son of Pedaiah. ²¹ Half Manasseh in Gilead: Iddo son of Zechariah. Benjamin: Jaasiel son of Abner. ²² Dan: Azarel son of Jeroham. These were the officers of the tribes of Israel.

²³ David did not take a census of those under twenty years of age, for the LORD had promised to make Israel as numerous as the stars of heaven. ²⁴ Joab son of Zeruiah did begin to count them, but he did not finish; wrath struck Israel on account of this, and the census was not entered into the account of the chronicles of King David.

²⁵ Over the royal treasuries: Azmaveth son of Adiel. Over the treasuries in the country—in the towns, the hamlets, and the citadels: Jonathan son of Uzziah. ²⁶ Over the field laborers in agricultural work: Ezri son of Chelub. ²⁷ Over the vineyards: Shi-

mei the Ramathite. And over the produce in the vineyards for wine-cellars: Zabdi the Shiphmite. 28 Over the olive trees and the sycamores in the Shephelah: Baal-hanan the Gederite. Over the oil-stores: Joash. 29 Over the cattle pasturing in Sharon: Shirtai the Sharonite. And over the cattle in the valleys: Shaphat son of Adlai. 30 Over the camels: Obil the Ishmaelite. And over the she-asses: Jehdeiah the Meronothite. 31 Over the flocks: Jaziz the Hagrite. All these were stewards of the property of King David. 32 Jonathan, David's uncle, was a counselor, a master, and a scribe: Jehiel son of Hachmoni was with the king's sons. 33 Ahitophel was a counselor to the king. Hushai the Archite was the king's friend. 34 After Ahitophel were Jehoiada son of Benaiah and Abiathar. The commander of the king's army was Joab.

28 David assembled all the officers of Israel—the tribal officers, the divisional officers who served the king, the captains of thousands and the captains of hundreds, and the stewards of all the property and cattle of the king and his sons, with the eunuchs and the warriors, all the men of substance—to Jerusalem. 2 King David rose to his feet and said, "Hear me, my brothers, my people! I wanted to build a resting-place for the Ark of the Covenant of the LORD, for the footstool of our God, and I laid aside material for building. 3 But God said to me, 'You will not build a house for My name, for you are a man of battles and have shed blood.' 4 The LORD God of Israel chose me of all my father's house to be king over Israel forever. For He chose Judah to be ruler, and of the family of Judah, my father's house; and of my father's sons, He preferred to make me king over all Israel; 5 and of all my sons—for many are the sons the LORD gave me— He chose my son Solomon to sit on the throne of the kingdom of the LORD over Israel. 6 He said to me, 'It will be your son Solomon who will build My House and My courts, for I have chosen him to be a son to Me, and I will be a father to him. 7 I will establish his kingdom forever, if he keeps firmly to the ob-

servance of My commandments and rules as he does now.' [8] And now, in the sight of all Israel, the congregation of the LORD, and in the hearing of our God, [I say:] Observe and apply yourselves to all the commandments of the LORD your God in order that you may possess this good land and bequeath it to your children after you forever.

[9] "And you, my son Solomon, know the God of your father, and serve Him with single mind and fervent heart, for the LORD searches all minds and discerns the design of every thought; if you seek Him He will be available to you, but if you forsake Him He will abandon you forever. [10] See then, the LORD chose you to build a House as the Sanctuary; be strong and do it."

[11] David gave his son Solomon the plan of the porch and its houses, its storerooms and its upper chambers and inner chambers; and of the place of the Ark-cover; [12] and the plan of all that he had by the spirit: of the courts of the House of the LORD and all its surrounding chambers, and of the treasuries of the House of God and of the treasuries of the holy things; [13] the divisions of priests and Levites for all the work of the service of the House of the LORD and all the vessels of the service of the House of the LORD; [14] and gold, the weight of gold for vessels of every sort of use; silver for all the vessels of silver by weight, for all the vessels of every kind of service; [15] the weight of the gold lampstands and their gold lamps, and the weight of the silver lampstands, each lampstand and its silver lamps, according to the use of every lampstand; [16] and the weight of gold for the tables of the rows of bread, for each table, and of silver for the silver tables; [17] and of the pure gold for the forks and the basins and the jars; and the weight of the gold bowls, every bowl; and the weight of the silver bowls, each and every bowl; [18] the weight of refined gold for the incense altar and the gold for the figure of the chariot—the cherubs—those with outspread wings screening the Ark of the Covenant of the LORD. [19] "All this that the LORD made me understand by His hand on me, I give you in writing—the plan of all the works."

²⁰ David said to his son Solomon, "Be strong and of good courage and do it; do not be afraid or dismayed, for the LORD God my God is with you; He will not fail you or forsake you till all the work on the House of the LORD is done. ²¹ Here are the divisions of the priests and Levites for all kinds of service of the House of God, and with you in all the work are willing men, skilled in all sorts of tasks; also the officers and all the people are at your command."

29

King David said to the entire assemblage, "God has chosen my son Solomon alone, an untried lad, although the work to be done is vast—for the temple*a* is not for a man but for the LORD God. ² I have spared no effort to lay up for the House of my God gold for golden objects, silver for silver, copper for copper, iron for iron, wood for wooden, onyx-stone and inlay-stone, stone of antimony and variegated colors—every kind of precious stone and much marble. ³ Besides, out of my solicitude for the House of my God, I gave over my private hoard of gold and silver to the House of my God—in addition to all that I laid aside for the holy House: ⁴ 3000 gold talents of Ophir gold, and 7000 talents of refined silver for covering the walls of the houses ⁵ (gold for golden objects, silver for silver for all the work)—into the hands of craftsmen. Now who is going to make a freewill offering and devote himself today to the LORD?"

⁶ The officers of the clans and the officers of the tribes of Israel and the captains of thousands and hundreds and the supervisors of the king's work made freewill offerings, ⁷ giving for the work of the House of God: 5000 talents of gold, 10,000 darics, 10,000 talents of silver, 18,000 talents of copper, 100,000 talents of iron. ⁸ Whoever had stones in his possession gave them to the treasury of the House of the LORD in the charge of Jehiel the Gershonite. ⁹ The people rejoiced over the freewill offerings they made, for with a whole heart they made freewill offerings to the LORD; King David also rejoiced very much.

ª Lit. "fortress."

10 David blessed the LORD in front of all the assemblage; David said, "Blessed are You, LORD, God of Israel our father, from eternity to eternity. 11 Yours, LORD, are greatness, might, splendor, triumph, and majesty—yes, all that is in heaven and on earth; to You, LORD, belong kingship and preeminence above all. 12 Riches and honor are Yours to dispense; You have dominion over all; with You are strength and might, and it is in Your power to make anyone great and strong. 13 Now, God, we praise You and extol Your glorious name. 14 Who am I and who are my people, that we should have the means to make such a freewill offering; but all is from You, and it is Your gift that we have given to You. 15 For we are sojourners with You, mere transients like our fathers; our days on earth are like a shadow, with nothing in prospect. 16 O LORD our God, all this great mass that we have laid aside to build You a House for Your holy name is from You, and it is all Yours. 17 I know, God, that You search the heart and desire uprightness; I, with upright heart, freely offered all these things; now Your people, who are present here—I saw them joyously making freewill offerings. 18 O LORD God of Abraham, Isaac, and Israel, our fathers, remember this to the eternal credit of the thoughts of Your people's hearts, and make their hearts constant toward You. 19 As to my son Solomon, give him a whole heart to observe Your commandments, Your admonitions, and Your laws, and to fulfill them all, and to build this temple*a* for which I have made provision."

20 David said to the whole assemblage, "Now bless the LORD your God." All the assemblage blessed the LORD God of their fathers, and bowed their heads low to the LORD and the king. 21 They offered sacrifices to the LORD and made burnt offerings to the LORD on the morrow of that day: 1000 bulls, 1000 rams, 1000 lambs, with their libations; [they made] sacrifices in great number for all Israel, 22 and they ate and drank in the presence of the LORD on that day with great joy. They again proclaimed Solomon son of David king, and they anointed him as ruler before the LORD, and Zadok as high priest. 23 Solomon successfully

a *Lit. "fortress."*

took over the throne of the LORD as king instead of his father David, and all went well with him. All Israel accepted him; ²⁴ all the officials and the warriors, and the sons of King David as well, gave their hand in support of King Solomon. ²⁵ The LORD made Solomon exceedingly great in the eyes of all Israel, and endowed him with a regal majesty that no king of Israel before him ever had.

²⁶ Thus David son of Jesse reigned over all Israel; ²⁷ the length of his reign over Israel was 40 years: he reigned 7 years in Hebron and 33 years in Jerusalem. ²⁸ He died at a ripe old age, having enjoyed long life, riches and honor, and his son Solomon reigned in his stead. ²⁹ The acts of King David, early and late, are recorded in the history of Samuel the seer, the history of Nathan the prophet, and the history of Gad the seer, ³⁰ together with all the mighty deeds of his kingship and the events that befell him and Israel and all the kingdoms of the earth.

דברי הימים ב

II CHRONICLES

דברי הימים ב

II CHRONICLES

1 [a]Solomon son of David took firm hold of his kingdom, for the LORD his God was with him and made him exceedingly great. [2] Solomon summoned all Israel—the officers of thousands and of hundreds, and the judges, and all the chiefs of all Israel, the heads of the clans. [3] Then Solomon, and all the assemblage with him, went to the shrine at Gibeon, for the Tent of Meeting, which Moses the servant of the LORD had made in the wilderness, was there. ([4] But the Ark of God David had brought up from Kiriath-jearim to the place which David had prepared for it; for he had pitched a tent for it in Jerusalem.) [5] The bronze altar, which Bezalel son of Uri son of Hur had made, was also there before the Tabernacle of the LORD, and Solomon and the assemblage resorted to it. [6] There Solomon ascended the bronze altar before the LORD, which was at the Tent of Meeting, and on it sacrificed a thousand burnt offerings.

[7] That night, the LORD appeared to Solomon and said to him, "Ask, what shall I grant you?" [8] Solomon said to God, "You dealt most graciously with my father David, and now You have made me king in his stead. [9] Now, O LORD God, let Your promise to my father David be fulfilled; for You have made me king over a people as numerous as the dust of the earth. [10] Grant me then the wisdom and the knowledge [b-]to lead this people,[-b] for who can govern Your great people?" [11] God said to Solomon, "Because you want this, and have not asked for wealth, property, and glory, nor have you asked for the life of your enemy, or long life for yourself, but you have asked for the wisdom and the knowledge to be able to govern My people over whom I have made you king,

[a] With vv. 3–13, cf. I Kings 3.4–15; with vv. 14–17, cf. I Kings 10.26–29.
[b-b] Lit. "that I may go out before this people and come in."

¹² wisdom and knowledge are granted to you, and I grant you also wealth, property, and glory, the like of which no king before you has had, nor shall any after you have." ¹³ From the shrine at Gibeon, from the Tent of Meeting, Solomon went to Jerusalem and reigned over Israel.

¹⁴ Solomon assembled chariots and horsemen; he had 1400 chariots and 12,000 horses that he stationed in the chariot towns and with the king in Jerusalem. ¹⁵ The king made silver and gold as plentiful in Jerusalem as stones, and cedars as plentiful as the sycamores in the Shephelah. ¹⁶ Solomon's horses were imported from Egypt and from Que; the king's traders would buy them from Que at the market price. ¹⁷ A chariot imported from Egypt cost 600 shekels of silver, and a horse 150. These in turn were exported by them*c* to all the kings of the Hittites and the kings of the Arameans.

¹⁸ Then Solomon resolved to build a House for the name of the
2 LORD and a royal palace for himself.

*a*Solomon mustered 70,000 basket carriers and 80,000 quarriers in the hills, with 3600 men supervising them. ² Solomon sent this message to King Huram of Tyre, "In view of what you did for my father David in sending him cedars to build a palace for his residence—³ see, I intend to build a House for the name of the LORD my God; I will dedicate it to Him for making incense offering of sweet spices in His honor, for the regular rows of bread, and for the morning and evening burnt offerings on sabbaths, new moons, and festivals, as is Israel's eternal duty. ⁴ The House that I intend to build will be great, inasmuch as our God is greater than all gods. ⁵ Who indeed is capable of building a House for Him! Even the heavens to their uttermost reaches cannot contain Him, and who am I that I should build Him a House—except as a place for making burnt offerings to Him? ⁶ Now send me a craftsman to work in gold, silver, bronze, and iron, and in purple, crimson, and blue yarn, and who knows how to engrave, alongside the craftsmen I have here in Judah and in

c That is, Solomon's dealers.

a Cf. I Kings 5.

Jerusalem, whom my father David provided. ⁷ Send me cedars, cypress, and algum wood from the Lebanon, for I know that your servants are skilled at cutting the trees of Lebanon. My servants will work with yours ⁸ to provide me with a great stock of timber; for the House which I intend to build will be singularly great. ⁹ I have allocated for your servants, the wood-cutters who fell the trees, 20,000 kor of crushed wheat and 20,000 kor of barley, 20,000 bath of wine and 20,000 bath of oil."

¹⁰ Huram, king of Tyre, sent Solomon this written message in reply, "Because the LORD loved His people, He made you king over them."

¹¹ Huram continued, "Blessed is the LORD, God of Israel, who made the heavens and the earth, who gave King David a wise son, endowed with intelligence and understanding, to build a House for the LORD and a royal palace for himself. ¹² Now I am sending you a skillful and intelligent man, my master*b* Huram,¹³ the son of a Danite woman, his father a Tyrian. He is skilled at working in gold, bronze, iron, precious stones, and wood; in purple, blue, and crimson yarn and in fine linen; and at engraving and designing whatever will be required of him, alongside your craftsmen and the craftsmen of my lord, your father David. ¹⁴ As to the wheat, barley, oil, and wine which my lord mentioned, let him send them to his servants. ¹⁵ We undertake to cut down as many trees of Lebanon as you need, and deliver them to you as rafts by sea to Jaffa; you will transport them to Jerusalem."

¹⁶ Solomon took a census of all the aliens who were in the land of Israel, besides the census taken by his father David, and they were found to be 153,600. ¹⁷ He made 70,000 of them basket carriers, and 80,000 of them quarriers, with 3600 supervisors to see that the people worked.

3 *a*Then Solomon began to build the House of the LORD in Jerusalem on Mount Moriah, where [the LORD] had appeared to his father David, at the place which David had designated, at the

ᵇ *Lit. "my father."*

ᵃ *With vv. 2–17, cf. I Kings 6, 7.1–22.*

563

threshing floor of Ornan the Jebusite. [2] He began to build on the second day of the second month of the fourth year of his reign. [3] These were the dimensions Solomon established for building the House of God: its length in cubits, by the former measure, was 60, and its breadth was 20. [4] The length of the porch in front [was equal] to the breadth of the House—20 cubits, and its height was 120. Inside he overlaid it with pure gold. [5] The House itself he paneled with cypress wood. He overlaid it with fine gold and embossed on it palms and chains. [6] He studded the House with precious stones for decoration; the gold was from Parvaim. [7] He overlaid the House with gold—the beams, the thresholds, its walls and doors; he carved cherubim on the walls. [8] He made the Holy of Holies: its length was [equal to] the breadth of the house —20 cubits, and its breadth was 20 cubits. He overlaid it with 600 talents of fine gold. [9] The weight of the nails was 50 shekels of gold; the upper chambers he overlaid with gold. [10] He made two sculptured cherubim in the Holy of Holies, and they were overlaid with gold. [11] The outspread wings of the cherubim were 20 cubits across: one wing five cubits long touching one wall of the House, and the other wing five cubits long touching the wing of the other cherub; [12] one wing of the other [cherub] five cubits long extending to the other wall of the House, and its other wing five cubits long touching the wing of the first cherub. [13] The wingspread of these cherubim was thus 20 cubits across, and they were standing up facing the House. [14] He made the curtain of blue, purple, and crimson yarn and fine linen, and he worked cherubim into it. [15] At the front of the House he made two columns 35 cubits high; the capitals*b* on top of them were five cubits high. [16] He made chainwork in the inner Sanctuary and set it on the top of the columns; he made a hundred pomegranates and set them into the chainwork. [17] He erected the columns in front of the Great Hall, one to its right and one to its left; the one to the right was called Jachin, and the one to the left, Boaz.

b *Meaning of Heb. uncertain.*

4 *a*He made an altar of bronze 20 cubits long, 20 cubits wide, and 20 cubits high.

2 He made the sea*b* of cast metal ten cubits across from brim to brim, perfectly round; it was five cubits high, and its circumference was 30 cubits. 3 Beneath were figures of oxen set all around it, of ten cubits, encircling the sea; the oxen were in two rows, cast in one piece with it. 4 It stood upon 12 oxen: three faced north, three faced west, three faced south, and three faced east, with the sea resting upon them; their haunches were all turned inward. 5 It was a handbreadth thick, and its brim was made like that of a cup, like the petals of a lily. It held 3,000 bath.

6 He made ten bronze lavers for washing; he set five on the right and five on the left; they would rinse off in them the parts of the burnt offering; but the sea served the priests for washing. 7 He made ten lampstands of gold as prescribed, and placed them in the Great Hall, five on the right and five on the left. 8 He made ten tables and placed them in the Great Hall, five on the right and five on the left. He made one hundred gold basins. 9 He built the court of the priests and the great court, and doors for the great court; he overlaid the doors with bronze. 10 He set the sea on the right side, at the southeast corner.

11 Huram made the pails, the shovels, and the basins. With that Huram completed the work he had undertaken for King Solomon in the House of God: 12 the two columns, the globes, and the two capitals on top of the columns; and the two pieces of network to cover the two globes of the capitals on top of the columns; 13 the 400 pomegranates for the two pieces of network, two rows of pomegranates for each network, to cover the two globes of the capitals on top of the columns; 14 he made the stands and the lavers upon the stands; 15 one sea with the twelve oxen beneath it; 16 the pails, the shovels, and the bowls.*c* And all the vessels made for King Solomon for the House of the LORD by Huram his master were of burnished bronze. 17 The king had them cast in

---

a *Cf. I Kings 7.23–50.*
b *I.e. a large basin.*
c *Or "forks."*

molds dug out of the earth, in the plain of the Jordan between Succoth and Zeredah. [18] Solomon made a very large number of vessels; the weight of the bronze used could not be reckoned. [19] And Solomon made all the furnishings that were in the House of God: the altar of gold; the tables for the bread of display; [20] the lampstands and their lamps, to burn as prescribed in front of the inner Sanctuary, of solid gold; [21] and the petals, lamps, and tongs, of purest gold; [22] the snuffers, basins, ladles, and fire pans, of solid gold; and the entrance to the House: the doors of the innermost part of the House, the Holy of Holies, and the doors of the Great Hall of the House, of gold.

5 [a]When all the work that King Solomon undertook for the House of the LORD was completed, Solomon brought the things that his father David had consecrated—the silver, the gold, and the utensils—and deposited them in the treasury of the House of God.

[2] Then Solomon convoked the elders of Israel—all the heads of the tribes and the ancestral chiefs of the Israelites—in Jerusalem, to bring up the Ark of the Covenant of the LORD from the City of David, that is, Zion.

[3] All the men of Israel assembled before the king at the Feast,[b] in the seventh month. [4] When all the elders of Israel had come, the Levites carried the Ark. [5] They brought up the Ark and the Tent of Meeting and all the holy vessels that were in the Tent— the Levite priests brought them up. [6] Meanwhile, King Solomon and the whole community of Israel, who had gathered to him before the Ark, were sacrificing sheep and oxen in such abundance that they could not be numbered or counted.

[7] The priests brought the Ark of the LORD's Covenant to its place in the inner Sanctuary of the House, in the Holy of Holies, beneath the wings of the cherubim; [8] for the cherubim had their wings spread out over the place of the Ark so that the cherubim covered the Ark and its poles from above. [9] The poles projected

[a] Cf. I Kings 7.51–8.11.
[b] I.e. of Tabernacles.

beyond the Ark and the ends of the poles were visible from the front of the inner Sanctuary, but they could not be seen from the outside; and there they remain to this day. [10] There was nothing inside the Ark but the two tablets which Moses placed [there] at Horeb, when the LORD made [a Covenant] with the Israelites after their departure from Egypt. [11] When the priests came out of the Sanctuary—all the priests present had sanctified themselves, without keeping to the set divisions—[12] all the Levite singers, Asaph, Heman, Jeduthun, their sons and their brothers, dressed in fine linen, holding cymbals, harps, and lyres, were standing to the east of the altar, and with them were 120 priests who blew trumpets. [13] The trumpeters and the singers joined in unison to praise and extol the LORD; and as the sound of the trumpets, cymbals, and other musical instruments, and the praise of the LORD, "For He is good, for His steadfast love is eternal," grew louder, the House, the House of the LORD, was filled with a cloud. [14] The priests could not stay and perform the service because of the cloud, for the glory of the LORD filled the House of God.

6 [a]Then Solomon declared:
"The LORD has chosen
To abide in a thick cloud;
[2] I have built for You
A stately House,
And a place where You
May dwell forever."
[3] Then, as the whole congregation of Israel stood, the king turned and blessed the whole congregation of Israel. [4] He said, "Blessed is the LORD God of Israel, [b]who made a promise to my father David and fulfilled it.[b] For He said, [5] 'From the time I brought My people out of the land of Egypt, I never chose a city from among all the tribes of Israel to build a House where My name might abide; nor did I choose anyone to be the leader of

[a] Cf. I. Kings 8.12–53.
[b-b] Lit. "who spoke with His own mouth a promise to my father David and has fulfilled with His own hands."

my people Israel. 6 But then I chose Jerusalem for My name to abide there, and I chose David to rule My people Israel.'

7 "Now my father David had wanted to build a House for the name of the LORD God of Israel. 8 But the LORD said to my father David, 'As for your wanting to build a House for My name, you do well to want that. 9 However, you shall not build the House; your son, the issue of your loins, he shall build the House for My name.' 10 Now the LORD has fulfilled the promise that He made. I have succeeded*c* my father David and have ascended the throne of Israel, as the LORD promised. I have built the House for the name of the LORD God of Israel, 11 and there I have set the Ark containing the Covenant which the LORD made with the Israelites."

12 Then, standing before the altar of the LORD in front of the whole congregation of Israel, he spread forth his hands. 13 Solomon had made a bronze platform*d* and placed it in the midst of the Great Court; it was five cubits long and five cubits wide and three cubits high. He stood on it; then, kneeling in front of the whole congregation of Israel, he spread forth his hands to heaven 14 and said, "O LORD God of Israel, there is no god like You in the heavens and on the earth, You who steadfastly maintain the Covenant with Your servants who walk before You with all their heart; 15 You who have kept the promises You made to Your servant, my father David; You made a promise and have fulfilled it—as is now the case. 16 And now, O LORD God of Israel, keep that promise that You made to Your servant, my father David, 'You shall never lack a descendant in My sight sitting on the throne of Israel if only your children will look to their way and walk in the [path] of My teachings as you have walked before Me.' 17 Now, therefore, O God of Israel, let the promise that You made to Your servant, my father David, be confirmed.

18 "Does God really dwell with man on earth? Even the heavens to their uttermost reaches cannot contain You, how much less this House that I have built! 19 Yet turn, O LORD my God, to the prayer and supplication of Your servant, and hear the cry and the

c Lit. "risen in place of."
d Meaning of Heb. uncertain.

prayer which Your servant offers to You. ²⁰ May Your eyes be open day and night toward this House, toward the place where You have resolved to make Your name abide; may You heed the prayers which Your servant offers toward this place. ²¹ And when You hear the supplications which Your servant and Your people Israel offer toward this place, give heed in Your heavenly abode—give heed and pardon.

²² "If a man commits an offense against his fellow, and an oath is exacted from him, causing him to utter an imprecation against himself, and he comes with his imprecation before Your altar in this House, ²³ may You hear in heaven and take action to judge Your servants, requiting him who is in the wrong by bringing down the punishment of his conduct on his head, vindicating him who is in the right by rewarding him according to his righteousness.

²⁴ "Should Your people Israel be defeated by an enemy because they have sinned against You, and then once again acknowledge Your name and offer prayer and supplication to You in this House, ²⁵ may You hear in heaven and pardon the sin of Your people Israel, and restore them to the land that You gave to them and to their fathers.

²⁶ "Should the heavens be shut up and there be no rain because they have sinned against You, and then they pray toward this place and acknowledge Your name and repent of their sins, because You humbled them, ²⁷ may You hear in heaven and pardon the sin of Your servants, Your people Israel, when You have shown them the proper way in which they are to walk, and send down rain upon the land which You gave to Your people as their heritage. ²⁸ So, too, if there is a famine in the land, if there is pestilence, blight, mildew, locusts, or caterpillars, or if an enemy oppresses them in any of the settlements of their land.

"In any plague and in any disease, ²⁹ any prayer or supplication offered by any person among all Your people Israel—each of whom knows his affliction and his pain—when he spreads forth his hands toward this House, ³⁰ may You hear in Your heavenly abode, and pardon. Deal with each man according to his ways as You know his heart to be—for You alone know the hearts of all men—³¹ so that they may revere You all the days that they live on the land that You gave to our fathers.

³² "Or if a foreigner who is not of Your people Israel comes from a distant land for the sake of Your great name, Your mighty hand, and Your outstretched arm, if he comes to pray toward this House, ³³ may You hear in Your heavenly abode and grant whatever the foreigner appeals to You for. Thus all the peoples of the earth will know Your name and revere You, as does Your people Israel; and they will recognize that Your name is attached to this House that I have built.

³⁴ "When Your people take the field against their enemies in a campaign on which You send them, and they pray to You in the direction of the city which You have chosen and the House which I have built to Your name, ³⁵ may You hear in heaven their prayer and supplication and uphold their cause.

³⁶ "When they sin against You—for there is no person who does not sin—and You are angry with them and deliver them to the enemy, and their captors carry them off to an enemy land, near or far; ³⁷ and they take it to heart in the land to which they have been carried off, and repent and make supplication to You in the land of their captivity, saying, 'We have sinned, we have acted perversely, we have acted wickedly,' ³⁸ and they turn back to You with all their heart and soul, in the land of their captivity where they were carried off, and pray in the direction of their land which You gave to their fathers and the city which You have chosen, and toward the House which I have built for Your name— ³⁹ may You hear their prayer and supplication in Your heavenly abode, uphold their cause, and pardon Your people who have sinned against You. ⁴⁰ Now My God, may Your eyes be open and Your ears attentive to prayer from this place, and now,

⁴¹ Advance, O LORD God, to your resting-place,
You and Your mighty Ark.
Your priests, O LORD God, are clothed in triumph;

Your loyal ones will rejoice in [Your] goodness.
42 O LORD God,
do not reject Your anointed one;
remember the loyalty of Your servant David."

7 *When Solomon finished praying, fire descended from heaven and consumed the burnt offering and the sacrifices, and the glory of the LORD filled the House. 2 The priests could not enter the House of the LORD, for the glory of the LORD filled the House of the LORD. 3 All the Israelites witnessed the descent of the fire and the glory of the LORD on the House; they knelt with their faces to the ground and prostrated themselves, praising the LORD, "For He is good, for His steadfast love is eternal."

4 Then the king and all the people offered sacrifices before the LORD. 5 King Solomon offered as sacrifices 22,000 oxen and 120,000 sheep; thus the king and all the people dedicated the House of God. 6 The priests stood at their watches; the Levites with the instruments for the LORD's music which King David had made to praise the LORD, "For His steadfast love is eternal," by means of the psalms of David that they knew. The priests opposite them blew trumpets while all Israel were standing.

7 Solomon consecrated the center of the court in front of the House of the LORD, because he presented there the burnt offerings and the fat parts of the offerings of well-being, since the bronze altar that Solomon had made was not able to hold the burnt offerings, the meal offerings, and the fat parts. 8 At that time Solomon kept the Feast for seven days—all Israel with him —a great assemblage from Lebo-hamath to the Wadi of Egypt.

9 On the eighth day they held a solemn gathering; they observed the dedication of the altar seven days, and the Feast seven days. 10 On the twenty-third day of the seventh month he dismissed the people to their homes, rejoicing and in good spirits over the goodness that the LORD had shown to David and Solomon and His people Israel.

ª *Cf. I Kings 8.54–9.9.*

[11] Thus Solomon finished building the House of the LORD and the royal palace; Solomon succeeded in everything he had set his heart on accomplishing with regard to the House of the LORD and his palace. [12] The LORD appeared to Solomon at night and said to him, "I have heard your prayer and have chosen this site as My House of sacrifice. [13] If I shut up the heavens and there is no rain; if I command the locusts to ravage the land; or if I let loose pestilence against My people, [14] when My people, who bear My name, humble themselves, pray, and seek My favor and turn from their evil ways, I will hear in My heavenly abode and forgive their sins and heal their land. [15] Now My eyes will be open and My ears attentive to the prayers from this place. [16] And now I have chosen and consecrated this House that My name be there forever. My eyes and My heart shall always be there. [17] As for you, if you walk before Me as your father David walked before Me, doing all that I have commanded you, keeping My laws and rules, [18] then I will establish your royal throne over Israel forever, in accordance with the Covenant I made with your father David, saying, 'You shall never lack a descendant ruling over Israel.' [19] But if you turn away from Me and forsake My laws and commandments which I set before you, and go and serve other gods and worship them, [20] then I will uproot them[b] from My land which I gave them, and this House which I consecrated to My name I shall cast out of my sight, and make it a proverb and a byword among all peoples. [21] And as for this House, once so exalted, everyone passing by it shall be appalled and say, 'Why did the LORD do thus to this land and to this House?' [22] And the reply will be, 'It is because they forsook the LORD God of their fathers who freed them from the land of Egypt, and adopted other gods and worshiped them and served them; therefore He brought all this calamity upon them.' "

---

[b] *I.e. Israel; cf. I Kings 9.7.*

8 ^aAt the end of twenty years, during which Solomon constructed the House of the LORD and his palace—² Solomon also rebuilt the cities that Huram had given to him,^b and settled Israelites in them—³ Solomon marched against Hamath-zobah and overpowered it. ⁴ He built Tadmor in the desert and all the garrison towns which he built in Hamath. ⁵ He built Upper Beth-horon and Lower Beth-horon as fortified cities with walls, gates, and bars, ⁶ as well as Baalath and all of Solomon's garrison towns, chariot towns, and cavalry towns—everything that Solomon desired to build in Jerusalem and in the Lebanon, and throughout the territory that he ruled. ⁷ All the people that were left of the Hittites, Amorites, Perizzites, Hivites, and Jebusites, none of whom were of Israelite stock—⁸ those of their descendants who were left after them in the land, whom the Israelites had not annihilated—these Solomon subjected to forced labor, as is still the case. ⁹ But the Israelites, none of whom Solomon enslaved for his works, served as soldiers and as his chief officers, and as commanders of his chariotry and cavalry. ¹⁰ These were King Solomon's prefects—250 foremen over the people. ¹¹ Solomon brought up Pharaoh's daughter from the City of David to the palace which he had built for her, for he said, "No wife of mine shall dwell in a palace of King David of Israel, for [the area] is sacred since the Ark of the LORD has entered it."

¹² At that time, Solomon offered burnt offerings on the altar which he had built in front of the porch. ¹³ What was due for each day he sacrificed according to the commandment of Moses for the sabbaths, the new moons, and the thrice-yearly festivals—the Feast of Unleavened Bread, the Feast of Weeks, and the Feast of Booths. ¹⁴ Following the prescription of his father David, he set up the divisions of the priests for their duties, and the Levites for their watches, to praise and to serve alongside the priests, according to each day's requirement, and the gatekeepers in their watches, gate by gate, for such was the commandment of David,

^a *Cf. I Kings 9.10–28.*
^b *Lit. "Solomon."*

the man of God. ¹⁵ They did not depart from the commandment of the king relating to the priests and the Levites in all these matters and also relating to the treasuries. ¹⁶ And all of Solomon's work was well executed from the day the House of the LORD was founded until the House of the LORD was completed to perfection.

¹⁷ At that time Solomon went to Ezion-geber and to Eloth on the seacoast of the land of Edom. ¹⁸ Huram sent him, under the charge of servants, a fleet with a crew of expert seamen; they went with Solomon's men to Ophir, and obtained gold there in the amount of 450 talents, which they brought to King Solomon.

9 ^aThe queen of Sheba heard of Solomon's fame, and came to Jerusalem to test Solomon with hard questions, accompanied by a very large retinue, including camels bearing spices, a great quantity of gold, and precious stones. When she came to Solomon, she spoke to him of all that she had on her mind. ² Solomon had answers for all her questions; there was nothing that Solomon did not know, nothing to which he could not give her an answer.

³ When the queen of Sheba saw how wise Solomon was and the palace he had built, ⁴ the fare of his table, the seating of his courtiers, the service and attire of his attendants, his butlers and their attire, and the procession with which he went up to the House of the LORD, it took her breath away. ⁵ She said to the king, "What I heard in my own land about you and your wisdom was true. ⁶ I did not believe what they said until I came and saw with my own eyes that not even the half of your great wisdom had been described to me; you surpass the report that I heard. ⁷ How fortunate are your men and how fortunate are these courtiers of yours who are always in attendance on you and can hear your wisdom! ⁸ Blessed is the LORD your God, who favored you and set you on His throne as a king before the LORD. It is because of your God's love for Israel and in order to establish them forever

^a *Cf. I. Kings 10, 11.41–43.*

that He made you king over them to execute righteous justice."

9 She presented the king with 120 talents of gold, and a vast quantity of spices and precious stones. There were no such spices as those which the queen of Sheba gave to King Solomon— 10 also, the servants of Huram and Solomon who brought gold from Ophir brought algum-wood and precious stones. 11 The king made of the algum-wood ramps for the House of the LORD and for the royal palace, and lyres and harps for the musicians, whose like had never before been seen in the land of Judah— 12 King Solomon, in turn, gave the queen of Sheba everything she expressed a desire for, exceeding a return for what she had brought to the king. Then she and her courtiers left and returned to her own land.

13 The gold which Solomon received every year weighed 666 gold talents, 14 besides what traders and merchants brought, and the gold and silver that all the kings of Arabia and governors of the regions brought to Solomon. 15 King Solomon made 200 shields of beaten gold—600 shekels of beaten gold for each shield, 16 and 300 bucklers of beaten gold—300 [shekels] of gold for each buckler. The king placed them in the Lebanon Forest House. 17 The king also made a large throne of ivory, overlaid with pure gold. 18 Six steps led up to the throne; and the throne had a golden footstool attached to it, and arms on either side of the seat. Two lions stood beside the arms, 19 and twelve lions stood on the six steps, six on either side. None such was ever made for any other kingdom. 20 All of King Solomon's drinking vessels were of gold, and all the utensils of the Lebanon Forest House were of pure gold; silver counted for nothing in Solomon's days. 21 The king's fleet traveled to Tarshish with Huram's servants. Once every three years, the Tarshish fleet came in, bearing gold and silver, ivory, apes, and peacocks.

22 King Solomon surpassed all the kings of the earth in wealth and wisdom. 23 All the kings of the earth came to pay homage to Solomon and to listen to the wisdom with which God had endowed him. 24 Each brought his tribute—silver and gold objects,

robes, weapons, and spices, horses and mules—in the amount
due each year. [25] Solomon had 4000 stalls for horses and chariots,
and 12,000 horsemen, which he stationed in the chariot towns
and with the king in Jerusalem. [26] He ruled over all the kings from
the Euphrates to the land of the Philistines and to the border
of Egypt. [27] The king made silver as plentiful in Jerusalem as
stones, and cedars as plentiful as sycamores in the Shephelah.
[28] Horses were brought for Solomon from Egypt and all the
lands. [29] The other events of Solomon's reign, early and late, are
recorded in the chronicle of the prophet Nathan and in the
prophecies of Ahijah the Shilonite and in the visions of Jedo the
seer concerning Jeroboam son of Nebat. [30] Solomon reigned
forty years over all Israel in Jerusalem. [31] Solomon slept with his
fathers and was buried in the city of his father David; his son
Rehoboam succeeded him as king.

10 [a]Rehoboam went to Shechem, for all Israel had come to
Shechem to acclaim him king. [2] Jeroboam son of Nebat learned
of it while he was in Egypt where he had fled from King Solomon,
and Jeroboam returned from Egypt. [3] They sent for him; and
Jeroboam and all Israel came and spoke to Rehoboam as follows:
[4] "Your father made our yoke heavy. Now lighten the harsh labor
and the heavy yoke which your father laid on us, and we will serve
you." [5] He answered them, "Come back to me in three days." So
the people went away.

[6] King Rehoboam took counsel with the elders who had served
during the lifetime of his father Solomon. He said, "What answer
do you counsel to give these people?" [7] They answered him, "If
you will be good to these people and appease them and speak to
them with kind words, they will be your servants always." [8] But
he ignored the counsel that the elders gave him, and took counsel
with the young men who had grown up with him and were serving
him. [9] "What," he asked, "do you counsel that we reply to these
people who said to me, 'Lighten the yoke that your father laid on
us'?" [10] And the young men who had grown up with him an-

[a] *Cf. I Kings 12.1–19.*

swered, "Speak thus to the people who said to you, 'Your father made our yoke heavy, now you make it lighter for us.' Say to them, 'My little finger is thicker than my father's loins. [11] My father imposed a heavy yoke on you, and I will add to your yoke; my father flogged you with whips, but I [will do so] with scorpions.' "

[12] Jeroboam and all the people came to Rehoboam on the third day, since the king had told them, "Come back on the third day." [13] The king answered them harshly; thus King Rehoboam ignored the elders' counsel. [14] He spoke to them in accordance with the counsel of the young men, and said, *b*-"I will make-*b* your yoke heavy, and I will add to it; my father flogged you with whips, but I [will do so] with scorpions." [15] The king did not listen to the people, for God had brought it about in order that the LORD might fulfill the promise which He had made through Ahijah the Shilonite to Jeroboam son of Nebat. [16] When all Israel [saw] that the king had not listened to them, the people answered the king:

"We have no portion in David,
No share in Jesse's son!
To your tents, O Israel!
Now look to your own house, O David."

So all Israel returned to their homes.*c* [17] But Rehoboam continued to reign over the Israelites who lived in the towns of Judah. [18] King Rehoboam sent out Hadoram, who was in charge of the forced labor, but the Israelites pelted him to death with stones. Thereupon, King Rehoboam hurriedly mounted his chariot and fled to Jerusalem. [19] Israel has been in revolt against the house of David to this day.

11 *a*When Rehoboam arrived in Jerusalem, he mustered the house of Judah and Benjamin, 180,000 picked fighting men, to make war with Israel in order to restore the kingdom to Rehoboam. [2] But the word of the LORD came to Shemaiah, the man of God, [3] "Say to Rehoboam son of Solomon king of Judah, and to all Israel in Judah and Benjamin: [4] Thus said the LORD: You shall

---

b-b *Some mss. and printed editions read "my father made"; cf. I Kings 12.14.*
c *Lit. "tents."*

a With 11.1–4, cf. I Kings 12.21–24.

not set out to make war on your kinsmen. Let every man return to his home, for this thing has been brought about by Me." They heeded the words of the LORD and refrained from marching against Jeroboam. ⁵ Rehoboam dwelt in Jerusalem and built fortified towns in Judah. ⁶ He built up Bethlehem, and Etam, and Tekoa, ⁷ and Beth-zur, and Soco, and Adullam, ⁸ and Gath, and Mareshah, and Ziph, ⁹ and Adoraim, and Lachish, and Azekah, ¹⁰ and Zorah, and Aijalon, and Hebron, which are in Judah and in Benjamin, as fortified towns. ¹¹ He strengthened the fortified towns and put commanders in them, along with stores of food, oil, and wine, ¹² and shields and spears in every town. He strengthened them exceedingly; thus Judah and Benjamin were his.

¹³ The priests and the Levites, from all their territories throughout Israel, presented themselves to him. ¹⁴ The Levites had left their pasturelands and their holdings and had set out for Judah and Jerusalem, for Jeroboam and his sons had prevented them from serving the LORD, ¹⁵ having appointed his own priests for the shrines, goat-demons, and calves which he had made. ¹⁶ From all the tribes of Israel, those intent on seeking the LORD God of Israel followed them to Jerusalem, to sacrifice to the LORD God of their fathers. ¹⁷ They strengthened the kingdom of Judah, and supported Rehoboam son of Solomon for three years, for they followed the ways of David and Solomon for three years.

¹⁸ Rehoboam married Mahalath daughter of Jerimoth son of David, and Abihail daughter of Eliab son of Jesse. ¹⁹ She bore him sons: Jeush, Shemariah, and Zaham. ²⁰ He then took Maacah daughter of Absalom; she bore him Abijah, Attai, Ziza, and Shelomith. ²¹ Rehoboam loved Maacah daughter of Absalom more than his other wives and concubines—for he took eighteen wives and sixty concubines; he begot twenty-eight sons and sixty daughters. ²² Rehoboam designated Abijah son of Maacah as chief and leader among his brothers, for he intended him to be his successor. ²³ He prudently distributed all his sons throughout the regions of Judah and Benjamin and throughout the fortified

towns; he provided them with abundant food, and he sought many wives for them.

12 When the kingship of Rehoboam was firmly established, and he grew strong, he abandoned the Teaching of the LORD, he and all Israel with him.
² In the fifth year of King Rehoboam, King Shishak of Egypt marched against Jerusalem—for they had trespassed against the LORD—³ with 1200 chariots, 60,000 horsemen and innumerable troops who came with him from Egypt: Lybians, Sukkites and Kushites. ⁴ He took the fortified towns of Judah and advanced on Jerusalem. ⁵ The prophet Shemaiah came to Rehoboam and the officers of Judah, who had assembled in Jerusalem because of Shishak, and said to them, "Thus said the LORD: You have abandoned Me, so I am abandoning you to Shishak." ⁶ Then the officers of Israel and the king humbled themselves and declared, "The LORD is in the right." ⁷ When the LORD saw that they had submitted, the word of the LORD came to Shemaiah, saying, "Since they have humbled themselves, I will not destroy them but will grant them some measure of deliverance, and My wrath will not be poured out on Jerusalem through Shishak. ⁸ They will be subject to him, and they will know the difference between serving Me and serving the kingdoms of the earth." King Shishak of Egypt marched against Jerusalem. ⁹ ᵃHe took away the treasures of the House of the LORD and the treasures of the royal palace; he took away everything; he took away the golden shields that Solomon had made. ¹⁰ King Rehoboam had bronze shields made in their place, and entrusted them to the officers of the guardᵇ who guarded the entrance to the royal palace. ¹¹ Whenever the king entered the House of the LORD, the guards would carry them and then bring them back to the armory of the guards. ¹² After he had humbled himself, the anger of the LORD was averted and He did not destroy him entirely; in Judah, too, good things were found.

ᵃ *With vv. 9–16, cf. I Kings 14.26–31.*
ᵇ *Lit. "runners."*

¹³ King Rehoboam grew strong in Jerusalem and exercised kingship. Rehoboam was forty-one years old when he became king, and he reigned seventeen years in Jerusalem—the city the LORD had chosen out of all the tribes of Israel to establish His name there. His mother's name was Naamah the Ammonitess. ¹⁴ He did what was wrong, for he had not set his heart to seek the LORD. ¹⁵ The deeds of Rehoboam, early and late, are recorded in the chronicles of the prophet Shemaiah and Iddo the seer, in the manner of genealogy. There was continuous war between Rehoboam and Jeroboam. ¹⁶ Rehoboam slept with his fathers and was buried in the City of David. His son Abijah succeeded him as king.

13 In the eighteenth year of King Jeroboam, Abijah became king over Judah. ² He reigned three years in Jerusalem; his mother's name was Micaiah daughter of Uriel of Gibeah. There was war between Abijah and Jeroboam. ³ Abijah joined battle with a force of warriors, 400,000 picked men. Jeroboam arrayed for battle against him 800,000 picked men, warriors. ⁴ Abijah stood on top of Mount Zemaraim in the hill country of Ephraim and said, "Listen to me, Jeroboam and all Israel. ⁵ Surely you know that the LORD God of Israel gave David kingship over Israel forever—to him and his sons—by a covenant of salt. ⁶ Jeroboam son of Nebat had been in the service of Solomon son of David, but he rose up and rebelled against his master. ⁷ Riffraff and scoundrels gathered around him and pressed hard upon Rehoboam son of Solomon. Rehoboam was inexperienced and fainthearted and could not stand up to them. ⁸ Now you are bent on opposing the kingdom of the LORD, which is in the charge of the sons of David, because you are a great multitude and possess the golden calves which Jeroboam made for you as gods. ⁹ Did you not banish the priests of the LORD, the sons of Aaron, and the Levites, and, like the peoples of the land, appoint your own priests? Anyone who offered himself for ordination with a young bull of the herd and seven rams became a priest of no-gods! [10] As for us, the LORD is our God, and we have not forsaken Him. The priests who minister to the LORD are the sons of Aaron, and the Levites are at their tasks. [11] They offer burnt offerings in smoke each morning and each evening, and the aromatic incense, the rows of bread on the pure table; they kindle the golden lampstand with its lamps burning each evening, for we keep the charge of the LORD our God, while you have forsaken it. [12] See, God is with us as our chief, and His priests have the trumpets for sounding blasts against you. O children of Israel, do not fight the LORD God of your fathers, because you will not succeed."

[13] Jeroboam, however, had directed the ambush to go around and come from the rear, thus *a*-the main body was-*a* in front of Judah, while the ambush was behind them. [14] When Judah turned around and saw that the fighting was before and behind them, they cried out to the LORD, and the priests blew the trumpets. [15] The men of Judah raised a shout; and when the men of Judah raised a shout, God routed Jeroboam and all Israel before Abijah and Judah. [16] The Israelites fled before Judah, and God delivered them into their hands. [17] Abijah and his army inflicted a severe defeat on them; 500,000 men of Israel fell slain. [18] The Israelites were crushed at that time, while the people of Judah triumphed because they relied on the LORD God of their fathers. [19] Abijah pursued Jeroboam and captured some of his cities—Bethel with its dependencies, Jeshanah with its dependencies and Ephrain with its dependencies. [20] Jeroboam could not muster strength again during the days of Abijah. The LORD struck him down and he died. [21] But Abijah grew powerful; he married fourteen wives and begat twenty-two sons and sixteen daughters.

[22] The other events of Abijah's reign, his conduct and his acts, are recorded in the story of the prophet Iddo. [23] Abijah slept with his fathers and was buried in the city of David; his son Asa succeeded him as king. The land was untroubled for ten years.

---

a-a Lit. "they were."

14 Asa did what was good and pleasing to the LORD his God. ² He abolished the alien altars and shrines; he smashed the pillars and cut down the sacred posts. ³ He ordered Judah to turn to the LORD God of their fathers and to observe the Teaching and the Commandment. ⁴ He abolished the shrines and the incense stands throughout the cities of Judah, and the kingdom was untroubled under him. ⁵ He built fortified towns in Judah, since the land was untroubled and he was not engaged in warfare during those years, for the LORD had granted him respite. ⁶ He said to Judah, "Let us build up these cities and surround them with walls and towers, gates and bars, while the land is at our disposal because we turned to the LORD our God—we turned [to Him] and He gave us respite on all sides." They were successful in their building.

⁷ Asa had an army of 300,000 men from Judah bearing shields and spears, and 280,000 from Benjamin bearing bucklers and drawing the bow; all these were valiant men. ⁸ Zerah the Cushite marched out against them with an army of a thousand thousand and 300 chariots. When he reached Mareshah ⁹ Asa confronted him, and the battle lines were drawn in the valley of Zephat by Mareshah. ¹⁰ Asa called to the LORD his God, and said, "O LORD, it is all the same to You to help the numerous and the powerless. Help us, O LORD our God, for we rely on You, and in Your name we have come against this great multitude. You are the LORD our God. Let no mortal hinder You." ¹¹ So the LORD routed the Cushites before Asa and Judah, and the Cushites fled. ¹² Asa and the army with him pursued them as far as Gerar. Many of the Cushites fell wounded beyond recovery, for they broke before the LORD and His camp. Very much spoil was taken. ¹³ All the cities in the vicinity of Gerar were ravaged, for a terror of the LORD seized them. All the cities were plundered, and they yielded much booty. ¹⁴ They also ravaged the encampment of herdsmen, capturing much sheep and camels. Then they returned to Jerusalem.

15 The spirit of God came upon Azariah son of Oded. ² He came to Asa and said to him, "Listen to me, Asa and all Judah and Benjamin; the LORD is with you as long as you are with Him. If you turn to Him, He will respond to you, but if you forsake Him, He will forsake you. ³ Israel has gone many days without the true God, without a priest to give instruction and without Teaching. ⁴ But in distress it returned to the LORD God of Israel, and sought Him, and He responded to them. ⁵ At those times, *ᵃ*no wayfarer*ᵃ* was safe, for there was much tumult among all the inhabitants of the lands. ⁶ Nation was crushed by nation and city by city, for God threw them into panic with every kind of trouble. ⁷ As for you, be strong, do not be disheartened, for there is reward for your labor."

⁸ When Asa heard these words, the prophecy of Oded the prophet, he took courage and removed the abominations from the entire land of Judah and Benjamin and from the cities which he had captured in the hill country of Ephraim. He restored the altar of the LORD in front of the porch of the LORD. ⁹ He assembled all the people of Judah and Benjamin and those people of Ephraim, Manasseh, and Simeon who sojourned among them, for many in Israel had thrown in their lot with him when they saw that the LORD his God was with him. ¹⁰ They were assembled in Jerusalem in the third month of the fifteenth year of the reign of Asa. ¹¹ They brought sacrifices to the LORD on that day; they brought 700 oxen and 7000 sheep of the spoil. ¹² They entered into a covenant to worship the LORD God of their fathers with all their heart and with all their soul. ¹³ Whoever would not worship the LORD God of Israel would be put to death, whether small or great, whether man or woman. ¹⁴ So they took an oath to the LORD in a loud voice and with shouts, with trumpeting and blasts of the horn. ¹⁵ All Judah rejoiced over the oath, for they swore with all their heart and sought Him with all their will. He responded to them and gave them respite on every side.

¹⁶ *ᵇ*He*ᶜ* also deposed Maacah mother of King Asa from the rank

---

ᵃ⁻ᵃ *Lit. "one who goes out and one who comes in."*
ᵇ *With vv. 16–19, cf. I Kings 15.13–16.*
ᶜ *I.e. Asa.*

of queen mother, because she had made an abominable thing for [the goddess] Asherah. Asa cut down her abominable thing, reduced it to dust, and burned it in the Wadi Kidron. [17] The shrines, indeed, were not abolished in Israel; however, Asa was wholehearted [with the LORD] all his life. [18] He brought into the House of God the things that he and his father had consecrated—silver, gold, and utensils. [19] There was no war until the thirty-fifth year of the reign of Asa.

16 [a]In the thirty-sixth year of the reign of Asa, King Baasha of Israel marched against Judah and built up Ramah to block [b-]all movement[-b] of King Asa of Judah. [2] Asa took all the silver and gold from the treasuries of the House of the LORD and the royal palace, and sent them to King Ben-hadad of Aram, who resided in Damascus, with this message: [3] "There is a pact between me and you, as there was between my father and your father. I herewith send you silver and gold; go and break your pact with King Baasha of Israel so that he may withdraw from me." [4] Ben-hadad acceded to King Asa's request; he sent his army commanders against the towns of Israel and ravaged Ijon, Dan, Abel-maim, and all the garrison towns of Naphtali. [5] When Baasha heard about it, he stopped building up Ramah and put an end to the work on it. [6] Then King Asa mustered all Judah, and they carried away the stones and timber with which Baasha had built up Ramah; with these King Asa built up Geba and Mizpah.

[7] At that time, Hanani the seer came to King Asa of Judah and said to him, "Because you relied on the king of Aram and did not rely on the LORD your God, therefore the army of the king of Aram has slipped out of your hands. [8] The Cushites and Lybians were a mighty army with chariots and horsemen in very great numbers, yet because you relied on the LORD He delivered them into your hands. [9] For the eyes of the LORD range over the entire earth, to give support to those who are wholeheartedly with Him.

[a] *Cf. I Kings 15.17–24.*
[b-b] *Lit. "one who goes out and one who comes in."*

You have acted foolishly in this matter, and henceforth you will be beset by wars." [10] Asa was vexed at the seer and put him into the stocks,[c] for he was furious with him because of that. Asa inflicted cruelties on some of the people at that time.

[11] The acts of Asa, early and late, are recorded in the annals of the kings of Judah and Israel. [12] In the thirty-ninth year of his reign, Asa suffered from an acute foot ailment; but ill as he was, he still did not turn to the LORD but to physicians. [13] Asa slept with his fathers. He died in the forty-first year of his reign [14] and was buried in the grave that he had made for himself in the City of David. He was laid in his resting-place, which was filled with spices of all kinds, expertly blended; a very great fire was made in his honor.

17 His son Jehoshaphat succeeded him as king, and took firm hold of Israel. [2] He stationed troops in all the fortified towns of Judah, and stationed garrisons throughout the land of Judah and the cities of Ephraim which his father Asa had captured. [3] The LORD was with Jehoshaphat because he followed the earlier ways of his father David, and did not worship the Baalim, [4] but worshiped the God of his father and followed His commandments— unlike the behavior of Israel. [5] So the LORD established the kingdom in his hands, and all Judah gave presents to Jehoshaphat. He had wealth and glory in abundance. [6] His mind was elevated in the ways of the LORD. Moreover, he abolished the shrines and the sacred posts from Judah.

[7] In the third year of his reign he sent his officers Ben-hail, Obadiah, Zechariah, Nethanel, and Micaiah throughout the cities of Judah to offer instruction. [8] With them were the Levites, Shemaiah, Nethaniah, Zebadiah, Asahel, Shemiramoth, Jehonathan, Adonijah, Tobijah and Tob-adonijah the Levites; with them were Elishama and Jehoram the priests. [9] They offered instruction throughout Judah, having with them the Book of the Teaching of

[c] *Meaning of Heb. uncertain.*

the LORD. They made the rounds of all the cities of the LORD and instructed the people. [10] A terror of the LORD seized all the kingdoms of the lands around Judah, and they did not go to war with Jehoshaphat. [11] From Philistia a load of silver was brought to Jehoshaphat as tribute. The Arabs, too, brought him flocks: 7700 rams and 7700 he-goats. [12] Jehoshaphat grew greater and greater, and he built up fortresses and garrison towns in Judah. [13] He carried out extensive works in the towns of Judah, and had soldiers, valiant men, in Jerusalem. [14] They were enrolled according to their clans. Judah: chiefs of thousands, Adnah the chief, who had 300,000 valiant men; [15] next to him was Jehohanan the captain, who had 280,000; [16] next to him was Amasiah son of Zichri, who made a freewill offering to the LORD. He had 200,000 valiant men. [17] Benjamin: Eliada, a valiant man, who had 200,000 men armed with bow and buckler; [18] next to him was Jehozabad, who had 180,000 armed men. [19] These served the king, besides those whom the king assigned to the fortified towns throughout Judah.

18

[a]So Jehoshaphat had wealth and honor in abundance, and he allied himself by marriage to Ahab. [2] After some years had passed, he came to visit Ahab at Samaria. Ahab slaughtered sheep and oxen in abundance for him and for the people with him, and persuaded him to march against Ramoth-gilead. [3] King Ahab of Israel said to King Jehoshaphat of Judah, "Will you accompany me to Ramoth-gilead?" He answered him, "I will do what you do; my troops shall be your troops and shall accompany you in battle." [4] Jehoshaphat then said to the king of Israel, "But first inquire of the LORD."

[5] So the king of Israel gathered the prophets, four hundred men, and asked them, "Shall I march upon Ramoth-gilead for battle, or shall I not?" "March," they said, "and God will deliver it into the king's hands." [6] Then Jehoshaphat asked, "Is there not another prophet of the LORD here through whom we can in-

[a] Cf. I Kings 22.

quire?" [7] And the king of Israel answered Jehoshaphat, "There is one more man through whom we can inquire of the LORD; but I hate him, because he never prophesies anything good for me but always misfortune. He is Micaiah son of Imlah." Jehoshaphat replied, "Let the king not say such a thing." [8] So the king of Israel summoned an officer and said, "Bring Micaiah son of Imlah at once."

[9] The king of Israel and King Jehoshaphat of Judah, wearing their robes, were seated on their thrones situated in the threshing floor at the entrance of the gate of Samaria; and all the prophets were prophesying before them. [10] Zedekiah son of Chenaanah had provided himself with iron horns; and he said, "Thus said the LORD: With these you shall gore the Arameans till you make an end of them." [11] All the other prophets were prophesying similarly, "March against Ramoth-gilead and be victorious! The LORD will deliver it into Your Majesty's hands."

[12] The messenger who had gone to summon Micaiah said to him, "Look, the words of the prophets are unanimously favorable to the king. Let your word be like that of the rest of them; speak a favorable word." [13] "By the life of the LORD," Micaiah answered, "I will speak only what my God tells me." [14] When he came before the king, the king said to him, "Micah,[b] shall we march against Ramoth-gilead for battle or shall we not?" He answered him, "March and be victorious! They will be delivered into your hands." [15] The king said to him, "How many times must I adjure you to tell me nothing but the truth in the name of the LORD?" [16] Then he said, "I saw all Israel scattered over the hills like sheep without a shepherd; and the LORD said, 'These have no master; let everyone return to his home in safety.'"

[17] The king of Israel said to Jehoshaphat, "Did I not tell you that he would not prophesy good fortune for me, but only misfortune?"

[18] Then [Micaiah] said, "Indeed, hear now the word of the LORD! I saw the LORD seated upon His throne, with all the host of heaven standing in attendance to the right and to the left of

[b] *A shortened form of Micaiah.*

Him. [19] The LORD asked, 'Who will entice King Ahab of Israel so that he will march and fall at Ramoth-gilead?' Then one said this and another said that, [20] until a certain spirit came forward and stood before the LORD and said, 'I will entice him.' 'How?' said the LORD to him. [21] And he replied, 'I will go forth and become a lying spirit in the mouth of all his prophets.' Then He said, 'You will entice with success. Go forth and do it.' [22] Thus the LORD has put a lying spirit in the mouth of all these prophets of yours; for the LORD has decreed misfortune for you.''

[23] Thereupon Zedekiah son of Chenaanah came up and struck Micaiah on the cheek, and exclaimed, "However did the spirit of the LORD pass from me to speak with you!'' [24] Micaiah replied, "You will see on the day when you try to hide in the innermost room.'' [25] Then the king of Israel said, "Take Micaiah and turn him over to Amon, the governor of the city, and to Prince Joash, [26] and say, 'The king's orders are: Put this fellow in prison, and let his fare be scant bread and scant water until I come home safe.' '' [27] To which Micaiah retorted, "If you ever come home safe, the LORD has not spoken through me.'' He said further, ᶜ-"Listen, all you peoples!''-ᶜ

[28] The king of Israel and King Jehoshaphat of Judah marched against Ramoth-gilead. [29] The king of Israel said to Jehoshaphat, ᵈ-"I will disguise myself and go-ᵈ into the battle, but you, wear your robes.'' So the king of Israel disguised himself, and they went into the battle. [30] The king of Aram had given these instructions to his chariot officers: "Do not attack anyone, small or great, except the king of Israel.'' [31] When the chariot officers saw Jehoshaphat, whom they took for the king of Israel, they wheeled around to attack him, and Jehoshaphat cried out and the LORD helped him, and God diverted them from him. [32] And when the chariot officers realized that he was not the king of Israel, they gave up the pursuit. [33] Then a man drew his bow at random and hit the king of Israel between the ᵉ-plates of the-ᵉ armor and he said to his charioteer, "Turn around and get me behind the lines; I am wounded.'' [34] The battle ᵉ-raged all day long,-ᵉ and the king

ᶜ-ᶜ *Cf. Mic. 1.2.*
ᵈ-ᵈ *Infinitives used for finite verb; cf. note at I Kings 22.30.*
ᵉ-ᵉ *Meaning of Heb. uncertain*

remained propped up in the chariot facing Aram until dusk; he died as the sun was setting.

19 King Jehoshaphat of Judah returned safely to his palace, to Jerusalem. ² Jehu son of Hanani the seer went out to meet King Jehoshaphat and said to him, "Should one give aid to the wicked and befriend those who hate the LORD? For this, wrath is upon you from the LORD. ³ However, there is some good in you, for you have purged the land of the sacred posts and have dedicated yourself to worship the LORD."

⁴ Jehoshaphat remained in Jerusalem awhile and then went out among the people from Beer-sheba to the hill country of Ephraim; he brought them back to the LORD God of their fathers. ⁵ He appointed judges in the land in all the fortified towns of Judah, in each and every town. ⁶ He charged the judges: "Consider what you are doing, for you judge not on behalf of man, but on behalf of the LORD, and He is with you when you pass judgment. ⁷ Now let the dread of the LORD be upon you; act with care, for there is no injustice or favoritism or bribe-taking with the LORD our God." ⁸ Jehoshaphat also appointed in Jerusalem some Levites and priests and heads of the clans of Israelites for rendering judgment in matters of the LORD, and for disputes. Then they returned to Jerusalem. ⁹ He charged them, "This is how you shall act: in fear of the LORD, with fidelity, and with whole heart. ¹⁰ When a dispute comes before you from your brothers living in their towns, whether about homicide, or about ritual, or laws or rules, you must instruct them so that they do not incur guilt before the LORD and wrath be upon you and your brothers. Act so and you will not incur guilt. ¹¹ See, Amariah the chief priest is over you in all cases concerning the LORD, and Zebadiah son of Ishmael is the commander of the house of Judah in all cases concerning the king; the Levitical officials are at your disposal; act with resolve and the LORD be with the good."

20 After that, Moabites, Ammonites, together with some Am-
monim,ᵃ came against Jehoshaphat to wage war. ² The report was
brought to Jehoshaphat: "A great multitude is coming against
you from beyond the sea, from Aram, and is now in Hazazon-
tamar"—that is, Ein-gedi. ³ Jehoshaphat was afraid; he decided to
resort to the Lord and proclaimed a fast for all Judah. ⁴ Judah
assembled to beseech the Lord. They also came from all the
towns of Judah to seek the Lord.

⁵ Jehoshaphat stood in the congregation of Judah and Jerusalem in the House of the Lord at the front of the new court. ⁶ He
said, "Lord God of our fathers, truly You are the God in heaven
and You rule over the kingdoms of the nations; power and
strength are Yours; none can oppose You. ⁷ O our God, you
dispossessed the inhabitants of this land before Your people
Israel, and You gave it to the descendants of Your friend
Abraham for ever. ⁸ They settled in it and in it built for You a
House for Your name. They said, ⁹ 'Should misfortune befall us
—the punishing sword, pestilence, or famine, we shall stand before this House and before You—for Your name is in this House
—and we shall cry out to You in our distress, and You will listen
and deliver us.' ¹⁰ Now the people of Ammon, Moab, and the hill
country of Seir, into whose [land] You did not let Israel come
when they came from Egypt, but they turned aside from them and
did not wipe them out, ¹¹ these now repay us by coming to expel
us from Your possession which You gave us as ours. ¹² O our
God, surely You will punish them, for we are powerless before
this great multitude that has come against us, and do not know
what to do, but our eyes are on You." ¹³ All Judah stood before
the Lord with their little ones, their womenfolk, and their children.

¹⁴ Then in the midst of the congregation the spirit of the Lord
came upon Jahaziel son of Zechariah son of Benaiah son of Jeiel
son of Mattaniah the Levite, of the sons of Asaph, ¹⁵ and he said,

ᵃ *Probably for* m'nym *"Meunites" (I Chron. 4.41); cf. Kimhi.*

"Give heed, all Judah and the inhabitants of Jerusalem and King Jehoshaphat; thus said the LORD to you, 'Do not fear or be dismayed by this great multitude, for the battle is God's, not yours. ¹⁶ March down against them tomorrow as they come up by the Ascent of Ziz; you will find them at the end of the wadi in the direction of the wilderness of Jeruel. ¹⁷ It is not for you to fight this battle; stand by, wait, and witness your deliverance by the LORD, O Judah and Jerusalem; do not fear or be dismayed; go forth to meet them tomorrow and the LORD will be with you.' " ¹⁸ Jehoshaphat bowed low with his face to the ground, and all Judah and the inhabitants of Jerusalem threw themselves down before the LORD to worship the LORD. ¹⁹ Levites of the sons of Kohath and of the sons of Korah got up to extol the LORD God of Israel at the top of their voices.

²⁰ Early the next morning they arose and went forth to the wilderness of Tekoa. As they went forth, Jehoshaphat stood and said, "Listen to me, O Judah and inhabitants of Jerusalem: Trust firmly in the LORD your God and you will stand firm; trust firmly in His prophets and you will succeed." ²¹ After taking counsel with the people, he stationed singers to the LORD extolling the One majestic in holiness as they went forth ahead of the vanguard, saying, "Praise the LORD, for His steadfast love is eternal." ²² As they began their joyous shouts and hymns, the LORD set ambushes for the men of Amon, Moab, and the hill country of Seir, who were marching against Judah, and they were routed. ²³ The Ammonites and Moabites turned against the men of the hill country of Seir to exterminate and annihilate them. When they had made an end of the men of Seir, each helped to destroy his fellow.

²⁴ When Judah reached the lookout in the wilderness and looked for the multitude, they saw them lying on the ground as corpses; not one had survived. ²⁵ Jehoshaphat and his army came to take the booty, and found an abundance of goods, corpses, and precious objects, which they pillaged, more than they could carry off. For three days they were taking booty, there was so much of

it. ²⁶ On the fourth day they assembled in the Valley of Blessing —for there they blessed the LORD; that is why that place is called the Valley of Blessing to this day. ²⁷ All the men of Judah and Jerusalem with Jehoshaphat at their head returned joyfully to Jerusalem, for the LORD had given them cause for rejoicing over their enemies. ²⁸ They came to Jerusalem to the House of the LORD, to the accompaniment of harps, lyres, and trumpets. ²⁹ The terror of God seized all the kingdoms of the lands when they heard that the LORD had fought the enemies of Israel. ³⁰ The kingdom of Jehoshaphat was untroubled, and his God granted him respite on all sides.

³¹ ᵇJehoshaphat reigned over Judah. He was thirty-five years old when he became king, and he reigned in Jerusalem for twenty-five years. His mother's name was Azubah daughter of Shilhi. ³² He followed the course of his father Asa and did not deviate from it, doing what was pleasing to the LORD. ³³ However, the shrines did not cease; the people still did not direct their heart toward the God of their fathers. ³⁴ As for the other events of Jehoshaphat's reign, early and late, they are recorded in the annals of Jehu son of Hanani, which were included in the Book of the Kings of Israel.

³⁵ Afterward, King Jehoshaphat of Judah entered into a partnership with King Ahaziah of Israel, thereby acting wickedly. ³⁶ He joined with him in constructing ships to go to Tarshish; the ships were constructed in Ezion-geber. ³⁷ Eliezer son of Dodavahu of Mareshah prophesied against Jehoshaphat, "As you have made a partnership with Ahaziah, the LORD will break up your work." The ships were wrecked and were unable to go to Tarshish.

21 ᵃJehoshaphat slept with his fathers and was buried with his fathers in the City of David; his son Jehoram succeeded him as king. ² He had brothers, sons of Jehoshaphat: Azariah, Jehiel,

ᵇ With vv. 31–37, cf. I Kings 22.41–49.

ᵃ Cf. II Kings 8.17–24.

Zechariah, Azariahu, Michael and Shephatiah; all these were sons of King Jehoshaphat of Israel. ³ Their father gave them many gifts of silver, gold, and [other] presents, as well as fortified towns in Judah, but he gave the kingdom to Jehoram because he was the firstborn.

⁴ Jehoram proceeded to take firm hold of his father's kingdom and put to the sword all his brothers, as well as some of the officers of Israel. ⁵ Jehoram was thirty-two years old when he became king, and he reigned in Jerusalem eight years. ⁶ He followed the practices of the kings of Israel doing what the House of Ahab had done, for he married a daughter of Ahab; he did what was displeasing to the LORD. ⁷ However, the LORD refrained from destroying the House of David for the sake of the covenant he had made with David, and in accordance with his promise to maintain a lamp for him and his descendants for all time. ⁸ During his reign, the Edomites rebelled against Judah's rule and set up a king of their own. ⁹ Jehoram advanced [against them] with his officers and all his chariotry. He arose by night and attacked the Edomites, who surrounded him and the chariot commanders. ¹⁰ Edom has been in rebellion against Judah, to this day; Libnah also rebelled against him at that time, because he had forsaken the LORD God of his fathers. ¹¹ Moreover, he built shrines in the hill country of Judah; he led astray the inhabitants of Jerusalem and made Judah wayward.

¹² A letter from Elijah the prophet came to him which read, "Thus says the LORD God of your father David: Since you have not followed the practices of your father Jehoshaphat and the practices of King Asa of Judah, ¹³ but have followed the practices of the kings of Israel, leading astray Judah and the inhabitants of Jerusalem as the House of Ahab led them astray, and have also killed your brothers of your father's house, who were better than you, ¹⁴ therefore, the LORD will inflict a great blow upon your people, your sons, and your wives and all your possessions. ¹⁵ As for you, you will be severely stricken with a disorder of the bowels year after year until your bowels drop out."

¹⁶ The LORD stirred up the spirit of the Philistines and the Arabs who were neighbors of the Cushites against Jehoram. ¹⁷ They marched against Judah, breached its defenses, and carried off all the property that was found in the king's palace, as well as his sons and his wives. The only son who remained was Jehoahaz, his youngest. ¹⁸ After this, the LORD afflicted him with an incurable disease of the bowels. ¹⁹ Some years later, when a period of two years had elapsed, his bowels dropped out because of his disease, and he died a gruesome death. His people did not make a fire for him like the fire for his fathers. ²⁰ He was thirty-two years old when he became king, and he reigned in Jerusalem eight years. He departed unpraised,ᵇ and was buried in the City of David, but not in the tombs of the kings.

22 ᵃThe inhabitants of Jerusalem made Ahaziah, his youngest son, king in his stead, because all the older ones had been killed by the troops that penetrated the camp with the Arabs. Ahaziah son of Jehoram reigned as king of Judah. ² Ahaziah was forty-two years old when he became king, and he reigned in Jerusalem one year; his mother's name was Athaliah daughter of Omri. ³ He too followed the practices of the house of Ahab, for his mother counseled him to do evil. ⁴ He did what was displeasing to the LORD, like the house of Ahab, for they became his counselors after his father's death, to his ruination. ⁵ Moreover, he followed their counsel and marched with Jehoram son of King Ahab of Israel to battle against King Hazael of Aram at Ramoth-gilead, where the Arameans wounded Joram. ⁶ He returned to Jezreel to recover from the wounds inflicted on him at Ramah when he fought against King Hazael of Aram. King Azariah son of Jehoram of Judah went down to Jezreel to visit Jehoram son of Ahab while he was ill. ⁷ The LORD caused the downfall of Ahaziah because he visited Joram. During his visit he went out with Jehoram to Jehu son of Nimshi, whom the LORD had anointed to cut off the house of Ahab. ⁸ In the course of bringing the house of Ahab to judg-

ᵇ Following Septuagint; cf. Arabic ḥamada, "praise."

ᵃ With vv. 1–6, cf. II Kings 8.25–29; with vv. 8–9, cf. II Kings 9.27–28; with vv. 10–12, cf. II Kings 11.1–3.

ment, Jehu came upon the officers of Judah and the nephews of
Ahaziah, ministers of Ahaziah, and killed them. ⁹ He sent in
search of Ahaziah, who was caught hiding in Samaria, was
brought to Jehu, and put to death. He was given a burial, because
it was said, "He is the son of Jehoshaphat who worshiped the
LORD wholeheartedly." So the house of Ahaziah could not muster the strength to rule.

¹⁰ When Athaliah, Ahaziah's mother, learned that her son was
dead, she promptly did away with all who were of the royal stock
of the house of Judah. ¹¹ But Jehoshabeath, daughter of the king,
spirited away Ahaziah's son Joash from among the princes who
were being slain, and put him and his nurse in a bedroom. Jehoshabeath, daughter of King Jehoram, wife of the priest Jehoiada
—she was the sister of Ahaziah—kept him hidden from Athaliah
so that he was not put to death. ¹² He stayed with them for six
years, hidden in the House of God, while Athaliah reigned over
the land.

23 ᵃIn the seventh year, Jehoiada took courage and brought
the chiefs of the hundreds, Azariah son of Jehoram, Ishmael son
of Jehohanan, Azariah son of Obed, Maaseiah son of Adaiah, and
Elishaphat son of Zichri, into a compact with him. ² They went
through Judah and assembled the Levites from all the towns of
Judah, and the chiefs of the clans of Israel. They came to Jerusalem ³ and the entire assembly made a covenant with the king in
the House of God. Heᵇ said to them, "The son of the king shall
be king according to the promise the LORD made concerning the
sons of David. ⁴ This is what you must do: One third of you,
priests and Levites, who are on duty for the week, shall be gatekeepers at the thresholds; ⁵ another third shall be stationed in the
royal palace, and the other third at the Foundation Gate. All the
people shall be in the courts of the House of the LORD. ⁶ Let no
one enter the House of the LORD except the priests and the
ministering Levites. They may enter because they are sanctified,

---

ᵃ *Cf. II Kings 11. 4–20.*
ᵇ *I.e. Jehoiada.*

but all the people shall obey the proscription of the LORD. ⁷ The Levites shall surround the king on every side, every man with his weapons at the ready; and whoever enters the House shall be killed. Stay close to the king in his comings and goings." ⁸ The Levites and all Judah did just as Jehoiada the priest ordered: each took his men—those who were on duty that week and those who were off duty that week, for Jehoiada the priest had not dismissed the divisions. ⁹ Jehoiada the priest gave the chiefs of the hundreds King David's spears and shields and quivers that were kept in the House of God. ¹⁰ He stationed the entire force, each man with his weapons at the ready, from the south end of the House to the north end of the House, at the altar and the House, to guard the king on every side. ¹¹ Then they brought out the king's son, and placed upon him the crown and the insignia. They proclaimed him king, and Jehoiada and his sons anointed him and shouted, "Long live the king!"

¹² When Athaliah heard the shouting of the people and the guards and the acclamation of the king, she came out to the people, to the House of the LORD. ¹³ She looked about and saw the king standing by his pillar at the entrance, the chiefs with their trumpets beside the king, and all the people of the land rejoicing and blowing trumpets, and the singers with musical instruments leading the hymns. Athaliah rent her garments and cried out, "Treason, treason!" ¹⁴ Then the priest Jehoiada ordered out the army officers, the chiefs of hundreds, and said to them, "Take her out between the ranks, and if anyone follows her, put him to the sword." For the priest thought, "Let her not be put to death in the House of the LORD." ¹⁵ They cleared a passage for her and she came to the entrance of the Horse Gate to the royal palace; there she was put to death.

¹⁶ Then Jehoiada solemnized a covenant between himself and the people and the king that they should be the people of the LORD. ¹⁷ All the people then went to the temple of Baal; they tore it down and smashed its altars and images to bits, and they slew Mattan, the priest of Baal, in front of the altars. ¹⁸ Jehoiada put

the officers of the House of the LORD in the charge of Levite priests whom David had assigned over the House of the LORD to offer up burnt offerings, as is prescribed in the Teaching of Moses, accompanied by joyful song as ordained by David. [19] He stationed the gatekeepers at the gates of the House of the LORD to prevent the entry of anyone unclean for any reason. [20] He took the chiefs of hundreds, the nobles, and the rulers of the people and all the people of the land, and they escorted the king down from the House of the LORD into the royal palace by the upper gate, and seated the king on the royal throne. [21] All the people of the land rejoiced, and the city was quiet. As for Athaliah, she had been put to the sword.

24 [a]Jehoash was seven years old when he became king, and he reigned in Jerusalem forty years. His mother's name was Zibiah of Beer-sheba. [2] All the days of the priest Jehoiada, Jehoash did what was pleasing to the LORD. [3] Jehoiada took two wives for him, by whom he had sons and daughters.

[4] Afterward, Joash decided to renovate the House of the LORD. [5] He assembled the priests and the Levites and charged them as follows: "Go out to the towns of Judah and collect money from all Israel for the annual repair of the House of your God. Do it quickly." But the Levites did not act quickly. [6] The king summoned Jehoiada the chief and said to him, "Why have you not seen to it that the Levites brought the tax imposed by Moses, the servant of the LORD, and the congregation of Israel from Judah and Jerusalem to the Tent of the Pact?" [7] For the children of the wicked Athaliah had violated the House of God and had even used the sacred things of the House of the LORD for the Baals. [8] The king ordered that a chest be made and placed on the outside of the gate of the House of the LORD. [9] A proclamation was issued in Judah and Jerusalem to bring the tax imposed on Israel in the wilderness by Moses, the servant of God. [10] All the officers

[a] Cf. II Kings 12.1–22.

and all the people gladly brought it and threw it into the chest till it was full. ¹¹ Whenever the chest was brought to the royal officers by the Levites, and they saw that it contained much money, the royal scribe and the agent of the chief priest came and emptied out the chest and carried it back to its place. They did this day by day, and much money was collected. ¹² The king and Jehoiada delivered the money to those who oversaw the tasks connected with the work of the House of the LORD. They hired masons and carpenters to renovate the House of the LORD, as well as craftsmen in iron and bronze to repair the House of the LORD. ¹³ The overseers did their work; under them the work went well and they restored the House of God to its original form and repaired it. ¹⁴ When they had finished, they brought the money that was left over to the king and Jehoiada; it was made into utensils for the House of the LORD: buckets and ladles, golden and silver vessels. Burnt offerings were offered up regularly in the House of the LORD all the days of Jehoiada. ¹⁵ Jehoiada reached a ripe old age and died; he was one hundred and thirty years old at his death. ¹⁶ They buried him in the City of David together with the kings, because he had done good in Israel, and on behalf of God and His House.

¹⁷ But after the death of Jehoiada, the officers of Judah came, bowing low to the king; and the king listened to them. ¹⁸ They forsook the House of the LORD God of their fathers to serve the sacred posts and idols; and there was wrath upon Judah and Jerusalem because of this guilt of theirs. ¹⁹ The LORD sent prophets among them to bring them back to Him; they admonished them but they would not pay heed. ²⁰ Then the spirit of God enveloped Zechariah son of Jehoiada the priest; he stood above the people and said to them, "Thus God said: Why do you transgress the commandments of the LORD when you cannot succeed? Since you have forsaken the LORD, He has forsaken you." ²¹ They conspired against him and pelted him with stones in the court of the House of the LORD, by order of the king. ²² King Joash disregarded the loyalty that his father Johoiada had shown to him, and

killed his son. As he was dying, he said, "May the LORD see and requite it."

²³ At the turn of the year, the army of Aram marched against him; they invaded Judah and Jerusalem, and wiped out all the officers of the people from among the people, and sent all the booty they took to the king of Damascus. ²⁴ The invading army of Aram had come with but a few men, but the LORD delivered a very large army into their hands, because they had forsaken the LORD God of their fathers. They inflicted punishments on Joash. ²⁵ When they withdrew, having left him with many wounds, his courtiers plotted against him because of the murder*b* of the sons of Jehoiada the priest, and they killed him in bed. He died and was buried in the City of David; he was not buried in the tombs of the kings. ²⁶ These were the men who conspired against him: Zabad son of Shimeath the Ammonitess, and Jehozabad son of Shimrith the Moabitess. ²⁷ As to his sons, and the many pronouncements against him, and his rebuilding of the House of God, they are recorded in the story in the book of the kings. His son Amaziah succeeded him as king.

25 *a*Amaziah was twenty-five years old when he became king, and he reigned twenty-nine years in Jerusalem; his mother's name was Jehoaddan of Jerusalem. ² He did what was pleasing to the LORD, but not with a whole heart. ³ Once he had the kingdom firmly under control, he executed the courtiers who had assassinated his father the king. ⁴ But he did not put their children to death for [he acted] in accordance with what is written in the Teaching, in the Book of Moses, where the LORD commanded, *b*-"Parents shall not die for children, nor shall children die for parents, but every person shall die only for his own crime."-*b*

⁵ Amaziah assembled the men of Judah, and he put all the men of Judah and Benjamin under officers of thousands and officers of hundreds, by clans. He mustered them from the age of twenty upward, and found them to be 300,000 picked men fit for service,

---

b Lit. "blood."

a Cf. II Kings 14.
b-b Cf. Deut. 24.16.

able to bear spear and shield. [6] He hired 100,000 warriors from Israel for 100 talents of silver. [7] Then a man of God came to him and said, "O king! Do not let the army of Israel go with you, for the LORD is not with Israel—all these Ephraimites. [8] But go by yourself and do it; take courage for battle, [else] God will make you fall before the enemy. For in God there is power to help one or make one fall!" [9] Amaziah said to the man of God, "And what am I to do about the 100 talents I gave for the Israelite force?" The man of God replied, "The LORD has the means to give you much more than that." [10] So Amaziah detached the force that came to him from Ephraim, [ordering them] to go back to their place. They were greatly enraged against Judah and returned to their place in a rage.

[11] Amaziah took courage and, leading his army, he marched to the Valley of Salt. He slew 10,000 men of Seir; [12] another 10,000 the men of Judah captured alive and brought to the top of Sela. They threw them down from the top of Sela and every one of them was burst open. [13] The men of the force that Amaziah had sent back so they would not go with him into battle made forays against the towns of Judah from Samaria to Beth-horon. They slew 3000 of them, and took much booty.

[14] After Amaziah returned from defeating the Edomites, he had the gods of the men of Seir brought, and installed them as his gods; he prostrated himself before them, and to them he made sacrifice. [15] The LORD was enraged at Amaziah, and sent a prophet to him who said to him, "Why are you worshiping the gods of a people who could not save their people from you?" [16] As he spoke to him, [Amaziah] said to him, "Have we appointed you a counselor to the king? Stop, else you will be killed!" The prophet stopped, saying, "I see God has counseled that you be destroyed, since you act this way and disregard my counsel."

[17] Then King Amaziah of Judah took counsel and sent this message to Joash son of Jehoahaz son of Jehu, king of Israel, "Come, let us confront each other!" [18] King Joash of Israel sent

back this message to King Amaziah of Judah, "The thistle in Lebanon sent this message to the cedar in Lebanon, 'Give your daughter to my son in marriage.' But a wild beast in Lebanon passed by and trampled the thistle. [19] You boast that you have defeated the Edomites and you are ambitious to get more glory. Now stay at home, lest, provoking disaster you fall, dragging Judah down with you." [20] But Amaziah paid no heed—it was God's doing, in order to deliver them up because they worshiped the gods of Edom. [21] King Joash of Israel marched up, and he and King Amaziah of Judah confronted each other at Beth-shemesh in Judah. [22] The men of Judah were routed by Israel, and they all fled to their homes. [23] King Joash of Israel captured Amaziah son of Joash son of Jehoahaz, king of Judah, in Beth-shemesh. He brought him to Jerusalem and made a breach of 400 cubits in the wall of Jerusalem, from the Ephraim Gate to the Corner Gate. [24] Then, with all the gold and silver and all the utensils that were to be found in the House of God in the custody of Obed-edom, and with the treasuries of the royal palace, and with the hostages, he returned to Samaria.

[25] King Amaziah son of Joash of Judah lived fifteen years after the death of King Joash son of Jehoahaz of Israel. [26] The other events of Amaziah's reign, early and late, are recorded in the book of the kings of Judah and Israel. [27] From the time that Amaziah turned from following the LORD, a conspiracy was formed against him in Jerusalem, and he fled to Lachish; but they sent men after him to Lachish and they put him to death there. [28] They brought his body back on horses and buried him with his fathers in the city of Judah.

26 Then all the people of Judah took Uzziah, who was sixteen years old, and proclaimed him king to succeed his father Amaziah. [2] It was he who rebuilt Eloth and restored it to Judah after King [Amaziah] slept with his fathers.

[3] Uzziah was sixteen years old when he became king, and he

reigned fifty-two years in Jerusalem; his mother's name was Jecoliah of Jerusalem. ⁴ He did what was pleasing to the LORD just as his father Amaziah had done. ⁵ He applied himself to the worship of God during the time of Zechariah, instructor in the visions^a of God; during the time he worshiped the LORD, God made him prosper. ⁶ He went forth to fight the Philistines, and breached the wall of Gath and the wall of Jabneh and the wall of Ashdod; he built towns in [the region of] Ashdod and among the Philistines. ⁷ God helped him against the Philistines, against the Arabs who lived in Gur-baal, and the Meunites. ⁸ The Ammonites paid tribute to Uzziah, and his fame spread to the approaches of Egypt, for he grew exceedingly strong. ⁹ Uzziah built towers in Jerusalem on the Corner Gate and the Valley Gate and on the Angle, and fortified them. ¹⁰ He built towers in the wilderness and hewed out many cisterns, for he had much cattle, and farmers in the foothills and on the plain, and vinedressers in the mountains and on the fertile lands, for he loved the soil.

¹¹ Uzziah had an army of warriors, a battle-ready force who were mustered by Jeiel the scribe and Maaseiah the adjutant under Hananiah, one of the king's officers. ¹² The clan chiefs, valiants, totaled 2600; ¹³ under them was the trained army of 307,500, who made war with might and power to aid the king against the enemy. ¹⁴ Uzziah provided them—the whole army—with shields and spears, and helmets and mail, and bows and slingstones. ¹⁵ He made clever devices in Jerusalem, set on the towers and the corners, for shooting arrows and large stones. His fame spread far, for he was helped wonderfully, and he became strong.

¹⁶ When he was strong, he grew so arrogant he acted corruptly: he trespassed against his God by entering the Temple of the LORD to offer incense on the incense altar. ¹⁷ The priest Azariah, with eighty other brave priests of the LORD, followed him in ¹⁸ and, confronting King Uzziah, said to him, "It is not for you, Uzziah, to offer incense to the LORD, but for the Aaronite priests, who have been consecrated, to offer incense. Get out of the

---

ª *Some Heb. mss. read* byr't; *compare ancient versions, "fear."*

Sanctuary, for you have trespassed; there will be no glory in it for you from the Lord God." ¹⁹ Uzziah, holding the censer and ready to burn incense, got angry; but as he got angry with the priests, leprosy broke out on his forehead in front of the priests in the House of the Lord beside the incense altar. ²⁰ When the chief priest Azariah and all the other priests looked at him, his forehead was leprous, so they rushed him out of there; he too made haste to get out, for the Lord had struck him with a plague. ²¹ King Uzziah was a leper until the day of his death. He lived in ᵇ⁻ isolated quarters-ᵇ as a leper, for he was cut off from the House of the Lord—while Jotham his son was in charge of the king's house and governed the people of the land.

²² The other events of Uzziah's reign, early and late, were recorded by the prophet Isaiah son of Amoz. ²³ Uzziah slept with his fathers in the burial field of the kings, because, they said, he was a leper; his son Jotham succeeded him as king.

27 Jotham was twenty-five years old when he became king, and he reigned sixteen years in Jerusalem; his mother's name was Jerushah daughter of Zadok. ² He did what was pleasing to the Lord just as his father Uzziah had done, but he did not enter the Temple of the Lord; however, the people still acted corruptly. ³ It was he who built the Upper Gate of the House of the Lord; he also built extensively on the wall of Ophel. ⁴ He built towns in the hill-country of Judah, and in the woods he built fortresses and towers. ⁵ Moreover, he fought with the king of the Ammonites and overcame them; the Ammonites gave him that year 100 talents of silver and 10,000 kor of wheat and another 10,000 of barley; that is what the Ammonites paid him, and [likewise] in the second and third years. ⁶ Jotham was strong because he maintained a faithful course before the Lord his God.

⁷ The other events of Jotham's reign, and all his battles and his conduct are recorded in the book of the kings of Israel and Judah. ⁸ He was twenty-five years old when he became king, and he

ᵇ⁻ᵇ *Meaning of Heb. uncertain.*

reigned sixteen years in Jerusalem. ⁹ Jotham slept with his fathers, and was buried in the City of David; his son Ahaz succeeded him as king.

28 Ahaz was twenty years old when he became king, and he reigned sixteen years in Jerusalem. He did not do what was pleasing to the LORD as his father David had done, ² but followed the ways of the kings of Israel; he even made molten images for the Baals. ³ He made offerings in the Valley of Ben-hinnom and burned his sons in fire, in the abhorrent fashion of the nations which the LORD had dispossessed before the Israelites. ⁴ He sacrificed and made offerings at the shrines, on the hills, and under every leafy tree. ⁵ The LORD his God delivered him over to the king of Aram, who defeated him and took many of his men captive, and brought them to Damascus. He was also delivered over to the king of Israel, who inflicted a great defeat on him. ⁶ Pekah son of Remaliah killed 120,000 in Judah—all brave men —in one day, because they had forsaken the LORD God of their fathers. ⁷ Zichri, the champion of Ephraim, killed Maaseiah the king's son, and Azrikam chief of the palace, and Elkanah, the second to the king. ⁸ The Israelites captured 200,000 of their kinsmen, women, boys, and girls; they also took a large amount of booty from them and brought the booty to Samaria.

⁹ A prophet of the LORD by the name of Oded was there, who went out to meet the army on its return to Samaria. He said to them, "Because of the fury of the LORD God of your fathers against Judah, He delivered them over to you, and you killed them in a rage that reached heaven. ¹⁰ Do you now intend to subjugate the men and women of Judah and Jerusalem to be your slaves? As it is, you have nothing but offenses against the LORD your God. ¹¹ Now then, listen to me, and send back the captives you have taken from your kinsmen, for the wrath of the LORD is upon you!" ¹² Some of the chief men of the Ephraimites—Azariah son of Jehohanan, Berechiah son of Meshillemoth, Jehizkiah son of Shallum, and Amasa son of Hadlai—confronted those return-

ing from the campaign [13] and said to them, "Do not bring these captives here, for it would mean our offending the LORD, adding to our sins and our offenses; for our offense is grave enough, and there is already wrath upon Israel." [14] So the soldiers released the captives and the booty in the presence of the officers and all the congregation. [15] Then the men named above proceeded to take the captives in hand, and with the booty they clothed all the naked among them—they clothed them and shod them and gave them to eat and drink and anointed them and provided donkeys for all who were failing and brought them to Jericho, the city of palms, back to their kinsmen. Then they returned to Samaria.

[16] At that time, King Ahaz sent to the king of Assyria for help. [17] Again the Edomites came and inflicted a defeat on Judah and took captives. [18] And the Philistines made forays against the cities of the Shephelah and the Negeb of Judah; they seized Beth-shemesh and Aijalon and Gederoth, and Soco with its villages, and Timnah with its villages, and Gimzo with its villages; and they settled there. [19] Thus the LORD brought Judah low on account of King Ahaz of Israel,[a] for he threw off restraint in Judah and trespassed against the LORD. [20] Tillegath-pilneser, king of Assyria, marched against him and gave him trouble, instead of supporting him. [21] For Ahaz plundered the House of the LORD and the house of the king and the officers, and made a gift to the king of Assyria—to no avail.

[22] In his time of trouble, this King Ahaz trespassed even more against the LORD, [23] sacrificing to the gods of Damascus which had defeated him, for he thought, "The gods of the kings of Aram help them; I shall sacrifice to them and they will help me"; but they were his ruin and that of all Israel. [24] Ahaz collected the utensils of the House of God, and cut the utensils of the House of God to pieces. He shut the doors of the House of the LORD and made himself altars in every corner of Jerusalem. [25] In every town in Judah he set up shrines to make offerings to other gods, vexing the LORD God of his fathers.

[a] *Some mss. and ancient versions read "Judah."*

²⁶ The other events of his reign and all his conduct, early and late, are recorded in the book of the kings of Judah and Israel. ²⁷ Ahaz slept with his fathers and was buried in the city, in Jerusalem; his body was not brought to the tombs of the kings of Israel. His son Hezekiah succeeded him as king.

29 Hezekiah became king at the age of twenty-five, and he reigned twenty-nine years in Jerusalem; his mother's name was Abijah daughter of Zechariah. ² He did what was pleasing to the LORD, just as his father David had done.

³ He, in the first month of the first year of his reign, opened the doors of the House of the LORD and repaired them. ⁴ He summoned the priests and the Levites and assembled them in the east square. ⁵ He said to them, "Listen to me, Levites! Sanctify yourselves and sanctify the House of the LORD God of your fathers, and take the abhorrent things out of the holy place. ⁶ For our fathers trespassed and did what displeased the LORD our God; they forsook Him and turned their faces away from the dwelling-place of the LORD, turning their backs on it. ⁷ They also shut the doors of the porch and put out the lights; they did not offer incense and did not make burnt offerings in the holy place to the God of Israel. ⁸ The wrath of the LORD was upon Judah and Jerusalem; He made them an object of horror, amazement, and hissing^a as you see with your own eyes. ⁹ Our fathers died by the sword, and our sons and daughters and wives are in captivity on account of this. ¹⁰ Now I wish to make a covenant with the LORD God of Israel, so that His rage may be withdrawn from us. ¹¹ Now, my sons, do not be slack, for the LORD chose you to attend upon Him, to serve Him, to be His ministers and to make offerings to Him."

¹² So the Levites set to—Mahath son of Amasai and Joel son of Azariah of the sons of Kohath; and of the sons of Merari, Kish son of Abdi and Azariah son of Jehallelel; and of the Gershonites, Joah son of Zimmah and Eden son of Joah; ¹³ and of the sons of

^a *See note at Jer. 18.16.*

Elizaphan, Shimri and Jeiel; and of the sons of Asaph, Zechariah and Mattaniah; ¹⁴ and of the sons of Heman, Jehiel and Shimei; and of the sons of Jeduthun, Shemaiah and Uzziel—¹⁵ and, gathering their brothers, they sanctified themselves and came, by a command of the king concerning the LORD's ordinances, to purify the House of the LORD. ¹⁶ The priests went into the House of the LORD to purify it, and brought all the unclean things they found in the temple of the LORD out into the court of the House of the LORD; [there] the Levites received them, to take them outside to Wadi Kidron. ¹⁷ They began the sanctification on the first day of the first month; on the eighth day of the month they reached the porch of the LORD. They sanctified the House of the LORD for eight days, and on the sixteenth day of the first month they finished. ¹⁸ Then they went into the palace of King Hezekiah and said, "We have purified the whole House of the LORD and the altar of burnt offering and all its utensils, and the table of the bread of display and all its utensils; ¹⁹ and all the utensils which King Ahaz had befouled during his reign, when he trespassed, we have made ready and sanctified. They are standing in front of the altar of the LORD."

²⁰ King Hezekiah rose early, gathered the officers of the city, and went up to the House of the LORD. ²¹ They brought seven bulls and seven rams and seven lambs and seven he-goats as a sin offering for the kingdom and for the Sanctuary and for Judah. He ordered the Aaronite priests to offer them on the altar of the LORD. ²² The cattle were slaughtered, and the priests received the blood and dashed it against the altar; the rams were slaughtered and the blood was dashed against the altar; the lambs were slaughtered and the blood was dashed against the altar. ²³ The he-goats for the sin offering were presented to the king and the congregation, who laid their hands upon them. ²⁴ The priests slaughtered them and performed the purgation-rite with the blood against the altar, to expiate for all Israel, for the king had designated the burnt offering and the sin offering to be for all Israel. ²⁵ He stationed the Levites in the House of the LORD with

cymbals and harps and lyres, as David and Gad the king's seer and Nathan the prophet had ordained, for the ordinance was by the LORD through His prophets.

²⁶ When the Levites were in place with the instruments of David, and the priests with their trumpets, ²⁷ Hezekiah gave the order to offer the burnt offering on the altar. When the burnt offering began, the song of the LORD and the trumpets began also, together with the instruments of King David of Israel. ²⁸ All the congregation prostrated themselves, the song was sung and the trumpets were blown—all this until the end of the burnt offering. ²⁹ When the offering was finished, the king and all who were there with him knelt and prostrated themselves. ³⁰ King Hezekiah and the officers ordered the Levites to praise the LORD in the words of David and Asaph the seer; so they praised rapturously, and they bowed and prostrated themselves.

³¹ Then Hezekiah said, "Now you have consecrated yourselves to the LORD; come, bring sacrifices of well-being and thanksgiving to the House of the LORD." The congregation brought sacrifices of well-being and thanksgiving, and all who felt so moved brought burnt offerings. ³² The number of burnt offerings that the congregation brought was 70 cattle, 100 rams, 200 lambs— all these for burnt offerings to the LORD. ³³ The sacred offerings were 600 large cattle and 3000 small cattle. ³⁴ The priests were too few to be able to flay all the burnt offerings, so their kinsmen, the Levites, reinforced them till the end of the work, and till the [rest of the] priests sanctified themselves. (The Levites were more conscientious about sanctifying themselves than the priests.) ³⁵ For beside the large number of burnt offerings, there were the fat parts of the sacrifices of well-being and the libations for the burnt offerings; so the service of the House of the LORD was properly accomplished. ³⁶ Hezekiah and all the people rejoiced over what God had enabled the people to accomplish, because it had happened so suddenly.

30 Hezekiah sent word to all Israel and Judah; he also wrote letters to Ephraim and Manasseh to come to the House of the Lord in Jerusalem to keep the Passover for the Lord God of Israel. ² The king and his officers and the congregation in Jerusalem had agreed to keep the Passover in the second month, ³ for at the time, they were unable to keep it,ᵃ for not enough priests had sanctified themselves, nor had the people assembled in Jerusalem. ⁴ The king and the whole congregation thought it proper ⁵ to issue a decree and proclaim throughout all Israel from Beer-sheba to Dan that they come and keep the Passover for the Lord God of Israel in Jerusalem—not often did they act in accord with what was written. ⁶ The couriers went out with the letters from the king and his officers through all Israel and Judah, by order of the king, proclaiming, "O you Israelites! Return to the Lord God of your fathers, Abraham, Isaac, and Israel, and He will return to the remnant of you who escaped from the hand of the kings of Assyria. ⁷ Do not be like your fathers and brothers who trespassed against the Lord God of their fathers and He turned them into a horror, as you see. ⁸ Now do not be stiff-necked like your fathers; submit yourselves to the Lord and come to His Sanctuary, which He consecrated forever, and serve the Lord your God so that His anger may turn back from you. ⁹ If you return to the Lord, your brothers and children will be regarded with compassion by their captors, and will return to this land; for the Lord your God is gracious and merciful; He will not turn His face from you if you return to Him."

¹⁰ As the couriers passed from town to town in the land of Ephraim and Manasseh till they reached Zebulun, they were laughed at and mocked. ¹¹ Some of the people of Asher and Manasseh and Zebulun, however, were contrite, and came to Jerusalem. ¹² The hand of God was on Judah, too, making them of a single mind to carry out the command of the king and officers concerning the ordinance of the Lord. ¹³ A great crowd assem-

---

ᵃ *I.e. on its proper date; cf. Num. 9.1–14.*

bled at Jerusalem to keep the Feast of Unleavened Bread in the second month, a very great congregation. [14] They set to and removed the altars that were in Jerusalem, and they removed all the incense stands and threw them into Wadi Kidron. [15] They slaughtered the paschal sacrifice on the fourteenth of the second month. The priests and Levites were ashamed, and they sanctified themselves and brought burnt offerings to the House of the LORD. [16] They took their stations, as was their rule according to the Teaching of Moses, man of God. The priests dashed the blood [which they received] from the Levites. [17] Since many in the congregation had not sanctified themselves, the Levites were in charge of slaughtering the paschal sacrifice for everyone who was not clean, so as to consecrate them to the LORD. [18] For most of the people—many from Ephraim and Manasseh, Issachar and Zebulun—had not purified themselves, yet they ate the paschal sacrifice in violation of what was written. Hezekiah prayed for them, saying, "The good LORD will provide atonement for [19] everyone who set his mind on worshiping God, the LORD God of his fathers, even if he is not purified for the sanctuary." [20] The LORD heard Hezekiah and healed the people.

[21] The Israelites who were in Jerusalem kept the Feast of Unleavened Bread seven days, with great rejoicing, the Levites and the priests praising the LORD daily with powerful instruments for the LORD. [22] Hezekiah persuaded all the Levites who performed skillfully for the LORD to spend the seven days of the festival making offerings of well-being, and confessing to the LORD God of their fathers. [23] All the congregation resolved to keep seven more days, so they kept seven more days of rejoicing. [24] King Hezekiah of Judah contributed to the congregation 1000 bulls and 7000 sheep. And the officers contributed to the congregation 1000 bulls and 10,000 sheep. And the priests sanctified themselves in large numbers. [25] All the congregation of Jerusalem and the priests and the Levites and all the congregation that came from Israel, and the resident aliens who came from the land of Israel and who lived in Judah rejoiced. [26] There was great rejoic-

ing in Jerusalem, for since the time of King Solomon son of David of Israel nothing like it had happened in Jerusalem. 27 The Levite priests rose and blessed the people, and their voice was heard, and their prayer went up to His holy abode, to heaven.

31 When all this was finished, all Israel who were present went out into the towns of Judah and smashed the pillars, cut down the sacred posts, demolished the shrines and altars throughout Judah and Benjamin, and throughout Ephraim and Manasseh, to the very last one. Then all the Israelites returned to their towns, each to his possession.

2 Hezekiah reconstituted the divisions of the priests and Levites, each man of the priests and Levites according to his office, for the burnt offerings, the offerings of well-being, to minister, and to sing hymns and praises in the gates of the courts of the LORD; 3 also the king's portion, from his property, for the burnt offerings—the morning and evening burnt offering, and the burnt offerings for sabbaths, and new moons, and festivals, as prescribed in the Teaching of the LORD.

4 He ordered the people, the inhabitants of Jerusalem, to deliver the portions of the priests and the Levites, so that they might devote themselves to the Teaching of the LORD. 5 When the word spread, the Israelites brought large quantities of grain, wine, oil, honey, and all kinds of agricultural produce, and tithes of all, in large amounts. 6 The men of Israel and Judah living in the towns of Judah—they too brought tithes of cattle and sheep and tithes of sacred things consecrated to the LORD their God, piling them in heaps. 7 In the third month the heaps began to accumulate, and were finished in the seventh month. 8 When Hezekiah and the officers came and saw the heaps, they blessed the LORD and his people Israel. 9 Hezekiah asked the priests and Levites about the heaps. 10 The chief priest Azariah, of the house of Zadok, replied to him, saying, "Ever since the gifts began to be brought to the House of the LORD, people have been eating to satiety and leav-

ing over in great amounts, for the LORD has blessed His people; this huge amount is left over!" [11] Hezekiah then gave orders to prepare store-chambers in the House of the LORD; and they were prepared. [12] They brought in the gifts and the tithes and the sacred things faithfully. Their supervisor was Conaniah the Levite, and Shimei his brother was second in rank. [13] Jehiel and Azaziah and Nahath and Asahel and Jerimoth and Jozabad and Eliel and Ismachiah and Mahath and Benaiah were commissioners under Conaniah and Shimei his brother by appointment of King Hezekiah; Azariah was supervisor of the House of God. [14] Kore son of Imnah the Levite, the keeper of the East Gate, was in charge of the freewill offerings to God, of the allocation of gifts to the LORD, and the most sacred things. [15] Under him were Eden, Miniamin, Jeshua, Shemaiah, Amariah, and Shecaniah, in offices of trust in the priestly towns, making allocation to their brothers by divisions, to great and small alike; [16] besides allocating their daily rations to those males registered by families from three years old and up, all who entered the House of the LORD according to their service and their shift by division; [17] and in charge of the registry of priests by clans, and of the Levites, from twenty years old and up, by shifts, in their divisions; [18] and the registry of the dependents of their whole company—wives, sons, and daughters—for, relying upon them, they sanctified themselves in holiness. [19] And for the Aaronite priests, in each and every one of their towns with adjoining fields, the above-named men were to allocate portions to every male of the priests and to every registered Levite. [20] Hezekiah did this throughout Judah. He acted in a way that was good, upright, and faithful before the LORD his God. [21] Every work he undertook in the service of the House of God or in the Teaching and the Commandment, to worship his God, he did with all his heart; and he prospered.

32 [a]After these faithful deeds, King Sennacherib of Assyria invaded Judah and encamped against its fortified towns with the aim of taking them over. [2] When Hezekiah saw that Sennacherib had come, intent on making war against Jerusalem, [3] he consulted with his officers and warriors about stopping the flow of the springs outside the city, and they supported him. [4] A large force was assembled to stop up all the springs and the wadi that flowed through the land, for otherwise, they thought, the king of Assyria would come and find water in abundance. [5] He acted with vigor, rebuilding the whole breached wall, raising towers on it, and building another wall outside it. He fortified the Millo of the City of David, and made a great quantity of arms and shields. [6] He appointed battle officers over the people; then, gathering them to him in the square of the city gate, he rallied them, saying, [7] "Be strong and of good courage; do not be frightened or dismayed by the king of Assyria or by the horde that is with him, for we have more with us than he has with him. [8] With him is an arm of flesh, but with us is the LORD our God, to help us and to fight our battles." The people were encouraged by the speech of King Hezekiah of Judah.

[9] Afterward, King Sennacherib of Assyria sent his officers to Jerusalem—he and all his staff being at Lachish—with this message to King Hezekiah of Judah and to all the people of Judah who were in Jerusalem: [10] "Thus said King Sennacherib of Assyria: On what do you trust to enable you to endure a siege in Jerusalem? [11] Hezekiah is seducing you to a death of hunger and thirst, saying, 'The LORD our God will save us from the king of Assyria.' [12] But is not Hezekiah the one who removed His shrines and His altars and commanded the people of Judah and Jerusalem saying, 'Before this one altar you shall prostrate yourselves, and upon it make your burnt offerings'? [13] Surely you know what I and my fathers have done to the peoples of the lands? Were the gods of the nations of the lands able to save their lands from me?

[a] Cf. II Kings 18–20; Isa. 36–39.

¹⁴ Which of all the gods of any of those nations whom my fathers destroyed was able to save his people from me, that your God should be able to save you from me? ¹⁵ Now then, do not let Hezekiah delude you; do not let him seduce you in this way; do not believe him. For no god of any nation or kingdom has been able to save his people from me or from my fathers—much less your God, to save you from me!" ¹⁶ His officers said still more things against the LORD God and against His servant Hezekiah. ¹⁷ He also wrote letters reviling the LORD God of Israel, saying of Him, "Just as the gods of the other nations of the earth did not save their people from me, so the God of Hezekiah will not save his people from me." ¹⁸ They called loudly in the language of Judah to the people of Jerusalem who were on the wall, to frighten them into panic, so as to capture the city. ¹⁹ They spoke of the God of Jerusalem as though He were like the gods of the other peoples of the earth, made by human hands. ²⁰ Then King Hezekiah and the prophet Isaiah son of Amoz prayed about this, and cried out to heaven.

²¹ The LORD sent an angel who annihilated every mighty warrior, commander, and officer in the army of the king of Assyria, and he returned in disgrace to his land. He entered the house of his god, and there some of his own offspring struck him down by the sword. ²² Thus the LORD delivered Hezekiah and the inhabitants of Jerusalem from King Sennacherib of Assyria, and from everyone; He provided for them on all sides. ²³ Many brought tribute to the LORD to Jerusalem, and gifts to King Hezekiah of Judah; thereafter he was exalted in the eyes of all the nations.

²⁴ At that time, Hezekiah fell deathly sick. He prayed to the LORD, who responded to him and gave him a sign. ²⁵ Hezekiah made no return for what had been bestowed upon him, for he grew arrogant; so wrath was decreed for him and for Judah and Jerusalem. ²⁶ Then Hezekiah humbled himself where he had been arrogant, he and the inhabitants of Jerusalem, and no wrath of the LORD came on them during the reign of Hezekiah. ²⁷ Hezekiah enjoyed riches and glory in abundance; he filled

treasuries with silver and gold, precious stones, spices, shields, and all lovely objects; [28] and store-cities with the produce of grain, wine, and oil, and stalls for all kinds of beasts, and flocks for sheepfolds. [29] And he acquired towns, and flocks of small and large cattle in great number, for God endowed him with very many possessions. [30] It was Hezekiah who stopped up the spring of water of Upper Gihon, leading it downward west of the City of David; Hezekiah prospered in all that he did. [31] So too in the matter of the ambassadors of the princes of Babylon, who were sent to him to inquire about the sign that was in the land, when God forsook him in order to test him, to learn all that was in his mind.

[32] The other events of Hezekiah's reign, and his faithful acts, are recorded in the visions of the prophet Isaiah son of Amoz and in the book of the kings of Judah and Israel. [33] Hezekiah slept with his fathers, and was buried on the upper part of the tombs of the sons of David. When he died, all the people of Judah and the inhabitants of Jerusalem accorded him much honor. Manasseh, his son, succeeded him.

33 [a]Manasseh was twelve years old when he became king, and he reigned fifty-five years in Jerusalem. [2] He did what was displeasing to the LORD, following the abhorrent practices of the nations which the LORD had dispossessed before the Israelites. [3] He rebuilt the shrines that his father Hezekiah had demolished; he erected altars for the Baals and made sacred posts. He bowed down to all the host of heaven and worshiped them, [4] and he built altars [to them] in the House of the LORD, of which the LORD had said, "My name will be in Jerusalem forever." [5] He built altars for all the host of heaven in the two courts of the House of the LORD. [6] He consigned his sons to the fire in the Valley of Ben-hinnom, and he practiced soothsaying, divination, and sorcery, and consulted ghosts and familiar spirits; he did much that was displeasing to the LORD in order to vex Him. [7] He placed a sculptured

[a] *Cf. II Kings 21.*

image that he made in the House of God, of which God had said to David and to his son Solomon, "In this House and in Jerusalem, which I chose out of all the tribes of Israel, I will establish My name forever. ⁸ And I will never again remove the feet of Israel from the land that I assigned to their fathers, if only they observe faithfully all that I have commanded them—all the teaching and the laws and the rules given by Moses." ⁹ Manasseh led Judah and the inhabitants of Jerusalem astray into evil greater than that done by the nations that the LORD had destroyed before the Israelites.

¹⁰ The LORD spoke to Manasseh and his people, but they would not pay heed, ¹¹ so the LORD brought against them the officers of the army of the king of Assyria, who took Manasseh captive in manacles, bound him in fetters, and led him off to Babylon. ¹² In his distress, he entreated the LORD his God and humbled himself greatly before the God of his fathers. ¹³ He prayed to Him, and He granted his prayer, heard his plea, and returned him to Jerusalem to his kingdom. Then Manasseh knew that the LORD alone was God. ¹⁴ Afterward he built the outer wall of the City of David west of Gihon in the wadi on the way to the Fish Gate, and it encircled Ophel; he raised it very high. He also placed army officers in all the fortified towns of Judah. ¹⁵ He removed the foreign gods and the image from the House of the LORD, as well as all the altars that he had built on the Mount of the House of the LORD and in Jerusalem, and dumped them outside the city. ¹⁶ He rebuilt the altar of the LORD and offered on it sacrifices of well-being and thanksgiving, and commanded the people of Judah to worship the LORD God of Israel. ¹⁷ To be sure, the people continued sacrificing at the shrines, but only to the LORD their God.

¹⁸ The other events of Manasseh's reign, and his prayer to his God, and the words of the seers who spoke to him in the name of the LORD God of Israel are found in the chronicles of the kings of Israel. ¹⁹ His prayer and how it was granted to him, the whole account of his sin and trespass, and the places in which he built

shrines and installed sacred posts and images before he humbled himself are recorded in the words of Hozai.[b] 20 Manasseh slept with his fathers and was buried on his palace grounds; his son Amon succeeded him as king.

21 Amon was twenty-two years old when he became king, and he reigned two years in Jerusalem. 22 He did what was displeasing to the LORD, as his father Manasseh had done. Amon sacrificed to all the idols that his father Manasseh had made and worshiped them. 23 He did not humble himself before the LORD, as his father Manasseh had humbled himself; instead, Amon incurred much guilt. 24 His courtiers conspired against him and killed him in his palace. 25 But the people of the land struck down all who had conspired against King Amon; and the people of the land made his son Josiah king in his stead.

34 [a]Josiah was eight years old when he became king, and he reigned thirty-one years in Jerusalem. 2 He did what was pleasing to the LORD, following the ways of his father David without deviating to the right or to the left. 3 In the eighth year of his reign, while he was still young, he began to seek the God of his father David, and in the twelfth year he began to purge Judah and Jerusalem of the shrines, the sacred posts, the idols, and the molten images. 4 At his bidding, they demolished the altars of the Baals, and he had the incense stands above them cut down; he smashed the sacred posts, the idols, and the images, ground them into dust, and strewed it onto the graves of those who had sacrificed to them. 5 He burned the bones of priests on their altars and purged Judah and Jerusalem. 6 In the towns of Manasseh and Ephraim and Simeon, as far as Naphtali, [lying] in ruins on every side, 7 he demolished the altars and the sacred posts and smashed the idols and ground them into dust; and he hewed down all the incense stands throughout the land of Israel. Then he returned to Jerusalem.

8 In the eighteenth year of his reign, after purging the land and

b *Or "seers."*

a *Cf. II Kings 22, 23.1–20.*

the House, he commissioned Shaphan son of Azaliah, Maaseiah the governor of the city, and Joah son of Joahaz the recorder to repair the House of the LORD his God. ⁹ They came to the high priest Hilkiah and delivered to him the silver brought to the House of God, which the Levites, the guards of the threshold, had collected from Manasseh and Ephraim and from all the remnant of Israel and from all Judah and Benjamin and *ᵇ*the inhabitants of Jerusalem.*ᵇ* ¹⁰ They delivered it into the custody of the overseers who were in charge at the House of the LORD, and the overseers who worked in the House of the LORD spent it on examining and repairing the House. ¹¹ They paid it out to the artisans and the masons to buy quarried stone and wood for the couplings and for making roof-beams for the buildings that the kings of Judah had allowed to fall into ruin. ¹² The men did the work honestly; over them were appointed the Levites Jahath and Obadiah, of the sons of Merari, and Zechariah and Meshullam, of the sons of Kohath, to supervise; while other Levites, all the master musicians, ¹³ were over the porters, supervising all who worked at each and every task; some of the Levites were scribes and officials and gatekeepers.

¹⁴ As they took out the silver that had been brought to the House of the LORD, the priest Hilkiah found a scroll of the LORD's Teaching given by Moses. ¹⁵ Hilkiah spoke up and said to the scribe Shaphan, "I have found a scroll of the Teaching in the House of the LORD"; and Hilkiah gave the scroll to Shaphan. ¹⁶ Shaphan brought the scroll to the king and also reported to the king, "All that was entrusted to your servants is being done; ¹⁷ they have melted down the silver that was found in the House of the LORD and delivered it to those who were in charge, to the overseers." ¹⁸ The scribe Shaphan also told the king, "The priest Hilkiah has given me a scroll"; and Shaphan read from it to the king. ¹⁹ When the king heard the words of the Teaching, he tore his clothes. ²⁰ The king gave orders to Hilkiah, and Ahikam son of Shaphan, and Abdon son of Micah, and the scribe Shaphan, and Asaiah the king's minister, saying, ²¹ "Go, inquire of the

ᵇ⁻ᵇ *With* kethib *and ancient versions;* qere *"they returned to Jerusalem."*

LORD on my behalf and on behalf of those who remain in Israel and Judah concerning the words of the scroll that has been found, for great indeed must be the wrath of the LORD that has been poured down upon us because our fathers did not obey the word of the LORD and do all that is written in this scroll."

²² Hilkiah and those whom the king [had ordered] went to the prophetess Huldah, wife of Shallum son of Tokhath son of Hasrah, keeper of the wardrobe, who was living in Jerusalem in the Mishneh,ᶜ and spoke to her accordingly. ²³ She responded to them: "Thus said the LORD God of Israel: Say to the man who sent you to Me, '²⁴ Thus said the LORD: I am going to bring disaster upon this place and its inhabitants—all the curses that are written in the scroll that was read to the king of Judah— ²⁵ because they forsook Me and made offerings to other gods in order to vex Me with all the works of their hands; My wrath shall be poured out against this place and not be quenched.' ²⁶ But say this to the king of Judah who sent you to inquire of the LORD: 'Thus said the LORD God of Israel: As for the words which you have heard, ²⁷ since your heart was softened and you humbled yourself before God when you heard His words concerning this place and its inhabitants, and you humbled yourself before Me and tore your clothes and wept before Me, I for My part have listened, declares the LORD. ²⁸ Assuredly, I will gather you to your fathers, and you will be laid in your grave in peace; your eyes shall see nothing of the disaster which I will bring upon this place and its inhabitants.' " They reported this back to the king.

²⁹ Then the king sent word and assembled all the elders of Judah and Jerusalem. ³⁰ The king went up to the House of the LORD with all the men of Judah and the inhabitants of Jerusalem and the priests and the Levites—all the people, young and old— and he read to them the entire text of the covenant scroll that was found in the House of the LORD. ³¹ The king stood in his place and solemnized the covenant before the LORD: to follow the LORD and observe His commandments, His injunctions, and His laws with all his heart and soul, to fulfill all the terms of the

ᶜ A quarter in Jerusalem; cf. Zeph. 1.10.

covenant written in this scroll. [32] He obligated all the men of Jerusalem and Benjamin who were present; and the inhabitants of Jerusalem acted in accord with the Covenant of God, God of their fathers. [33] Josiah removed all the abominations from the whole territory of the Israelites and obliged all who were in Israel to worship the LORD their God. Throughout his reign they did not deviate from following the LORD God of their fathers.

35 [a]Josiah kept the Passover for the LORD in Jerusalem; the passover sacrifice was slaughtered on the fourteenth day of the first month. [2] He reinstated the priests in their shifts and rallied them to the service of the House of the LORD. [3] He said to the Levites, consecrated to the LORD, who taught all Israel, "Put the Holy Ark in the House that Solomon son of David, king of Israel, built; as you no longer carry it on your shoulders, see now to the service of the LORD your God and His people Israel, [4] and dispose yourselves by clans according to your divisions, as prescribed in the writing of King David of Israel and in the document of his son Solomon, [5] and attend in the Sanctuary, by clan divisions, on your kinsmen, the people—by clan divisions of the Levites. [6] Having sanctified yourselves, slaughter the passover sacrifice and prepare it for your kinsmen, according to the word of God given by Moses." [7] Josiah donated to the people small cattle— lambs and goats, all for passover sacrifices for all present—to the sum of 30,000, and large cattle, 3000—these from the property of the king. [8] His officers, priests, and Levites gave a freewill offering to the people, to the priests and to the Levites. Hilkiah and Zechariah and Jehiel, the chiefs of the House of God, donated to the priests for passover sacrifices 2600 [small cattle] and 300 large cattle. [9] Conaniah, Shemaiah, and Nethanel, his brothers, and Hashabiah and Jeiel and Jozabad, officers of the Levites, donated 5000 [small cattle] and 500 large cattle to the Levites for passover sacrifices.

[10] The service was arranged well: the priests stood at their posts

[a] *Cf. II Kings 23.21–30.*

and the Levites in their divisions, by the king's command. [11] They slaughtered the passover sacrifice and the priests [received its blood] from them and dashed it, while the Levites flayed the animals. [12] They removed the parts to be burnt, distributing them to divisions of the people by clans, and making the sacrifices to the LORD, as prescribed in the scroll of Moses; they did the same for the cattle. [13] They roasted the passover sacrifice in fire, as prescribed, while the sacred offerings they cooked in pots, cauldrons, and pans, and conveyed them with dispatch to all the people. [14] Afterward they provided for themselves and the priests, for the Aaronite priests were busy offering the burnt offerings and the fatty parts until nightfall, so the Levites provided both for themselves and for the Aaronite priests. [15] The Asaphite singers were at their stations, by command of David and Asaph and Heman and Jeduthun, the seer of the king; and the gatekeepers were at each and every gate. They did not have to leave their tasks, because their Levite brothers provided for them. [16] The entire service of the LORD was arranged well that day, to keep the Passover and to make the burnt offerings on the altar of the LORD, according to the command of King Josiah. [17] All the Israelites present kept the Passover at that time, and the Feast of Unleavened Bread for seven days. [18] Since the time of the prophet Samuel, no Passover like that one had ever been kept in Israel; none of the kings of Israel had kept a Passover like the one kept by Josiah and the priests and the Levites and all Judah and Israel there present and the inhabitants of Jerusalem. [19] That Passover was kept in the eighteenth year of the reign of Josiah.

[20] After all this furbishing of the Temple by Josiah, King Necho of Egypt came up to fight at Carchemish on the Euphrates, and Josiah went out against him. [21] [Necho] sent messengers to him, saying, "What have I to do with you, king of Judah? I do not march against you this day but against the kingdom that wars with me, and it is God's will that I hurry. Refrain, then, from interfering with God who is with me, that He not destroy you." [22] But Josiah would not let him alone; instead, [b]-he donned [his armor]-[b]

[b-b] *With Targ.*

to fight him, heedless of Necho's words from the mouth of God; and he came to fight in the plain of Megiddo. ²³ Archers shot King Josiah, and the king said to his servants, "Get me away from here, for I am badly wounded." ²⁴ His servants carried him out of his chariot and put him in the wagon of his second-in-command, and conveyed him to Jerusalem. There he died, and was buried in the grave of his fathers, and all Judah and Jerusalem went into mourning over Josiah. ²⁵ Jeremiah composed laments for Josiah which all the singers, male and female, recited in their laments for Josiah, as is done to this day; they became customary in Israel and were incorporated into the laments. ²⁶ The other events of Josiah's reign and his faithful deeds, in accord with the Teaching of the LORD, ²⁷ and his acts, early and late, are recorded in the book of the kings of Israel and Judah.

36 ^{*a*}The people of the land took Jehoahaz son of Josiah and made him king instead of his father in Jerusalem. ² Jehoahaz was twenty-three years old when he became king and he reigned three months in Jerusalem. ³ The king of Egypt deposed him in Jerusalem and laid a fine on the land of 100 silver talents and one gold talent. ⁴ The king of Egypt made his brother Eliakim king over Judah and Jerusalem, and changed his name to Jehoiakim; Necho took his brother Joahaz and brought him to Egypt.

⁵ Jehoiakim was twenty-five years old when he became king, and he reigned eleven years in Jerusalem; he did what was displeasing to the LORD his God. ⁶ King Nebuchadnezzar of Babylon marched against him; he bound him in fetters to convey him to Babylon. ⁷ Nebuchadnezzar also brought some vessels of the House of the LORD to Babylon, and set them in his palace in Babylon. ⁸ The other events of Jehoiakim's reign, and the abominable things he did, and what was found against him, are recorded in the book of the kings of Israel and Judah. His son Jehoiachin succeeded him as king.

⁹ Jehoiachin was eight years old when he became king, and he

---

^a *With vv. 1–13, cf. II Kings 23.28–37, II Kings 24.1–20.*

reigned three months and ten days in Jerusalem; he did what was displeasing to the LORD. [10] At the turn of the year, King Nebuchadnezzar sent to have him brought to Babylon with the precious vessels of the House of the LORD, and he made his kinsman Zedekiah king over Judah and Jerusalem.

[11] Zedekiah was twenty-one years old when he became king, and he reigned eleven years in Jerusalem. [12] He did what was displeasing to the LORD his God; he did not humble himself before the prophet Jeremiah, who spoke for the LORD. [13] He also rebelled against Nebuchadnezzar, who made him take an oath[b] by God; he stiffened his neck and hardened his heart so as not to turn to the LORD God of Israel. [14] All the officers of the priests and the people committed many trespasses, following all the abominable practices of the nations. They polluted the House of the LORD which He had consecrated in Jerusalem. [15] The LORD God of their fathers had sent word to them through His messengers daily without fail, for He had pity on His people and His dwelling-place. [16] But they mocked the messengers of God and disdained His words and taunted His prophets until the wrath of the LORD against His people grew beyond remedy. [17] He therefore brought the king of the Chaldeans upon them, who killed their youths by the sword in their Sanctuary; He did not spare youth, maiden, elder, or graybeard, but delivered all into his hands. [18] All the vessels of the House of God, large and small, and the treasures of the House of the LORD and the treasures of the king and his officers were all brought to Babylon. [19] They burned the House of God and tore down the wall of Jerusalem, burned down all its mansions, and consigned all its precious objects to destruction. [20] Those who survived the sword he exiled to Babylon, and they became his and his sons' servants till the rise of the Persian kingdom, [21] in fulfillment of the word of the LORD spoken by Jeremiah, until the land paid back its sabbaths; as long as it lay desolate it kept sabbath, till seventy years were completed.

[22] And in the first year of King Cyrus of Persia, when the word of the LORD spoken by Jeremiah was fulfilled, the LORD roused

[b] *Viz. a vassal oath.*

the spirit of King Cyrus of Persia to issue a proclamation throughout his realm by word of mouth and in writing, as follows: 23 "Thus said King Cyrus of Persia: The LORD God of Heaven has given me all the kingdoms of the earth, and has charged me with building Him a House in Jerusalem, which is in Judah. Anyone of you of all His people, the LORD His God be with him and let him go up."